Essentials of
Business Communication

KENT SERIES IN BUSINESS COMMUNICATION

Essentials of
Business Communication

Second Edition

MARY ELLEN GUFFEY

Los Angeles Pierce College

PWS-KENT PUBLISHING COMPANY
Boston

PWS–KENT
Publishing Company

20 Park Plaza
Boston, Massachusetts 02116

ISBN 0-534-92555-3 Students Edition

ISBN 0-534-92613-4 Instructor's Edition

Cover Art: "Iris 4" is a silk-screen print used with the permission of the artist, Jane de Sausmarez, London, England.

Sponsoring Editor: Rolf A. Janke
Production Coordinator: Robine Andrau
Manufacturing Coordinator: Peter D. Leatherwood
Interior and Cover Designer: Julia Gecha
Cover Illustration: Jane de Sausmarez
Cover Printer: New England Book Components, Inc.
Typesetter: Beacon Graphics Corporation
Printer and Binder: Courier Book Companies

Printed in the United States of America

91 92 93 94 95 — 10 9 8 7 6 5 4 3 2 1

PREFACE

Tell me, I forget. Show me, I remember. Involve me, I understand.
—Chinese proverb

Essentials of Business Communication, Second Edition, is founded upon this proverb. This book involves students in the learning process so that they *understand* what's being taught. As one instructor who is using the text said, "This is a hands-on book." Writing skills receive particular emphasis because these skills are in great demand and because such skills are difficult to achieve.

This textbook will be especially helpful to postsecondary, college, and adult students with outdated, inadequate, or weak language arts training. Numerous features facilitate the teaching/learning process.

Text-Workbook Format

The convenient text-workbook format presents an all-in-one teaching/learning package that includes concepts, workbook application exercises, writing problems, and a combination handbook/reference manual. Readers need to purchase only one volume.

Four-Stage Plan

Essentials of Business Communication, Second Edition, develops communication skills in a carefully designed four-stage plan. Stage 1 lays a foundation by presenting communication theory, by introducing electronic tools, and by providing an optional review of basic grammar, punctuation, usage, and style. Stage 2 introduces writing techniques, including "tricks of the trade" for writers. Stage 3 teaches writing strategies and helps students apply these strategies in composing business letters and memos. Stage 4 adapts basic communication strategies and techniques to varying communication problems.

Grammar/Mechanics Checkups

Each chapter includes intructions for a systematic review of the Grammar/ Mechanics Handbook, along with a short quiz. In this way students receive continual review and reinforcement of the fundamentals of correct writing.

Writing Improvement Exercises and Cases

Two unique features help readers develop writing skills. First, writing improvement exercises break down the total writing process into simple components. Second, many writing improvement cases enable students to rewrite realistic business messages, thereby helping them concentrate on applying strategies and solving writing problems rather than struggling to provide unknown details to unfamiliar, hypothetical writing cases.

Letters and Memorandum Writing

Students learn to write letters and memos that request information, order goods, make claims, respond to inquiries, respond to claims, refuse requests, and refuse credit. They also learn to apply practical psychology in persuasion and sales, as well as to develop goodwill with letters of appreciation, congratulation, sympathy, and recommendation.

Report Writing

The expanded report-writing section now includes two chapters. Chapter 11 concentrates on informal, short reports. Chapter 12 covers formal, long reports and includes a model long report.

Listening and Speaking Skills

Students learn to reduce barriers to effective listening, as well as to become more active listeners. They also study methods of organizing and delivering oral presentations; and they refine telephone, dictation, and meeting skills.

Employment Skills

Successful résumés, letters of application, and other employment documents are among the most important topics in a good business communication course. The Second Edition provides expanded coverage of both traditional and functional résumés.

Diagnostic Test

The optional grammar/mechanics diagnostic test helps students and instructors systematically pinpoint specific student writing weaknesses. Students may be directed to the Grammar/Mechanics Handbook for remediation.

Grammar/Mechanics Handbook

The comprehensive Grammar/Mechanics Handbook supplies a thorough review of English grammar, punctuation, capitalization style, and number usage. Its self-teaching exercises may be used for classroom instruction or for supplementary assignments. The handbook also serves as a convenient reference throughout the course.

New in the Second Edition

■ **Redesigned Format** For improved readability this edition features a second color, new heading and text fonts, and more white space on the page.

■ **"How-to" Articles** Included throughout the text are short boxed items on useful topics, such as "How to Increase Your Vocabulary in Six Steps," "How to Overcome the Fear of Writing," "How to Measure Readability: The Fog Index," and "How to Respond to Ten Frequently Asked Interview Questions."

■ **More Reports** Coverage of information, recommendation, justification, and progress reports has been expanded. Proposals, minutes of meetings, summaries, and to-file reports, as well as increased coverage of library techniques and procedures for writing long, formal reports, have also been added.

■ **Letter Models** An increase in the number of fully formatted letters and memos and the addition of the simplified letter style provide clear illustrations.

■ **Electronic Tools** Chapter 1 now includes a section entitled "Technology and Communication Tools Today," so that readers are introduced to electronic communication technology early in their writing training.

■ **Telephone, Meeting Skills** Chapter 14, "Listening and Speaking," incorporates new tips for improving telephone techniques and for developing successful meetings and conferences.

■ **More Résumés** To provide comprehensive employment skills, more student résumé models and successful interviewing ideas are provided.

■ **Software** A template diskette of writing improvement exercises and cases is provided to help students develop word processing and text editing skills as they learn writing techniques and strategies.

Instructor Support

As a practicing business communication instructor—who also teaches four other classes each week—I know how difficult it is to prepare all the auxiliary materials necessary to provide students with a challenging and effective course. For that reason, this textbook contains an extensive instructional package filled with practical, classroom-oriented support materials. Moreover, I continue to develop new materials, which I share with instructors who adopt the book.

Facsimile Key The *Instructor's Manual* includes a facsimile key so that instructors have an easy-to-read, all-in-one manual from which to teach.

Transparencies A packet of 150 ready-to-use acetate transparencies is provided by PWS-KENT to all adopters.

Lecture Extras Supplementary minilectures covering topics not presented in the textbook (such as doublespeak and nonverbal communication) enrich classroom discussions. Transparency acetates accompany many of these lecture extras.

Solutions   Nearly every writing improvement exercise and case has a prepared solution available both in the *Instructor's Manual* and in the *Testing Materials and Transparencies* packet.

Tests   Chapter quizzes, unit tests, and a final examination, along with keys, are available.

Chapter Teaching Plans   The *Instructor's Manual* details a complete lesson plan for presenting each chapter.

Textbook Coordination   The principles of grammar and usage incorporated in *Essentials of Business Communication* coordinate with and reinforce those presented in Guffey's *Business English*, Third Edition, and Clark and Clark's *HOW6: Handbook for Office Workers*, Sixth Edition.

Software Options   As mentioned earlier, a diskette for IBM-compatible computers contains all writing improvement exercises and selected cases from the textbook. Instructors may provide diskette solutions for immediate reinforcement or may withhold solutions so that responses may be discussed in the classroom.

Acknowledgments

Sincere thanks are extended to the reviewers whose excellent advice and constructive suggestions helped shape the second edition of *Essentials of Business Communication*. I am grateful for the consultation of Edna Jellesed, Lane Community College; Ron Kapper, College of DuPage; Keith Kroll, Kalamazoo Valley Community College; Bonnie Miller, Los Medanos College; Joseph Schaffner, SUNY College of Technology at Alfred; and Beverly Wickersham, Central Texas College.

For their especially insightful contributions, I thank Jeanette Dostourian, Cypress College; Nancy J. Dubino, Greenfield Community College; Valerie Evans, Cuesta College; Margaret E. Gorman, Cayuga Community College; Jackie Ohlson, University of Alaska—Anchorage; Vilera Rood, Concordia College; and Lois A. Wagner, Southwest Wisconsin Technical College.

For sharing their expertise regarding *Essentials of Business Communication*, Second Edition, warm appreciation also goes to the following educators: Karen Bounds, Boise State University; Cecile Earle, Heald College; Pat Fountain, Coastal Carolina Community College; Marlene Frederich, New Mexico State University—Carlsbad; L. P. Helstrom, Rochester Community College; Nedra Lowe, Marshall University; Jane Mangrum, Miami-Dade Community College; Willie Minor, Phoenix College; Carl Perrin, Casco Bay College; Jeanette Purdy, Mercer County College; Cinda Skelton, Central Texas College; Marilyn Theissman, Rochester Community College; Linda Weavil, Elan College; Leopold Wilkins, Anson Community College; Almeda Wilmarth, State University of New York—Delhi; and Barbara Young, Skyline College.

The perceptive comments and encouragement of reviewers for the first edition were instrumental in creation of this hands-on writing approach to business communication. Thanks to Patricia Beagle, Bryant & Stratton Business Institute; Edwina Jordan, Illinois Central College; Nancy Moody, Sinclair Community College; Nancy Mulder, Grand Rapids Junior College; Carlita Robertson,

Northern Oklahoma College; Clara Smith, North Seattle Community College; and Judy Sunayama, Los Medanos College.

I commend the following dedicated professionals at PWS-KENT Publishing Company for their care, patience, and expertise: Executive Editor Richard Crews, Managing Editor Rolf Janke, Senior Production Editor Robine Andrau, Product Manager Robert Wolcott, and all the enthusiastic, hard-working PWS-KENT sales representatives. Finally, for his inestimable counsel and support, I salute my husband, Dr. George R. Guffey, professor of English, University of California, Los Angeles.

Instructor Networking

Each year I develop and distribute new classroom teaching materials for business communication instructors. To ensure that you receive notice of these materials, please send me your name and address—and any comments regarding your course and this book.

Dr. Mary Ellen Guffey
Los Angeles Pierce College
6201 Winnetka Avenue
Woodland Hills, CA 91371

CONTENTS

*Tests are included in *Testing Materials and Transparencies* packet.

*Tests are included in *Testing Materials and Transparencies* packet.

*Tests are included in *Testing Materials and Transparencies* packet.

*Tests are included in *Testing Materials and Transparencies* packet.

Laying Communication Foundations

CHAPTER 1

Communicating in Business Today

In this chapter you will learn to do the following:

- Explain why communication skills are valuable both to employers and to employees.
- Analyze the process of communication.

- Describe how communication skills can be developed in four stages.
- List ten new communication and decision-making tools available to today's business communicator.

Communicating and the Information Age

We are now living in the Information Age. Our lives and our jobs revolve around information—its development, management, manipulation, processing, and exchange. To exchange information, we must communicate. This book is about understanding how we communicate and learning how to improve our communication skills.

Knowing how to communicate successfully will be invaluable to you both professionally and personally. In your professional life language skills are vital for three employment phases: in obtaining the job you want, in performing the tasks of your employment well, and in securing promotions within your profession. Aside from employment, good communication skills enable you to create a rich and satisfying personal life.

Some things about ourselves we can't change—our height, our complexion, our disposition, even our native intelligence. But other characteristics we can change, and proficiency in communication is one of them. Frank Carey, former board chairman of IBM, once said that the four qualities of truly successful top executives are intelligence, integrity, empathy, and the ability to communicate. Of the four, only the last, communication, is a learnable skill. Aspiring employees, as well as top executives, can learn to communicate well through instruction and practice.

This chapter takes a broad look at communication today. First, it discusses the importance of communication skills in the workplace. Next, the chapter examines communication theory, followed by a glimpse of the effects of technol-

Of all new jobs created, the U.S. Government estimates that 95 percent will be information- or service-related. Only 5 percent will be product- or manufacturing-related. What does this situation mean for you?

ogy on communicating today. Finally, it outlines a plan to help you improve your skills.

Wanted: Good Communication Skills

Possessing effective communication skills is highly regarded in the business world. Employers, aware of the dollar-and-cents value of clear expression, increasingly identify and require oral and writing skills in job announcements. Examine the following excerpts from employment advertisements taken from two of the nation's largest newspapers, *The New York Times* and the *Los Angeles Times*. Notice how these ads for diverse positions in professional, managerial, technical, and secretarial fields specifically designate good communication skills.

Director of Personnel

400-bed metropolitan New York hospital seeks highly motivated, sensitive, results-oriented personnel generalist. Must be a hands-on self-starter with *effective communication skills.*

Management Trainee

Leading, innovative financial organization seeks energetic, organized, detail-oriented individual to monitor . . . programs. Candidates must have initiative, *excellent written and verbal skills*, and strong analytical ability.

Classified ads reflect a growing concern for good verbal and writing skills.

Manager, Business Systems

National organization seeks project manager to develop, coordinate, and provide automated tracking and control systems . . . An outgoing, congenial personality and *exceptional communication skills* essential. Salary $60,000 plus.

Executive Secretary

Expanding engineering firm. Applicant must have 5 years of secretarial experience and excellent typing and *communication skills.*

Word Processing Specialists

Immediate openings for operators with Word, WordPerfect, or WordStar experience. *Communication skills tested.*

Administrative Assistant

Beverly Hills cosmetic firm seeks capable administrative assistant to work with our dynamic team. Requirements include typing, computer, and *excellent communication skills.*

Why Employers Value Good Communicators

Business needs good communicators because these employees stimulate additional business. They are persuasive. They are able to sell ideas, services, and products. Good communicators know how to analyze, organize, and clarify information. Not only do they promote business for their organizations, but they also keep administrative costs down because their messages are not misunderstood and do not have to be repeated. Good communicators produce goodwill for their organizations. They feel positive about themselves and about their organizations.

Warren Yerks, an executive in a California aerospace firm, warns that employees have little chance in industry if they can't process and present information in writing. Everyone in his organization must be able to write: engineers, secretaries, managers, production personnel, and equipment operators. Employees who cannot write effectively probably wouldn't be hired in the first place; but if they are, according to Yerks, they often end up in a "professional eddy." These unproductive employees are frustrated and unhappy, out of the mainstream of corporate life, going nowhere professionally.[1]

Estimates indicate that more than one third of all business letters do nothing more than seek clarification of earlier correspondence.

In locating individuals with good communication skills, some organizations require job candidates to submit a writing sample. Other employers test communication skills. All personnel officers judge a job applicant's performance in the interview. How well you answer questions, communicate your ideas, explain your qualifications, and promote yourself determine whether you are hired. A survey of employers who hired recent college graduates revealed that the two characteristics in which employers were most interested were poise and communication skills.[2] Others stress the applicant's ability to get along with other people as indicated by extracurricular activities or community activities. Clearly, if you can communicate well, you will get along better with others than will those who do not communicate well.

~~

Communicating on the Job

Once you have been hired, you'll need good speaking, listening, and writing skills to get your work done. How much communication skill you will need depends on the field you enter and on the stage of your career. Jobs such as selling insurance and managing investments demand excellent communication skills for entry-level positions. Other positions may not require exceptional writing and speaking skills at first.

However, as one advances into supervisory and management roles, the demand for communication skills increases. Studies show, as you might expect, that supervisors, managers, and executives spend a much higher percentage of their time writing memos, letters, and reports than do their employees. Promotions are often given to those employees who demonstrate that they are effective communicators. In a national study of vice presidents selected from *Fortune 500* corporations, 98 percent reported that effective communication skills had positively affected their advancement to top executive positions.[3]

Individuals who are promoted into supervisory and managerial positions require better communication skills than do entry-level employees.

[1]Robert Mehaffy and Constance Warloe, "Corporate Communications: Next Step for the Community Colleges," *The Technical Writing Teacher* (Winter 1989): 1.

[2]Allen Blitstein, "What Employers Are Seeking in Business Graduates," *The Collegiate Forum* (Winter 1980–81).

[3]James C. Bennett and Robert J. Olney, "Executive Priorities for Effective Communication in an Information Society," *The Journal of Business Communication* (Spring 1986): 15.

~~

But Not for Accountants?

"But," you may protest, "I'm going to be an accountant (or computer specialist or financial analyst or health care specialist). In my field, language skills are unimportant."

Even in business activities that center on technical concepts, skill in communicating ideas rates highly among employers. In a study of accounting academics and professionals, an average of 70 percent of professional accountants reported that the written communication skills of the typical newly graduated accountant were inadequate. One employer in this study made the following revealing comment:

Workers in technical areas must be able to communicate their ideas to both technical and nontechnical colleagues.

> The most neglected skill apparent in entry-level accountants is the ability to write effectively. For the most part, these "new" accountants have excellent technical preparation. However, they are unable to communicate the results of their technical procedures in a clear and concise manner.[4]

Promotion from technical jobs into supervisory or managerial positions brings increased administrative responsibilities. Consider the duties of the director of budgets and controls for a major American airline. In addition to working with figures, this individual is responsible for the "preparation, consolidation, and distribution of budgets; the analysis and interpretation of results; and the preparation of financial and operating statistical reports to provide a basis of management planning and operating controls." In other words, the budget director must be proficient in writing financial reports that other managers can understand.

~~

On the Personal Side

Aside from professional considerations, good communication skills benefit us personally. Since we spend the better part of our waking existence communicating with others, it is reasonable to assume that individuals who express ideas easily and clearly are better understood and experience greater satisfaction in interpersonal relationships than do those with weak skills.

The impressions you make on others are largely determined by the way you communicate.

Moreover, good communicators create favorable impressions. For better or worse, we all make judgments about others based on a number of factors, including the way they speak and the way they write. Our judgments, then, are influenced to a great extent by communication skills. Individuals who speak and write well convey the impression of intelligence, education, and success. They command respect, whether deserved or not. They are also happier because they are productive.

[4]J. Douglas Andrews and Norman B. Sigband, "How Effectively Does the 'New' Accountant Communicate? Perceptions by Practitioners and Academics," *The Journal of Business Communication* (Spring 1984): 20.

≈≈

What Is Communication?

Communication skills play an important part in our personal lives and in our business careers. Before we begin our plan for improving those skills, it would be wise to explore briefly the general process of communication. What does the word *communication* mean? This complex term has no single definition. Webster's *New Collegiate Dictionary* lists at least three considerably different meanings for the word *communication*, which is derived from the Latin *communis* meaning "common." When we communicate, we make something common; that is, we share something with others with or without a response.

1. An *act* of transmitting
2. *Information* transmitted, such as a verbal or written message
3. A *process* by which information is exchanged between individuals through a common system of symbols, signs, or behavior

To make the term less abstract, let's try to illustrate each of the preceding definitions. The act of transmitting might be as simple as voicing the word *hello* to a friend or handing a coworker a memo. Both of these are examples of the act of transmitting. Notice that *communication* in this sense requires no response on the part of a receiving individual.

The second sense of the word emphasizes a product. This product might be a new work schedule announced by an office manager. It might be a business letter sent to a customer. Again, no response is required for this sense of *communication*.

In the third sense, however, *communication* is described as a process in which information is *exchanged*. This exchange of information cannot be accomplished unless individuals, or machines, use a system of symbols or signs that both parties understand. It is with this last sense of the definition that we will be most concerned in our study of the essentials of business communication. Improving the process of communication is our goal. To achieve this goal, we need to understand better the components of the communication process.

Communication is both a process and the product of that process.

≈≈

Understanding the Communication Process

Only in comparatively recent times has the communication process been studied. In the past fifty years, theories of communication have been developed. Theories, by the way, seldom solve immediate problems. Rather, they help us view our experiences in a fresh way. Theories and models enable us to organize experiences so that relationships are simplified and more easily comprehended.

The model shown in Figure 1.1 breaks down the process of communication into its component parts and illustrates its cycle. When we consider communication to be the *exchange* of information, feedback becomes an important part of the cycle. Let's look more carefully at each of the five parts of the communication process.

Effective communication is a *cyclic* rather than a *linear* process.

FIGURE 1.1   Communication Model

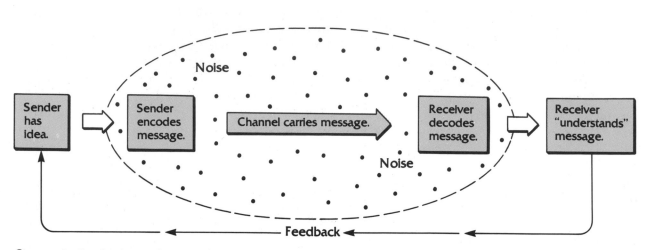

Communication barriers and noise may cause the communication cycle to break down.

Sender

Messages may be conveyed verbally (with spoken or written words) or nonverbally (with actions or pictures).

The communication cycle begins with a sender who has an idea to transmit to another individual. How can the sender shape that idea into a message that the receiver will understand? The sender must make choices regarding the length, emphasis, tone, and organization of the message. The words the sender selects to convert, or *encode*, the idea into an appropriate form require careful thought. The sender considers the purpose, the subject, and the intended receiver of the message.

The message that the sender encodes will be influenced by the communication skills, attitudes, experiences, and, to some degree, culture of the sender. The goal of a good communicator is to create a message that is understood as he or she intended.

To ensure understanding, the sender chooses words and concepts that are not beyond the receiver's knowledge and experience. For example, a telecommunication software sales representative presenting a new product to an office manager with little knowledge of computers would wisely avoid descriptions like

Source: Reprinted by permission of Johnny Hart and Creators Syndicate, Inc.

"it's a file-transfer-level protocol designed for dial-up asynchronous transmission." Even though such language may be clear to the sales rep, it's probably not so clear to the office manager.

In the communication cycle, the sender may fail to communicate with the receiver when the code or symbols are not understood by both. It is the responsibility of the sender to prepare a message that is within the comprehension of the receiver. Moreover, the sender should strive for feedback, which will be discussed shortly.

Message

The message created to represent an idea may be verbal or nonverbal. A nod of the head delivers a simple message of agreement. When a smile accompanies that nod, it signifies approval as well. Nonverbal communication is often subtle and may be culture-dependent. Throughout most of the world, shaking of the head back and forth indicates a negative response, but in certain regions of India it means just the opposite. Culture affects both nonverbal and verbal messages.

In this textbook, we will be most concerned with verbal messages, that is, those that are expressed with spoken or written words. The words the sender chooses, the way they are arranged, their number, their meaning, and their length all contribute to the effect a message has on the listener or reader. Consider Howard Hightower, the national sales manager for a publisher. He must tell all salespeople that declining sales necessitate reducing their commissions; however, he also wants to encourage them to increase their sales. He could make this announcement in a blunt statement of 15 words. But if he desires comprehension, compliance, and cooperation, he will probably create a message with well-considered words organized into an effective strategy. The same information delivered by a Japanese sales manager to salespeople in his or her firm might be presented quite differently. Messages, then, are determined by the sender's objective, audience, subject, communication skills, attitudes, and culture.

Channel

The medium over which the message is physically transmitted is the channel. Messages may be delivered by computer, telephone, letter, memorandum, report, announcement, picture, face-to-face exchange, fax, or through some other channel.

How should a message be sent? Several factors determine the choice of channel, the most important of which are these:

The selection of an appropriate channel for a message is determined by its complexity, importance, expected response, immediacy, degree of formality, audience, and cost.

- **Complexity of the message**. Is the information so detailed that the receiver will need to read and study it?

- **Importance of the message**. Is the content of this message such that it requires a permanent record?

- **Anticipated reaction**. Will this message create a positive or negative receiver response?

- **Immediacy of the situation**. Is a quick response needed?

- **Degree of formality**. Does a personal relationship exist between the sender and the receiver?

- **Size and location of the audience**. Is the message intended for a single receiver nearby or for hundreds of distant receivers?
- **Comparative costs**. Does the message warrant a costly channel in terms of time, equipment, and people?

Let's say, for example, that you are an executive in a large company and you are announcing a profit-sharing plan to employees. The best channel for your message would probably be a memo, rather than a personal interview with or a telephone call to each employee. If, however, you wish to convince a director of the company that certain options in the profit-sharing plan should be revised, then a personal conference, along with a factual report, would be most effective. If you were inviting a colleague to lunch, the most appropriate communication channel would be the telephone.

Physical transmission of a message can affect the receiver's perception of that message. If you receive a letter addressed to "Occupant," you may dismiss its contents as junk mail. The same message, however, addressed to you by name and delivered on quality stationery may command your attention. You perceive the message as important; you have a favorable mind-set toward it.

Receiver

The receiver's reaction to a message is determined by a number of external and internal factors, including the following:

- **Form and appearance of the message**. Is the channel appropriate? Is the message attractive and clear?
- **Subject of the message**. How much does the receiver know about the subject?
- **Attitude toward the message**. Does the receiver have an open, closed, or neutral attitude toward the message? Is the receiver in a receptive mood?
- **Communication skills**. Does the receiver possess sufficient communication skills to comprehend the message?
- **Physical conditions**. Is the receiver free of physical distractions so that it is possible to concentrate on the message?

Successful communication results when a receiver understands a message as the sender intended and responds as expected. To do this, the receiver must decode the symbols and ascribe to them the same general meanings as the sender ascribes.

Feedback

To ensure that receivers comprehend their messages, skilled communicators provide opportunities for feedback during and after the delivery of their messages.

The final step in the communication cycle is the response of the receiver. Nonverbal feedback may consist of a puzzled frown if, for example, the receiver does not understand the message. Verbal feedback may be a spoken comment or a written message. Even no response to a message is, in a sense, a form of feedback.

Feedback helps the sender evaluate the effectiveness of the original message. If the desired results were not achieved, the sender selects other words organized in an alternate strategy to repeat the communication attempt.

Skillful communicators recognize the importance of feedback and consciously provide for it. In conversation they watch facial expressions and respond accordingly. They don't dominate; conversation is two-way. They encourage questions. In letters and memos they conclude by asking for a specific action that indicates comprehension of the idea communicated.

Barriers

For an infinite number of reasons, the communication cycle is not always successful. Barriers may cause the breakdown of communication in any of the encoding, transmitting, decoding, and responding stages of the process. A message sender who lacks awareness of the receiver or who possesses poor communication skills will have difficulty sending clear messages.

Barriers in transmitting messages are created by physical distractions and by long communication chains. Messages become distorted when too many people must process them. In the decoding stage, communication is disrupted if the receiver lacks interest in or knowledge of the topic in the message. Emotional distractions may interfere with both the encoding and the decoding of messages. These disruptions, sometimes called "noise," can create failure in any step of the communication cycle.

> **Communication barriers and noise prevent effective communication.**

~~

Technology and Communication Tools Today

Despite extraordinary technological advances in the field of communication today, the process of communication remains largely unchanged—that is, individuals still have ideas that must be encoded properly and transmitted through appropriate channels to receivers. However, in this Information Age, we are witnessing remarkable changes in the tools of communication. Advances in technology have altered the way we gather information, store data, make decisions, create messages, transmit ideas, and respond to those ideas.

Does the following description of a business executive's day sound like a futurist's fairy tale?

> **The process of encoding and decoding messages changes little, but the tools that enhance the process are changing greatly.**

> After arriving at his downtown Los Angeles office on a given morning, George Moody, president of Security Pacific Corporation, the fifth-largest bank holding company in the United States, decides that he would like to review the profitability of his 1,000 retail branches and check the status of third-world loans. Instead of turning to a pile of reports and printouts or ordering studies that get bucked down the chain of command, he turns to his desktop computer, clears his throat and, using simple oral commands, calls up the data he wants in the depth and quantity he requires. The computer responds to his voice alone and displays the information in precisely the graphic format he prefers. If he doesn't want to squint at little green numbers on a tiny monitor, he can adjourn to the management committee room just down the hall and ponder branch-office P&Ls [profit and loss statements] and third-world-loan schedules on two giant 67-inch screens—the kind sports nuts use to watch football games . . . .
>
> What if he closed Security Pacific's 50 least profitable branches? What if he agreed to stretch out its Mexican loans by two years? By uttering a

few more commands, he summons up computer models simulating Security Pacific's branch operations and third-world-loan portfolios to test his management options. For each move he proposes, a projected outcome flashes onto the big screen. Moreover, once he has decided on a course of action, there is no need to wait for memos to be dictated, typed, proofread, retyped, photocopied, and delivered. Moody simply taps out new orders on his computer's word-processing program and fires them off via electronic mail.[5]

No, this is not an imaginary scenario dreamed up by a science fiction writer. George Moody actually uses very sophisticated technology to manage Security Pacific's operations in 46 states and 27 countries. Although most executives today are not so advanced as Moody, future top managers and other workers will be using an amazing array of decision-making and communication tools.

Computer skills will be required of nearly all white-collar workers in the future. Office automation is rising floor by floor, from word and data processing specialists, into executive suites. Clerical workers, middle managers, and executives alike find that being comfortable with technology is a requisite for success in business today.

Chuck Gibson, of the Boston-based consulting firm The Index Group, says that he used to tell chief executives that computer skills depended on the individual and how he or she sees the job. "Today," he says, "it's different. Now we tell him, 'Find a reason, any reason, but learn how to use one.' Being comfortable with technology in a personal way is going to be the *sine qua non* [absolutely indispensable element] of management in the 1990s."[6]

The area of communication technology is vast and grows larger every day. Since we are most concerned with automation as it affects today's communicator, this chapter will concentrate on what is technologically available to today's business communicator. We'll look at communication tools for business writers, tools for business managers, and tools for overall business performance. Bear in mind, however, that because this highly dynamic scene changes rapidly, it is nearly impossible to keep printed information up to date.

Tools for Today's Business Communicators

In creating and exchanging information today, business communicators employ dictation, word processing systems, word-processing accessories, and desktop publishing.

Dictation.   Some business writers, especially professionals and executives with heavy correspondence, dictate their memos, letters, and reports into voice-recording machines. They may use desktop, portable, or centralized units. Many machines include indexing capability for comments to transcribers and dictation review. To use dictation equipment effectively, most individuals need a little instruction and practice. Tips on how to give dictation can be found on page 000.

Dictation of documents is more efficient than handwriting, although a surprising number of business writers still compose first drafts by hand. Younger

---

[5]Stephen W. Quickel, "Management Joins the Computer Age," *Business Month* (May 1989): 42.
[6]Robin Nelson, "CEOs: Computing in High Places," *Personal Computing* (April 1989): 71.

employees, many of whom grew up with computers, are turning to word processing systems to generate documents. Many are like Thomas G. Plaskett, chief executive officer (CEO) of Pan American Airlines. Rather than dictate, he prefers to use a computer for writing his notes, letters, outlines, speeches, and position papers. "I find [dictation] to be a terrible waste of two individuals' time," Plaskett says.[7]

Word Processing Systems.   Probably the single most important tool for business communicators today comes in the form of word processing systems. Documents may be keyboarded on microcomputers or terminals connected to mainframe computers. The writer's composition can be edited, corrected, revised, and manipulated until it's perfect on the screen. Documents can then be printed or stored externally on floppy disks or internally on hard disks. The documents may be called back to the screen for revision. Sophisticated software programs (computer instructions) enable the writer to incorporate graphs and illustrations into documents. Completed documents may be printed on local or distant printers. They may even be distributed electronically without printed hard (paper) copies at all. Some of the most popular word processing packages at this writing are WordPerfect, WordStar, Word, and Xywrite.

Word Processing Accessories.   Today's microcomputer writers have a number of electronic tools to enhance output. Spelling programs accompany many word processing packages. The best are quite effective in locating and correcting spelling or typographical errors. Thesaurus programs, whether resident or external, enable the writer to search and select synonyms when the precise word does not immediately come to the writer's mind. For example, in checking the word *immediately* with my thesaurus program, I found 33 alternatives in an instant. Outlining features help a writer organize a topic according to a traditional outline form.

Grammar and style checkers perform proofreading and editing tasks. Grammatik IV, a currently available aid, identifies the following problems: doubled words and punctuation marks, wordy phrases, passive-voice constructions, and redundant or misused words. It even locates some (but not all) problems in subject-verb agreement and faulty possessive constructions. Although marginally useful to practicing writers, grammar and style checkers are probably most helpful in learning environments, such as the classroom, where an instructor can interpret and evaluate the advice of the software program.

Desktop Publishing.   Microcomputer programs now go far beyond simple word processing. For writers who need to produce bulletin board notices, announcements, brochures, newsletters, pamphlets, or even books—desktop publishing enters the scene. Formerly, only printshops could produce camera-ready copy. New software with printer drivers that control type styles, sizes, and graphic images now allow writers to produce masters that are nearly professional in typeset quality. Desktop publishing requires not only page layout software but also laser printers. Skillful operators enjoy all the advantages of in-house typesetting without its expenses.

New employees, from clerks to managers, find that computer skills are necessary both for entry-level employment and for promotion.

---

[7]Nelson: 79.

Business Manager's Tools

Business managers and executives increase their productivity by using spreadsheet and data-base management programs. Teleconferencing enables them to meet with others electronically.

Spreadsheet.   An electronic spreadsheet is like a large, lined pad of paper used by an accountant. Horizontal columns might show figures for the years, while vertical rows could show income and expenses. This matrix of figures is used to project future costs and revenues or to analyze past performance. Manual calculation is slow and tedious. Computer spreadsheet programs perform these tasks electronically. When one figure is changed, the computer automatically recalculates all entries. Spreadsheets enable managers to forecast or predict future income, expenses, and cash flow. Spreadsheets are invaluable for budgeting and decision making.

> **More spreadsheet programs are sold annually than any other form of computer software.**

Jerry Pearlman, CEO of Zenith Electronics Corporation, says, "There's no substitute for a computer and a good spreadsheet . . . . There are decisions we make now from accumulated data and manipulated data where, once or twice a week, I find myself saying, 'Amazing. We could not have made this decision 10 years ago.' "[8]

Data-base Management.   Programs that sort data into files and records are called data-base management software. If you have placed any telephone orders for merchandise from mail-order catalogs recently, you were probably asked to give the number on your catalog along with your zip code. With that information, your name and previous record could be found in the merchandiser's data base. Data bases are used for customer mailing lists, membership lists, sales leads, equipment inventories, student records, and numerous other applications. Data-base management programs can sort and locate information very quickly from among millions or even billions of files.

Teleconferencing.   Traditionally, businesspeople meet face-to-face to exchange information, discuss variables, and work out decisions. Such one-on-one communication can now be accomplished through the technology of teleconferencing. Rather than travel to distant locations, individuals may conduct a conference electronically. An audioconference involves voice only. It's like a conference call except that individuals at each location are generally together. A videoconference allows two-way audio/video transmission. Participants often go to a nearby hotel where facilities are available for telecasting the conference. The transmission can be in full color with full motion or slow-scan or freeze-frame video. Participants enjoy the benefits of face-to-face communication without paying the heavy price of travel: employee fatigue, lost time, and transportation expenses.

Business Office Tools

Developments in communication technology that serve the entire business office include electronic mail, facsimile, electronic voice messaging, and local area networks (LANs).

[8]Nelson: 77.

Electronic Mail. *Electronic mail* is a broad term that indicates the transmission of messages by means of telephone wire, microwave, satellite, or hardwired cable. To send E-mail messages over hardwired networks, one needs only a computer or a terminal. To send messages using telephone systems, one must have a computer, communication software, and a modem (a device that allows a computer to connect to a telephone). Here's how E-mail works: A computer operator keyboards a message to another individual with a computer or terminal. (This message may be transmitted within the same building or across the country or around the world—instantaneously.) At its destination, the message remains in the receiver's computer until it is read, deleted, filed, or forwarded. The receiver may respond immediately or when convenient.

At Coca-Cola Foods in Houston, Texas, Cheryl Currid, director of applied information technology, found that E-mail has begun to supplant voice communications, as well as meetings in some cases. Before E-mail was introduced, telephone tag was the rule. Now, coworkers are easy to reach, and it usually takes only ten minutes to receive an answer to a message.[9]

As offices become more computer oriented and local area networks become more effective, E-mail may eventually replace most internal forms of communication.

> In offices of the future, E-mail may one day replace most internal forms of communication—including telephone calls, meetings, and "snail mail" (paper mail).

Facsimile. Transmission of documents, charts, graphs, drawings, letters, and photographs may now be accomplished by means of facsimile, or fax, machines. Fax sales are brisk; more than one million standard fax machines were in place in 1990. Law firms use fax to exchange documents, radio stations to take requests, purchasing agents to order goods, and restaurants to receive menu choices. Facsimile transmission is considered a form of electronic mail because it uses telephone wires. However, it is different from other forms of electronic mail in that it transmits an exact duplicate of the original document. Fax copies are so accurate that they are accepted in place of originals in courts of law. E-mail fax is available through many services, such as AT&T Mail, CompuServe, MCI Mail, and Western Union.

LANs. A local area network is a system for transmitting data between electronic devices at one location. Within a business, LANs allow dissimilar computers to "talk" to each other. Such networks are necessary to link large computers, microcomputers, printers, workstations, and other devices so that they can exchange messages. Networks also enable microcomputers to share the resources of large data banks. LANs are required if organizations are to use E-mail services for distributing messages among employees.

Voice Mail. Voice messaging systems allow users to send and receive messages from telephones at any time or to any destination. The computerized voice storage and forward system provides natural voice messages when callers are unable to speak directly. For example, many calls made during business hours in the United States will reach Japan in the middle of the night. With voice mail, the sender's voice is converted to electronic signals that are sent to a mailbox or callback system. The recipient takes the call when convenient. Messages can be

---

[9]Emily Kay, "E-Mail for LANs: Redefining Corporate Networking," *Personal Computing* (November 1989): 127–28.

replayed, edited, stored, erased, or forwarded to another individual. Another benefit of voice mail is that one voice message can be sent to many people at once.

≋

Developing Your Communication Skills

Thus far in this chapter you've learned that communication skills are vital both in the business world and in your personal life. You've become familiar with the communication process, and you've had a brief introduction to some of the communication tools that technology has produced.

What does all this mean to you? It means that to be successful, you need well-developed communication skills. But the ability to communicate effectively is not a universal trait. Most of us require instruction, practice, supervision, and feedback to develop and improve these communication skills.

Effective communication includes oral, listening, and writing skills. All these topics will be presented in this book, along with numerous opportunities to apply the concepts presented. In addition to techniques, you will learn to apply practical psychological principles in solving communication problems. Many of the suggestions intended for analyzing business communication problems are equally helpful in resolving personal problems.

Emphasis on Writing

For many reasons, special emphasis will be directed to writing skills. The most significant information in business and industry eventually must be committed to writing. Although data may be shared by telephone and decisions arrived at in conversations, businesspeople frequently say, "Put it in writing" or "Get it on paper." A written record is necessary for permanence and for legal purposes.

Good writers are not born with their writing skills; they develop such skills through training and practice.

The process of "putting it in writing" can be painful. Writing is not easy, especially if the writer has little instruction or supervised practice. Effective writing techniques, however, can be learned, and real skill can be developed.

Four Stages of Development

Good writers learn the craft of writing in much the same way that other skilled artisans or professionals learn their trades. Each of them typically follows a four-stage plan.

The first stage involves learning how to use the *tools of the trade*. For the writer these tools are the basic rules of language, including grammar, punctuation, and capitalization, as well as number, spelling, and syntax conventions.

In the second stage the writer learns the *proper techniques* for efficient and coherent combination of these basic tools. These techniques involve learning how to use words skillfully and precisely, how to write effective sentences and paragraphs, and how to develop appropriate style and tone.

After learning these techniques, the writer needs a *plan of action*. For example, what procedures or strategies are known to be effective in writing a business letter? The third stage, then, involves learning and applying strategies for producing the desired result.

Finally, in the fourth stage, the writer practices *applying the tools, techniques, and strategies* in varying situations. In this way writers improve their skills in producing satisfactory results.

Textbook Parallel

This textbook is organized to parallel and amplify these four stages of skill development. Stage 1 (Chapter 1 and the Grammar/Mechanics Handbook) lays a foundation for communication by introducing communication theory and concepts. Some students will need to review the basic tools in language. Your instructor may assign the Grammar/Mechanics Diagnostic Test so that you can assess your strengths and weaknesses. The Grammar/Mechanics Handbook, following the diagnostic test, provides a review of grammar and punctuation, as well as exercises to enable you to sharpen your basic skills.

Stage 2 (Chapters 2, 3, and 4) presents writing techniques, the "tricks of the trade" for authors. Stage 3 (Chapters 5 through 9) develops communication strategies. Stage 4 (Chapters 10 through 14) applies and adapts these techniques and strategies in varying communication situations.

The emphasis throughout this volume is on developing communication skills in practical business applications.

APPLICATION AND PRACTICE—1

Discussion

1. How do communication skills affect promotion to and within management?

2. Discuss the statement that managers or executives with good secretaries do not have to be concerned with their own communication skills.

3. Describe the communication cycle. Why should it be considered a cycle rather than a line?

4. Select two of the newer communication tools and describe how they might be useful in increasing productivity in a given business field.

5. It's been said that individuals can operate cars without knowing how to build or repair them. How does that statement relate to today's computerized communication tools?

Short Answers

6. Name three jobs in which good communication skills would be important for entry-level positions.

7. Name three positions to which an employee with good communication skills could be promoted.

8. Name two or more ways in which an individual with good communication skills could be valuable to an organization.

9. Name two reasons for putting a business message in writing.

10. What are three definitions for the word *communication*?

11. Give a brief definition or explanation of the following words:
    a. Encode
    b. Channel
    c. Decode

12. Name four tools for today's business communicator. Be ready to discuss how each might be useful in your career.

13. Name three tools for today's business manager. Be ready to discuss how each might be useful in your career.

14. Name four new communication tools for today's offices. Be ready to discuss how each might be useful in your career.

15. List four stages in developing the craft of writing.

Activities

16. Get to know your classmates. Since a successful communication class begins with open lines of communication among and between class members, learn something about your classmates. Your instructor may choose one of the following two techniques.

    a. For larger classes your instructor may divide the class into groups of four or five. Take one minute to introduce yourself briefly (name, major academic interest, hobbies, goals). Spend five minutes in the first group session. Record the first name of each individual you meet. Then informally regroup. In new groups, again spend five minutes on introductions. After three or four sessions, study your name list. How many names can you associate with faces?

    b. For smaller classes, your instructor may ask each student to introduce himself or herself in a two-minute oral presentation while standing before the class at the rostrum. Where are you from? What are your educational goals? What are your interests? This informal presentation can serve as the first of two or three oral presentations correlated with Chapter 14, *Listening and Speaking*.

17. From the Sunday classified section of your local newspaper (or the newspaper of a larger city nearby), select five or more advertisements for

positions that require good communication skills. Bring them to class for discussion.

18. Analyze the communication process for a vice president of sales who must send an announcement to the sales staff regarding a new product. Using the communication model on page 8, discuss the components of the process. How might noise interfere with successful communication? How could the vice president reduce or prevent such noise? How could he or she ensure feedback?

19. Imagine a business in which you have been employed or an organization in which you have participated. Suggest five specific ways in which this organization could improve its communication with employees or members. Your instructor may ask you to report your suggestions in memo form. See Appendix 1 for memo formatting.

20. Imagine that classmates of yours are unconvinced of the need for good communication skills in your major. They believe that such skills are unnecessary in this field. Moreover, they claim that they will have secretaries or word processors to clean up weak writing. Do you agree or disagree?

21. At the direction of your instructor, make an oral or written report based on an interview with a businessperson. Gather information on these topics: (a) types and frequency of communication within the business, (b) importance of written communication to the individual and to the business, (c) importance of oral communication to the individual and to the business, and (d) types of technological tools used to enhance decision making and communication.

22. Begin reading articles in business magazines and newspapers. Some possibilities are *Business Week, Consumer Reports, Entrepreneur, Forbes, Fortune, Money, The Economist, The Monthly Labor Review, U.S. News and World Report,* and *Venture.* Two good newspapers are *The Wall Street Journal* and *Barron's National Business and Financial Weekly.* Consult the *Business Periodicals Index* for articles listed by subject. Reading well-written articles will not only help you improve your vocabulary and provide examples of good writing but will also expand your knowledge of events in the business world. Your instructor may direct you to write a memo summarizing each article. Your memo should introduce the topic, summarize main points, describe weaknesses and strengths, identify the audience for whom the article was intended, and conclude with your reactions to what you have learned. See Appendix 1 for memo formatting.

23. Make an informal study of technology in your field. Talk with two or more individuals who are familiar with your career field. Ask them which, if any, of the new communication and decision-making technologies they are using. What reactions do they have to the effectiveness of these technologies? What recommendations do they have for individuals training to enter the field? Be prepared to present your findings in an oral or written report.

GRAMMAR/MECHANICS CHECKUP—1

Nouns

These checkups are designed to improve your control of grammar and mechanics. They systematically review all sections of the Grammar/Mechanics Handbook. Answers are given for odd-numbered statements; answers to even-numbered statements will be provided by your instructor.

Review Sections 1.01 through 1.06 in the Grammar/Mechanics Handbook. Then study each of the following statements. Underscore any inappropriate form, and write a correction in the space provided. Also record the appropriate G/M section and letter to illustrate the principle involved. If a sentence is correct, write *C*. When you finish, compare your responses with those provided. If your answers differ, study carefully the principles shown in parentheses.

companies   (1.05e)

Example: Two surveys revealed that many <u>companys</u> will move to the new industrial park.

_____   1. Several attornies investigated the case and presented their opinions.

_____   2. At the counter we are busier on Saturday's, but telephone business is greater on Sundays.

_____   3. Some of the citys in Mr. Graham's report offer excellent opportunities.

_____   4. Frozen chickens and turkies are kept in the company's basement lockers.

_____   5. All secretaries were asked to check supplies and other inventorys immediately.

_____   6. Both the Finchs and the Lopezes agreed to attend the business meeting.

_____   7. In the 1980s profits slowly grew; in the 1990's we anticipate greater growth.

_____   8. The two father-in-laws kept silent during the civil and religious ceremonies.

_____   9. Luxury residential complexs are part of the architect's overall plan.

_____   10. Voters in three countys are likely to approve increasing gas taxes.

_____   11. The instructor was surprised to find three Jennifer's in one class.

_____   12. California's interior valleys become quite warm in August.

_____   13. All of the bosses of the secretarys attended the luncheon.

_____   14. The sign was difficult to read because one could not distinguish between its *o's* and *a's*.

_____   15. Two runner-ups complained that they should have won the contest.

---

1. attorneys (*1.05d*)   3. cities (*1.05e*)   5. inventories (*1.05e*)   7. 1990s (*1.05g*)
9. complexes (*1.05b*)   11. Jennifers (*1.05a*)   13. secretaries (*1.05e*)   15. runners-up (*1.05f*)

CHAPTER 2

Using Words Skillfully

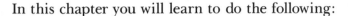

In this chapter you will learn to do the following:

- Make your writing more readable by substituting familiar words for unfamiliar words.
- Recognize and avoid unnecessary jargon, legalese, foreign expressions, and slang.
- Achieve a forceful style by using precise verbs, concrete nouns, vivid adjectives, and other specific forms.
- Avoid clichés, buzz words, repetitious words, and redundancies.
- Identify and employ idiomatic expressions.

We usually take the words we use for granted, seldom thinking consciously about choosing them carefully. We use whatever words come to mind. In this chapter we will ask you to become more aware of the words that you write.

Most of us seldom choose our words carefully.

Writers are totally dependent on their words to convey meaning. If the speaker's words are not understood in conversation, the listener will signal verbally or nonverbally that more information is needed to clarify an idea being expressed. If a writer's words are unclear, the reader cannot immediately seek clarification.

Because words commonly have different meanings for different individuals, the communicator must be judicious in word selection and usage. We can never be certain that our words will have the exact effect intended. We can, however, improve our chances for successful communication by following specific word-selection and writing techniques. The techniques presented here include practical suggestions encouraging the use of familiar and vivid words. We'll also show you how to avoid overworked, redundant, and improper words.

Familiar Words

Clear messages contain words that are familiar and meaningful to the reader. How can we know what is meaningful to a given reader? Although we can't know with certainty, we can avoid certain groups of words that are likely to create misunderstanding.

Familiar words are more meaningful to readers.

Avoid long, difficult, unfamiliar words. Substitute short, simple, common words. Here are some examples:

Difficult, Unfamiliar Words	Simple Alternatives
ascertain	find out
conceptualize	see
encompass	include
hypothesize	guess
monitor	check
operational	working
option	choice
perpetuate	continue
perplexing	troubling
reciprocate	return
stipulate	require
terminate	end
utilize	use

Jargon

Jargon, which is terminology unique to a certain profession, should be reserved for individuals who understand it.

Avoid jargon and unnecessary technical terms. Jargon is special terminology that is peculiar to a particular activity or profession. For example, geologists speak knowingly of *exfoliation*, *calcareous ooze*, and *siliceous particles*. Aerospace engineers are familiar with phrases like *infrared processing flags*, *output latches*, and *movable symbology*. Telecommunication experts use such words and phrases as *protocol*, *mode*, and *asynchronous transmission*.

"It could mean 'Men at Work'?"

Source: From *The Wall Street Journal*. Reprinted with permission of the Cartoon Features Syndicate.

Every field has its own special vocabulary. Using that vocabulary within the field is acceptable and even necessary for accurate communication. Don't use special terms, however, if you have reason to believe that your reader may misunderstand them.

〰 Plain Language

Good writers use plain language to express clear meaning. They do not use showy words and ambiguous expression in an effort to dazzle or confuse readers. They write to express ideas, not to impress others.

Some business, legal, and government documents are written in an inflated style that obscures meaning. This style of writing has been given various terms, such as *legalese*, *federalese*, *bureaucratese*, *doublespeak*, and the *official style*. It may be used intentionally to mask meaning, or it may simply be an attempt to show off the writer's intelligence and learning. What do you think the manager's intention was in writing the following message?

Inflated, unnatural writing that is intended to impress readers more often confuses them.

> Personnel assigned vehicular space in the adjacent areas are hereby
> advised that utilization will be suspended temporarily Friday morning.

Employees will probably have to read that sentence several times before they understand that they are being advised not to park in the lot next door Friday morning.

Legal documents and contracts often suffer from this same inflated, ambiguous style. In response, some state governments have passed "plain English" laws. These laws require that consumer contracts be written in a clear and coherent style using everyday words. One New York firm specializes in producing "de-jargonized" forms for banks, government offices, insurance companies, and real estate firms.

What does plain English mean? Although it's difficult to define precisely, it generally means writing that is clear, simple, and understandable. It suggests writing that is easy to follow, well organized, and appropriately divided. A plain English document should include many of the writing techniques you are about to study (active voice, positive form, parallel construction, use of headings).

Don't be impressed by high-sounding language and legalese, such as *herein*, *thereafter*, *hereinafter*, *whereas*, and similar expressions. Your writing will be better understood if you use plain expressions.

〰 Foreign Expressions

To many readers, foreign expressions are like a code; they hold secret meanings known only to the select few. Writers who use foreign expressions risk offending readers who cannot decipher the code. Although such expressions as *crème de la crème* may flavor the prose of world travelers, they have little justification in business writing.

Slang

Slang sounds
fashionable, but it
lacks precise
meaning and should
be avoided in
business writing.

Like foreign expressions, slang usually has precise meaning for only a favored few. Slang is composed of informal words with arbitrary and extravagantly changed meanings. Slang words quickly go out of fashion because they are no longer appealing when everyone begins to understand them. The following statement, quoted by the *Los Angeles Times*, was made by a government official. He had been asked why his department was dropping a proposal to lease offshore oil lands, and he responded: "The Administration has an awful lot of other things in the pipeline, and this has more wiggle room so they just moved it down the totem pole." He added, however, that the proposal might be offered again since "there is no pulling back because of hot-potato factors."

The meaning here, if the speaker really intended to impart any, is considerably obscured by the use of slang. Good communicators, of course, aim at clarity and avoid unintelligible slang.

Forceful Words

Effective writing creates meaningful images in the mind of the reader. Such writing is sparked by robust, concrete, and descriptive words. Ineffective writing is often dulled by insipid, abstract, and generalized words. To produce messages that communicate your intentions, use precise verbs, concrete nouns, and vivid adjectives.

Precise Verbs

The most direct way to improve lifeless writing is through effective use of verbs. Verbs not only indicate the action of the subject but also deliver the force of the sentence. Select verbs carefully so that the reader can visualize precisely what is happening.

Precise verbs make
your writing forceful
and intelligible.

General: Our salesperson will *contact* you next month.

Precise: Our salesperson will (*telephone, write, visit*) . . . .

General: The vice president *said* that we should contribute.

Precise: The vice president (*urged, pleaded, demanded*) . . . .

General: We must *consider* this problem.

Precise: We must (*clarify, remedy, rectify*) . . . .

General: The newspaper was *affected* by the strike.

Precise: The newspaper was (*crippled, silenced, demoralized*) . . . .

The power of a verb is diminished when it is needlessly converted into a noun. This happens when verbs such as *acquire, establish,* and *develop* are made into nouns (*acquisition, establishment,* and *development*). These nouns then receive the central emphasis in the sentence. In the following pairs of sentences, observe how forceful the original verbs are as compared with their noun forms.

Verb: The city *acquired* park lands recently.

Noun: *Acquisition* of park lands was made recently by the city.

Verb: Mr. Miller and Mrs. Lopez *discussed* credit card billing.

Noun: Mr. Miller and Mrs. Lopez had a *discussion* concerning credit card billing.

Verb: Both companies must *approve* the merger.

Noun: Both companies must grant *approval* of the merger.

Concrete Nouns

Nouns name persons, places, and things. Abstract nouns name concepts that are difficult to visualize, such as *automation, function, justice, institution, integrity, form, judgment,* and *environment.* Concrete nouns name objects that are more easily imagined, such as *desk, car,* and *light bulb.* Nouns describing a given object can range from the very abstract to the very concrete; for example, *object, motor vehicle, car, convertible, Mustang.* All of these words or phrases can be used to describe a Mustang convertible. However, a reader would have difficulty envisioning a Mustang convertible when given just the word *object* or even *motor vehicle* or *car.*

Concrete nouns help readers visualize the meanings of words.

In business writing, help your reader "see" what you mean by using concrete language.

General	Concrete
a *change* in our budget	a *10 percent reduction* in our budget
that company's product	*Panasonic's Sensicolor videotape*
a *person* called	*Mrs. Swain, the administrative assistant,* called
we *improved* the assembly line	we *installed 26 advanced Unimate robots* on the assembly line

Vivid Adjectives

Including highly descriptive, dynamic adjectives is the easiest way to make writing more vivid and concrete. Be careful, though, not to overuse them nor to lose objectivity in selecting them.

General: The report was on time.

Vivid: The *detailed 12-page* report was submitted on time.

General: John needs a better truck.

Vivid: John needs a *rugged, four-wheel-drive Dodge* truck.

General: We enjoyed the movie.

Vivid: We enjoyed the *entertaining* and *absorbing* movie.

Overkill: We enjoyed the *gutsy, exciting, captivating,* and *thoroughly marvelous* movie.

A good writer combines precise verbs, concrete nouns, and vivid adjectives with other carefully selected words to give the reader specific facts rather than

A thesaurus (on your computer or in a book) helps you select precise words and also increases your vocabulary.

flabby generalizations. Notice how much more meaningful the concrete version is in each of the following sentence pairs:

General: One of the company's officers has proved unworthy of corporate trust.

Concrete: Don DeSoto, treasurer, embezzled $25,000 of Datacom's funds.

General: The computer is portable and handy.

Concrete: The 5-pound, notebook-sized MicroOffice "RoadRunner" portable computer uses removable, reusable cartridges.

General: The implementation of improved operations may change company vitality soon.

Concrete: By improving packaging, shipping, and distribution procedures, we expect to increase gross profits by 14 percent within three months.

General: A new management official was recently hired to improve the division.

Concrete: Appointed senior vice president of marketing on August 27, Jeffrey Bamford launched a comprehensive program to retrain sales representatives in his Market Services Division.

By describing facts with precise verbs, concrete nouns, and vivid adjectives, you can make sure your readers understand your message.

Clichés

Clichés are dull and sometimes ambiguous.

Clichés are expressions that have become exhausted by overuse. These expressions not only lack freshness but also frequently lack clarity for some individuals who misunderstand their meaning. The following partial list contains representative clichés you should avoid in business writing.

below the belt	keep your nose to the grindstone
better than new	last but not least
beyond the shadow of a doubt	make a bundle
easier said than done	pass with flying colors
exception to the rule	quick as a flash
fill the bill	shoot from the hip
first and foremost	stand your ground
hard facts	true to form

Can you think of any clichés to add to this list? How about, *it goes without saying*—(and it probably should)?

Buzz words are overworked expressions taken from industry or government.

Buzz Words

Another category of overworked expressions is that of so-called buzz words. These expressions, often borrowed from industry or government, are words and phrases of fashion. They seem to be used more often to impress the reader than to express the user's meaning.

commonality	parameter
configuration	productionwise (profitwise, budgetwise, and other *-wise* words)
dysfunction	
impact on	prioritize
incremental	scenario
interface	state of the art
interrelationships	subsystem
logistical	systematized
orientate	unilateral

Repetitious Words

Good communicators vary their words to avoid unintentional repetition. Observe how heavy and monotonous the following personnel announcement seems:

> Employees will be able to elect an additional six employees to serve with the four previously elected employees who currently comprise the employees' board of directors. To ensure representation, swing-shift employees will be electing one swing-shift employee as their sole representative.

The unconscious repetition of words creates monotonous and boring reading.

The preceding version uses the word *employee* six times. In addition, the last sentence begins with the word *representation* and ends with the similar word *representative*. An easier-to-read version follows:

> Employees will be able to elect an additional six representatives to serve with the four previously elected members of the employees' board of directors. To ensure representation, swing-shift workers will elect their own board member.

In the second version, synonyms (*representatives, members, workers*) replaced *employee*. The last sentence was reworked by using a pronoun (*their*) and by substituting *board member* for the repetitious *representative*. Variety of expression can be achieved by searching for appropriate synonyms and by substituting pronouns.

Good writers are also alert to the overuse of the articles *a, an,* and particularly *the*. Often the word *the* can simply be omitted. Articles can also be eliminated by changing singular constructions to plurals. In the following revision, for example, *a change in the price of gas* becomes *changes in gas prices*:

Wordy: The deregulation of the natural gas industry has caused a change in the price of gas.

Improved: Deregulation of the natural gas industry caused changes in gas prices.

Notice the efficiency of the second sentence.

≈≈

Redundant Words

Repetition of words to achieve emphasis or effective transition is an important writing technique we'll discuss in forthcoming chapters. The needless repetition, however, of words whose meanings are clearly implied by other words is a writing fault called *redundancy*. For example, in the expression *final outcome*, the word *final* is redundant and should be omitted, since *outcome* implies finality. Learn to avoid redundant expressions such as the following:

absolutely essential	*final* outcome
adequate *enough*	*grateful* thanks
advance warning	*mutual* cooperation
basic fundamentals	*necessary* prerequisite
big *in size*	*new* beginning
combined *together*	*past* history
consensus *of opinion*	reason *why*
continue *on*	red *in color*
each *and every*	refer *back*
exactly identical	repeat *again*
few *in number*	*true* facts

≈≈

Idiomatic Words

Every language has its own *idiom*, that is, its own special way of combining words. In English, as in any language, it's important to use combinations of words that "sound right" to the typical native speaker. Particularly important is the use of the right prepositions with certain words. Study the following examples:

acquainted *with* (not *on* or *about*)	guard *against* (not *from*)
agree *to* (not *with*) a proposal	in accordance *with* (not *to*)
agree *with* a person	independent *of* (not *from*)
angry *at* (not *with*) a thing	interest *in* (not *about*)
angry *with* a person	plan *to* (not *on*)
authority *on* (not *about* or *in*)	retroactive *to*
buy *from* (not *off of*)	sensitive *to*
capable *of*	try *to* (not *and*)

≈≈≈≈≈

How to Increase Your Vocabulary in Six Steps

Success in your education, career, and personal life is enhanced by possessing a precise vocabulary. The number one learning difficulty among college students is deficient vocabulary. Word skills are also important in the workplace. A direct correlation exists between vocabulary and success in employment. Studies show that managers and executives have larger vocabularies than the employees they direct. Often individuals are hired or promoted because they are able to express their ideas persuasively and precisely. If you are serious about improving your vocabulary, here are six steps that research shows are most effective in helping adults increase their knowledge of words.[1]

- **Make a commitment.** Decide that you want to increase your vocabulary and that you are willing to work toward that goal. Without a goal or a commitment, little is achieved. Vague feelings regarding self-improvement and half-hearted attempts seldom produce significant change.

- **Select your own material.** Research with post-secondary students shows that long-term vocabulary gains are greatest when learners choose the target words themselves instead of attempting to memorize isolated words on lists developed by others. Moreover, words drawn from a unifying content, such as your major subject area, allow you to integrate your previous knowledge and provide a framework within which you can use the new words.

- **Choose five good words.** From your assigned homework reading in any course, select five good words each week. The words should be ones that you feel are important in your field and ones whose meanings you do not know. Record the words in a vocabulary journal, following this format: word, source, pronunciation, sentence in which you found the word (underline the word), and dictionary definition. Use a journal or keep the same information on 3 × 5 cards.

- **Use the key image method.** Research with learners of all ages reveals that we can remember a new word better if we form a mental picture of its definition or an image of some part of the word that will relate to the definition. For example, the word *acrophobia* has two parts: *acro* means height and *phobia* means fear. Imagine the word *acrobat*, which starts with the same letters and could suggest a performer high in the air, a performer who conquered his or her fear of height. Form a mental picture of the acrobat. Make a sentence

[1]Based on Michele L. Simpson, Sherrie L. Nist, Kate Kirby, "Ideas in Practice: Vocabulary Strategies Designed for College Students," *Journal of Developmental Education* (November 1987): 20.

using this picture and the new word: *The acrobat performed skillfully on the high wire showing absolutely no acrophobia, a fear of heights.* Close your eyes; recall the picture and the sentence.

- **Make concept cards.** If no key image comes to mind, try another strategy. Record the targeted word in bold letters on the front of a 3 × 5 card. In the upper right-hand corner record the topic or category into which the word could be classified. For example, the word *boilerplate* would be classified under the concept of *word processing.* On the back of the card, record the definition in your own words. Then show examples of the word, if possible, such as "Examples—form letter paragraphs used by insurance companies—one kind of boilerplate." Add any other personal associations or clues that will help you remember this word.

- **Practice your words.** Concentrate on your five weekly words, and then pronounce them. Look for other occurrences of these words in your assignments. Use the words in sentences. Review your vocabulary journal and/or cards several times a week.

College students and other adults using these steps are much more successful in increasing their vocabularies than in memorizing word lists. Remember, though, that nothing substantial is achieved without effort.

APPLICATION AND PRACTICE—2

Discussion

1. Writers should always use familiar words. Discuss.

2. Because legal documents are written to be extremely precise, everyone should write like an attorney. Discuss.

3. How can dull, lifeless writing be made forceful?

4. Because clichés are familiar and have stood the test of time, they help clarify writing. Discuss.

5. Why is idiom one of the hardest elements of language for foreign speakers to master?

Short Answers

6. Define *jargon*.

7. Provide at least three examples of jargon from your chosen field of specialization.

8. Define *slang*.

9. Give at least three examples of current slang.

10. Verbs are the most important words in sentences because they do what?

11. What happens when verbs are converted to nouns (for example, when *acquire* becomes "to make an acquisition")?

12. Define *cliché* and provide at least one example (other than those shown in the chapter) that you have heard frequently.

13. What are articles, and what problem do they present to writers?

14. Define *redundant* and provide an example.

15. Define *idiom* and provide an illustration.

Writing Improvement Exercises

Familiar Words. Revise the following sentences using simpler language for unfamiliar terms. Assume that you are writing at a level appropriate for typical business communication. Use a dictionary if necessary.

Example: Please ascertain the extent of our fiscal liability.
Revision: Please find how much we owe.

16. Profits are declining because our sales staff is insufficiently cognizant of our competitor's products.

    We are losing money because our sales STAFF is NOT aware of our competitors products

17. He hypothesized that the vehicle was not operational because of a malfunctioning gasket.

    He decided the vehicle was NOT working because of a bad gasket

18. It may be necessary to ~~terminate the employment~~ of Mr. Sims.

    fire

19. The contract stipulates that management must perpetuate the present profit-sharing plan.

    IT is required that management must join the profit-sharing plan.

20. Numerous employee options are encompassed in the recently revised benefit package.

    The new benefit package includes many choices.

Jargon, Slang. Revise the following sentences using simpler language that would be clear to an average reader. Avoid jargon, foreign expressions, and slang.

Example: Because of a glitch in the program, the printout appears *sans* statistics.
Revision: Because of an error in the program, the printout appears without statistics.

21. This contract contains a ~~caveat~~ *stipulation* stipulating that vendors must utilize ~~bona fide~~ *real* parts.

22. Quality products had heretofore helped this organization perpetuate its central market position.

    The marketing of quality products has helped ~~this organ~~ us

23. Although there ~~is little wiggle-room~~ *are few allowances* in our budget, by ~~keeping a tight ship~~ *being thrifty* we should have this project ~~operational right~~ on target.

24. In regard to our advertising budget, Mr. Hargrove says that TV is going down the tubes because audiences are being fractionalized into special interest groups.

    To safeguard our T.V. advertising budget, Mr. Hargrove says we'll need to change to include special interest groups.

25. This half-price ~~promotional~~ *advertising* ~~campa~~ign sounds ~~real gutsy~~ *courageous*, but I ~~don't~~ think we should ~~touch it with a 10-foot pole.~~ *leave it alone.* *forget it.*

Precise Verbs.   Rewrite these sentences, centering the action in the verbs.

Example: Mrs. Kinski gave an appraisal of the equipment.

Revision: Mrs. Kinski appraised the equipment.

26. The engineer ~~made a description of~~ *described* the project.

27. Can you ~~bring about a~~ change ~~in~~ our company travel policy?

28. In writing this proposal, we must ~~make application~~ *include* of the new government regulations.

29. *By* Streamlin~~ed~~*ing* procedures will ~~produce the effect of reduction in~~ *we cut* labor costs.

30. The board of directors ~~made a~~ recommend~~ation~~*ed* ~~affirming~~ *that we abandon* ~~abandonment of~~ the pilot project.

31. An investigator ~~made a determination of~~ *determined* the fire damage~~s~~.

32. We hope to have ~~production of~~ our new line of products by January.

33. The duty of the comptroller is ~~verification of~~ *to verify* departmental budgets.

34. Please ~~make a correction in~~ *credit* my account ~~to reflect~~ *with* my late payment.

35. The compilation of tax returns is the function of our accountant.

Our accountant compiles tax returns

Vivid Words.   Revise the following sentences to include vivid and concrete language. Add appropriate words.

Example: They said it was a long way off.

Revision: Management officials announced that the merger would not take place for two years.

36. Our new copier is ~~fast.~~

efficient

37. Mr. Grant's record indicates that he is a good worker.

Mr. Grant is efficient, effective, on-time and without complaint

38. An employee from that company called about our new computer.

Mrs. Smith, the hardware ~~hardware~~ specialist at ~~from~~ Univac called about our new Univac 10,000.

39. Please contact them soon.

Please notify the specialist soon.

40. They said that the movie they saw was very interesting.

Susie & Tom said the movie "Gone w/ the Wind" moved them to tears

Clichés, Buzz Words, Repetition.   Revise the following sentences to avoid clichés, buzz words, and unnecessary repetition.

Example: The president said that it was the president's job to spearhead the drive for energy conservation.

Revision: The president said that it was his job to lead the drive for energy conservation.

41. The production manager arrived ~~just~~ in ~~the nick of~~ time to prevent the oil ~~damage~~ from damaging the floor.

42. New ~~corporate~~ taxes will impact ~~on~~ corporations ~~in the course of events.~~ _soon._

43. The contract will be considered ~~a~~ valid ~~contract~~ if the terms ~~of said contract are configured to~~ meet with ~~the~~ approval of all parties who ~~will~~ sign ~~the contract.~~

44. Employees receive ~~employee~~ raises in ~~orderly incremental~~ step ~~raises.~~ _s_

45. ~~Without rhyme or reason~~ Sales Manager, Shimada, refused to interface ~~or have personal conferences~~ with ~~any~~ sales reps ~~face to face.~~

Redundant Words, Idiomatic Expressions.   Rewrite the following sentences to correct the use of redundant words and unidiomatic expressions.

Example: In accordance to your wishes, we have completely eliminated tipping.

Revision: In accordance with your wishes, we have eliminated tipping.

46. ~~First and foremost,~~ _First,_ ~~W~~e plan on emphasizing an instructional training program.

47. _In refering to her file_ ~~If you will refer back to her file~~, you will see ~~that the reason~~ why Carmen Campis was chosen ~~is that she has~~ _because of her_ experience ~~in~~ _that_ many different fields.

48. It was ~~the consensus of opinion of the~~ _agreed_ committee ~~that it~~ _that the committee_ should meet at 11 a.m. in the morning.

49. Although ~~she was angry with the report,~~ Lucy Williams, _she_ collected together ~~her~~ facts to make a last and final effort.

50. ~~One~~ _A_ local resident asked for all the ~~important~~ _important details_ ~~essentials~~ regarding small business loans.

Legalese, Bureaucratese, Jargon.   Find examples of legalese, bureaucratese, or jargon in newspapers, magazines, or other documents. Bring them to class for discussion. Continue to search for such examples as your course continues.

GRAMMAR/MECHANICS CHECKUP—2

Pronouns

Review Sections 1.07 through 1.09 in the Grammar/Mechanics Handbook. Then study each of the following statements. In the space provided, write the word that completes the statement correctly and the number of the G/M principle illustrated. When you finish, compare your responses with those shown below. If your responses differ, study carefully the principles in parentheses.

its   (1.09d)
_____

Example: The Recreation and Benefits Committee will be submitting (its, their) report soon.

_____ 1. I was expecting Mr. Marks to call. Was it (he, him) who left the message?

_____ 2. Every one of the members of the men's bowling team had to move (his car, their cars) before the tournament could begin.

_____ 3. A serious disagreement between management and (he, him) caused his resignation.

_____ 4. Does anyone in the office know for (who, whom) this paper was ordered?

_____ 5. It looks as if (her's, hers) is the only report that contains the sales figures.

_____ 6. Mrs. Simmons asked my friend and (I, me, myself) to help her complete the work.

_____ 7. My friend and (I, me, myself) were also asked to work on Saturday.

_____ 8. We sent both printers in for repair, but (yours, your's) should be returned shortly.

_____ 9. Give the budget figures to (whoever, whomever) asked for them.

_____ 10. Everyone except the broker and (I, me, myself) claimed a share of the commission.

_____ 11. No one knows that problem better than (he, him, himself).

_____ 12. Investment brochures and information were sent to (we, us) shareholders.

_____ 13. If any one of the women tourists has lost (their, her) scarf, please see the driver.

_____ 14. Neither the glamour nor the excitement of the position had lost (its, it's, their) appeal.

_____ 15. Any new subscriber may cancel (their, his or her) subscription within the first month.*

*Note: How could the last statement be reworded to avoid the awkward *his-or-her* construction? See 1.09b.

---

1. he (*1.08b*)   3. him (*1.08c*)   5. hers (*1.08d*)   7. I (*1.08a*)   9. whoever (*1.08j*)
11. he (*1.08f*)   13. her (*1.09c*)   15. his or her (*1.09b*)

CHAPTER 3

Developing Tone and Style

~~~~~~~

In this chapter you will learn to do the following:

- Appreciate how writing tone and style affect goodwill.
- Recognize and develop reader benefits in your writing.
- Distinguish between formal and conversational language.
- Avoid outdated expressions.

- Improve your writing by condensing wordiness.
- Use positive language.
- Project confidence.
- Replace sexist terms with appropriate alternatives.

In addition to using words skillfully, good writers and communicators practice other techniques that make messages effective. They are aware of the tone and style of their messages. They know—consciously or unconsciously—how their words sound to listeners and readers. In this chapter techniques for developing and improving tone and style will be featured. These techniques include using conversational and current language, writing concisely, including reader benefits, expressing ideas positively, showing confidence, and being sensitive to sexist terms.

Cultivating Goodwill

Before we turn to specific techniques for improving tone and style, let's consider the concept of *goodwill*. Goodwill is an abstract quality defined as "a kindly feeling of approval and support." It represents the favor, prestige, and good reputation that a business enjoys. Some companies develop goodwill by making donations to local projects and charities. Some offer special discounts to students and senior citizens. Still others train their employees to greet all customers by name. Businesses know that such actions create a feeling of approval toward them. They strive to develop goodwill because it's a valuable asset. It can even be assigned a monetary value when businesses calculate their worth.

Goodwill reflects the favorable attitude of customers toward a business.

Developing goodwill is worthwhile not only for business organizations but for individuals as well. As individuals, we appreciate being treated with courtesy and tact. We enjoy working and living in environments that are harmonious. Most of us dislike causing unhappiness, disappointment, or enmity. We feel better and we make others feel better when our actions promote harmony and goodwill.

The techniques for developing goodwill that you will learn in this chapter and throughout the book are aimed at helping you communicate effectively. You will find, moreover, that many of these same techniques may be applied in your personal life to enable you to get along better with people and to help you achieve your life goals.

In business messages goodwill is achieved through appropriate tone and style. Tone in a business letter describes the mood of a message; it reflects the writer's attitude toward the reader. The tone of a letter may be constructive or destructive, casual or formal, patronizing or sincere, arrogant or helpful, objective or subjective, pompous or humble, subtle or blunt, demanding or conciliatory, old-fashioned or contemporary. Notice how harsh and patronizing the following sentence sounds:

> If you would take the time to read your operator's manual, you will see that your car should have received full servicing at 10,000 miles.

The writer's feelings toward the reader come through in the tone of this message. Here are techniques for helping you cultivate appropriate tone and style in your business communication.

> *One of the best ways to enlarge your vocabulary is to look up meanings of unfamiliar words. For example, in the second line check out the meaning of enmity.*

～ Conversational Language

Business letters and memos replace conversation. Therefore, they are most effective when they convey an informal, conversational tone instead of a formal, artificial tone.

A casual, conversational tone in letters is harder to achieve than it may appear. Many writers tend to become formal, unnatural, and distant when they put words on paper. They seem to undergo personality changes, taking on a different persona when their fingers pick up a pencil or approach a keyboard. Perhaps this is a result of composition training in schools. Many students learned to develop a writing style that impressed the instructor. They were rewarded when they used big words, complex sentences, and abstractions, even if their ideas were not altogether clear. After leaving school, some writers continue to use words that inflate ideas, making them sound important and intellectual. Instead of writing as they would speak in conversation, their sentences become long and complex, and expression of their thoughts is confusing. Rather than using familiar pronouns such as *I*, *we*, and *you*, they depersonalize their writing by relying on third-person constructions such as *the undersigned, the writer*, and *the affected party*.

To develop a warm, friendly tone in your letters, imagine that you are sitting next to the reader. *Talk* to the reader with words that sound comfortable to you. Don't be afraid to use an occasional contraction such as *We're* or *I'll*. Avoid legal terminology, technical words, and formal constructions. Your writing will be

> *Do you go through a Dr. Jekyll–Mr. Hyde personality change when you begin writing?*

easier to read and understand if it sounds like the following conversational examples:

Formal language	Conversational language
All employees are herewith instructed to return the appropriately designated contracts to the undersigned.	Please return your contracts to me.
Pertaining to your order, we must verify the sizes that your organization requires prior to consignment of your order to our shipper.	We'll send your order as soon as we confirm the sizes you need.
The writer wishes to inform the above-referenced individual that subsequent payments may henceforth be sent to the address cited below.	Your payments should now be sent to us in Lakewood.
To facilitate ratification of this agreement, your negotiators urge that the membership respond in the affirmative.	We urge you to approve the agreement by voting *yes*.
It may interest you to be informed that your account has been credited in the aforementioned amount, and a copy of your account showing the newly calculated balance is enclosed.	I am happy to send you a copy of your June bill showing your credit of $37.14.
Although service operations have been terminated at our El Segundo branch, customers are herewith notified that their claims may be submitted to the Santa Monica branch.	Although we're no longer operating our El Segundo branch, you may now submit your claims to our Santa Monica branch.

You can develop a conversational tone in your written messages by using familiar words, an occasional contraction, and first-person pronouns (*I*, *me*) instead of third-person expressions (*the writer*).

The preceding examples illustrate effective conversational style. Although friendly, the tone of these messages is businesslike and objective. Successful letter writers are able to make their business letters conversational without becoming chatty, friendly without becoming familiar, and warm without becoming intimate. Strive to achieve a proper balance between objectivity and friendliness.

Business letters can be warm and friendly without becoming familiar and intimate.

~~

Outdated Expressions

The world of business has changed greatly in the past century or two. Yet, some business writers continue to use antiquated phrases and expressions borrowed from a period when the "language of business" was exceedingly formal and flowery. In the 1800s letter writers "begged to state" and "trusted to be favored with" and assured their readers that they "remained their humble servants." Such language suggests powdered wigs, quill pens, sealing wax, tall stools, green eye shades, and sleeveguards.

Compare these two versions of a letter acknowledging an order. The first uses old-fashioned, flowery language that was appropriate a century ago. The second represents a modern, efficient style.

Dear Sirs,

Outdated, flowery style

Your esteemed favor of the 10th has been received and contents duly noted. Please be advised that your shipment is forthcoming. Trusting to be favored by future orders and assuring you of my cooperation,

I remain, Dear Sirs,
Yours respectfully,

The same message today might sound like this:

Gentlemen:

Modern, efficient style

Your order for 75 Datacom Desk Planners should reach you by July 1. Call me collect at (212) 757-7008 to place future orders. We appreciate your business.

Sincerely,

The letters of few modern writers sound as dated as the first example shown here, yet some time-worn, stale expressions linger from the past and should be avoided. Replace outdated expressions such as these shown here with more modern phrasing shown in parentheses.

Outdated expressions

Outdated expressions sound stale and insincere to readers.

are in receipt of (have received)

as per your request (at your request)

attached hereto (attached)

enclosed please find (enclosed)

kindly advise (please write)

pursuant to your request (at your request)

thanking you in advance (thank you)

I trust that (I think, I believe)

under separate cover (separately)

Source: Duffy. Copyright 1985 Universal Press Syndicate. Reprinted with permission. All rights reserved.

Concise Wording

In business, time is indeed money. Translated into writing, this means that concise messages save reading time and, thus, money. In addition, messages that are written directly and efficiently are easier to read and comprehend. Say what you have to say and then stop.

Developing a concise writing style requires conscious effort. The scientist and philosopher Blaise Pascal once apologized for the length of a letter, explaining to his correspondent that the letter would have been shorter if he had more time.

Taking the time to make your writing concise means that you look for other—shorter—ways to say what you intend. Examine every sentence that you write. Could the thought be conveyed in fewer words? In addition to eliminating repetitious words (Chapter 2), you should concentrate on shortening flabby phrases, eliminating expletives, deleting excessive prepositions, revising negatives, avoiding long lead-ins, and omitting needless adverbs.

Improve your writing by imagining that you will be fined $5 for every unnecessary word.

Shorten Flabby Phrases

Eliminate wasted words by boiling a phrase down to its essence. Consider the flabby expressions shown here and the more concise forms shown in parentheses.

at a later date (later)	in addition to the above (also)
at this point in time (now)	in spite of the fact that (even though)
afford an opportunity (allow)	in the event that (if)
are of the opinion that (believe)	in the amount of (for)
at the present time (now, presently)	in the near future (soon)
despite the fact that (though)	in view of the fact that (because)
due to the fact that (because, since)	inasmuch as (since)
during the time (while)	more or less (about)
feel free to (please)	until such time as (until)
for the period of (for)	
fully cognizant of (aware)	

Rewrite sentences with flabby expressions, omitting the wasted words.

Wordy: Inasmuch as you have had an excellent credit history previous to your illness, we are willing to extend your due date until a later date.

Concise: Since you had an excellent credit history before your illness, we are willing to extend your due date.

Wordy: In regard to your request for a parking decal, we would like to tell you that first of all we must see your motor vehicle registration.

Concise: We can issue a parking decal after we see your registration.

Eliminate Expletives

Expletives are sentence fillers such as *there* and occasionally *it*. Avoid expletives that fatten sentences with excess words.

Wordy: There are three vice presidents who report directly to the president.
Concise: Three vice presidents report directly to the president.

Wordy: It was the federal government that protected the health of workers.
Concise: The federal government protected the health of workers.

Delete Excessive Prepositions

Some wordy prepositional phrases may be replaced by single adverbs. For example, *in the normal course of events* becomes *normally* and *as a general rule* becomes *generally*.

Wordy: Datatech approached the merger *in a careful manner*.
Concise: Datatech approached the merger *carefully*.

Wordy: The merger will *in all probability* be effected.
Concise: The merger will *probably* be effected.

Wordy: We have taken this action *in very few cases*.
Concise: We have *seldom* taken this action.

Revise Wordy Negatives

Shorten negative expressions by using the prefixes *un-* and *dis-* (for example, *unclear* for *not clear* and *dissatisfied* for *not satisfied*), or shorten negative constructions by using a positive construction (for example, *didn't have any excuse* becomes *had no excuse*).

Wordy: James was *not happy* with his bonus.
Concise: James was *unhappy* with his bonus.

Wordy: Dr. Francisco did *not agree* with the report.
Concise: Dr. Francisco *disagreed* with the report.

Wordy: Although he *did not have* a parking permit, he entered the lot.
Concise: Although he *had no* parking permit, he entered the lot.

Avoid Long Lead-ins

Thomas Jefferson said, "The most valuable of all talents is that of never using two words when one will do."

Delete unnecessary introductory words. The meat of the sentence often follows the words *that* or *because*.

Wordy: *I am sending you this announcement to let you all know that* the office will be closed Monday.
Concise: The office will be closed Monday.

Wordy:	*You will be interested to learn that* you may now use the automatic teller at our Lynwood branch.
Concise:	You may now use the automatic teller at our Lynwood branch.
Wordy:	*I am writing this letter because* Professor Lydia Brunton suggested that your organization was hiring trainees.
Concise:	Professor Lydia Brunton suggested that your organization was hiring trainees.

Omit Needless Adverbs

Eliminating adverbs like *very, definitely, quite, completely, extremely, really, actually, somewhat,* and *rather* streamlines your writing and makes the tone more businesslike.

Wordy:	We *actually* did not *really* give his plan a *very* fair trial.
Concise:	We did not give his plan a fair trial.
Wordy:	Professor Schaffner offered an *extremely* fine course that students *definitely* appreciated.
Concise:	Professor Schaffner offered a fine course that students appreciated.

Reader Benefit

It is human nature for individuals to be most concerned with matters that relate directly to themselves. This is a natural and necessary condition of existence. If we weren't interested in attending to our own needs, we could not survive.

Most of us are also concerned with others. We are interested in their lives, and we care about their feelings. Individuals who are successful in the business world—and in their personal lives—often possess a trait called *empathy. Empathy* is the capacity to put yourself into another's position and experience that person's feelings.

Empathetic business writers care about readers and express that concern in their communication. They try to see the reader's viewpoint. Place yourself in the reader's position. How would you react? How would you feel? When you read a message, you're very likely thinking, consciously or unconsciously, "What's in it for me?" When you write a message, say to yourself, "What's in it for the reader?" In what aspect of your message would the reader be most interested? How will it benefit the reader? Once you've answered these questions, write your message so that it emphasizes the benefits to the reader.

Look at your message from the reader's position.

Be especially alert to the overuse of first-person pronouns like *I, my, we,* and *our.* These words indicate that the writer is most interested in only one narrow view—the writer's. On the other hand, you should not sacrifice fluency, brevity, and directness to avoid an occasional *I* or *me.*

Overemphasis of the pronouns I and me reflect the writer's interests instead of the reader's.

Compare the following sets of statements. Notice how first-person pronouns are deemphasized and second-person pronouns (*you, your*) become more obvious when the focus shifts to benefits and interests of the reader. Some authorities refer to this emphasis as the *you-attitude*.

Instead of	Try this
I am very pleased that I am able to offer my customers a new investment program.	You are the first of our customers to be offered our new investment program.
We are happy to announce the opening of our new bank branch in Newton to meet all banking needs.	You will now be able to use our new Newton branch for all your banking needs.
I have been an insurance agent for over 25 years, and I am confident that I can serve all the insurance needs of business executives.	You will benefit by dealing with an agent who has more than 25 years of experience in serving the insurance needs of successful executives like you.
All new employees are required to complete and return the attached parking application if they want to park in our lot.	You may begin enjoying company parking privileges as soon as you complete and return the attached card.
Before we can allow you to write checks on your account, we request that you sign the enclosed signature card.	For your protection, please sign the enclosed signature card before you begin to write checks on your account.
We have produced a new brand of cookies called Choco-Chunks, and we think you should carry them.	Once your customers have tried our new Choco-Chunk cookies, they'll be back for more of this rich chocolate-nut confection.

Develop the *you-attitude* by emphasizing reader benefits.

Positive Language

The tone of a letter is considerably improved if you use positive rather than negative language. It's uplifting and pleasant to focus on the positive. Moreover, positive language generally conveys more information than negative language does. Positive wording tells what *is* and what *can be done* rather than what *isn't* and what *can't be done*. For example, "Your order cannot be shipped by January 10," is not nearly so informative as "Your order will be shipped January 20."

Readers learn more when you write positively.

Analyze what you have to say, and then present it in positive language. Here are examples of statements in which the negative tone can be revised to reflect a positive impression.

Negative: We are unable to send your shipment until we receive proof of your payment.

Positive: We are happy to have your business and look forward to sending your shipment as soon as we receive your payment.

Negative: We are sorry that we must reject your application for credit at this time.

Positive: At this time we can serve you on a cash basis only.

Negative: You will never regret opening a charge account with us.

Positive: Your new charge account will enable you to purchase executive suits at reasonable prices.

Negative: We cannot use this computer keyboard efficiently until we receive the proper template.

Positive: After we receive the proper computer template, we will be able to use this computer keyboard efficiently.

Negative: Although I've never had a paid position before, I have worked as an intern in an attorney's office while completing my degree requirements.

Positive: My experience in an attorney's office and my recent training in legal procedures and office automation can be assets to your organization.[1]

Confidence

Your business letters should sound as if you have confidence in yourself, your organization, and your ideas. Expect your reader to be persuaded by your words. Listen to the tone of each of the following examples:

Lacks confidence: If you think that you may be able to be our speaker, we can arrange for you to stay at the Mission Inn.

Confident: When you speak before our Riverside group, we will arrange for you to stay at the Mission Inn.

Lacks confidence: Although some employees have complained about the proposed flexible work schedule, most employees will find that it gives them greater freedom.

Confident: Most employees are looking forward to the proposed flexible work schedule because they expect greater freedom in arranging their work hours.

Lacks confidence: Would you like to have our representative call?

Confident: Our representative will be in your area June 9 and will be able to visit you in your showroom.

Appear confident but not overconfident. Avoid expressions that sound presumptuous, such as *I am sure that, We know that you will*, and *You will agree*.

Sexist Terms

Sexist words suggest prejudice or discrimination based on sex. For example, notice the use of the masculine pronouns *he* and *his* in the following sentences:

If a physician is needed, *he* will be called.

Every homeowner must read *his* insurance policy carefully.

---

[1]Note: This sentence not only uses positive language but also emphasizes the reader's benefit.

Sensitive writers today try to use sex-neutral terms, such as *letter carrier* instead of *mailman*.

These sentences illustrate an age-old grammatical rule called "common gender." When a speaker or writer did not know the gender (sex) of an individual, masculine pronouns (such as *he* and *his*) were used. Masculine pronouns were understood to indicate both men and women.

Today, however, sensitive writers and speakers have become increasingly uncomfortable about the use of common-gender pronouns. To refer automatically to a physician or a homeowner as *he* may be misleading and even offensive. A sensitive writer today may wish to avoid common-gender pronouns by using an alternate construction.

Source: Reprinted with special permission of North America Syndicate, Inc.

Instead of	Try this
Every attorney has ten minutes for *his* summation.	All *attorneys* have ten minutes for *their* summations. (Use a plural noun and plural pronoun.)
	Attorneys have ten minutes for summations. (Omit the pronoun entirely.)
	Every attorney has ten minutes for *a* summation. (Use an article instead of a pronoun.)
	Every attorney has ten minutes for his or her summation. (Use both a masculine and a feminine pronoun.)

A stereotype is a standardized, usually oversimplified opinion.

The last alternative—including a masculine and a feminine pronoun—is wordy and awkward. Don't use it too frequently.

Other words are considered sexist because they suggest stereotypes. For example, the nouns *fireman* or *mailman* suggest that only men hold these positions. Avoid offending your listener or reader by using nonsexist job titles or functions such as the following: *firefighter, letter carrier, salesperson, flight attendant, department head, committee chair, technician,* and *law enforcement officer.*

How to Overcome the Fear of Writing

Cynthia W., a personnel specialist, was recently promoted to a supervisory position that required the writing of regular reports and some correspondence. She confessed to a communication consultant, "I've always been able to express myself quite adequately orally. But having to write a letter or, worse yet, a report paralyzes me with fear. I recognize my weaknesses, so I took a course at a local college. It improved my grammar and punctuation, but I still have an enormous fear of writing."

The following techniques will help Cynthia and other individuals who fear writing and can't start a document.

- **Don't expect to be a Hemingway.** Professional writers, like novelists, are practicing an art. Business writers, however, are practicing a craft. And crafts are skills that can be learned by using the right tools, following instructions, seeing models, and practicing. The first step in overcoming a fear of writing is developing a realistic level of expectation.

- **Start with small, easy tasks.** Begin by writing short memos and letters that respond to previous documents. If you have longer projects, such as reports, break these tasks into smaller, more manageable parts.

- **Jot down major ideas.** Usually, you are responding to something—letters, memos, reports. In the margin of these documents, make notes of your thoughts. These notes need not be a formal outline, but they will give you a guide to information you want to include.

- **"Talk" your writing.** Imagine you are chatting with a friend or colleague at lunch. Would you say, "It has come to my attention that questions are being asked by many employees in regard to our parking policy"? Of course not. Probably you'd say something like, "Many employees are asking questions about our parking policy." If you're able to express your ideas orally, you'll have no problems getting started in writing. Later, you'll rewrite.

- **Don't write backwards.** Many writers fall into the trap of writing a message in the same order in which they thought it. They begin with explanations and background information and end with the most important idea. But readers need to learn the primary idea (action to be taken or the solution to a problem) first so that they know immediately why they are reading this message. Instead of writing backwards, start out directly with the big idea.

- **Embrace the KISS formula.** *Keep It Simple, Stupid,* is good advice for both novice and experienced writers. Short sentences (17 words is average), short paragraphs, and familiar words produce messages that anyone can understand. And that should be your goal—writing that anyone can comprehend. Some writers change personalities when they begin to write. Thinking that writing must be formal to be correct, they sabotage their writing with long, impressive-sounding words and gobbledygook.

- **Expect to revise.** Your first "quick-and-dirty" version, whether on paper or on a computer, will not be perfect. Don't expect it to be. Plan to read it again to listen to its sound, to add punctuation, and to revise sentence structure. Professional writers revise many, many times. You should reread and revise at least two or three times, depending upon how important the document is.

- **Switch places.** Put yourself in the shoes of the receiver as you read your message. Will that person understand what you have written? Don't be a lazy writer, willing to let an unclear phrase pass, hoping the reader will understand what you meant. Add a word or rephrase a statement to make it absolutely clear. Then, ask yourself, "Does this message sound like me?" Remember that you are not present to smile and soften the effect of your words. Nor can you observe the face of the reader to assess comprehension.

By observing these techniques, anyone can overcome a fear of writing. And with supervised practice, a novice writer can make great progress.

APPLICATION AND PRACTICE—3

Discussion

1. The establishment of goodwill in business communications requires time, energy, and skill. Such effort produces extra costs for an organization. Justify this expenditure.

2. Why is the flowery, formal language used in business communication a century ago no longer appropriate today?

3. Explain why and how empathetic business writers try to see the reader's viewpoint.

4. If it's easier to state an idea negatively, why should a writer make an effort to state it positively?

5. Why is a conversational tone in business writing hard to achieve?

Short Answers

6. List two objectives that successful business messages accomplish.

   reader benefits, expressing ideas positively

7. Define *goodwill*.

   a kindly feeling of approval and support

8. List three ways to define or characterize tone in a business letter.

   constructive or destructive, casual or formal, PATRONIZING OR SINCERE.

9. List seven ways to make writing more concise.

   Eliminating repetitious words, concentrate on shortening flabby phrases, eliminating expletives, deleting excessive prepositions, revising negatives, avoiding long lead-ins, and omitting needless adverbs.

10. What is an *expletive*?

    sentence fillers such as there and occasionally it.

11. Give an original example of a long and wordy lead-in to a sentence.

    I would say

12. Define *empathy*.

    Is the capacity to put yourself into another's position and experience that person's feelings

13. List five examples of sexist pronouns and nouns.

he, his, hers
fireman, mailman

14. Supply shorter words for the expressions shown below:

in addition to the above
in view of the fact that
until such time as

15. Make the following negative constructions positive (and concise):

He didn't have time.
She doesn't say anything.
We don't have a reason.

Writing Improvement Exercises

Reader Benefits.   Revise the following sentences to emphasize benefits to the reader.

Example: We have just designed an amazing computer program that automatically computes income tax.

Revision: You will be amazed by our computer program that automatically computes your income tax.

16. To prevent us from possibly losing large sums of money, our bank now requires verification of any large check presented for immediate payment.

We thank you for payments that are prompt and require verification of any large checks for our banking purposes.

17. Our extensive experience in investments enables us to find our customers the most profitable programs.

You at Because of our extensive experience in investments we will provide our customers with the most profitable programs.

18. Our company policy demands that individuals who rent power equipment must demonstrate a proficiency in its use.

Our company will gladly rent power equipment to those who show proper use.

19. We are offering a new series of short-term loans that may be used for carrying accounts receivable and for stocking inventory.

If you are in need Short-term loans are being offered for carrying accts. receivable and stocking inventory.

20. For just $150 per person, ~~we have arranged~~ *you can enjoy* a three-day trip to Las Vegas that includes deluxe accommodations, the "City Lights" show, and selected meals.

Conversational Language.   Revise the following sentences to make the tone more conversational.

Example: As per your recent request, the undersigned is happy to inform you that we are sending you forthwith the brochures you requested.

Revision: I'm happy to send you the brochures you requested.

21. ~~Kindly inform the undersigned whether or not~~ *Please let us know if* your representative will be making a visitation in the near future.

22. ~~As you requested~~ *Thank you for your order,* ~~Pursuant to your letter of the 12th, please be advised that~~ your shipment *your shipment was sent June 9.* was sent June 9.

23. Kindly be informed that your vehicle has been determined to require corrective work.
your vehicle needs repairs

24. As ~~per your recent request,~~ *you requested attached is the price for the three-board set.* attached herewith please find our quotation for the three-board computer set.

25. ~~The undersigned respectfully reminds affected individuals~~ that Employees ~~desirous of~~ chang~~ing~~ health plans must do so before December 30.
desiring to

Outdated Expressions.   Revise the following sentences to eliminate outdated expressions and to improve tone.

Example: This is to inform you that we are sending you under separate cover one dozen printwheels as per your request.

Revision: We're sending you one dozen printwheels.

26. ~~We are in receipt of your letter~~ of October 3, and ~~as per your request,~~ *We* are sending to you two ~~complimentary~~ passes to Expo 2000.

27. Attached ~~please find~~ *are* instructions for completing the ~~above-referenced~~ claim.

28. ~~Please allow the writer to take the liberty of offering his~~ Congratulations on your recent promotion!

We thank you ~~and we~~
29. ~~Thanking you in advance,~~ ~~we genuinely~~ hope ~~that~~ you ~~can~~ accept this invitation to ~~address~~ our organization. ~~and thank~~
    speak to

30. We trust that our letter under date of July 17 reached you and that its contents were duly noted.
    and responded to
    We hope you received, our letter ~~and~~ dated
    ~~you responded to~~   July 17.

Flabby Phrases.   Revise the following sentences to eliminate flabby phrases. Be particularly alert to negative constructions, long lead-ins, imprecise words, and needless adverbs like *very* and *quite*.

Example: This is to notify you that our accountant actually couldn't find anything wrong with your report.

Revision: Our accountant could find no fault with your report.

31. This memorandum is to inform you that all books and magazines must be taken back to the library by June 1.
    Please return all books & magazines by June 1.

32. This is to let you know that you should feel free to use your credit card for the purpose of purchasing household items for a period of 60 days.
    Letting you know your credit card can be
    used to purchase household items for up to 60 days

33. You may be interested to learn that there are a number of references in medical literature citing support for higher-dose aspirin.
    There is much support in medical literature
    for higher-dose aspirin.

34. ~~As you may possibly be aware,~~ Nordstroms is opening a discount fashion center ~~in the~~ Fallbrook ~~area~~ December 1.
    Near

35. ~~Filling out~~ an application is ~~not really~~ *only* necessary ~~unless~~ *if* you are ~~basically~~ interested in that position.

Expletives.   Revise the following sentences to avoid wordy expressions using the expletives *there* and *it*.

Example: *There are* four major fields in accounting. They are public accounting, private accounting, government accounting, and auditing.

Revision: The four major fields in accounting are public accounting, private accounting, government accounting, and auditing.

36. There are ~~at least~~ *more than* five advantages ~~that~~ computers have over the human *mind* ~~decision maker.~~

37. The report shows ~~that~~ there are numerous employers looking for qualified ~~job~~ applicants.

38. ~~As a result of our research,~~ *we* we learned ~~that~~ ~~there is~~ *we have* ~~no single factor~~ *Nothing* ~~causing the~~ decline of interest in our product. *has* *a*

39. ~~There are~~ Specialized areas one can branch off into, ~~such as~~ *are* tax accounting, teaching, management advisory services, and investment banking.

40. There is ~~a~~ great demand for legal secretaries ~~Because~~ of the growing number of attorneys beginning law practices.→

   because attorneys are on the increase there is great demand for legal secretaries.

Prepositional Phrases, Wordy Phrases. Revise the following sentences to eliminate flabby expressions. Be alert to prepositional phrases that could be reduced to an adverb or adjective, and watch for wordy expletives.

Example: Under ordinary circumstances, there are two technicians to repair appliances.

Revision: Ordinarily, two technicians repair appliances.

41. ~~There are~~ *we have* two sources of funding ~~that we have~~ available for your business.

42. ~~At an early date you may be sure~~ that Mr. Benson will see you ~~in regard to~~ *soon* *regarding* ~~providing~~ supplies for your office.

43. ~~In very few cases~~ *Rarely* do we revoke ~~the~~ privileges ~~of our~~ credit cards.

44. ~~During our spring sale~~ there is a week ~~of~~ private previews ~~that~~ may be enjoyed by our preferred customers.

45. If the form is filled out ~~in a~~ satisfactory~~ly~~ ~~manner,~~ we can process it ~~with~~ *immediately* ~~immediacy.~~

Positive Language.   Revise the following sentences to use positive language. Add information if needed.

46. ~~We regret to inform you that your order did not reach us immediately, so we cannot ship~~ your electrical conduits ~~until~~ August 1.
    we shipped

47. Parking is ~~not~~ permitted in ~~any lot other than~~ South Lot D.
    ed

48. We are ~~sorry to~~ inform *ing* you that *currently* you do not qualify for a charge account ~~at this time~~.

49. Because your name was overlooked, you will not receive our introductory packet until we make our second mailing.
    you will receive our introductory packet as soon as possible ~~we can send it to you~~.

50. You will ~~never be sorry that you~~ applied for a federally insured student loan at Pacific Bank.
    be happy for you
    you will be happy you applied

Expressing Confidence and Avoiding Sexist Language.   Revise the following sentences to show confidence and to avoid sexist expressions.

51. If y~~ou~~ *you're* ~~might be~~ interested in our new SX-10 copier, I *will* ~~could~~ have a sales representative call on you.

52. Every employee has the right to examine his personnel file under ~~the most recent~~ federal regulation~~s~~.

53. ~~When you can spare the time,~~ Please look at our catalog of computer and office supplies.

54. Any applicant for the position of fireman *fire fighter* must submit a medical report signed by ~~his~~ physician.
    their

55. At most hospitals in this area a nurse provides ~~her~~ *his or her* own uniform.

Outside Reading. Bring in three to five examples of writing that demonstrates (or fails to demonstrate) concepts from this chapter: reader benefits, concise writing, gender-free expression, and so forth.

GRAMMAR/MECHANICS CHECKUP—3

Verbs

Review Sections 1.10 through 1.15 of the Grammar/Mechanics Handbook. Then study each of the following statements. Underline any verbs that are used incorrectly. In the space provided write the correct form and the number of the G/M principle illustrated. If a sentence is correct, write *C*. When you finish, compare your responses with those provided below. If your responses differ, study carefully the principles in parentheses.

Example: Our inventory of raw materials <u>were</u> presented as collateral for a short-term loan.

was   (1.10c)

1. Located across town is a research institute and our product-testing facility. _____

2. The deposits in nearly every single bank in the United States is insured by the Federal Deposit Insurance Corporation. _____

3. First Federal Savings, along with 20 other large national banks, offer a variety of savings plans. _____

4. Locating a bank and selecting a savings/checking plan often require considerable research and study. _____

5. Neither the plans that this bank offers nor the service just rendered by the teller are impressive. _____

6. The budget analyst wants to know if the Equipment Committee are ready to recommend a product. _____

7. Either of the products that the committee selects is acceptable to the budget analyst. _____

8. If Mr. Davis had chose the Maximizer Plus savings plan, his money would have earned maximum interest. _____

9. Although the applications have laid there for two weeks, they may still be used. _____

10. Mrs. Gebhardt acts as if she was the manager. _____

11. One of the reasons that our Alaskan sales branches have been so costly are high transportation and living costs. _____

In the space provided write the letter of the sentence that illustrates consistency in subject, voice, and mood.

12. (a) If you will read the instructions, the answer can be found.
    (b) If you will read the instructions, you will find the answer. _____

_____ 13. (a) All employees must fill out application forms; only then will you be insured.

(b) All employees must fill out application forms; only then will they be insured.

_____ 14. (a) First, take an inventory of equipment; then, order supplies.

(b) First, take an inventory of equipment; then, supplies must be ordered.

_____ 15. (a) Select a savings plan that suits your needs; deposits may be made immediately.

(b) Select a savings plan that suits your needs; begin making deposits immediately.

---

1. *are* instead of *is* (*1.10e*)   3. *offers* instead of *offer* (*1.10d*)   5. *is* instead of *are* (*1.10g*)
7. C (*1.10h*)   9. *lain* instead of *laid* (*1.15*)   11. *is* instead of *are* (*1.10c*)   13. b (*1.15c*)
15. b (*1.15c*)

Applying the Direct Strategy

CHAPTER 4

The Process of Writing Effective Sentences, Paragraphs, and Messages

In this chapter you will learn to do the following:

- Avoid three basic sentence faults.
- Vary the length and structure of sentences.
- Emphasize important ideas.
- Match sentence parts in achieving parallelism.

- Use active- and passive-voice verbs appropriately.
- Develop clear, unified, and coherent paragraphs.
- Organize the process of writing.

Good writers have mastered a number of effective techniques regarding sentence and paragraph formation. These techniques are some of the "tricks of the trade" that can be acquired through study and practice. In this chapter you will practice techniques that help you achieve variety, emphasis, and unity in your writing. You will learn how to make effective use of parallelism and active- and passive-voice verbs. In addition, you will study how to compose unified and coherent paragraphs developed deductively and inductively. Finally, you will examine the total process of writing. A logical place to start is with a review of sentence components.

Successful writers master numerous techniques as their "tricks of the trade."

Phrases and Clauses

The construction of effective sentences begins with an understanding of the role of phrases and clauses. A *phrase* is a group of related words without a subject and a verb. Study the phrases in the following example:

We will be making a decision about the case in two weeks.

      verb phrase   prepositional prepositional
                                        phrase   phrase

Clauses have subjects and verbs; phrases do not.

A group of related words including a subject and a verb is a *clause*.

Mr. Lee is our shipping manager, and he will call you.

$\underbrace{\qquad\qquad\qquad\qquad\qquad}_{\text{clause}}$ $\underbrace{\qquad\qquad\qquad}_{\text{clause}}$

An *independent clause* makes sense and is complete in itself. A *dependent clause*, although it has a subject and a verb, depends for its meaning upon an independent clause.

If you are able to attend, the meeting is next Tuesday.

$\underbrace{\qquad\qquad\qquad}_{\text{dependent clause}}$ $\underbrace{\qquad\qquad\qquad}_{\text{independent clause}}$

Understanding the difference between phrases and clauses will help you avoid writing unclear, faulty sentences.

~~~

Three Basic Sentence Faults

Beginning or careless writers sometimes produce sentences with one or more of the following three glaring faults.

Three common sentence faults are (1) fragments, (2) run-on sentences, and (3) comma splices.

1. **Fragment.** A fragment is part of a sentence, usually a phrase or a dependent clause, punctuated as if it were an independent clause. Notice how the following fragments do not make sense by themselves.

   Persuading employees to support the United Fund, to learn how to program a computer, or to prepare for an assignment in a new department. These activities all require human change. (The italicized fragment is a series of phrases.)

   Federal regulations in the financial field have been changed. *Which explains why savings and loans, thrifts, and other financial institutions are now more competitive.* (The italicized fragment is a dependent clause.)

   Most attempts at change are likely to meet some resistance. *Change that brings about doubt and that may be seen as a threat to a worker's security and salary.* (The italicized fragment is an incomplete sentence.)

Do not capitalize and punctuate a broken-off portion of a sentence as if it were complete.

2. **Run-on sentence.** When one independent clause follows another without appropriate punctuation, a run-on sentence results.

   The Intel Corporation makes computer chips *it serves a large portion of the computer industry.* (The clause beginning with *it* should be capitalized to form a new sentence, and a period should follow *chips*.)

3. **Comma Splice.** When two independent clauses are joined together inappropriately with a comma, a comma splice results.

Comma splice: We are sorry that your order was delayed, your shipment will be sent out this afternoon.

Comma splice: The titles of the jobs were quite similar, the duties of the jobs were substantially different.

Sentences with comma splices can be revised in several ways, as you see here:

Comma splice: The workshops for the managers start on Tuesday, the sessions for representatives begin Wednesday.

Revision: The workshops for managers start on Tuesday. The sessions for representatives begin Wednesday.

Revision: The workshops for managers start on Tuesday; the sessions for representatives begin Wednesday.

Revision: The workshops for managers start on Tuesday, and the sessions for representatives begin Wednesday.

Sentence Variety and Length

Good writers vary the length and structure of their sentences. Messages composed totally of sentences that sound the same are monotonous to read. Such messages may also divert the reader's attention from what is being said to how it is being said. Compare these two versions of the same paragraph:

Lacks variety: We congratulate you on the purchase of your new home. It will be a source of pride and enjoyment for many years. It will increase in value. It can provide a valuable hedge against inflation. We encourage you to protect that investment.

Shows variety: Congratulations on the purchase of your new home. We know that it will be a source of pride and enjoyment for many years. As it increases in value, it can provide a valuable hedge against inflation. We encourage you to protect that investment.

Sentences with varied structures are interesting to readers.

The first paragraph bores the reader because it relies solely on simple sentences of about the same length with the same subject-verb-object structure. The second paragraph is more interesting because it includes both short, emphatic sentences and longer sentences with dependent clauses. As a result of its varied sentence structures, the second paragraph is less choppy and more fluent.

Generally, it's best to write short sentences since they are more easily understood. What happens to comprehension as sentence length increases? The American Press Institute makes the following estimates:

Sentence Length	Percent of People Who Understand
0 to 8 words	100%
9 to 15 words	90%
16 to 19 words	80%
20 to 28 words	50%

Average sentences contain between 15 and 20 words.

The average sentence length is between 15 and 20 words. This doesn't mean that all sentences should be 15 or 20 words long, however. Effective paragraphs contain a mixture of sentences, some shorter and some longer.

≈

Emphasis

Speakers can emphasize main ideas by saying them loudly or by repeating them slowly or by pounding the table as they speak. They can signal the importance or unimportance of an idea by raising their eyebrows or by shaking their heads or by whispering in a low voice. Writers, however, must rely upon other means to tell their readers what ideas are more important than others. Emphasis in writing can be achieved primarily in two ways: mechanically or stylistically.

Writers may emphasize their ideas by using mechanical or stylistic devices.

Emphasis Through Mechanics

To emphasize an idea in print, a writer may use any of the following devices:

Underlining:	<u>Underlining</u> draws the eye to a word.
Typeface:	Using a different typeface, such as **boldface**, is like shouting a word.
All caps:	Notice how the words FREE GIFT stand out when typed in all caps.
Dashes:	Dashes—if used sparingly—can be effective in capturing attention.
Tabulation:	Listing items vertically makes them stand out:

      1. First item
      2. Second item
      3. Third item

Other means of achieving mechanical emphasis include the arrangement of space, color, lines, boxes, columns, titles, headings, and subheadings to set off ideas.

Emphasis Through Style

Although mechanical means are occasionally appropriate, more often a writer achieves emphasis stylistically. That is, the writer chooses words carefully and constructs sentences skillfully to emphasize main ideas and deemphasize minor or negative ideas. Here are four suggestions for emphasizing ideas stylistically:

1. **Use vivid words.** Vivid words, as you recall from Chapter 2, are emphatic because the reader can picture ideas clearly.

General:	*One business* uses *personal* selling techniques.
Vivid and emphatic:	*Avon* uses *face-to-face* selling techniques.
General:	A *customer said* that he wanted the contract returned *soon*.
Vivid and emphatic:	*Mr. Santos insisted* that the contract be returned *July 1.*

2. **Label the main idea.** If an idea is significant, tell the reader.

> Unlabeled: Explore the possibility of leasing a site, but also hire a business consultant.
>
> Labeled: Explore the possibility of leasing a site; but most importantly, hire a business consultant.

3. **Place the important idea first or last in the sentence.** Ideas have less competition from surrounding words when they appear first or last in a sentence. Observe how the concept of *productivity* is emphasized in the first and second examples:

> Emphatic: *Productivity* is more likely to be increased when profit-sharing plans are linked to individual performance than to group performance.
>
> Emphatic: Profit-sharing plans that are linked to individual performance rather than to group performance are more effective in increasing *productivity*.
>
> Unemphatic: Profit-sharing plans are more effective in increasing *productivity* when they are linked to individual performance rather than to group performance.

4. **Place the important idea in a simple sentence or in an independent clause.** Don't dilute the effect of the idea by making it share the spotlight with other words and clauses.

> Emphatic: You are the first trainee that we have hired for this program. (Use a simple sentence for emphasis.)
>
> Emphatic: Although we considered many candidates, you are the first trainee that we have hired for this program. (Independent clause contains main idea.)
>
> Unemphatic: Although you are the first trainee that we have hired for this program, we had many candidates and expect to expand the program in the future. (Main idea is lost in a dependent clause.)

Deemphasis

To deemphasize an idea, such as bad news, try one of the following stylistic devices:

The word *stylistic* refers to literary or artistic style as opposed to content.

1. **Use general words.** Just as vivid words emphasize, the use of general words can soften an unpleasant point when necessary.

> Vivid: Our records indicate that *you recently were fired.*
>
> General: Our records indicate that *your employment status has changed.*

2. **Bury the bad news in the middle of a sentence or in a dependent clause.** Instead of placing a negative point where it is conspicuous and perhaps painful to the reader, include it in a dependent clause.

Bad news can be made less painful by deemphasizing its presentation.

> Emphasizes bad news: We cannot issue you credit at this time, but we do have a plan that will allow you to fill your immediate needs on a cash basis.
>
> Deemphasizes bad news: We have a plan that will allow you to fill your immediate needs on a cash basis since we cannot issue you credit at this time.

Additional tips and strategies for announcing bad news will be provided in Chapter 8.

~~

Unity

Unified sentences contain only related ideas.

Unified sentences contain thoughts that are related to only one main idea. The following sentence lacks unity because the first clause has little or no relationship to the second clause:

Lacks unity: Our insurance plan is available in all states, and you may name anyone as a beneficiary for your coverage.

Three factors that destroy sentence unity are zigzag writing, mixed constructions, and misplaced modifiers. Let's consider each of these faults.

Zigzag Writing

Sentences that twist or turn unexpectedly away from the main thought are examples of zigzag writing. Such confusing writing may result when too many thoughts are included in one sentence or when one thought does not relate to another. To rectify a zigzag sentence, revise it so that the reader understands the relationship between the thoughts. If that is impossible, move the unrelated thoughts to a new sentence.

Zigzag sentence: I appreciate the time you spent with me last week, and I have purchased a personal computer that generates graphics.

Revision: I appreciate the time you spent with me last week. As a result of your advice, I have purchased a personal computer that generates graphics.

Zigzag sentences often should be broken into two sentences.

Zigzag sentence: The stockholders of a corporation elect a board of directors, although the chief executive officer is appointed by the board and the CEO is not directly responsible to the stockholders.

Revision: The stockholders of a corporation elect a board of directors, who in turn appoints the chief executive officer. The CEO is not directly responsible to the stockholders.

Mixed Constructions

Writers who fuse two different grammatical constructions destroy sentence unity and meaning.

Mixed construction: The reason I am late is *because* my car battery is dead.

Revision: The reason I am late is *that* my car battery is dead. (The construction introduced by *the reason is* should be a noun clause beginning with *that*, not an adverbial clause beginning with *because*.)

Mixed construction: When the stock market index rose five points was our signal to sell.

Revision: When the stock market index rose five points, we were prepared to sell. *Or*, Our signal to sell was an increase of five points in the stock market index.

Misplaced Modifiers

Sentence unity can also be destroyed by the separation of phrases or clauses from the words that they modify.

Keep phrases and clauses close to the words they describe.

Misplaced modifier:	We will be happy to send a park map for all motorists *reduced to a 1-inch scale.*
Revision:	We will be happy to send all motorists a park map *reduced to a 1-inch scale.*
Misplaced modifier:	Whether you travel for business or for pleasure, charge everything to your credit card *in the United States.*
Revision:	Whether you travel for business or for pleasure *in the United States,* charge everything to your credit card.

In each of the preceding sentences, the sentence made sense once the misplaced phrase was moved closer to the words it modified.

"Do you want the grammatical errors in or out?"

Source: From *The Wall Street Journal.* Reprinted with permission of the Cartoon Features Syndicate.

Another modifier fault results when an introductory verbal phrase is not followed immediately by a word that it can logically modify. This is called a "dangling modifier." Notice in each of the following revisions of dangling modifiers that the sentence makes sense once we place the logical modifier after the introductory phrase.

Beware of introductory verbal phrases that are not immediately followed by the words they describe.

Dangling modifier:	To receive a degree, 120 credits are required. (This sentence reads as if *120 credits* are receiving a degree.)
Revision:	To receive a degree, a student must earn 120 credits.
Dangling modifier:	When filling out an employment application, the personnel manager expects each applicant to use ink. (The personnel manager is not filling out the application.)
Revision:	When filling out an employment application, each applicant is expected to use ink.

Parallelism

Balanced wording helps the reader anticipate your meaning.

Parallelism is a skillful writing technique that involves balanced writing. Sentences written so that their parts are balanced or parallel are easy to read and understand. To achieve parallel construction, use similar structures to express similar ideas. For example, the words *computing, coding, recording,* and *storing* are parallel because the words all end in *-ing*. To express the list as *computing, coding, recording,* and **storage** is disturbing because the last item is not what the reader expects. Try to match nouns with nouns, verbs with verbs, phrases with phrases, and clauses with clauses. Avoid mixing active-voice verbs with passive-voice verbs. Keep the wording balanced in expressing similar ideas.

Lacks parallelism:	The market for industrial goods includes manufacturers, contractors, wholesalers, and *those concerned with the retail function.*
Revision:	The market for industrial goods includes manufacturers, contractors, wholesalers, and *retailers.* (Parallel construction matches nouns.)
Lacks parallelism:	Our primary goals are to increase productivity, reduce costs, and *the improvement of product quality.*
Revision:	Our primary goals are to increase productivity, reduce costs, and *improve product quality.* (Parallel construction matches verbs.)
Lacks parallelism:	We are scheduled to meet in Dallas on January 5, *we are meeting in Houston on the 15th of March,* and in Austin on June 3.
Revision:	We are scheduled to meet in Dallas on January 5, *in Houston on March 15,* and in Austin on June 3. (Parallel construction matches phrases.)
Lacks parallelism:	Mrs. Horne audits all accounts lettered A through L; accounts lettered M through Z are audited by Mr. Shapiro.
Revision:	Mrs. Horne audits all accounts lettered A through L; Mr. Shapiro audits accounts lettered M through Z. (Parallel construction matches active-voice verbs in balanced clauses.)

All items in a list should be expressed in balanced constructions.

In presenting lists of data, whether shown horizontally or tabulated vertically, be certain to express all the items in parallel form. Which item in the following tabulated list is not parallel?

Lacks parallelism:	Three primary objectives of advertising are as follows:
	  1. Increase frequency of product use
	  2. Introduce complementary products
	  3. Enhancement of the corporate image

Active and Passive Voice

In sentences with active-voice verbs, the subject is the doer of the action. In passive-voice sentences, the subject is acted upon.

Active verb:	Mr. Johnson *completed* the tax return before the April 15 deadline. (The subject is the doer of the action.)
Passive verb:	The tax return *was completed* before the April 15 deadline. (The subject, *tax return,* is acted upon.)

In the first sentence, the active-voice verb emphasizes Mr. Johnson. In the second sentence, the passive-voice verb emphasizes the tax return. In sentences with passive-voice verbs, the doer of the action may be revealed or left unknown.

Most writers prefer active verbs because such verbs tell the reader clearly what the action is and who or what is performing that action.

On the other hand, passive verbs can be employed to perform certain necessary functions. They are helpful in (1) emphasizing an action or the recipient of the action (*You have been selected to represent us*); (2) deemphasizing negative news (*Your watch has not been repaired*); and (3) concealing the doer of an action (*A major error was made in the estimate*). In business writing, as well as in our personal relations, some situations demand tact and sensitivity. Instead of using a direct approach with active verbs, we may prefer the indirectness that passive verbs allow. Rather than making a blunt announcement with an active verb (*Mr. Sullivan made a major error in the estimate*), we can soften the sentence with a passive construction (*A major error has been made in the estimate*).

How can you tell if a verb is active or passive? Identify the subject of the sentence and decide if the subject is doing the acting or if it is being acted upon. For example, in the sentence *An appointment was made for January 1*, the subject is *appointment*. The subject is being acted upon; therefore, the verb (*was made*) is passive. Another clue in identifying passive-voice verbs is this: they always have a *to be* helping verb, such as *is, are, was, were, being,* or *been*.

Although active-voice verbs are preferred in business writing, passive-voice verbs perform useful functions.

Paragraphs

We have thus far concentrated on the basic unit of writing, the sentence. The next unit of writing is the paragraph. A paragraph is a group of sentences with a controlling idea, usually stated first. Paragraphs package ideas into meaningful groups for readers. Often when you're writing the first draft of a message, the idea units are not immediately clear. In revising, though, you see that similar ideas should be placed together. You recognize ways to improve the sequencing of thoughts so that the reader better understands. Here are suggestions for working with paragraph unity, coherence, length, and organization.

Paragraph Unity

Just as sentences require unity, so do paragraphs. When is a paragraph unified? A paragraph is unified when all its sentences concern just one topic or idea. Any sentence that treats a new topic should begin a new paragraph or be revised to relate to the paragraph topic.

Paragraph Coherence

Effective paragraphs are coherent; that is, they hold together. Coherence is a quality of good writing that does not happen accidentally. It is consciously achieved through effective organization and through skillful use of three devices.

1. **Repetition of key ideas or key words.** Repeating a word or key thought from a preceding sentence helps guide a reader from one thought to the next. This redundancy is necessary to build cohesiveness into writing.

Three ways to create paragraph coherence are (1) repetition of key ideas, (2) use of pronouns, and (3) use of transitional expressions.

Quality control problems in production are often the result of poor-quality raw materials. Some companies have strong programs for ensuring the *quality* of *incoming production materials and supplies.*

The second sentence of the preceding paragraph repeats the key idea of *quality.* Moreover, the words *incoming production materials and supplies* refer to *raw materials* mentioned in the preceding sentence. Good writers find other words to describe the same idea, thus using repetition to clarify a topic for the reader.

2. **Use of pronouns.** Pronouns such as *this, that, they, these,* and *those* promote coherence by connecting the thoughts in one sentence to the thoughts in a previous sentence. To make sure that the pronoun reference is clear, consider joining the pronoun with the word to which it refers, thus making the pronoun into an adjective.

Xerox has a four-point program to assist suppliers. *This program* includes written specifications for production materials and components.

Be very careful in using pronouns. A pronoun without a clear antecedent can be most annoying. The reader doesn't know precisely to what the pronoun refers.

Faulty: When company profits increased, employees were given a bonus, either a cash payment or company stock. *This* became a real incentive to employees.

Improved: When company profits increased, employees were given a bonus, either a cash payment or company stock. *This profit-sharing plan* became a real incentive to employees.

3. **Use of transitional expressions.** One of the most effective ways to achieve paragraph coherence is through the use of transitional expressions. These expressions act as road signs: they indicate where the message is headed, and they help the reader anticipate what is coming. Here are transitional expressions grouped according to uses:

Time Association	Contrast	Illustration
before, after	although	for example
first, second	but	in this way
meanwhile	however	
next	instead	
until	nevertheless	
when, whenever	on the other hand	

Cause, Effect	Additional Idea
consequently	furthermore
for this reason	in addition
hence	likewise
therefore	moreover

Used appropriately, transitional expressions help the reader see how ideas and sentences are related, thus achieving paragraph coherence.

Paragraph Length

Have you ever avoided reading a document because the paragraphs were forbiddingly long? If so, you're like most readers, who find short paragraphs more inviting than long ones. As a writer, you can make your messages more attractive by controlling paragraph length. In business letters, first and last paragraphs are often very short (one to four typed lines). Other paragraphs in letters and most paragraphs in reports should average about six lines, with ten lines being the maximum.

Paragraph Organization

Sentences within paragraphs are usually arranged either deductively (directly) or inductively (indirectly).

Deductive method. In this arrangement a topic sentence appears first, followed by other information. A topic sentence serves to orient readers so that they know what this paragraph is going to be about. It may be a summarizing statement followed by explanation and amplification of the main idea. This orienting sentence provides an introduction so that readers can better understand the following sentences. Without a topic sentence, readers must guess at why the paragraph is being written. Readers need a frame of reference provided by a topic sentence. Notice how the topic sentence in the following paragraph provides an overview:

> Personnel administrators for large companies are changing their preferences for items included in résumés of prospective employees. Recent surveys show that today's companies want to see evidence of achievement such as grade-point average, work experience, and college activities. They are less interested in personal items such as birth date, marital status, health, and number of dependents. A new category that many personnel officers said they would like to see is a summary of qualifications.

Inductive method. The inductive (indirect) plan supplies examples and reasons first and then draws conclusions from them. Paragraphs or entire messages may be arranged inductively. This technique, discussed more fully in Chapters 8 and 9, is especially useful when bad news is being presented or when persuasion is necessary. Instead of bluntly announcing the primary idea in the first sentence of a paragraph, the author delays the big idea. The topic sentence comes at the end of the paragraph. If you were a student about to ask your parents for a new car, would you make the request immediately? Or would you first build a case by discussing many solid reasons why you deserve and need a new car, followed by the big idea? Clever individuals have learned that indirectness has value in certain instances. In the following paragraph, notice that the topic sentence comes last. It is a conclusion drawn from the previous sentences.

> Employees have rightfully complained recently of a lack of parking space in our company lots. As more employees are needed and hiring escalates, it's more difficult for us to provide guaranteed parking for everyone. *For this reason, we've purchased two company vans that will be used in a carpooling plan.*

Most paragraphs and most business messages are organized deductively with primary ideas presented first. However, when tactfulness or persuasion is necessary, inductive organization is appropriate. You'll learn more about these strategies in forthcoming chapters.

Process of Writing

Now that we've considered using words skillfully, developing effective sentences, and organizing unified paragraphs, let's look at the total process of writing. Experienced business writers generally follow a series of five steps in producing messages and documents. These five steps, which we'll call the POWER plan, include Planning, Organizing, Writing, Editing, and Reexamining.

- **Planning.** Every successful document begins with planning. Examine your message in relation to the communication cycle. What is your purpose, and what effect do you hope to achieve? Consider your audience, and anticipate reader reaction to the message. Decide on the medium for your message, considering noise and feedback. Decide what ideas to emphasize and which to deemphasize or omit. This planning process should take place whether you are responding to another message or initiating communication. In its simplest form, planning occurs when the writer reads an incoming letter and underlines significant points or makes marginal notes regarding the response. In a more complex form, planning may involve research to solve a problem.

- **Organizing.** The next step in the process of writing is organizing the message. Follow a deductive (direct) strategy, shown more fully in Chapter 5, for good news and for neutral messages. Use an inductive (indirect) strategy, presented in Chapter 8, for negative messages and persuasion. Novice writers often need help in organizing messages effectively. To give you practice in developing this skill, we will provide writing plans and organizational tips for a variety of business writing situations in forthcoming chapters. As you develop your skills, though, fewer organizational suggestions are provided. Learn to jot down a brief outline or list of points to be covered before you begin to write any message.

- **Writing.** Once you have planned a document and organized its content, begin writing. Some writers compose a rough draft at a typewriter; others prefer pencil and paper. Increasingly, writers are learning the joys of word processing for ease in composition and revision. Your first version should be considered a rough draft only. If you have time and if the document is significant, put it aside for a day before revising it. Fresh insights may help you see the subject differently—perhaps more clearly. Apply the principles you have learned in writing effective sentences and paragraphs.

- **Editing.** Read over your rough draft critically. Is the tone appropriate? Will the reader understand what you have said? Will this message achieve your purpose? Edit your message by crossing out awkward and unclear sections. Replace dull or meaningless words with precise, vivid ones. Look for ways to polish the content and structure of your message. Many experts consider the editing phase the most important step in the process of writing. After prudent editing, prepare the final copy.

- **Reexamining.** The final step is a careful reexamination of the message. Proofread the final copy not only for meaning and expression but also for typographical errors, as well as spelling, grammar, capitalization, and other errors. Consider its appearance. Is it attractive and neat? Is it balanced on the page? Are names, addresses, and numbers expressed accurately?

As you start writing business documents in the next chapter, apply this POWER formula. Too often, inexperienced writers begin writing a document immediately, without preparing and without aiming toward a goal.

How to Measure Readability: The Fog Index

Everyone would agree that articles in *Time Magazine* or *U.S.A. Today* are much easier to read than articles in scientific journals, such as *The Journal of Abnormal Psychology* or *Science*. Exactly why is that? It's because magazines for popular audiences concentrate on material with two common elements: short words and short sentences. To measure the readability of writing, Robert Gunning developed a formula, called the Fog Index, based on these two elements. Read the following paragraph, taken from *Innovation and Entrepreneurship*,[1] by Peter F. Drucker, noted authority on management. How readable is this segment of Drucker's writing? When you finish, we'll apply the Fog Index to determine its readability. The underscored words will be explained as part of the analysis to follow.

[1]"Planning" as the term is commonly understood is actually incompatible with an entrepreneurial society and economy. [2]Innovation does indeed need to be purposeful and [3]entrepreneurship has to be managed. [4]But innovation, almost by definition, has to be decentralized, *ad hoc*, autonomous, specific, and micro-economic. [5]It had better start small, tentative, flexible. [6]Indeed, the opportunities for innovation are found, on the whole, only way down and close to events. [7]They are not to be found in the massive aggregates with which the planner deals of necessity, but in the deviations therefrom—in the unexpected, in the incongruity, in the difference between "The glass is half full" and "The glass is half empty," in the weak link in a process.

To determine the readability of this passage (or any of your choosing), select a section of contextual material (sentences) with 100 to 150 words. Then follow these steps:

1. Count the total number of words. Count hyphenated words, such as *micro-economic*, as two words. (Our sample has 119 words.)

2. Count the number of sentences. Independent clauses are considered separate sentences. Therefore, count compound sentences as two sentences. (Our sample has 7 clauses that count as sentences.)

3. Divide the total number of words (119) by the number of clauses (7), resulting in the average sentence length (17 words).

4. Underscore the long words (25). A word is *long* if it has three or more syllables. However, do not count the following:

   a. Proper nouns (capitalized words)
   b. Combinations of easy words (such as *understood*)
   c. Verbs made three syllables by the addition of *ed* or *es*

[1]Peter F. Drucker, *Innovation and Entrepreneurship: Practice and Principles*, Harper & Row, Publishers (New York, 1985): 255.

5. Divide the number of long words (25) by the total number of words in the passage (119). This results in the percentage of long words (.21 or 21%).

6. Add the average sentence length (17) and the percentage of long words (21%), dropping the decimal point. The result is 38.

7. Multiply the answer in Step 6 by 0.4. The result is 15.2. Therefore, the Fog Index for this passage is 15.2.

If you thought this passage was fairly difficult to read, you were right. Its readability score of 15.2 indicates a level between the third and fourth year of college. Level 12 indicates the last year of high school.

Although readability indexes are not exact scientific measures, they are helpful in providing a general sense of reading ease or difficulty. Many magazines including *Time* and *Newsweek* are written at tenth and eleventh high school grade levels to appeal to their wide readership.

Most business writing is between grade levels 8 and 12. Keep your sentences short, but not choppy. Strive to use short words, but don't necessarily sacrifice a long word if it is precise. Try to make your writing readable without being monotonous.

Recap of Fog Index Calculation

1. Count total words.

2. Count total sentences.

3. Find average sentence length. (Divide number of words by sentences.)

4. Count long words.

5. Find percentage of long words. (Divide total number of words by long ones.)

6. Add number of long words and percentage.

7. Multiply by 0.4.

APPLICATION AND PRACTICE—4

Discussion

1. How are speakers and writers different in the manner in which they emphasize ideas?

2. Why is parallelism an important technique for writers to master?

3. Why are active-voice verbs preferred in business writing?

4. How does a writer achieve paragraph unity?

5. Differentiate between the deductive and inductive methods for organizing paragraphs.

Short Answers

6. Write definitions for these words.

   a. Phrase
   b. Clause

7. What is the difference between an independent and a dependent clause?

8. Write definitions for these sentence faults.

   a. Fragment
   b. Run-on sentence

   c. Comma splice

9. Name the five steps in the POWER formula that describe the process of writing.

10. What is the average length of a sentence?

11. List five techniques for achieving emphasis through mechanics.

12. List four techniques for achieving emphasis through style.

13. List two stylistic techniques for deemphasizing an idea.

14. Define zigzag writing.

15. How can a writer achieve parallelism? Give an example.

Writing Improvement Exercises

Sentence Structure.   Each of the following groups of words could be classified as a fragment, comma splice, or run-on sentence. In the space provided, name the fault. Be prepared to discuss how to remedy sentence faults.

fragment _____ **Example:**   Since the trip originates in Los Angeles and makes one stop in Chicago.

_____ 16. We would like to inspect your car, please contact your authorized dealer immediately.

_____ 17. If the necessary work has already been done or if you no longer own your Volkswagen.

_____ 18. We would very much appreciate your completing the enclosed questionnaire return it in the postage-paid envelope.

_____ 19. Because they know they can save money and time when they shop with us.

_____ 20. Bills are mailed on the 16th of each month, they are payable by the 10th of the next month.

_____ 21. We are happy to grant your request for a credit account with us we welcome you as a charge customer.

_____ 22. Accounts that are payable by the 10th of each month and subject to a finance charge of $1\frac{1}{2}$ percent if unpaid.

_____ 23. Your credit record, Mr. Deckman, is excellent, therefore, we are happy to welcome you as a charge customer.

_____ 24. A service representative was dispatched immediately he found that the computer had been programmed incorrectly.

_____ 25. As long as you are able to make a rush delivery of pottery to arrive before February 28.

Emphasis.   For each of the following sentences, circle (a) or (b).

26. Which is more emphatic?

    (a) It is a good idea that we advertise more.
    (b) It is critical that we advertise heavily.

27. Which is more emphatic?

    (a) The committee was powerless to act.
    (b) The committee was unable to take action.

28. Which sentence places more emphasis on *product loyalty*?

    (a) Product loyalty is the primary motivation for advertising.
    (b) The primary motivation for advertising is loyalty to the product,
         although other purposes are served also.

29. Which is more emphatic?

    (a) We need a faster, more efficient distribution system.
    (b) We need a better distribution system.

30. Which sentence places more emphasis on the seminar?

    (a) An executive training seminar that starts June 1 will include four
         candidates.
    (b) Four candidates will be able to participate in an executive training
         seminar that we feel will provide a valuable learning experience.

31. Which sentence places more emphasis on the date?

    (a) The deadline is December 30 for applications for overseas assignments.
    (b) December 30 is the deadline for applications for overseas assignments.

32. Which is *less* emphatic?

    (a) Miss Curtis said that her financial status had worsened.
    (b) Miss Curtis said that she had lost her job and owed $2,000.

33. Which sentence *deemphasizes* the credit refusal?

    (a) We are unable to grant you credit at this time, but we will reconsider
         your application later.
    (b) Although we welcome your cash business, we are unable to offer you
         credit at this time; but we will be happy to reconsider your application
         later.

34. Which sentence gives more emphasis to *judgment*?

    (a) He has many admirable qualities, but most important is his good
         judgment.
    (b) He has many admirable qualities, including good judgment and
         patience.

35. Which is more emphatic?

    (a) Three departments are involved: (1) Legal, (2) Accounting, and
        (3) Distribution.
    (b) Three departments are involved:
        (1) Legal
        (2) Accounting
        (3) Distribution

Sentence Unity. The following sentences lack unity. Rewrite, correcting the identified fault.

Example: (Dangling modifier) By advertising extensively, all the open jobs were filled quickly.

Revision: By advertising extensively, we were able to fill all the open jobs quickly.

36. (Dangling modifier) To open a money market account, a deposit of $3,000 is required.

37. (Mixed construction) The reason why Mrs. Harris is unable to travel extensively is because she has family responsibilities.

38. (Misplaced modifier) Identification passes must be worn at all times in offices and production facilities showing the employee's picture.

39. (Misplaced modifier) The editor in chief's rules were to be observed by all staff members, no matter how silly they seemed.

40. (Zigzag sentence) The business was started by two engineers, and these owners worked in a garage, which eventually grew into a million-dollar operation.

Parallelism.   Revise the following sentences so that their parts are balanced.

41. (Hint: Match verbs.) Some of our priorities include linking employee compensation to performance, keeping administrative costs down, the expansion of computer use, and the improvement of performance-review skills of supervisors.

42. (Hint: Match active voice of verbs.) Sally Strehlke, of the Newport office, will now supervise our Western Division; and the Eastern Division will be supervised by our Baltimore office manager, James McFee.

43. (Hint: Match nouns.) Word processing is being used in the fields of health care, by attorneys, by secretaries in insurance firms, for scripts in the entertainment industry, in the banking field, and in many other places.

44. If you have decided to cancel our service, please cut your credit card in half, and the card pieces should be returned to us.

45. We need more laboratory space, additional personnel is required, and we also need much more capital.

46. The application for a grant asks for this information: funds required for employee salaries, how much we expect to spend on equipment, and what is the length of the project.

47. To lease an automobile is more expensive than buying one.

48. Mr. Claiborne's attorney said that a will should contain three elements: distribution of property, some way for an executor to be appointed, and you must provide for administration of the will.

49. To use the copier, insert your meter, the paper trays must be loaded, indicate the number of copies needed, and your original sheet should be inserted through the feeder.

50. The new teleconferencing service allows on-line users to send data, data can be received by users, they can discuss it, and data is clarified.

Active-Voice Verbs.   Business writing is more forceful if it uses active-voice verbs. Revise the following sentences so that verbs are in the active voice. Put the emphasis upon the doer of the action. Add subjects if necessary.

Example: The computers were powered up each morning at 7 a.m.

Revision: Kevin powered up the computers each morning at 7 a.m.

51. Initial figures for the bid were submitted before the June 1 deadline.

52. A separate bill from AT&T will be sent to customers who continue to lease their equipment from AT&T.

53. Substantial sums of money were saved by customers who enrolled early in our stock option plan.

54. A significant financial commitment has been made by us to ensure that our customers will be able to take advantage of our discount pricing.

55. Smaller-sized automated equipment was ordered so that each manager could have an individual computer.

Passive-Voice Verbs.   When indirectness or tact is required, use passive-voice verbs. Revise the following sentences so that they are in the passive voice.

Example: Mrs. Murdock did not turn in the accounting statement on time.

Revision: The accounting statement was not turned in on time.

56. Mr. Kelly made a computational error in the report.

57. We cannot ship your order for 50 motors until June 15.

58. The government first issued a warning regarding the use of this pesticide over 15 months ago.

59. The private laboratory rated products primarily on the basis of their performance.

60. We will notify you immediately if we make any changes in your travel arrangements.

Inductive/Deductive Organization.   Read the lettered statements below and answer the following questions. Be prepared to justify your responses.

61. If you were organizing the lettered ideas in a deductive strategy, with   _____
    which statement would you logically begin?

62. If you were organizing the lettered ideas in an inductive memo, with   _____
    which statement would you conclude?

   (a) The Los Angeles Convention Center has facilities to accommodate over 250 exhibitors and thousands of visitors.
   (b) Los Angeles is a large metropolitan center that will attract a sizable audience for the conference.
   (c) The Los Angeles Convention Center has excellent parking facilities and better-than-average transportation connections.
   (d) The conference planning committee recommends that the next National Automation Conference be held in Los Angeles.

Readability.   From a magazine or textbook select a passage of 100 to 150 words. Determine its readability level by applying the Fog Index. Write a paragraph describing your findings. Do you think the level is appropriate for the intended audience? How could the author alter the readability of the passage?

CASE 4–1

Paragraph Unity

The following paragraph is poorly organized and lacks unity and coherence. On a separate sheet of paper, revise the paragraph following the suggestions provided in the text. Add or delete information as necessary. Pay particular attention to the use of transitions to connect thoughts coherently.

> We are pleased to welcome you to First National. Our family of banking customers is satisfied with First National. Group term life insurance is offered. This is one of the services we make available to our customers. This group term life insurance program has many benefits. It is low in cost. No medical examination is necessary to qualify for this program. The cost of living is steadily rising, and our premium rates remain reasonable. Take a look at the enclosed outline describing our group term life insurance.

CASE 4–2

Paragraph Organization

The following material is part of a letter of application. It lacks organization, emphasis, and coherence. Its unity could be improved by including only relevant information. Revise this paragraph to remedy its faults. (Do not rewrite the entire letter.)

> You will see that I have wide variety in the field of communications in course work, and I have some work experience. My résumé that is enclosed shows this. I had a course in media analysis, one in business writing, one in communications law, and television ethics. I was active in the Scouts, 4-H, the Band Club, and my church. I worked with a newspaper for a while, television special events, and did a radio show. I have studied reporting, how to edit, and public relations.

CASE 4–3

Paragraph Organization

Select *one* of the topics below to write a well-organized, unified 100- to 150-word paragraph. Identify your topic sentence and method of organization.

1. Explain to a professor why you feel a grade you received should be changed.

2. Explain to an employer why you feel you should work different hours or be given a different assignment.

GRAMMAR/MECHANICS CHECKUP—4

Adjectives and Adverbs

Review Sections 1.16 and 1.17 of the Grammar/Mechanics Handbook. Then study each of the following statements. Underscore any inappropriate forms. In the space provided write the correct form and the number of the G/M principle illustrated. You may need to consult your dictionary for current practice regarding some compound adjectives. When you finish, compare your responses with those shown below. If your answers differ, study carefully the principles in parentheses.

live-and-let-live (1.17e)
_____

Example: He was one of those individuals with a <u>live and let live</u> attitude.

_____ 1. Most large corporations do not rely upon one source of long term financing only.

_____ 2. Many subscribers considered the $25 per year charge to be a bargain.

_____ 3. Other subscribers complained that $25 per year was exorbitant.

4. The computer supplied the answer so quick that we were all amazed. _____

5. He only had $1 in his pocket. _____

6. If you expect double digit inflation to return, look for safe investments. _____

7. Jeremy found a once in a lifetime opportunity. _____

8. Although the house was four years old, it was in good condition. _____

9. Of the two sample colors shown in the brochure, which do you think is best? _____

10. Professor Roberts is very well-known in his field. _____

11. Channel 12 presents up to the minute news broadcasts. _____

12. Lower tax brackets would lessen the after tax yield of some bonds. _____

13. The conclusion drawn from the statistics couldn't have been more clearer. _____

14. The new investment fund has a better than fifty fifty chance of outperforming the older fund. _____

15. If you feel badly about the transaction, contact your portfolio manager. _____

---

1. long-term (*1.17e*)   3. C (*1.17e*)   5. had only (*1.17f*)   7. once-in-a-lifetime (*1.17e*)
9. better (*1.17a*)   11. up-to-the-minute (*1.17e*)   13. have been clearer (*1.17b*)   15. bad (*1.17c*)

CHAPTER 5

Memorandums That Inform, Request, and Respond

～～～～

In this chapter you will learn to do the following:

- Distinguish between direct and indirect writing strategies.
- Recognize functions, characteristics, and kinds of memorandums.
- Write memorandums that deliver information.
- Write memorandums that make requests.
- Write memorandums that respond to other documents.

Memorandums (memos) are forms of internal communication; that is, they deliver information within an organization. In many organizations more internal memos are written than letters addressed outside the company. One study revealed that executives rank memos first in frequency among 20 forms of written communication.[1] Another study indicated that the typical manager writes seven memos a week.[2]

Memos deliver messages within organizations.

～～

A Word About Strategies

Before we continue our discussion of memos, we need to consider plans or strategies. Business writing usually follows one of two strategies: the direct (deductive) plan or the indirect (inductive) plan. In Chapter 4, you learned to organize paragraphs inductively and deductively. Now we'll apply those same strategies to complete messages. How do you know which strategy to use? By analyzing your

[1]Donna Stine and Donald Skarzenski, "Priorities for the Business Communication Classroom: A Survey of Business and Academe," *The Journal of Business Communication* 16 (1979): 17.

[2]Martha H. Rader and Alan P. Wunsch, "A Survey of Communication Practices of Business School Graduates by Job Category and Undergraduate Major," *The Journal of Business Communication* 17 (1980): 39.

message and the anticipated reader reaction to that message, you can determine whether to use the direct or the indirect strategy. Most messages can be divided into three categories:

Most messages can be divided into three categories.

1. **Positive or neutral messages.** Expect the reader to be pleased or at least not displeased.

2. **Negative messages.** Expect the reader to be displeased.

3. **Persuasive messages.** Expect the reader to be initially uninterested.

The anticipated reader reaction determines whether a message should be written directly or indirectly.

For positive or neutral messages, the direct strategy is most effective. You will learn to apply the direct strategy in writing informational memos in this chapter. In Chapters 6 and 7, you will use the direct strategy for routine request letters and for routine replies. In Chapters 8 and 9, you will learn to use the indirect strategy for negative letters and for persuasive messages.

Functions of Memos

Memos are a vital means of conducting business within an organization. They explain policies, procedures, and guidelines. They make announcements, request information, and follow up conversations. They provide a written record of decisions, telephone conversations, and meetings. They save time by relaying information to many people without the need for a meeting. Moreover, they ensure that all concerned individuals receive the *same* message, which would be unlikely if the message were transmitted orally.

Memos can save time and provide a written record.

When used judiciously, memos serve useful functions. When misused, however, they waste time, energy, and resources. A memo should not be written if a telephone call or a short note would function as well. Memos should not be written as self-serving attention-getters. Some individuals churn out lengthy memos on the slightest pretense, such as the need for additional wastepaper baskets or catered coffee service or assigned parking spaces. Moreover, copies of memos should be sent only to concerned individuals. The fact that the office has an excellent copy machine does not justify sending copies of memos to all employees.

Memos should be used for producing a permanent record, for gathering information, and for transmitting information when a personal meeting is impossible or unnecessary.

Kinds of Memos

Most memos can be classified into four groups: (1) memos that inform, (2) memos that request, (3) memos that respond, and (4) memos that persuade. In this chapter we will be concerned with the first three groups because they use the direct strategy. The fourth group, persuasive memos, uses the indirect strategy, which will be presented in Chapters 8 and 9.

Characteristics of Memos

Well-considered memos have the following characteristics:

1. They begin with *To*, *From*, *Date*, and *Subject*.

2. They cover just one topic.

3. They are informal.

4. They are concise.

Memos use an efficient standardized format, as shown in Figure 5.1. See page 371 for more information about formatting memos. You may prepare memos on printed forms or keyboard them on word processsors. Use of the headings *To*, *From*, *Date*, and *Subject* has two benefits. First, headings force the sender to organize his or her thoughts in order to compose the subject of the message. Second, headings are invaluable aids for filing and retrieving memos.

A memo normally covers only one topic. This facilitates action and filing. If an executive, for example, discusses both the faulty exhaust system on the company car and the approaching company banquet in the same memo, the reader may place the memo in a stack of paper relating to company cars and forget the details of the company banquet.

To facilitate action and filing, memos should cover a single topic only.

Memos may be written somewhat more informally than letters addressed outside the organization. Because you usually know and work with the reader, you do not have to build goodwill nor strive to create a favorable image. Like business letters, memos should sound like conversation. For example, *Please be informed that* is much more formal than *I'd like you to know that*. Which would you be more likely to say in conversation?

Although informality is appropriate in memos, the degree of informality depends upon the relationship between the employees. When a close working relationship exists between the sender and the receiver, a warm personal tone is fitting.

The techniques that you learned in Chapters 2, 3, and 4 for writing concisely will help make your memos succinct. Memos are more likely to be read and acted upon if they are just long enough to say what is necessary.

Direct Strategy

Memos that carry neutral or positive messages are most effective when written directly.

Direct Strategy

- Big idea first

- Details or explanation

- Closing thought

FIGURE 5.1   Sample Memorandum

DT DATATECH, INC.

Internal Memorandum

TO: Carlita Robertson

Writers of memos usually place their initials here.

FROM: Edwina Jordan

DATE: February 6, 19xx

SUBJECT: FORMATTING COMPUTER MEMORANDUMS

Here is the information you requested regarding appropriate formatting for memorandums keyed at computers and printed on plain paper.

1. Use 1 to 1 1/4-inch side margins.

2. Leave a top margin of 1 to 2 inches.

3. Type in all caps the headings TO, FROM, DATE, and SUBJECT.

4. Single-space within paragraphs but double-space between them.

We prefer to make a master memo document with all the format settings. Then we read that command file into any new memo. This method is fast and accurate.

Notice that memos do not end with a closing such as *Sincerely.*

If you'd like to discuss formatting computer memos further, please call me at Ext. 606.

The direct strategy gets right down to business quickly; it uses the BIF approach: Big Idea First. If your memo has a new procedure to announce, summarize that announcement in the first sentence. Don't explain why the new procedure is being introduced or what employee reactions to the new procedure might be. Save explanations and details for later.

> **The direct strategy starts with the Big Idea First.**

Providing the main idea first has several advantages:

- It saves time for readers. They don't have to skim the first part of the message quickly to find a key sentence telling what the message is about.

- It enables readers to develop the proper mind-set. After they learn the main idea, the following explanations and details make sense. Readers comprehend more quickly because they anticipate what is coming.

- It helps the writer organize the message logically. Once the writer has stated the main idea, the rest of the message is easier to write.

Remember, however, that the direct strategy is useful only if you expect that the reader will not be displeased by the content of the message. If the announcement of a new procedure might generate resistance, then persuasion is necessary and the indirect strategy (Chapter 9) would be more effective.

Developing a Memo-Writing Plan

Once you have decided upon the strategy for your message, proceed to a writing plan. In this book you will be shown a number of writing plans appropriate for different messages. These plans provide a skeleton; they are the bones of a message. Writers provide the flesh. Simply plugging in phrases or someone else's words won't work. Good writers provide details and link together their ideas with transitions to create fluent and meaningful messages. However, a writing plan helps you get started and gives you ideas about what to include. At first, you will probably rely on these plans considerably. As you progress, they will become less important. Later in the book no plans are provided. Here is the writing plan for a memo that is not expected to create displeasure or resistance.

Writing Plan for Memos

- **Subject line**—summarizes memo contents.
- **First sentence**—states the main idea.
- **Body**—provides background data and explains the main idea.
- **Closing**—requests action or summarizes the message.

> **A writing plan helps you organize a complete message.**

Writing the Subject Line

Probably the most important part of a memo is the subject line, which summarizes the contents of the memo in concise language. It should be brief, but not so brief that it is senseless. The subject line *Revised Procedures* is probably meaningless to a reader. An improved subject line might read, *Revised Procedures for Scheduling Vacations*.

> **A subject line must be concise but meaningful.**

A subject line is like a newspaper headline. It should attract attention, create a clear picture, and present an accurate summary. It should not be a complete sentence and should rarely occupy more than one line. Cramming comprehensive information into one dense line is a challenge that many writers enjoy because it tests their word and organizational skills.

Beginning With the Main Idea

Although an explanation occasionally must precede the main idea, the first sentence usually states the primary idea of the memo. An appropriate opening sentence for a memo that announces a new vacation procedure is as follows:

> Here are new guidelines for employees taking two- or three-week vacations between June and September.

It's better to attach a copy of previous correspondence than to ask the reader to find it.

Don't open a memo by asking the reader to refer to another memo. Attach a copy of that document if necessary. Or provide a brief review of the relevant points. Asking the reader to dig out previous correspondence is inefficient and inconsiderate.

The first sentence may constitute the entire first paragraph. If more information is needed to present the main idea, write a unified paragraph using the techniques suggested in Chapter 4. In many memos, however, the first paragraph consists of a single sentence.

Explaining in the Body

In the body of the memo, explain the main idea. If you are asking for detailed information, arrange the questions in logical order. If you are providing information, group similar information together. When considerable data are involved, use a separate paragraph for each topic. Work for effective transitions between paragraphs.

The tone of memos is informal. Don't be self-conscious about using contractions (*won't, didn't, couldn't*), conversational language, and occasional personal pronouns (*I, me, we*). Make an effort, though, to deemphasize first-person pronouns. Concentrate on developing the *you*-attitude.

Memos are most effective when they are concise. For this reason, lists often appear in memos. Lists boil down information into readable and understandable form. See page 97 for tips about writing effective lists.

Closing the Memo

End the memo with a request for action, a summary of the contents of the memo, or a closing thought. If action on the part of the reader is sought, spell out that action clearly. A vague request such as *Drop by to see this customer sometime* is ineffective because the reader may not understand exactly what is to be done. A better request might be worded as follows: *Please make an appointment to see John Ayers before August 5*. Another way to close a memo is by summarizing its major points. This is particularly helpful if the memo is complicated.

End a memo with a request for action, a summary, or a closing remark.

If no action request is made and a closing summary is unnecessary, the writer may prefer to end the memo with a simple closing thought. Although it is unnecessary to conclude memos with goodwill statements such as those found in letters to customers, some closing statement is useful to prevent a feeling of abruptness. For example, a memo might end with *I'll appreciate your assistance* or *What do you think of this proposal?*

≈ Memos That Inform

The memo format is useful to explain organization policies, procedures, and guidelines. As policy-making documents, memos that inform should be particularly clear and concise.

The memo shown in Figure 5.2 informs employees about a new storewide policy. It begins directly by telling the reader what the memo is about. The next paragraph explains why the new policy is needed; a list enumerates policy information and guidelines, making them easy to read and understand.

≈ Memos That Request

Memos that make requests are most effective when they use the direct approach. The reader learns immediately what is being requested. However, if you have any reason to suspect that the reader may resist the request, then an indirect approach would probably be more successful.

Requests should be courteous and respectful, not demanding or dictatorial. The tone of the following request would likely antagonize its recipient:

The tone of a request memo should encourage cooperation.

> I want you to find out why the Davis account was not included in this report, and I want this information before you do anything else.

So that the intent of the memo is not misunderstood, requests should be considered carefully and written clearly. What may seem clear to the writer may not always be clear to a reader. Therefore, it's wise to have a fellow worker read a critical memo for clarity before it is sent out.

Whenever possible, the closing paragraph of a request memo should be *end dated*. An end date sets a deadline for the requested action and gives a reason for this action to be completed by the deadline. Such end dating prevents procrastination and allows the reader to plan a course of action to ensure completion by the date given. For example, a request that an employee order mailing labels might conclude with the following:

End dating includes a deadline and, if possible, a reason explaining the deadline.

> Please submit your order by December 1 so that sufficient labels will be on hand for mailing the year-end reports January 15.

Many requests within organizations relate to the collection of information necessary for decision making. The memo shown in Figure 5.3 requests data about personal computers.

FIGURE 5.2   Memo With Enumerated List

DATE: December 2, 19xx

TO: Pat Walker, Cecille Cabanne, Don Deonne, Gil Sweeney, and
                  Kathy Pedroza

FROM: E. W. Lauderman, Store Manager   *E.W.L.*

Summarizes contents of memo. SUBJECT: STORE POLICY REGARDING OFF-PLANET DOLLS

Combines main idea with brief explanation.   Because we anticipate heavy customer interest in the popular Off-Planet dolls, I would like you to share the following information and newly developed GemMart policy with all your employees.

Explains why new policy is needed.   I've just learned that a GemMart buyer recently appeared in a taped television interview that will be aired nationally this week. Apparently our buyer said that the Off-Planet dolls would be available in some GemMart stores. Since we expect our stores to be swamped with telephone calls from customers asking specifically about this series of dolls, we have decided that all employees in all of our area stores should have the same policy information to help them answer questions consistently. Please note the following points:

Lists items in parallel form for easy reading.
■ GemMart currently has no Off-Planet dolls.

■ We do not know if we will receive any in the future.

■ We will neither issue rainchecks nor take any orders for these dolls.

Closes with directions and promise.   Please discuss this policy with your employees. I'll be sure to let you know immediately if we receive a shipment of Off-Planet dolls.

des

≈≈

FIGURE 5.3   Survey Request Memo

TO: All Department Heads   DATE: February 20, 19xx

FROM: Joseph Ferguson *J.F.*
             Vice President, Operations

SUBJECT: SURVEY OF PERSONAL COMPUTER EQUIPMENT

Please answer the questions below regarding the kinds of personal computers your department is now using.

Because many of our departments now find it necessary to exchange data disks, we are considering the purchase of software that will enable us to make the data disks from various computer manufacturers compatible. Your answers to the following questions will help us select the proper software.

States request courteously.

1. What kinds of personal computers does your department currently use?

Lists questions for ease in reading.

2. What size data disks are you using?

3. What software programs are you now using?

4. Are you anticipating the purchase of additional computer equipment in the near future? If so, what kind?

I'll appreciate your answers by March 7 so that we can analyze your responses before our budget requests are due March 15.

Provides end date and reason.

≈≈

Memos That Respond

Much office correspondence reacts or responds to other memos or documents. When responding to a document, follow these preparatory steps: (1) collect whatever information is necessary, (2) organize your thoughts, and (3) make a brief outline of the points you plan to cover. You may wish to make your outline or notes right on the document you are answering.

Before answering a memo or letter, gather the necessary data, organize your ideas, and make an outline of your response.

Begin the memo with a clear statement of the big idea, which often is a summary of the contents of the memo. For example, the following wordy and dated opening begins with an outdated expression: *Pursuant to your request of January 20, I am herewith including the information you wanted.*

FIGURE 5.4   Memo That Responds

TO: Joseph Ferguson   DATE: March 5, 19xx
                Vice President, Operations

FROM: Lois R. Jones, *L.R.J.*
                Manager, Legal Support Services

SUBJECT: SURVEY OF COMPUTER EQUIPMENT IN LEGAL SUPPORT
                SERVICES

Identifies response immediately.   Here is the information you requested regarding personal computers in Legal Support Services.

Lists numbered answers in same order they were asked.   1. Our staff members are now using three Martech ATs, one Astro XS100, one Computer Deskpro, and one Everex Turbo.

2. The Martech ATs, the Astro XS100, and the Computer Deskpro use $5\frac{1}{4}$-inch floppy disks; the Turbo uses $3\frac{1}{2}$-inch disks.

3. Our software includes WordPerfect, CalcStar, Lotus 1-2-3, and Symphony.

4. We are considering purchasing two more personal computers soon, but we have not yet decided on a vendor.

Closes with reassuring remark.   We, too, are interested in making our data disks compatible. Let me know if I may offer additional information.

Lois Jones, manager of Legal Support Services, responded to Bill Dixon's request for computer information with the memo shown in Figure 5.4. Notice that the memo begins directly with a clear reference to Mr. Dixon's request. It also answers his questions in the same order in which they were asked.

Memorandums serve as vital channels of information within business offices. They use a standardized format to request and deliver information. In this chapter you learned to apply the direct strategy in writing informational memos. In the next chapter you will extend the direct strategy to writing letters that make requests.

How to Write Winning Lists

A list is a group or series of related items, usually three or more. Business and professional writers have learned that presenting similar information in list form improves readability and emphasis. Because lists require fewer words than complete sentences, they are faster to read and easier to understand. Listed information stands out; therefore, it's swiftly located and quickly reviewed. Professional writers who strive for readability, comprehension, and emphasis frequently use lists.

How can you write good lists? Concentrate on two concepts: (a) the list itself, and (b) the paragraph or sentence that introduces it.

Items in List

Use lists only if the items that are related can be shown in the same form. If one item is a single word but the next item requires a paragraph of explanation, the items are not suitable for listing.

Items in a list must be balanced, or parallel, in construction. Use similar grammatical form.

Instead of This	Try This
Her primary pastimes are sleeping, eating, and work.	Her primary pastimes are sleeping, eating, and working.
We are hiring the following: sales clerks, managers who will function as supervisors, and people to work in offices.	We are hiring the following: sales clerks, supervising managers, and office personnel.
Some of the most pressing problems are refunds that are missing, payments directed to the wrong place, and numerous lost documents.	These are the most pressing problems: missing refunds, misdirected payments, and lost documents.

A list of instructions snaps to attention if each item is a command starting with a verb. Notice in the next example that bullets (periods) signal each item.

Here are instructions for using the copy machine:

- Insert the departmental meter in the slot.
- Load paper, curved upward, in the upper tray.
- Feed flat copies through the feed chute.

Some items are most efficiently shown with headings:

Date	City	Speaker
September 16	Portland	Dr. Roietta Fulgham
October 30	Seattle	Professor Iva Upchurch

Occasionally, listed items are longer, requiring more than one sentence. Strive for consistency in construction within the items. For example,

McDonald's was able to increase its productivity and profits with three effective techniques.

1. Unnecessary and redundant tasks in the work-place were identified and eliminated, resulting in simplification.

2. Functions not requiring face-to-face customer contact were centralized in an administrative center.

3. Routine tasks, such as bill-paying and simple customer service questions, were automated with a touch-tone voice-response system.

Items may be listed vertically or horizontally. Items shown vertically, obviously, stand out more—but they require more space. To use less space and to show less separation from the surrounding paragraph, arrange items horizontally. In horizontal lists, items are usually part of one sentence. Notice that each item is followed by a comma and that the word *and* precedes the last item in the series. If the items are too long for incorporation in one sentence, use a vertical list or rewrite the material without a list. Using letters or numbers for listed items gives them more importance and separation.

Many individuals backslide on their resolutions regarding fitness. To keep exercising, you should (a) make a written commitment to yourself, (b) set realistic goals for each day's workout, and (c) enlist the support of your spouse or a friend.

The health club has four sign-up months: January, May, August, and October.

Welcome to the following new members. They all signed up for aerobics exercises beginning in January.

Jeffrey Moss	Chandell Handley
Cindy Hunter	Tim Hansen

Introductory Words

The introductory words to a list must make sense with each item in the list. The introduction should be as complete as possible so that the same words do not have to be repeated in each item.

Instead of This	Try This
Our goal	Our goal is to recruit sales reps who are
■ Is to recruit intensely competitive sales reps	■ Intensely competitive
■ Is to use reps who are familiar with our products	■ Familiar with our products
■ Recruit intelligent reps who learn quickly	■ Intelligent and learn quickly

Punctuating and Capitalizing Lists

Although some flexibility exists, most writers follow similar guidelines in punctuating and capitalizing words in lists. Study the examples above for illustration of the following suggestions.

1. Use a colon following the introduction to most lists. However, there are three exceptions.

   ■ Do not use a colon if the listed items follow verbs or prepositions (thus functioning as complements or objects to elements in the introduction).

   ■ Do not use a colon after the introduction if another sentence comes before the list.

   ■ You may choose to use a period (or a colon) after the introduction if both the introductory statement and the listed items are complete sentences, as shown in the McDonald's example above.

2. Omit punctuation after any item listed vertically. Use a period *only* if the item is a complete sentence.

3. Capitalize the initial letter of any item listed vertically.

APPLICATION AND PRACTICE—5

Discussion

1. Explain the functions of memos within organizations.

2. Distinguish between the direct and indirect strategies.

3. How can memos waste time, money, and resources?

4. What are the differences between internal and external correspondence for an organization?

5. Name four classifications of memos and explain what strategy each should follow.

Short Answers

6. List three categories into which most messages can be divided.

7. Explain what reader reaction you might expect for each of the three categories of messages you listed above.

8. What are the four guide words that appear at the top of most printed memo forms?

9. The use of a standardized memo format benefits whom?

10. Why should a memo cover only one topic?

11. List three ways to close a memo.

12. List three advantages of the BIF approach.

13. List and describe briefly the four parts of the writing plan for a memo.

14. What is *end dating*?

15. Most memos will use which strategy?

Writing Improvement Exercises

Memo Openers and Organizations.   Compare the sets of memo openers below. Circle the letter of the opener that illustrates the BIF plan. Be prepared to discuss the weaknesses and strengths of each opener shown.

16. a. For some time now we have been thinking about the possibility of developing an in-service training program for some of our employees.
    b. Employees interested in acquiring and improving computer skills are invited to an in-service training program beginning October 4.

17. a. I am asking our Customer Relations Department to conduct a study and make recommendations regarding the gradual but steady decline of customer checking accounts.
    b. We have noticed recently a gradual but steady decline in the number of customer checking accounts. We are disturbed by this trend, and for this reason I am asking our Customer Relations Department to conduct a study and make recommendations regarding this important problem.

18. a. Some of the customer representatives in the field have suggested that they would like to dictate their reports from the field instead of coming back to the office to dictate them here. For this reason, we're going to make some changes.
    b. Customer representatives may now dictate their field reports using the following procedures.

Opening Paragraphs.   The following opening paragraphs to memos are wordy and indirect. After reading each paragraph, identify the big idea. Then, write an opening sentence that illustrates the BIF plan. Use a separate sheet if necessary.

19. Some of our staff members are interested in computer software that might lessen our work here in Accounting. Several staff members asked if they could attend a seminar February 11. This seminar previews accounting software that might be effective in our department. I am allowing the following employees to attend the seminar: Artie Miller, Ethel Martin, and Aurelia Gomez.

20. Your TechData Employees Association has secured for you discounts on auto repair, carpet purchases, travel arrangements, and many other services. These services are available to you if you have a Buying Power Card. All TechData employees are eligible for their own private Buying Power Cards.

Lists

21. Use the following information to compose a horizontal list with an introductory statement.

    Please follow in the plant at all times the following rules and restrictions. Hard hats should be worn at all times. Refrain from horseplay please. Smoking is prohibited for the good of all.

22. Use the following information to compose a vertical list with an introductory statement.

    Traditional employee suggestion programs often fail—for a number of reasons. To make them more successful, participation must be increased. Try to get more people to participate. For one thing, invitations should be extended to managers, part-timers, temporary workers, and even representatives of suppliers. But the rules must be simple—so simple that anyone may suggest anything at any time. And when they do submit a suggestion, they should be rewarded immediately. It's easy to give a simple reward, such as a button or a coffee mug, to anyone as soon as a suggestion is made.

23. Use the following information to compose a horizontal list with an introductory statement.

    Your lease is about to mature. When it does, you must make a decision. Three options are available to you. If you like, you may purchase the equipment at fair market value. Or the existing lease may be extended, again at fair market value. Finally, if neither of these options is appealing, the equipment could be sent back to the lessor.

Memo Format.   Study memo formatting and parts in Appendix 1 (p. 370). Then answer these questions:

24. Are memos usually single- or double-spaced?

25. How many inches should you leave for side margins when typing a memo?

26. Where does an author sign a memo?

27. If you have no printed stationery on which to type a memo, on what line should you begin typing?

CASE 5–1

Memo That Requests

Play the part of Gordon Burns, president of Alloy Products. You must send a memo to Stacy Stafford, assistant personnel director, asking her to write a report comparing group health insurance plans. The Board of Directors of Alloy Products has authorized this study in preparation for the eventual adoption of a plan for your employees. The board has specific key factors to consider in the comparison: the cost to the company for each employee covered; kinds of illnesses and/or injuries covered; total annual health benefits allowed per employee; the costs to employees; and the coverage for hospital, out-patient, and home visits. You want Stacy to make a thorough investigation of the plans offered by seven or eight companies in your area. You need the report by July 1. In her report she should recommend three plans that are most appropriate. The board will make the final selection.

   To help you organize your memo according to the principles you have learned in this chapter, read the options suggested here. Circle appropriate responses.

1. From the point of view of the person receiving the memo, what is the big idea in this memo?
   a. The Board of Directors is considering a health plan for employees.
   b. Stacy is to make a comparative study of group health plans.
   c. The Board of Directors has certain key factors to consider.
   d. Stacy's report must be submitted by July 1.

2. An effective opening sentence for your memo might be
   a. At its last meeting the Board of Directors considered adopting an employee group health insurance plan.
   b. We are very interested in employee group health insurance plans.
   c. Please make a comparative study of employee group health insurance plans as a preliminary step in selecting a suitable program for our employees.
   d. I have been authorized by the Board of Directors to begin an investigation of employee group health insurance plans.

3. The body of your memo should include
   a. An explanation of what the Board of Directors has authorized.
   b. A description of the Board of Directors' meeting.
   c. An inquiry about the personnel file of Jack Hays, which you gave her last week.
   d. References to complaints from employees regarding the lack of health benefits.

4. An effective closing for this memo might be
   a. Thanks for your assistance in this matter, Stacy.
   b. Please submit your comparison report to me by July 1.
   c. If I may be of assistance to you, please do not hesitate to call on me.
   d. I wonder, Stacy, if you would be able to speak to a group of high school students who asked us to supply a speaker on the topic of high-tech employment.

Use this memo for class discussion or use it as a writing assignment. If your instructor so directs, write the entire memo to Stacy on a separate sheet. Begin with an appropriate subject line. You may wish to incorporate some of the sentences you selected here. Add other information and join your thoughts with logical transitions. Be sure that your list of key factors is concise and parallel.

CASE 5–2

Memo That Requests

Analyze the following poorly written memo. List its faults in the space provided. Outline an appropriate plan for a memo that requests. Then, on a separate sheet, write an improved version of this memo, rectifying its faults.

TO: Susan Richardson   DATE: April 3, 19xx
            Community Relations Coordinator

FROM: H. W. Rosenblum
            President

SUBJECT: SUMMER INTERNSHIP PROGRAM

As you know, Susan, we at TechData have not been altogether pleased with the quality of the new employees we attract each year. We do not feel that we are getting the crème de la crème of the college graduates on the market, so to speak.

Our Management Council has suggested that we make a consideration of the possibility of adding a summer internship program for the express purpose of attracting superior college students to our company.

A number of questions arise. Accordingly, this memo is to make a request that you do some research on this possibility. Here are some things I want you to find out about. How much would such a program cost? I would like this question and the others answered in a report that you submit to me by June 15. Has this kind of program been tried in other companies? Do you think colleges and universities would participate? And if so, which ones would participate? We need to know if such a plan is likely to improve our present situation. We're also wondering if the company would be obligated to offer permanent positions to these summer interns.

If you'd like to talk with me about this project, Susan, just give me a jingle.

1. List at least five faults:

2. Outline a writing plan for this memo.

CASE 5–3

Memo That Responds

Cynthia Chomsky, secretary of the Management Council of DataTech, wrote a first draft of the following memo. Then she attended a company workshop on improving communication techniques. She wrote comments to herself based on some of the things she learned. Revise the memo using her suggestions.

TO: Martin Reid, Sal Alvarez, Kim Rockenrader

FROM: Cynthia Chomsky

DATE: February 3, 19xx

SUBJECT: Reminder   *really vague... must improve*

long-winded memo... wastes everyone's time!

this first ¶ is a real drag!!

As you know, the Management Council is very concerned about our employee hiring techniques. This has become a problem in our company. I heard many of you say at our last meeting in January that you felt we had to improve our selection of employees. I understand that some new employees are hired for positions for which they are unsuited, and we don't seem to learn about the problem until it's too late. We really need to improve the entire personnel selection process, beginning with the writing of job specifications to the interviewing process. One area where we have been particularly lax is the checking of applicants' references.

they already know all this stuff... condense or leave out

I was asked at our last meeting in January to find speakers I spent a lot of time finding individuals who I thought would bring us valuable information about improving our interviewing and other hiring techniques. I think you're all really going to benefit from the programs I've arranged. Please be reminded that the Management Council meets at 2:30 p.m. in Conference Room C.   *move to end*   *need this?*   *add end date*

too much "I" - not enough "you"

If for some reason you cannot attend any of these meetings, you must call me. We also voted, if you will recall, to include outside guests at these last three sessions. So, if you would like to invite anyone, tell me his name so I can send him an invitation.   *— by when?*   *sexist!*

what a dictator I sound like!   *should come last*

check spelling of names

Here are the three speakers I have arranged. The first is Norman J. Withers, from ABC Consultants. He will speak February 20 on the topic of "Job Specifications." Ann D. Seaman, Ph.D., Weber State University, is the next speaker. She will speak on the topic of "The Interviewing Process," and her date is March 28. Last but not least is Erick Basil, from Smith & Burney, Inc. The title of his talk is "Reference Checking" set for April 30.

arrange in list... use headings?

cliché   *shorten entire memo!*

CASE 5-4

Personal Writing Situation

Write the following memo from your own work or personal experience. Some employees have remarked to the boss that they are working more than other employees. Your boss has decided to study the matter by collecting memos from everyone and asks you to write a memo describing your current duties and the skills required for your position. If some jobs are found to be overly demanding, your boss may redistribute job tasks or hire additional employees. Write a well-organized memo describing your duties, approximately how much time you spend on each task, and the skills needed for what you do. Provide enough details to make a clear record of your job. Use actual names and describe actual tasks. If you have no work experience, use experience from an organization or institution to which you belong. Report to the head of the organization, describing the duties of an officer or of a committee. Your boss or organization head appreciates brevity. Keep your memo under one page.

Additional Problems

1. Assume you are Stephanie Adams and you work for Petro Products, Inc. The office manager, Sharon Chambers, asks you to go to a U.S. Post Office to gather information about current formatting of envelopes. Ms. Chambers wants to know how envelopes should be prepared and why they are no longer prepared the way they were 20 years ago. Get the information, and write a memo summarizing your findings. Your memo should be no more than one page.

2. You have been asked to draft a memo to the office staff about the company's Christmas party. Include information about where the party will be held, when it is, what the cost will be, a description of the food to be served, whether guests are allowed, and whom to make reservations with.

3. Assume you are Pamela Haas, marketing director, United Foods, Inc. Write a memo to V. A. McFee, vice president, informing him about the following advertising program. You have just completed the planning stages of a promotion campaign for your pasta product, Creamettes. Together with Sunkist Growers, Inc., you have worked out an agreement to launch a joint campaign aimed at combining the use of Creamettes with Sunkist lemons. The details for the planned campaign were formulated by your advertising agency, McFarlaine and Becker, over the past two months. The promotion will concentrate on light recipes for summer consumption. Along with the recipes, discount coupons on Creamettes will be offered. The coupons and recipes will be published in appropriate magazines and in the Thursday food sections of 48 daily newspapers in the Western states. The campaign will be concentrated in June, July, and August. You expect this campaign to cost $190,000 for advertising in newspapers and magazines, $90,000 for redeemed coupons (300,000 coupons at 30 cents each), and $37,000 to McFarlaine and Becker. Sunkist will provide one fifth of these costs. Mr. McFee has no prior knowledge of this promotion; he'll need all the details you can provide.

4. As director of employee relations of United Foods, write a memo to all employees informing them of new banking services soon to be available. You have arranged with First National Bank of your city to install an automated teller machine (ATM) in your lobby. It will operate from 6 a.m. to 9 p.m., six days a week, beginning next week. Describe the advantages of ATMs. Tell employees that a representative from First National will be present in the lobby for the next two weeks. This representative will be able to open accounts for employees who want to take advantage of their banking services, including a range of combination checking and savings accounts. NOW (negotiable order of withdrawal) accounts, CDs (certificates of deposit), and time deposits are available. The company has also arranged with First National to enable employees to deposit their paychecks directly to the bank. Describe the advantages of direct deposits. Encourage employees to visit the First National representatives in the next two weeks.

5. As Sanford Henry, vice president for personnel at United Foods, write a memo to Kathleene Basil, director of information services. Tell her that you have attended a conference on ergonomic office environments. You learned of employee complaints in some organizations where automated information processing equipment has been introduced. Ask her if she is aware of any dissatisfaction among word processing specialists regarding muscular discomfort or eyestrain. Has she noticed increased absenteeism among word processors? Have operators expressed unhappiness with their jobs? Do we have a high turnover rate? Have any steps been taken to reduce job discomfort and dissatisfaction? You are very concerned about the health and happiness of employees. Ask Ms. Basil to give this matter her immediate consideration. You want a quick response. You don't expect her to conduct an elaborate investigation.

6. As Kathleene Basil, director of information services, respond to Mr. Henry's memo request described in No. 5 above. You don't know of any employee complaints about aching necks and shoulders. Only one employee, Edith Yen, the chief editor/proofreader, complained of eye trouble. You tried to solve that problem by rotating the task of editing among all word processing operators. You are concerned, too, about providing an ergonomically satisfactory work environment. You encourage employees who are performing eye-straining tasks to take 10-minute breaks every hour. You make sure that furniture is adjusted to the body size of users. You've checked on the absenteeism of your division compared with other divisions, and you find that yours is lower. You have also installed glare-resistant screens on your monitors to reduce eyestrain. You admit that you have had a higher turnover rate than you would like, but employees seem to be leaving for better-paying word processing positions elsewhere. You are also experimenting with job-enrichment tasks to try to reduce any employee dissatisfaction in the Information Services Division. If Mr. Henry has any suggestions for you, you'd be glad to hear them. Encourage him to come to visit your division.

7. Again as Sanford Henry, vice president for personnel, write a memo to all department managers of United Foods. The city of Milwaukee has mandated that employees "shall adopt, implement, and maintain a written smoking policy which shall contain a prohibition against smoking in restrooms and infirmaries." Employers must also "maintain a nonsmoking area of not less than two thirds of the seating capacity in cafeterias, lunchrooms, and employee lounges, and make efforts to work out disputes between smokers and nonsmokers." Make this announcement to your department managers. Tell the managers that you want them to set up departmental committees to mediate any smoking conflicts before the complaints surface. Explain why this is a good policy.

8. You are Mike O'Dell, manager of accounting services for United Foods, responding to Mr. Henry's memo in No. 7. You could have called Mr. Henry, but you prefer to have this problem in writing. The problem is the difficulty you are experiencing in enforcing the smoking ban in restrooms. Only one men's room serves your floor, and 15 of your 27 male employees are smokers. You have already received complaints, and you see

no way to enforce the ban in the restrooms. Nonsmokers are also muttering about the smoke in the office, which is quite heavy because of your 15 smokers. What suggestions does Mr. Henry have for dealing with the smoke problem in your large, open office? The air circulation system is unable to remove all the smoke. Your committee members can find no solutions; in fact, they have become polarized in their meetings to date. You need help from a higher authority. Appeal to Mr. Henry for solutions. Perhaps he should visit your department.

GRAMMAR/MECHANICS CHECKUP—5

Prepositions and Conjunctions

Review Sections 1.18 to 1.19 in the Grammar/Mechanics Handbook. Then study each of the following statements. Write *a* or *b* to indicate the sentence that is expressed more effectively. Also record the number of the G/M principle illustrated. When you finish, compare your responses with those provided below. If your answers differ, study carefully the principles shown in parentheses.

b_____ (1.18a)   **Example:** (a) Tiffany will graduate college this spring.
                              (b) Tiffany will graduate from college this spring.

_____   1. (a) DataTech enjoyed greater profits this year then it expected.
               (b) DataTech enjoyed greater profits this year than it expected.

_____   2. (a) I hate it when we have to work overtime.
               (b) I hate when we have to work overtime.

_____   3. (a) Dr. Simon has a great interest and appreciation for the study of robotics.
               (b) Dr. Simon has a great interest in and appreciation for the study of robotics.

_____   4. (a) Gross profit is where you compute the difference between total sales and the cost of goods sold.
               (b) Gross profit is computed by finding the difference between total sales and the cost of goods sold.

_____   5. (a) We advertise to increase the frequency of product use, to introduce complementary products, and to enhance our corporate image.
               (b) We advertise to have our products used more often, when we have complementary products to introduce, and we are interested in making our corporation look better to the public.

_____   6. (a) What type computers do you prefer?
               (b) What type of computers do you prefer?

_____   7. (a) Many of our new products are selling better then we anticipated.
               (b) Many of our new products are selling better than we anticipated.

_____   8. (a) The sale of our San Antonio branch office last year should improve this year's profits.

(b) The sale of our branch office in San Antonio during last year should improve the profits for this year.

9. (a) Do you know where the meeting is at?
   (b) Do you know where the meeting is? _____

10. (a) The cooling-off rule is an FTC rule that protects consumers from making unwise purchases at home. _____
    (b) The cooling-off rule is where the FTC has made a rule that protects consumers from making unwise purchases at home.

11. (a) Meetings can be more meaningful if the agenda is stuck to, the time frame is followed, and if someone keeps follow-up notes. _____
    (b) Meetings can be more meaningful if you stick to the agenda, follow the time frame, and keep follow-up notes.

12. (a) They printed the newsletter on yellow paper like we asked them to do. _____
    (b) They printed the newsletter on yellow paper as we asked them to do.

13. (a) A code of ethics is a set of rules spelling out appropriate standards of behavior. _____
    (b) A code of ethics is where a set of rules spells out appropriate standards of behavior.

14. (a) We need an individual with an understanding and serious interest in black-and-white photography. _____
    (b) We need an individual with an understanding of and serious interest in black-and-white photography.

15. (a) The most dangerous situation is when employees ignore the safety rules. _____
    (b) The most dangerous situation occurs when employees ignore the safety rules.

CHAPTER 6

Letters That Make Routine Requests

In this chapter you will learn to do the following:

- Analyze letter content and select an appropriate writing strategy.
- Write letters that request information concisely.
- Order merchandise clearly and efficiently.
- Write letters that make justified claims.

External Communication

Written communication outside an organization is conducted largely by letters. Executives, managers, and supervisors at all levels of management, as well as nonmanagement employees, typically are called upon daily to exchange information with customers and other organizations. Although information is also exchanged verbally, written communication in the form of letters is essential to provide a convenient, well-considered, and permanent communication record.

Content and Strategy

Like memos, letters are easiest to write when you have a strategy or plan to follow. The plan for letters, just as for memos, is determined by the content of the message and its anticipated effect on the receiver. Letters delivering bad news require an indirect approach (Chapter 8). Many letters, however, carry good or neutral news. Because such letters will not produce a negative effect on their readers, they follow the deductive or direct strategy.

The content of a message and its anticipated effect on the reader determine the strategy you choose.

Direct Strategy

- Big idea first
- Details or explanation
- Closing thought

The routine business of an organization often involves three kinds of letters: (1) information requests, (2) order requests, and (3) claim requests. These three

113

kinds of letters will be presented in this chapter. Each follows the direct strategy, but each has its own writing plan. Therefore, you will find three different writing plans in this chapter.

Information Requests

The first kind of letter to be described in this chapter is the information request. Although the specific subject of each inquiry may differ, the similarity of purpose in routine requests enables writers to use the following writing plan.

Writing Plan for an Information Request

- **Opening**—asks the most important question first, or expresses a polite command. *Please send or could you please send*

- **Body**—explains the request logically and courteously, and asks other questions. *One sentence, maybe two.*

- **Closing**—requests specific action with end date, if appropriate, and shows appreciation.

Opening Directly

Readers find the openings and closings of letters most interesting.

The most emphatic positions in a letter are the first and last sentences. Readers tend to look at them first. The writer, then, should capitalize upon this tendency by putting the most significant statement first. The first sentence of an information request is usually a question or a polite command. It should not be an explanation or justification, unless resistance to the request is expected. When the information requested is likely to be forthcoming, immediately tell the reader what you want. This saves the reader's time and may ensure that the message is read. A busy executive who skims the mail, quickly reading subject lines and first sentences only, may grasp your request rapidly and act upon it. A request that follows a lengthy explanation, on the other hand, may never be found. This inquiry about a computer program gets off to a slow start.

> I read about the A-plusTax program in the June 5 issue of *The Wall Street Journal*. Because I have a personal computer and because I have a business preparing tax returns primarily for construction contractors, I am very interested in this program. Would you please send me information about it.

The same request with the big idea first, expressed as a polite command, is far more effective because the reader knows immediately what is being requested.

> Please send me information about your A-plusTax program that was advertised in *The Wall Street Journal* on June 5.

Open with a question when you seek specific information.

When a request demands exact information, the first sentence of the inquiry letter will probably be a question. For example,

> Will the A-plusTax preparation program advertised in *The Wall Street Journal* run on my Astro computer?

If several questions must be asked, use one of two approaches: ask the most important question first, or introduce the questions with a summary statement. The following example poses the most important question first, followed by other questions.

> Will the Dun & Bradstreet seminar at the Hyatt Regency in San Francisco
>   July 30 offer college credit?
> How much of the total expense for this seminar is tax deductible?
> If I make a reservation and then must cancel, may I receive a refund?

If you want to ask many questions that are equally important, begin with a summarizing statement.

> Will you please answer the following questions about the Dun & Bradstreet
> seminar in San Francisco.

Notice that the summarizing statement sounds like a question, but it has no question mark. That's because it's really a command disguised as a question. Rather than bluntly demanding information (*Answer the following questions*), we often prefer to soften commands by posing them as questions. Such statements (some authorities call them rhetorical questions) should not be punctuated as questions because they do not demand answers.

A rhetorical question is one for which no answer is expected.

Details in the Body

The body of a letter that requests information should provide necessary details. For example, if you want information about the type of printer that is appropriate for your personal computer, you must explain what kind of computer you have and what your requirements are. Requesting general information without pinpointing your exact demands may produce a general response that requires a second inquiry.

The body of a request letter may carry an explanation or a list of questions.

If a summarizing statement opens the letter, the body of your request may consist of a list of specific questions. Compare the two following methods of requesting information. The first is ineffective and generalized.

> I am interested in the cash value of my insurance policy. I am also
> thinking of borrowing against this policy. How do I do this? Too, a friend
> told me that if I didn't pay the premium, it would be automatically paid
> from the cash value of the policy. Is this true?

This second request asks the same questions but enumerates them.

1. What is the current cash value of my insurance policy?

2. What is the current loan value of this policy?

3. What is the procedure for borrowing against this policy?

4. If I do not pay the policy premium, is it automatically paid from the
   policy's cash value?

The enumerated request is more effective for these reasons: (1) each question stands by itself and is numbered, (2) each request is phrased as a question that

Would you rather read items enumerated in a list or items bunched in a paragraph?

requires a specific answer, and (3) each item is structured in parallel form so that the reader may anticipate and grasp its meaning quickly.

The quality of the information obtained from a request letter depends upon the clarity of the inquiry. If you analyze your needs, organize your ideas, and frame your request logically, you are likely to receive a meaningful answer.

Closing With an Action Request

The ending of a request letter should tell the reader what you want done and when.

Use the last paragraph to ask for specific action, to set an end date, if appropriate, and to express appreciation.

As you learned in working with memos, a request for action is most effective when an end date and reason for that date are supplied. If it's appropriate, use this kind of end dating:

> Please have your accountant fill out the enclosed survey and return it to me by February 15. In this way we may update your file before you come in for your tax preparation.

It's always appropriate to end a request letter with appreciation for the action taken. However, don't fall into a cliché trap, such as *Thanking you in advance, I remain . . .* or the familiar *Thank you for any information you can send me*. Your appreciation will sound most sincere if you avoid mechanical, tired expressions. Here's a simple but sincere closing to a request for insurance information:

> I'll be most appreciative if you will send me this information by July 10, when I will be reevaluating my entire insurance program.

Illustrating the Plan

The letter shown in Figure 6.1 requests information about conference accommodations and illustrates the writing plan you have learned. The writer has many questions to ask and begins with the most important one.

Appendix 1, p. 365, shows letter formats and styles.

The letter also illustrates block style, the most popular letter style.

≈≈

Order Requests

The second category of letter to be presented in this chapter is that of order requests. Orders for merchandise are usually made by telephone or by filling out an order form. On occasion, though, you may find it necessary to write a letter ordering merchandise. For example, if you had a merchandise catalog but couldn't find its order forms, or if you were responding to an advertisement in a magazine, you'd have to write a letter to place an order.

Ordering merchandise may occasionally require a letter.

Order requests use the direct strategy, beginning with the big idea.

Writing Plan for an Order Request

- **Opening**—authorizes purchase, and suggests method of shipping.
- **Body**—lists items vertically; provides quantity, order number, description, and unit price; and shows total price of order.
- **Closing**—requests shipment by a specific date; tells method of payment; and expresses appreciation.

FIGURE 6.1 Letter That Requests Information—Block Style, Mixed Punctuation

GEOTECH   **Letterhead**

770 Airport Boulevard
Burlingame, CA 94010

August 20, 19xx   **Dateline**

Ms. Jane Mangrum, Manager   **Inside address**
Scottsdale Hilton Hotel
6333 North Scottsdale Road
Scottsdale, AZ 85253-4310

Dear Ms. Mangrum: **Salutation**

Can the Scottsdale Hilton provide meeting rooms and accommodations for   **Body**
about 250 Geotech sales representatives from May 25 through May 29?

It is my responsibility to locate a hotel that offers both resort and
conference facilities appropriate for the spring sales meeting of my
company. Please answer these additional questions regarding the
Scottsdale Hilton:

1. Does the hotel have a banquet room that can seat 250?

2. Do you have at least four smaller meeting rooms, each to
   accommodate a maximum of 75?

3. Do you provide public address systems, audio-visual equipment, and
   ice water in each meeting room?

4. Do you offer special room rates for conferees?

5. What is the nearest airport, and do you provide transportation to and
   from it?

I will be most grateful for answers to these questions and for any other
information you can provide regarding your resort facilities. May I please
have your response by September 1 so that I can meet with our planning
committee September 4.

Sincerely yours,   **Complimentary close**

Marlene Frederick

Marlene Frederick   **Author's name**
Corporate Travel Department   **Identification**

mef   **Reference initials**

Authorizing Purchase in the Opening

Let the reader know immediately that your letter is an order and not a request for information.

The first sentence of an order letter should authorize the purchase and shipment of merchandise. It should specify that the letter is an *order* and not a request for information. It should not be an explanation or an ambiguous expression of interest, such as *I was fascinated by your advertisement describing your microcassette dictation system*; nor should an order letter begin, *I certainly liked my friend's solar calculator and would like to have one for myself.* These two examples give no indication that the letter is intended to place an order. They leave the reader wondering about the intent and purpose of the writer.

A more effective opening begins with specific order language, such as *Please send me.* The opening should also tell how the order is to be shipped, unless you have no preference, and may include the source of the information for the order. This opening sentence leaves no doubt about the intent of the letter:

Please *send by UPS the* following *items listed in* your *1990 price* list.

Listing Items in the Body

If you are ordering more than one item, list them vertically rather than describing them in a paragraph. Include as much of the following information as possible: quantity, order number, complete description, unit price, and total price. Here's an example of a vertical order list for several items:

2	No. 9A57313 ionization smoke alarms @ $24.99	$ 49.98
2	No. 9A5709 Diehard 9-volt batteries @ 2.39	4.78
1	No. 9A58031 Zytel fire extinguisher @ 51.99	51.99
1	No. 9A58051 heavy-duty mounting bracket @ 3.99	3.99
	Subtotal	$110.74
	Estimated tax at $6\frac{1}{2}$ percent	7.20
	Estimated shipping costs	4.50
	Total	$122.44

Closing With Specifics

End an order letter by stating how you plan to pay for the merchandise and when you expect to receive it.

In closing an order letter, tell how you plan to pay for the shipment. Since tax and shipping costs may be unknown, some individuals prefer to provide a credit card number so that the order can be shipped immediately. Organizations may have credit agreements that allow the manufacturer to ship goods without prior payment.

In addition to including payment information, the closing of an order letter should indicate when the goods should be sent (end dating) and may express appreciation. Observe how the following closing achieves the goal:

We would appreciate your sending these items before May 5. Please bill us at our usual terms of 2/10, n/30.

The term *2/10, n/30* means that a 2 percent discount will be given if the invoice is paid within 10 days; the total bill (*net*) is due in 30 days.

Order Letters That Succeed and Fail

The ineffective order letter shown in Figure 6.2 is faulty for many reasons. Its opening is too general, failing to show that the letter authorizes the purchase of goods. The first sentence is also 43 words long, making its meaning difficult to comprehend. Most sentences should average 15 to 20 words. In addition, this letter does not describe sufficiently the items being ordered, and it fails to mention a method of payment.

An improved version of this order letter (Figure 6.3) begins with specific order language, itemizes and describes the goods clearly, includes shipping and payment information, and closes with an end date.

This letter illustrates modified block style, second only to block (page 117) style in popularity. Notice that in modified block style, the date and closing lines begin approximately at the center of the page. Notice, too, that this letter uses a company name in its closing. When included in the closing lines, company names are typed in all capital letters and are double spaced below the complimentary close.

"It's a combination word processor and food processor, in case you have to eat your words."

Source: From *The Wall Street Journal*. Reprinted with permission of the Cartoon Features Syndicate, Inc.

Simple Claim Requests

The third category of letters to be presented in this chapter is that of simple claim requests. A claim is a demand for something that is due or is believed to be due. A simple claim is one to which the writer believes the reader will agree—or *should* agree. For example, a purchaser has a legitimate claim for warrantied products that fail, for goods that are promised but not delivered, for damaged

FIGURE 6.2   Poor Order Letter

Uses outdated salutation.	Dear Sirs:
Fails to use order language.	My company has never been able to find a way to print our business checks at our microcomputer, but I notice in your catalog that just arrived in the mail that you have check forms that are compatible with a number of computers.
Lacks sufficient description of goods.	I would be interested in 500 multipurpose checks at the price listed in the catalog. I am also interested in your multipurpose microcomputer forms for invoices. These are listed at 500 for $36.79.
Omits method of payment and end date.	May I have both of these items at your convenience.
	Sincerely,

The direct strategy is best for simple claims that require no persuasion.

products, or for poor service. When the writer feels that the claim is justified and that persuasion is not required, a claim request should follow the direct strategy.

Writing Plan for a Simple Claim

- **Opening**—describes clearly the desired action.
- **Body**—explains the nature of the claim, tells why claim is justified, and provides details regarding action requested.
- **Closing**—ends pleasantly with goodwill statement, and includes end dating, if appropriate.

Opening With Action

Start with a clear statement of the action you want taken.

In a simple claim request, tell the reader immediately what action you would like taken. Such directness may appear to be blunt, but actually it's businesslike and efficient. Don't begin a claim letter with an attempt to establish goodwill or an explanation, such as

> We've used Pentack tools for years and have always appreciated the quality product that you produce and the prompt service that we have received when we placed our orders.

Save the explanation for the body and the goodwill for the closing. Tell the reader what you want in the opening sentence:

> Please send us two ½-inch socket sets to replace the two ⅜-inch sets sent with our order shipped October 23.

With this direct opening, the reader knows what you want and can read the remainder of the letter in the proper context.

〜

FIGURE 6.3   Improved Order Letter—Modified Block Style, Mixed Punctuation

DUXLER SHEET METAL FABRICATION, INC.

12890 West Dixie Highway
North Miami, Florida 33181

January 24, 19xx

Quill Corporation
100 South Shelter Road
P.O. Box 4700
Lincolnshire, IL 60197-4700

Ladies and Gentlemen:

SUBJECT: ORDER FOR COMPUTER CHECK FORMS AND INVOICES

Please send by UPS the following items shown in your April sale catalog:

500 No. 202-82411-1 checks for the Turbo-PC	$61.14
500 No. 292-85011 invoice forms for the Turbo-PC	36.79
Total	$97.93

This order letter includes all the elements necessary for a successful transaction.

I would greatly appreciate your prompt handling of this order so that we may have these forms by February 10. The enclosed check for $102.68 includes shipping costs of $4.75. If there are additional charges, please bill my company.

Sincerely,

DUXLER SHEET METAL FABRICATION, INC.

Melba Herrick

Melba Herrick
Vice President

jf
Enclosure

How to Approach The Salutation Dilemma

Letters usually begin with a salutation, a greeting to the reader. This greeting is included to personalize a letter. If the name of the individual receiving the letter is known, the salutation is easy: *Dear Kevin* or *Dear Mr. Roberts* or *Dear Mrs. Hayden.* But what should be used when no name is known? The salutation dilemma perplexes many writers today. Grammar hotline services all across the country report that one of their most frequent inquiries concerns proper salutations.

In the past we used *Dear Sirs* or *Gentlemen* to address an organization and *Dear Sir* for anonymous individuals. With increasing numbers of women entering the workplace and a new sensitivity to the power of language, writers are reconsidering business letter salutations. No clearcut pattern has emerged, and many authorities are not ready to be pinned down. Here are some of the many possibilities and a few thoughts about each.

Dear Sirs. This salutation is definitely out. Nearly everyone agrees that it's old-fashioned as well as sexist.

Dear Sir or Madam or **Sir/Madam.** Both greetings sound obsolete, and the word *Madam* has an additional stigma. In English it is associated with the keeping of a brothel.

Gentlemen. This salutation survives and is commonly used for all-male organizations. If women are known to be in management, however, many authorities prefer *Ladies and Gentlemen.*

Ladies and Gentlemen. Although this salutation is acceptable for addressing organizations with men and women in management, it is cumbersome and conspicuous. It seems to call attention to itself. Moreover, some feminists take exception to the term *Ladies.*

Gentlepersons, Gentlefolk, Gentle/wo/men. These greetings, along with *Gentles* from Shakespeare, may solve the problem of sexism; but they sound archaic, frivolous, and certainly unbusinesslike. Serious business writers are wary of these.

Dear [company name]. *Dear General Motors* sounds childlike and depersonalized, yet many private individuals seem to prefer using company names when addressing business organizations in general. However, when one company addresses another, this greeting seems inappropriate. It is doubtful that *Dear General Mills* or *Dear Honda Motor Company* will fill the void left by the overthrow of *Dear Sirs.*

Dear [job title]. *Dear Honda Motor Company Service Manager* as a letter greeting is a somewhat acceptable compromise if all else fails. But it seems to dehumanize the correspondence.

Greetings, Salutations, Hail, Please, People, Howdy. These one-word openers all have their champions among individual letter writers across the country. The favorite of William Safire, *New York Times* language columnist, is *Greetings* because it "smiles a welcome."[1] It's also appealing because of its brevity.

Whenever possible, of course, try to use the name of the individual to whom you're writing. Just how much of the name should you use in the salutation? Generally, include only a courtesy title and the last name, as *Dear Ms. Jones*. Include the entire name only if gender is uncertain and you cannot decide on the title, as *Dear Leslie Jones*.

One way to avoid the problem with greetings is to use the simplified letter style (Figure 6.5). This letter style omits the salutation, thus saving time and sidestepping the entire salutation dilemma.

[1]William Safire, *New York Times Magazine* (June 25, 1989): 10–12.

Justifying in the Body

Explain the reasons that justify your claim without becoming angry or emotional.

Here's where you explain why you feel your claim is justified. Provide the necessary details so that the problem can be rectified without misunderstanding. Avoid the tendency to fix blame. Instead of saying *You failed to send the items we ordered*, describe the situation objectively. Omit negative or angry words that offend the reader and may prevent compliance with your claim.

An objective explanation of the reason for replacing merchandise could read as follows:

> On October 10 we placed a telephone order requesting, among other things, two ½-inch socket sets. However, when the order arrived yesterday, we noted that two ⅜-inch socket sets had been sent. Because we cannot use that size, we are returning the ⅜-inch sets by UPS.

This unemotional presentation of the facts is more effective in achieving the writer's goal than an angry complaint.

After you have presented the circumstances of your claim objectively, you may wish to suggest alternatives to solving the problem; for example, *If it is impossible to send ½-inch socket sets, please credit my account.* When goods are being returned, you should inquire about the proper procedure. Some companies will allow returns only with prior authorization.

Closing Pleasantly

End the claim letter pleasantly with an effort toward maintaining goodwill. If appropriate, include a date by which you want the claim satisfied.

> We realize that mistakes in ordering and shipping sometimes occur. Because we've been impressed by your prompt delivery in the past, we hope that you will be able to send the ½-inch socket sets to us by November 1.

Effective and Ineffective Claim Letters

The claim letter shown in Figure 6.4 is unlikely to achieve its goal. In demanding that a tire warranty be honored, the writer failed to provide sufficient information. The account of what happened to the tire is incoherent, and the reader is not totally clear about what action the writer wants. In addition, the tone of the letter is angry and harsh.

An improved version of the irritating letter takes a different tone and approach. In the first sentence this improved letter (Figure 6.5) forthrightly asks for a refund under the tire warranty. The letter includes an unemotional, logical explanation of the problem. Its rational tone and sensible expression are more appealing to the reader, who needs to understand the problem before the organization can resolve it.

The improved letter shown in Figure 6.5 illustrates the simplified letter style. Like block style, all lines begin at the left margin. Notice, however, that the salutation is replaced by a subject line in all caps. The complimentary close

~~~

FIGURE 6.4   Angry, Ineffective Claim Letter

Gentlemen:

What good is a warranty if it's not honored? I don't agree with your dealer that the damage to my tire was caused by "road hazards." This tire was defective, and I am entitled to a refund.

My company purchased a GasSaver tire September 5, and it had been driven only 14,000 miles when a big bubble developed in its side. The gas station attendant said that its tread had separated from its body. But the dealer where my company bought it (Harbor Tire Company) refused to give us a refund. The dealer said that the damage was caused by "road hazards." They also said that they never make refunds, only replacements.

My company has always purchased GasSaver tires, but you can be sure that this is our last. Unless we get the refund to which we are rightfully entitled, I intend to spread the word about how we were treated.

Yours truly,

Begins with emotional, illogical, unclear demand.

Provides inadequate explanation of what happened.

Ends with threat instead of an attempt to establish goodwill.

---

is omitted, and the writer's name and identification appear on one line in all caps. Some writers prefer this streamlined style because it eliminates the problem of choosing an appropriate salutation for the receiver.

The claim letter shown in Figure 6.6 seeks permission to return a microcomputer to the manufacturer for repair. Normally, repairs are made locally, but this computer defies diagnosis. The letter writer does not angrily blame the local dealer for ineptness nor criticize the manufacturer for producing a faulty product. Instead, the letter cleverly invites the manufacturer to help solve a "mystery." Notice that the letter opens by asking for instructions on *how* to return the computer rather than by asking for *permission* to return the computer. The request for shipping instructions suggests the writer's confidence that the manufacturer will want to do the right thing and repair the malfunctioning computer.

This personal letter is shown with the return address typed above the date. Use this style when typing on paper without a printed letterhead.

The three types of letters presented in this chapter (information requests, order letters, and claim letters) all use the direct strategy. They open directly with the big idea first followed by details and explanations. In the next chapter you will learn how to use the direct strategy in responding to these same kinds of letters.

~~~

FIGURE 6.5   Simple Claim Letter—Simplified Style

R. KAPPER INDUSTRIES

255 Cherry Street
Milford, Connecticut 06460-6301

March 4, 19xx

Goodday Tire Manufacturers
770 Broad Street
Newark, NJ 07101-5210

WARRANTY REFUND ON GASSAVER TIRE

Simplified style uses subject line but no salutation.

Please honor the warranty and issue a refund for one GasSaver radial tire that was purchased for my company car at Harbor Tire Company on September 5.

Provides rational, coherent explanation.

This whitewall tire cost $109.13 and carried a warranty for 42,000 miles. It had only 14,000 miles of wear when trouble developed. On a business trip to Detroit recently, I noticed that the tire made a strange sound. When I stopped the car and inspected the tire, it had an ugly bulge protruding from its rim. A service station attendant said that the tread had separated from the tire body. I was forced to purchase a replacement tire at considerably more than the price we paid for the GasSaver tire.

When I returned the GasSaver tire to Harbor, they would not honor the warranty. They said the tire was damaged by "road hazards" and that refunds could not be made.

Ends courteously with specific request for action.

My company generally purchases GasSaver tires, and we have been pleased with their quality and durability. Enclosed are copies of the sales invoice and the tire warranty for the tire in question. Also enclosed is a receipt showing that the defective tire was returned to Harbor Tire Company.

I am confident that you will honor my request for a refund of the purchase price of $109.13 prorated for 14,000 miles of wear.

Ron Kapper

Simplified style omits complimentary close.

RON KAPPER, PRESIDENT

eha

Enclosures

~~~

FIGURE 6.6   Simple Claim Letter—Modified Block Style, Mixed Punctuation

23956 Hamlin Street
Canoga Park, CA 91307
August 14, 19xx

Return address is typed above date.

CompuCap, Inc.
2308 Borregas Avenue
Sunnyvale, CA 94088-3565

Ladies and Gentlemen:

SUBJECT: RETURN OF MALFUNCTIONING COMPUCAP 2-X

Please tell me how I may return my malfunctioning CompuCap 2-X microcomputer to you for repair.

Opens confidently, requesting instructions for return of computer.

I am sure you will be able to solve a problem that puzzles my local dealer. After about 45 minutes of normal activity, the screen on my 2-X computer suddenly becomes filled with a jumble of meaningless letters, numbers, and symbols. Computers For You, the dealer from whom I purchased my 2-X, seems to be unable to locate or correct the malfunction.

Describes malfunction coherently.

Although I am expected to have my computer serviced locally, my dealer has been unable to repair it. I am confident that you can solve the mystery and that you will repair my 2-X quickly.

Closes pleasantly with assurance that manufacturer will want to do the right thing.

Sincerely yours,

Carole Eustice

(Mrs.) Carole Eustice

APPLICATION AND PRACTICE—6

Discussion

1. How are letters like memos? How are they different?

2. Why should routine letters, such as inquiries and orders, follow the direct strategy?

3. Which is more effective in claim letters—anger or objectivity? Defend your position.

4. Why should the writer of a claim letter offer alternatives for solving the problem?

5. The quality of the information obtained from a request depends upon the clarity of the inquiry. Discuss.

Short Answers

6. List three reasons for exchanging business information in letter form rather than in oral form.

7. When a request seeks exact information, the first sentence of the inquiry letter will probably be what?

   question

8. Consider the situations below. Which strategy would be most effective? Write *Direct* or *Indirect* to indicate your choice.

   a. You need information about skiing equipment advertised in a magazine.   *direct*
   b. You want to convince your boss to change your assigned work schedule.   *INDIRECT*
   c. You want a replacement for a defective cassette tape recorder, still under warranty, that you ordered by mail.   *direct*
   d. You want to find out how much it costs to rent a houseboat in the Mississippi Delta region for you and your family.   *direct*
   e. As credit manager of a department store, you must tell a customer that he has been denied credit.   *indirect*
   f. You wish to order merchandise from a catalog.   *DIRECT*

9. What are the two most emphatic positions in a letter?

   Beginning and close

10. What is the most popular letter style?

    Block

11. List two ways that you could begin an inquiry letter that asks many questions.

    ASK THE most important question first
    or use summary STATEMENT to introduce many questions.

12. What is an enumerated request?

    questions are numbered, each inquiry is phrased as a question that requires a specific answer. Each item is structured in PARALLEL form for easier reading.

13. What three elements are appropriate in the closing of a request for information?

    ① Requests shipment by a certain date,
    ② Tells method of payment
    ③ expresses appreciation

14. The first sentence of an order letter should include what information?

    authorizes purchase and suggests method of shipping.

15. The closing of an order letter should include what information?

    ① Request specific action, ② to set an end date ③ to express appreciation.

Writing Improvement Exercises

Routine Request Openers.　Revise the following openers from routine request letters so that they are more direct.

16. I am interested in your rental rates for a three-bedroom cabin on Devil's Lake in August.

    If you have a three-bedroom cabin available on Devil's Lake in August what are the rental rates.

17. Recently I purchased a Country Manor linen tablecloth at Robinson's. I haven't been pleased with it, and I am interested in a replacement.

    I would like a replacement of the Country Manor linen tablecloth purchased from your store.

18. The Hi-Sound stereo set that I ordered from you has arrived, and it seems to have a problem in the amplifier. I'm wondering if you can tell me where I may take it for repair.

    I need a repair shop for the amplifier of the Hi-Sound stereo set I just received from you.

19. Your spring sale catalog shows a number of items in which I am interested. I would like the following items.

Order Request Letter.　Analyze the following poorly written order letter and respond to the questions following it.

Gentlemen:

I need an electronic typewriter called The Communicator shown in your fall catalog. Its catalog number is 3G5301C and it costs $599.95. This includes the carrying case and Prestige daisy wheel, but I would like to add some other daisy wheels, including Courier 10 (No. 3G54012) and Script 12 (No. 3G54014). Each of these daisy wheels costs $6.99. I'll need some ribbons—about six (No. 3G5455) at $6.99 for a package of two. I'll pay for this with MasterCharge; I need everything by September 1.

20. What does the opening lack?

command, polite

21. Write an appropriate opening for this order letter.

Please send me the typewriter and items listed below.

22. How would you group the order information so that it is orderly and logical? Name five headings you could use.

1 No. 3G5301C   "The Communicator" typewriter @ 599.95
1 No. 3G54012   "Courier 10" daisy wheel   @ 6.99
1 No. 3G54014   Script 12 Daisy wheel   @ 6.99
6 No. 3G5455   ribbons   @ 6.99
*   Subtotal*

23. Write an appropriate closing for this order request.

It will be much appreciated if you could send 655.87
by Sept. 1 and also this will be paid by Masterchage

Letter Format. Read about letter formats and parts in Appendix 1 (page 365). Then answer the following questions.

24. If you are typing a letter for yourself on plain paper, what items appear above the date?

address your represent and address

25. How is simplified letter style different from block style, and why do some writers prefer simplified style?

26. In what two places could an attention line be typed?

27. If you write a letter to Data General Corp., what salutation would be appropriate?

28. When letters are addressed to individuals, should their names always contain a courtesy title, such as *Mr., Ms., Miss,* or *Mrs.?*

CASE 6-1

Information Request

Assume that you are Mrs. Stephanie Jones. Based on an ad that you saw in a magazine, you wish to write to Mary Powell, Manager, Garden Court Rentals, Carmel-by-the-Sea, CA 93921. You want information about renting a two-bedroom condominium with an ocean view. You'd like to be there from July 17 through July 25, which is the time of the Carmel Bach Festival. You'll need accommodations for three (you, your husband, and your daughter). You're interested in having kitchen utensils, dishes, and bedding. Your husband is interested in nearby golf courses, and your daughter wants to know how close the beach is. You'll need to know what time you can arrive July 17 and how much the rental fee is. You'd like this information by April 1 so that you can complete your summer plans.

Before writing the letter, answer the following questions:

1. What should you include in the opening of an information request?

2. What should the body of your letter contain?

3. How should you close the letter?

4. What is the most important question Mrs. Jones has to ask?

5. How can the other questions be handled effectively?

On a separate sheet, write the letter. Use modified block style, and write on plain paper. Be sure to include your return address above the date. (See Appendix 1, page 367.)

CASE 6-2

Claim Request

Play the role of Joseph Albanese. On June 24 your company had the basement walls of its office building sealed with Modac II, an acrylic coating. This sealant was applied to reduce moisture in the basement so that you could store company files in this area. The contractor, Peter Muscarelli, promised that this product would effectively seal the walls and prevent moisture penetration, as well as prevent peeling, chalking, and color fading for many years. He said that if you had any trouble, he might have to give it a second coat. After the first rain in September, the walls of the basement leaked, making it necessary for you to remove the files stored there. Write a claim letter to Mr. Muscarelli asking that he correct the situation. Let him know that you want the basement effectively sealed by October 30 because heavy seasonal rains usually begin in November.

To help you organize your letter according to the principles you studied in this chapter, read the following suggestions and circle the most appropriate responses. Be prepared to discuss each of the possible responses that follow.

1. To open this letter directly, you might
   a. Remind Mr. Muscarelli that he recommended Modac II and that it just wasn't doing the job.
   b. Describe your disappointment in the ineffectiveness of Modac II and angrily demand that Mr. Muscarelli repeat this job and do it right this time.
   c. Ask Mr. Muscarelli to apply a second coat of Modac II to the basement walls of your company to prevent moisture penetration.
   d. Review chronologically the beginning of this project and your initial dealings with Mr. Muscarelli.

2. The body of this letter would probably
   a. Review the sealing process and your understanding of how you expected Modac II to make your walls moisture proof.
   b. Threaten to sue if Mr. Muscarelli doesn't rectify this matter immediately.
   c. Explain that the June 24 coat was ineffective and that he promised to apply a second coat if necessary.
   d. Blame Mr. Muscarelli for doing a poor job and specify clearly what he must do to satisfy your claim.

3. The closing of this letter should
   a. Explain when and why you want the second coat applied, and express appreciation for Mr. Muscarelli's efforts to keep your basement dry.
   b. Summarize all your dealings with Mr. Muscarelli and reiterate your dissatisfaction with Modac II and with his workmanship as well.
   c. Tell Mr. Muscarelli that you need this storage space badly and that you'd like to use it as soon as possible.
   d. Thank Mr. Muscarelli for his past work and express confidence that he will do the right thing for your company.

Use this letter for class discussion, or write the entire letter on a separate sheet to Mr. Peter Muscarelli, 5807 Redwood Highway, Grants Pass, OR 97526–5807. Add any information that you feel is necessary. Assume that you are writing this letter on letterhead stationery. Use block style. (See Appendix 1, page 367.)

CASE 6–3

Order Request

Analyze the following ineffective request for merchandise, and list its faults. Outline a writing plan for an order request. Then, on a separate sheet, rewrite this request. Use modified block style, and place your return address above the date. Send the letter to Cameratone, Inc., 140 Northern Boulevard, Flushing, NY 11354–1400. Add any necessary information.

Dear Sir:

I saw a number of items in your summer/fall catalog that would fit my Lentax ME camera. I am particularly interested in your Super Zoom 55-200mm lens. Its number is SF39971, and it costs $139.95. To go with this lens I will need a polarizing filter. Its number is SF29032 and costs $22.95 and should fit a 52mm lens. Also include a 05CC magenta filter for a 52mm lens. That number is SF29036 and it costs $9.95. Please send also a Hikemaster camera case for $24.95. Its number is SF28355.

I am interested in having these items charged to my credit card. I'd sure like to get them quickly because my vacation starts soon.

Sincerely,

1. List at least five faults in this letter:

2. Outline a writing plan for an order.

Opening:

Body:

Closing:

CASE 6–4

Personal Order

Write a letter ordering items advertised in a magazine, newspaper, or catalog. Assume that no order form is available. Attach the advertisement to your letter. Be sure to use an appropriate letter style for a personal business letter.

CASE 6–5

Personal Routine Claim

Write a routine claim letter for a product or service you have purchased. Assume that the product or service required a claim to the dealer or manufacturer because the product was defective or the service was not what you expected. Use a situation where you can reasonably expect the manufacturer to honor your claim.

Additional Problems

1. Assume that you are Marc Vannault, manager of a health spa and also an ardent backpacker. You are organizing a group of hikers for a wilderness trip to Canada. One item that must be provided is freeze-dried food for the three-week trip. You are unhappy with the taste and quality of backpacking food products currently available. You expect to have a group of hikers who are older, affluent, and natural-food enthusiasts. Some are concerned about products containing preservatives, sugar, and additives. Others are on diets restricting cholesterol and salt. You heard that Oregon High, Box 51, McMinnville, Oregon 97128, offers a new line of freeze-dried products. You want to know what they offer and if they have sufficient variety to serve all the needs of your group. You need to know where their products can be purchased and the range of cost. You'd also like to try a few of their items before placing a large order. You are interested in how they produce the food products and what kind of ingredients they use. If you have any items left over, you wonder how long they can be kept and still be usable. Write an inquiry letter to Oregon High.

2. Play the role of Edith Sterling, assistant vice president, Bank of Virginia. You have been given the responsibility of developing an employee suggestion program for the bank, which employs over 15,000 workers in the state. You have done some research and have collected helpful ideas, but now you'd like to gather reactions from an organization with first-hand experience. A friend suggested that you write Clifford Bianchi, director, Employee Development Division, Pratt and Whitney, P.O. Box 25438, Minneapolis, MN 55424. Pratt and Whitney implemented a suggestion program three years ago, and Mr. Bianchi has indicated that he would be happy to share details of how successful the Pratt and Whitney employee suggestion program has been. You are interested in the "nuts and bolts" of the program. You need to know how employees are encouraged to participate, how they submit their suggestions, who evaluates them, and what kind of awards are made. You wonder if suggestions should go to supervisors or local administrators first, or if they should go directly to an evaluation committee. You are concerned about legal problems. Also, should you have minimum and maximum awards? You wonder if you must respond to every suggestion. What if an employee protests the decisions of the evaluation committee? You have many questions, but you realize that you can't burden Mr. Bianchi with all of them. However, he was reported to be quite enthusiastic about employee suggestion programs. Write an inquiry letter to him.

3. You are Greg Fontecilla, manager, Datatronics, Inc. You want to order some items from an office supply catalog, but your catalog is one year old and you have lost the order form. You're in a hurry. Rather than write for a new catalog, you decide to take a chance and order items from the old catalog (Fall, 1990), realizing that prices may be somewhat different. You want three Panasonic electric pencil sharpeners, Item 22–A, at $19.95 each. You want one steel desktop organizer, 60 inches long, Item No. 23–K. Its price is $117.50. Order two Roll-a-Flex files for 2 by 4-inch cards at $14.50 each. This is Item 23–G. The next item is No. 29–H, file folders, box of 100, letter size, at $5.29. You need ten boxes. You would like to be invoiced for this purchase, and you prefer UPS delivery. Even though the prices may be somewhat higher, you decide to list the prices shown in your catalog so that you have an idea of what the total order will cost. Write a letter to Blackfield's Discount Office Furniture, 2890 Post Road, Warwick, RI 02886.

4. Play the part of Susan Lee, who lives at 845 Wainee Street, Lahaina, Maui, HI 96761. When you were in California recently, you saw an unusual toy (use your imagination to describe it) at Toys-R-Us in San Dimas. Now that you're back on Maui, you'd like to have that toy as a present for your nephew, but you have not been able to locate it. Write to Toys-R-Us and describe the toy. To save time, you want to order it and have it charged to your Visa credit card (supply the number and expiration date). You expect the toy to cost about $30, but you would go as high as $40 to purchase it. You would like to receive the toy within three weeks, so they should ship it by whatever method will ensure a timely delivery. If they can't ship it immediately, you would appreciate hearing from them so that you can purchase a present locally. Write to Toys-R-Us, 194 West Terrace Avenue, San Dimas, CA 91773, ordering the toy.

5. Assume that you are Sandra Fenwick, president of Fenwick Consulting Services. Since your consulting firm is doing very well, you decided to splurge and purchase a fine executive desk for your own office. You ordered an expensive desk described as "North American white oak embellished with hand-inlaid walnut cross-banding." Although you would not ordinarily purchase large, expensive items by mail, you were impressed by the description of this desk and by the money-back guarantee promised in the catalog. When the desk arrived, you knew that you had made a mistake. The wood finish was rough, the grain looked splotchy, and many of the drawers would not pull out easily. The advertisement had promised "full suspension, silent ball-bearing drawer slides." You are disappointed with the desk and decide to send it back, taking advantage of the money-back guarantee. You want your money refunded. You're not sure whether they will refund the freight charges, but it's worth a try. Supply any details needed. Write a letter to Idaho Wood Products, P.O. Box 488, Sandpoint, Idaho 83864.

6. Assume that you are Paul Friedman, purchase manager, Datatronics, Inc., 2569 Missouri Street, Mesa, AZ 85016. You purchased for your company two Ever-Cool window air conditioners, Model D–2, Serial Nos. 38920 and 38921. One of the units, Serial No. 38920, is not working properly. It worked when it first arrived, but after two weeks it is malfunctioning. The

compressor comes on and off from time to time, but the room does not cool down nor remain cool. Perhaps the thermostat is the problem. The control knob is also defective. You would not normally mention such a small matter, but since the entire unit needs repair, it seems worth mentioning the control knob too. No service representative is convenient to you in Mesa. You have a six-month warranty. How can this unit be repaired? It's very warm in Mesa at this time of the year, and employees are complaining about the lack of air conditioning. Write a claim letter and send a copy of your sales invoice and warranty to Ever-Cool Manufacturing Company, 951 Lawrence Drive, Newbury Park, CA 91320.

GRAMMAR/MECHANICS CHECKUP—6

Commas, 1

Review the Grammar/Mechanics Handbook Sections 2.01 to 2.04. Then study each of the following statements and insert necessary commas. In the space provided write the number of commas that you add; write *0* if no commas are needed. Also record the number of the G/M principle illustrated. When you finish, compare your responses with those shown below. If your answers differ, study carefully the principles shown in parentheses.

Example: In this class students learn to write business letters memos and reports clearly and concisely.   2   (2.01)

1. We do not as a rule allow employees to take time off for dental appointments.   _____

2. You may be sure Mrs. Schwartz that your car will be ready by 4 p.m.   _____

3. Anyone who is reliable conscientious and honest should be very successful.   _____

4. A conference on sales motivation is scheduled for May 5 at the Anaheim Marriott Hotel beginning at 2 p.m.   _____

5. As a matter of fact I just called your office this morning.   _____

6. We are relocating our distribution center from Memphis Tennessee to Des Moines Iowa.   _____

7. In the meantime please continue to address your orders to your regional office.   _____

8. The last meeting recorded in the minutes is shown on February 4 1990 in Chicago.   _____

9. Mr. Silver Mrs. Adams and Ms. Horne have been selected as our representatives.   _____

10. The package mailed to Ms. Leslie Holmes 3430 Larkspur Lane San Diego CA 92110 arrived three weeks after it was mailed.   _____

11. The manager feels needless to say that the support of all employees is critical.   _____

_____ 12. Eric was assigned three jobs: checking supplies replacing inventories and distributing delivered goods.

_____ 13. We will work diligently to retain your business Mr. Lopez.

_____ 14. The vice president feels however that all sales representatives need training.

_____ 15. The name selected for a product should be right for that product and should emphasize its major attributes.

1. (2) not, rule, (2.03)   3. (2) reliable, conscientious, (2.01)   5. (1) fact, (2.03)
7. (1) meantime, (2.03)   9. (2) Silver, Adams, (2.01)   11. (2) feels, say, (2.03)
13. (1) business, (2.02)   15. (0)

CHAPTER 7

Letters That Respond Positively

In this chapter you will learn to do the following:

- Apply the direct strategy in letters that respond positively.
- Write clear and efficient letters and memos that deliver information.
- Promote goodwill in acknowledging order requests.
- Grant claims efficiently and effectively.

Letters that respond positively bring good news to the reader. They answer requests for information and action, they acknowledge orders, and they agree to claims. These letters deliver positive news that the reader expects and wants. Therefore, they follow the direct strategy with the big idea first.

Deliver good news early in a response letter.

Responding to Information Requests

Applying the direct strategy to replies for information results in the following writing plan:

Writing Plan for an Information Response

- **Subject line**—identifies previous correspondence.
- **Opening**—delivers the most important information first.
- **Body**—arranges information in a logical sequence, explains and clarifies, provides additional information, and builds goodwill.
- **Closing**—ends pleasantly.

Subject Line Efficiency

Although it's not mandatory, a subject line is handy in responding to requests. It allows the writer to identify quickly and efficiently the previous correspondence, and it jogs the reader's memory regarding the request. By putting identifying information in a subject line, the writer reserves the first sentence (one of the most

Use the subject line to refer to previous correspondence.

139

important spots in a letter) for the big idea. Here's an effective subject line that responds to a request for interest information:

SUBJECT: YOUR JULY 2 LETTER ABOUT INTEREST RATES ON SAVINGS

Opening Strength

Reveal immediately what the reader expects to learn.

As the most emphatic position in the letter, the first sentence should carry the most important information. A response to an inquiry about the current interest rate on a customer's savings plan would reveal the rate immediately:

> The current interest rate on our Golden Passbook savings account is 7 percent.

Compare the preceding direct opening with the following indirect opening:

> We have received your letter of July 17 requesting information regarding interest rates on our savings programs.

If you are responding to a number of questions, use one of two approaches. The most direct approach is to answer the most important question in the first sentence. Other answers may be supplied in the body of the letter. For example, the following response to a complex request with many questions begins directly:

> Yes, the Dun & Bradstreet seminar at the Hyatt Regency in San Francisco July 30 will offer college credits from San Francisco State University.

A less direct approach starts with a summary statement that shows the reader you are complying with the request:

> Here is the information you requested about the Dun & Bradstreet seminar at the Hyatt Regency in San Francisco on July 30.

Then, answers to the questions are contained in the body of the letter.

Either of these two approaches is superior to the familiar openings *Thank you for your letter of* . . . or *I have received your letter asking for* . . . . These openings are indirect, overworked, and obvious. Stating that you received the customer's letter is obvious, because you are answering it.

Logic in the Body

Give explanations and additional information in the body of a letter that responds to an information request, if necessary. If you are answering a number of questions or providing considerable data, arrange your information logically. It may be possible to enumerate information, as shown in this response to the inquiry about the Dun & Bradstreet seminar:

1. The seminar is authorized to offer .6 CEUs (continuing education units) from San Francisco State University.

2. Because the seminar helps participants maintain or improve professional skills, the total cost (fees, travel, meals, lodging) is tax deductible.

3. Reservations cancelled less than 5 working days prior to the seminar are subject to a $25 service charge.

If your responses require more explanation, devote an entire paragraph to each.

In answering request letters, you have an opportunity to build goodwill toward yourself and toward your organization by offering additional advice or data. Don't confine your response to the questions presented. If you recognize that other facts would be helpful, present them. For example, if a special rate applies for a seminar participant who registers early, include that information. If a customer asks many questions about a printer for a computer but neglects to ask its price, you might include pricing data. If a student inquires about a course of study at your college, you could include answers to the particular questions as well as information about career possibilities in the field.

Provide extra information if you think it would be helpful.

Tailor-made Closing

To avoid abruptness, include a pleasant closing remark that shows your willingness to help the reader. Tailor your remarks to fit this letter and this reader. Since everyone appreciates being recognized as an individual, avoid form-letter closings such as *If we may be of any further assistance, do not hesitate to call upon us.*

Readers appreciate personalized remarks instead of all-purpose form-letter language.

"I liked it better when it listed all of our names!"

Source: From *The Wall Street Journal*. Reprinted with permission of the Cartoon Features Syndicate, Inc.

I appreciate your interest, Mrs. Kuwata, in our bank's savings programs and cordially invite you to stop in to discuss them with our customer service representative, Judy Lane.

Just call me at 899–3032 if you need additional information about the Dun & Bradstreet seminar July 30 in San Francisco.

Good luck in your survey of computer software programs. I hope that my answers contribute to the accuracy and completeness of your results.

Good and Bad Responses to Information Requests

The letter shown in Figure 7.1 is a reply to a bank that has requested information from an insurance company about a customer's policy that is about to be as-

Ineffective writing

FIGURE 7.1   Poor Information Response Letter

Dear Sir:

Wastes the reader's time by stating the obvious.

I have before me your bank's request dated November 5 in which you ask about the insurance policy of Wallace W. Mower. His policy number is 230-38-6958M. This request has been referred to my attention, and I am happy to supply herewith the information you request.

Presents information in disorganized manner.

Mr. Mower's policy has an approximate cash value of $15,500 as of September 1 of this year. According to our records, no liens exist against this policy at this time. On June 1 and again on January 1 of each year the policy has premium due dates.

We do not know of any contingent beneficiaries that would preclude assignment of this policy to your bank.

Closes with overworked, meaningless expression.

If we may be of further assistance, please do not hesitate to call upon us.

Sincerely,

A poor letter demonstrates what to avoid in responding to an information request.

signed to the bank. Since the insurance company does business with the bank and is able to supply the information, the response should be direct. However, the approach in this letter is indirect.

This letter suffers from a number of weaknesses. It begins poorly with *Dear Sir*, a salutation that is dated, impersonal, and perhaps offensive to some readers. It's always better to address the reader by name. This should be easy to do because the inquiry letter was probably signed. Beyond the salutation, the first paragraph is indirect and wordy. Much of this information could be handled efficiently in a subject line. The body of this letter presents in narrative form information that would be easier to read if it were enumerated. The letter makes no effort to develop goodwill, and the closing is a tired cliché.

An improved version of this letter, shown in Figure 7.2, opens with a personal salutation and a time-saving subject line. Although the first sentence does not begin directly with an answer to one of the questions posed in the inquiry, it does offer a summary statement introducing the responses. The body of the letter enumerates logically and in parallel form the information requested. It uses familiar language instead of jargon. This improved letter also includes unsolicited information that may be helpful to the reader. The cordial closing is individualized so that the reader knows it was written just for this letter.

A well-organized response begins directly and enumerates answers to questions asked.

The poorly expressed letter shown in Figure 7.3 responds to a telephone call requesting information about the location of two electronic calculators.

FIGURE 7.2   Information Response Letter—Simplified Style

Equity America Inc.

4350 Ontario Avenue
Detroit, Michigan 48305–4350
(517) 310–5910

February 12, 19xx

Mr. T. Kenneth Young
Customer Services Division
First Michigan Indemnity Bank
2307 East M Avenue
Kalamazoo, MI 49009–2487

YOUR NOVEMBER 5 REQUEST FOR INFORMATION REGARDING
POLICY NO. 230-38-6958M

Here is the information you requested about the insurance policy of
Wallace W. Mower.

Begins directly and provides answers in logical listing.

1. The September 1 cash value of this policy was about $15,500.

2. No liens exist against this policy.

3. Six-month premiums are due on January 1 and June 1.

Uses familiar language.

4. We have no knowledge of possible beneficiaries that would prevent
   assignment of this policy to your bank.

Although you did not ask, you may be interested to know that it is our
practice to notify the assigned bank if policy premiums are not paid. We
would also notify the assigned bank automatically if a premium loan is
made against the policy.

Offers helpful, extra information.

I am pleased to be able to help you obtain information about Mr. Mower's
insurance policy.

Keith Kroll

KEITH KROLL, EXECUTIVE VICE PRESIDENT

obm

Ineffective writing

FIGURE 7.3   Poor Information Response Letter

Dear Mr. Meyers:

Opens indirectly and uses legalese.

Pursuant to our telephone conversation of yesterday morning, this is to advise you about the two (2) electronic calculators in which you are interested.

Sounds harsh and needlessly formal.

The writer has been in contact with Mike Waldon, our office manager, and he has no record of these machines. These machines are not now on our premises nor have they been on our premises for almost two years. He is convinced that someone from your organization (he knows not who) picked these machines up some time ago.

Uses tired, insincere-sounding closing.

It is my hope that this answers your question. If I may be of further assistance, please let me know.

Sincerely,

The first sentence of this ineffective letter uses dated language (*pursuant to*), a wordy expression (*this is to advise you about*), and needless repetition [*two (2)*]. In addition, the first sentence does not deliver the information requested. The second paragraph opens with *the writer*, a formal expression, instead of the more conversational *I*. Moreover, the tone of the body of the letter is rather harsh and negative, and the closing sounds insincere.

The information conveyed in the preceding message could be more effectively delivered by using the direct strategy and by improving the tone of the letter. Notice how the letter shown in Figure 7.4 achieves its objective.

Responding to Order Requests

Letters that follow up orders create excellent opportunities to improve the company image and to sell products.

Many companies acknowledge orders by sending a printed postcard that merely informs the customer that the order has been received. Other companies take advantage of this opportunity to build goodwill and to promote new products and services. A personalized letter responding to an order is good business, particularly for new accounts, large accounts, and customers who haven't placed orders recently. An individualized letter is also necessary if the order involves irregularities, such as delivery delays, back-ordered items, or missing items.

Letters that respond to orders should deliver the news immediately; therefore, the direct strategy is most effective. Here's a writing plan that will achieve the results you want in acknowledging orders.

~~

FIGURE 7.4   Improved Information Response Letter

Dear Mr. Meyers:

Apparently the two electronic calculators about which you called yesterday are not on our premises.

I checked with Mike Waldon, our office manager, and he feels that these two machines were picked up by your organization nearly two years ago. It is possible, however, that the machines were transferred to our Newbury Park facility without Mike's knowledge. I suggest that you call Barbara Merton, our Newbury Park office manager, at (818) 582-8902 to make further inquiries.

You know that I'll be happy to help if I can.

Sincerely,

Gives requested information immediately.

Explains courteously and informally.

Suggests way to obtain additional information.

Ends cordially.

Writing Plan for an Order Response

- **Opening**—tells when and how shipment will be sent.
- **Body**—explains details of shipment if necessary, discusses any irregularities in the order, includes resale information, and promotes other products and services if appropriate.
- **Closing**—builds goodwill and uses friendly, personalized closing.

Give Delivery Information in the Opening

Customers want to know when and <u>how</u> their orders will be sent. Since that news is most important, put it in the first sentence. It is unnecessary to say that you have received an order. An inefficient opener such as *We have received your order dated June 20* wastes words and the reader's time by providing information that could be inferred from more effective openers. Even a seemingly courteous opening like *Thank you for your recent order* does not really tell readers what they want to know. Instead of stating that an order has been received, imply it in a first sentence that provides delivery details. Here's an example:

> We are sending your checks and invoice forms by Z Express air freight service, and these forms should arrive by February 8.

The first sentence should tell when and how an order will be sent.

This opening sentence provides delivery information, and it is certainly superior to the two perfunctory openers shown above. However, it could still be improved. Notice that it emphasizes "we" instead of "you." Because this letter is

A perfunctory opening is routine, superficial, mechanical.

primarily a goodwill effort, its effect can be enhanced by presenting its message from the viewpoint of the reader. Notice how the following version suggests reader benefits and emphasizes the you-attitude.

> Your checks and invoice forms for your IBM-PC were sent by Z Express air freight service. They should reach you by February 8—two days ahead of your deadline.

Put Details in the Body

You should include details relating to an order in the body of a letter that acknowledges the order. You should also discuss any irregularities about the order. If, for example, part of the order will be sent from a different location or prices have changed or items must be back-ordered, present this information.

When a sales clerk tells you how good you look in the new suit you just purchased, the clerk is practicing "resale."

The body of an order response is also the appropriate place to include resale information. *Resale* refers to reselling or reassuring customers that their choices were good ones. You can use resale in an order letter by describing the product favorably. You might mention its features or attributes, its popularity among customers, and its successful use in certain applications. Perhaps your competitive price recommends it. Resale information confirms the discrimination and good judgment of your customers and encourages repeat business. After an opening statement describing delivery information, resale information such as the following is appropriate:

> The multipurpose checks you have ordered allow you to produce several different check formats, including accounts payable and payroll. Customers tell us that these computerized checks are the answer to their check-writing problems.

Resale emphasizes a product already sold; promotion emphasizes additional products to be sold.

Order acknowledgment letters are also suitable vehicles for sales-promotion material. An organization often has other products or services that it wishes to highlight and promote. For example, a computer supply house might include the following sales feature:

> Another good buy from Quill is our popular 3½-inch disk available in our "mini" bulk pack of 25 disks at only $1.69 each. And we will send you free a desk storage tray for your disks.

Use sales-promotion material, however, in moderation. Too much can be a burden to read and therefore irritating.

Show Appreciation in the Closing

The best closings are personalized; that is, they relate to one particular letter.

The closing should be pleasant, forward-looking, and appreciative. Above all, it should be personalized. That is, it should relate to one particular letter. Don't use all-purpose form-letter closings such as *We appreciate your interest in our company* or *Thank you for your order* or *We look forward to your continued business*.
Notice that the following personalized closings refer to the customers personally and to their current orders.

> You may be certain that your checks and invoice forms will reach you before your February 10 deadline. We genuinely appreciate your business and look forward to serving you again.

We appreciate the payment you enclosed with your order. It is always a pleasure to do business with your organization.

You have our appreciation for this order and our assurance, Mr. Johnson, that your future orders will be processed as efficiently and as promptly as this one.

We are confident that you will be pleased with the quality and durability of your Super-Grip 4-ply tires. Your satisfaction with our products and our service, Mr. Steiner, is our primary concern. We hope it will be our privilege to serve you again.

Skillful and Faulty Letters That Respond to Orders

The letter shown in Figure 7.5 reflects a wordy and inefficient style that some businesspeople still use. This letter has many faults. Can you spot them all?

You're right if you said that this order letter starts out poorly with an impersonal salutation. It continues to progress slowly in the first sentence with obvious information that could be implied. It also gives the reader no hint of when the books will arrive. The second paragraph of the letter is unnecessarily negative. Instead of capitalizing upon the popularity of the books ordered, the writer uses negative language (*sorry to report, we will be forced*), implying that the shipment might be delayed. The letter contains a number of outdated and wordy expressions (*pursuant to your request, every effort will be made, attached please find*). The writer does not use resale or sales promotion to encourage repeat orders. Finally, the closing is wordy and overly formal.

~~~

FIGURE 7.5   Faulty Order Acknowledgment Letter

Ineffective writing

Dear Customer:

We are in receipt of your Purchase Order No. 2980 under date of March 15.

I'm sorry to report that the books you have ordered are selling so quickly that we cannot keep them in stock. Therefore, we will be forced to send them from our Nashville distribution center. Pursuant to your request, every effort will be made to ship them as quickly as possible.

Attached please find a list of our contemporary issues.

May I take the liberty to say that we thank you for allowing us to serve your book needs.

Sincerely,

Here's a good example of what should not appear in a letter that responds to an order.

≈≈

FIGURE 7.6   Letter That Responds to Order—Block Style, Mixed Punctuation

CHARTWELL'S BOOKS

5390 Tompkins Hill Road
Eureka, California 95502–7350
(707) 445–2378

March 20, 19xx

Ms. Judy Dresser
2319 Nevada Street
San Leandro, CA 94952–4390

Dear Ms. Dresser:

SUBJECT: YOUR MARCH 15 PURCHASE ORDER NO. 2980 FOR BOOKS

Opens with information the reader wants most to learn.

The books requested in your Purchase Order No. 2980 will be shipped from our San Francisco distribution center and should reach you by April 1.

Includes resale by reassuring reader of wise selections and also promotes future business.

The volumes you have ordered are among our best-selling editions and will certainly generate good sales for you at your spring book fair.

For your interest we are enclosing with this letter a list of contemporary issues recently released. If you place an order from this list or from our general catalog, you will be eligible for special terms that we are offering for a limited time. For each $10 worth of books ordered at full list price, we will issue a $4 credit toward the purchase of additional books—as long as all the books are ordered at the same time.

Ties in appreciation for order with content of letter.

We are genuinely pleased, Ms. Dresser, to be able to help supply the books for your fair. Please take advantage of our special terms in placing your next order soon.

Sincerely,

Charles Bailey

Charles Bailey
Marketing Division

wuh

The improved version of this letter (Figure 7.6) is written in an upbeat style that promotes good feelings between the writer and the customer. Notice that the letter contains a personal salutation, and the first sentence reveals immediately when the books should arrive. The body of the letter confirms the wise selection of the reader by mentioning the successful sales of the books ordered. To promote future sales, this letter includes sales-promotion information. It closes with sincere appreciation that ties in directly with the content of the letter. Notice throughout the letter the emphasis upon the you-attitude and benefits to the reader.

Responding to Claims

A claim is usually bad news to the organization receiving it. A claim means that something went wrong—goods were not delivered, a product failed to perform, a shipment was late, service was poor, or billing was fouled up. Large organizations have customer service departments that handle most claims. Smaller organizations respond individually to customer claims.

An individual who writes letters responding to claims has three goals: (1) to rectify the wrong, if one exists, (2) to regain the confidence of the customer, and (3) to promote future business.

The writer has three important aims when responding to customer claims.

When a claim is received, you must first gather information to determine what happened and how you will respond. Some organizations automatically comply with customer claims—even when the claim may be unjustified—merely to maintain good public relations.

Once you have gathered information, you must decide whether to say yes or no to the claim. If you respond positively, your letter will represent good news to the reader. Use the direct strategy in revealing the good news. If your response is negative, arrange the message indirectly (Chapter 8). Here's a writing plan that responds favorably to a claim.

Writing Plan for Granting a Claim

- **Subject line (optional)**—identifies the previous correspondence.

- **Opening**—grants the request or announces the adjustment immediately, and includes resale or sales promotion, if appropriate.

- **Body**—provides details about how you are complying with the request, tries to regain the customer's confidence, and includes resale or sales promotion, if appropriate.

- **Closing**—ends positively with a forward-looking thought, expresses confidence in future business relations, and avoids apologizing or referring to unpleasantness.

Subject Line Streamlines Reference

A subject line streamlines the reference to the reader's correspondence. Although it is optional, a subject line enables you to reserve the first sentence for

A subject line enables you to save the first sentence for the big idea.

announcing the most important information. Here are examples of subject lines that effectively identify previous correspondence.

SUBJECT: YOUR JUNE 3 INQUIRY REGARDING INVOICE 3569

SUBJECT: REQUEST FOR EXTENSION OF WEAREVER TIRE WARRANTY

SUBJECT: YOUR DECEMBER 7 LETTER ABOUT YOUR SNO-FLAKE ICE CRUSHER

Opening Reveals Good News

Since you have decided to comply with the reader's claim, reveal the good news immediately.

Readers want to learn the good news immediately.

A second shipment of green bar computer paper has been sent by UPS and should reach you by April 25.

We agree with you that the warranty on your Arizona Instruments programmable calculator Model AI 25C should be extended for six months.

You may take your Sno-Flake ice crusher to Ben's Appliances at 310 First Street, Myrtle Beach, where it will be repaired at no cost to you.

The enclosed check for $325 demonstrates our desire to satisfy our customers and earn their confidence.

In announcing that you will grant a claim, do so without a grudging tone—even if you have reservations about whether the claim is legitimate. Once you decide to comply with the customer's request, do so happily. Avoid half-hearted or reluctant responses like the following:

Although the Sno-Flake ice crusher works well when it is used properly, we have decided to allow you to take yours to Ben's Appliances for repair at our expense.

Apologies are usually counterproductive in that they needlessly stir up unpleasant emotions.

Don't begin your letter with an apology such as *We are sorry that you are having trouble with your Sno-Flake ice crusher.* This negative approach reminds the reader of the problem and may rekindle the heated emotions or unhappy feelings experienced when the claim was written. Also, such an opening is indirect. It doesn't tell the reader the good news first.

Body Explains Compliance With Claim

Most businesses comply with claims because they want to promote customer goodwill.

In responding to claims, most organizations sincerely want to correct a wrong. They want to do more than just make the customer happy. They want to stand behind their products and services; they want to do what's right.

In the body of the letter, then, explain how you are complying with the claim. In all but the most routine claims, you should also seek to regain the confidence of the customer. You might reasonably expect that a customer who has experienced difficulty with a product, with delivery, with billing, or with service has lost faith in your organization. Rebuilding that faith is important for future business. How to rebuild lost confidence depends upon the situation and the claim. If procedures need to be revised, explain what changes will be made. If a product has defective parts, tell how the product is being improved. If service is faulty, describe genuine efforts to improve it. Sincere and logical explanations do much to reduce hard feelings.

Sometimes the problem is not with the product but with the way it's being used. In other instances, customers misunderstand warranties or inadvertently cause delivery and billing mix-ups by supplying incorrect information. Again, rational and sincere explanations will do much to regain the confidence of unhappy customers.

In your explanation, avoid using negative words that convey the wrong impression. Words like *trouble*, *regret*, *misunderstanding*, *fault*, *defective*, *error*, *inconvenience*, and *unfortunately* carry connotations of blame and wrongdoing. Try to use as few negative words as possible. Keep your message positive and upbeat.

> **Because negative words suggest blame and fault, avoid them in letters that attempt to build customer goodwill.**

In regaining the confidence of the reader, it may be appropriate to include resale information. If a customer is unhappy with a product, explain its features and applications in an effort to resell it. Depending upon the situation, new product information could also be promoted.

Closing Shows Confidence

End positively with confidence that the problem has been resolved and that continued business relations will result. Don't apologize excessively or call the customer's attention to unpleasantness associated with the claim. You might mention the product in a favorable light, suggest a new product, express your appreciation for the customer's business, or look forward to future business. It's often appropriate to refer to the desire to be of service and to satisfy customers. Do the following closings achieve the objectives suggested here?

> **End your letter by looking ahead positively, not apologizing.**

> Your Sno-Flake ice crusher will help you remain cool and refreshed this summer. For your additional summer enjoyment, consider our Smokey Joe tabletop gas grill shown in the enclosed summer catalog. We genuinely value your business and look forward to your future orders.

> We hope that this refund check convinces you of our sincere desire to satisfy our customers. Our goal is to earn your confidence and continue to justify that confidence with quality products and matchless service.

> You were most helpful in telling us about this situation and giving us an opportunity to correct it. We sincerely appreciate your cooperation.

> In all your future dealings with us, you will find us striving our hardest to merit your confidence by serving you with efficiency and sincere concern.

Good and Bad Examples

The letter in Figure 7.7 is a response to an angry letter from Bud Stubbs of Sound, Inc., who did not receive a shipment of electronic equipment from Electronic Warehouse. Mr. Stubbs wants his shipment sent immediately. When Glenda Emerson of Electronic Warehouse investigated, she found that the order was sent to the address shown on Sound, Inc., stationery. The claim letter Ms. Emerson just received was written on Sound, Inc., stationery with a different address. Mr. Stubbs seems to be unaware of the discrepancy.

> **A confused address causes a shipping mix-up that necessitates a claim.**

Ineffective writing   **FIGURE 7.7**   Poor Response to a Customer's Claim

Gentlemen:

**Starts negatively
with effusive
apology.**

We deeply regret the inconvenience you suffered in relation to your recent order for speakers, receivers, headphones, and other electronic equipment.

Our investigators looked into this problem and determined that the shipment in question was indeed shipped immediately after we received the order. According to the shipper's records, it was delivered to the warehouse address given on your stationery: 3590 University Avenue, St. Paul, Minnesota 55114. No one at that address would accept delivery, so the shipment was returned to us. I see from your current stationery that your company has a new address. With the proper address, we probably could have delivered this shipment.

**Blames customer for
problem situation.**

**Uses grudging and
reluctant tone.**

Although we feel that it is entirely appropriate to charge you shipping and restocking fees, as is our standard practice on returned goods, in this instance we will waive those fees.

**Fails to promote
future business.**

Once again, please accept our apologies for the delay in filling this order. We hope this second shipment finally catches up with you at your current address.

Sincerely,

This response gets off to a bad start by failing to address Mr. Stubbs personally. Then, instead of telling Mr. Stubbs when he might expect this shipment, the opening sentence contains an apology. This serves only to remind him of the unpleasant emotions he felt when he wrote his orginal letter.

The tone of the letter does not promote goodwill. In a subtle way, it blames Sound, Inc., for the shipping problem as it grudgingly agrees to send the second shipment. The closing apologizes again—and insincerely at that—while at the same time sharply reminding Mr. Stubbs of the address difficulty.

The claim from Mr. Stubbs does represent a problem to Electronic Warehouse. Ms. Emerson must decide if a second shipment is justified. If so, who should pay the shipping and restocking fee? In this instance, Ms. Emerson decides to promote goodwill by sending a second shipment and by having her company absorb the extra costs. Once this decision was made, the good news should be announced immediately and positively.

**An effective claim
response does not
blame the customer
nor begrudge
compliance with the
claim.**

Figure 7.8 shows an improved version of the response to Mr. Stubbs. In this letter Ms. Emerson explains what happened to the first shipment. She graciously

E_W *ELECTRONIC WAREHOUSE*

930 Abbott Park Place
Providence, RI 02903-5309

February 21, 19xx

Mr. Bud Stubbs
Sounds, Inc.
2293 Second Avenue
St. Paul, MI 55120

Dear Mr. Stubbs:

SUBJECT: YOUR FEBRUARY 18 LETTER REGARDING YOUR
            JANUARY 20 PURCHASE ORDER

You should receive by February 25 a second shipment of the speakers, receivers, headphones, and other electronic equipment that you ordered January 20.

Announces good news immediately.

The first shipment of this order was delivered January 28 to 3590 University Avenue, St. Paul, Minnesota 55114. When no one at that address would accept the shipment, it was returned to us. Now that I have your letter, I see that the order should have been sent to 2293 Second Avenue, St. Paul 55120. When an order is undeliverable, we usually try to verify the shipping address by telephoning the customer. Somehow the return of this shipment was not caught by our normally painstaking shipping clerks. You can be sure that I will investigate shipping and return procedures with our clerks immediately to see if we can improve existing methods.

Regains confidence of customer by explaining what happened and by suggesting plans for improvement.

As you know, Mr. Stubbs, our volume business allows us to sell wholesale electronics equipment at the lowest possible prices. However, we do not want to be so large that we lose touch with our customers. Over the years it is our customers' respect that has made us successful, and we hope that the prompt delivery of this shipment will earn yours.

Closes confidently with genuine appeal for customer's respect.

Sincerely,

Glenda Emerson

Glenda Emerson
Distribution Manager

c David Cole
  Shipping Department

≈≈

FIGURE 7.9   Simple But Effective Response

Dear Mrs. Eustice:

Announces good news in first sentence.

We are indeed intrigued by your CompuCap 2-X computer mystery and authorize you to send your 2-X to our Diagnostic Department for inspection.

Explains company procedures and provides details on how company is complying with customer request.

Normally, we try to have our computers repaired locally to minimize transportation costs and to reduce stress to internal parts. However, your mystery case may require our special attention. We are enclosing a return authorization slip with instructions on how to pack your computer for shipping.

Ends confidently and promises quick return of computer.

Most 2-X users find that they can't get along without their computers for even a day. We will do our best to have your 2-X on its way back to you within four working days of its receipt here in Sunnyvale. We hope that this speedy service indicates to you our sincere interest in satisfying our customers.

Sincerely,

---

accepts blame for the incident. In reality the customer is probably equally guilty for not providing the proper shipping address.

Notice in Ms. Emerson's improved letter how effectively she achieves two of the three goals of an adjustment letter. She rectifies the wrong suffered by the customer and successfully regains his confidence. She treats the third goal—promoting future business—tactfully in the closing, without the use of resale or sales promotion.

Some claims involve minimal loss of customer confidence. In the letter above (Figure 7.9) Mrs. Eustice (see her request letter, Figure 6.6, in Chapter 6) is happy with her computer but asks a favor of the company. She wants the company to solve her computer's mystery malfunction. In responding to her request, the company could merely have sent Mrs. Eustice instructions for packing and shipping the computer. Instead, it took this opportunity to maintain and promote customer goodwill with a friendly letter explaining the company's service policy. Notice that the letter avoids mentioning negatives, such as the malfunctioning computer. In the closing, rather than dwelling on the loss of her computer while it's being repaired, the letter uses this opportunity to confirm the customer's happiness with her computer by referring to her dependence on it. The letter ends with a forward-looking promise of the computer's speedy return.

In this chapter you learned to write letters that respond favorably to information requests, orders, and claims. These messages employ deductive strategy; that is, they begin directly with the primary idea. In the next chapter you will learn to use the inductive strategy in conveying negative news.

APPLICATION AND PRACTICE—7

Discussion

1. Why is it advisable to use a subject line in responding to requests?

2. Since brevity is valued in business writing, is it ever advisable to respond with more information than requested? Discuss.

3. Why is it a good business practice to send a personalized acknowledgment of an order?

4. Distinguish between resale and sales promotion.

5. Discuss the policy of granting all customer claims, regardless of merit.

Short Answers

6. What is the most important position in a letter?

7. Name two ways to open a letter that responds to multiple questions.

8. Name three instances when it is particularly appropriate to send a personalized order acknowledgment.

9. What do customers want to know first about their orders?

10. Give an example of resale.

11. List five situations when claim letters might be written by customers.

12. What are three goals that the writer strives to achieve in responding to customer claims?

13. Name at least five negative words that carry impressions of blame and wrongdoing.

14. What should be included in the subject line of a response to a claim?

15. What's wrong with a salutation like *Dear Sirs*?

Writing Improvement Exercises

Subject Lines. Write effective subject lines for the following messages that appeared in this chapter.

16. Information response letter addressed to Mr. Meyers, page 145.

17. Simple but effective response addressed to Mrs. Eustice, page 154.

Letter Openers. Place a check mark to indicate whether the following letter openers are direct or indirect. Be prepared to explain your choices.

	Direct	Indirect
18. Thank you for your letter of December 2 in which you inquired if we have No. 19 bolts in stock.	____	____
19. We have an ample supply of No. 19 bolts in stock.	____	____
20. This will acknowledge receipt of your letter of December 2.	____	____
21. Yes, the Omni Cruise Club is planning a 15-day Mediterranean cruise beginning October 20.	____	____
22. I am pleased to have the opportunity to respond to your kind letter of July 9.	____	____
23. Your letter of July 9 has been referred to me because Mr. Halvorson is away from the office.	____	____
24. We sincerely appreciate your recent order for plywood wallboard panels.	____	____
25. The plywood wallboard panels that you requested were shipped today by Coastal Express and should reach you by August 12.	____	____

Opening Paragraph

26. Revise the following opening paragraph of an information response.

Thank you for letter of March 3 inquiring about the RefreshAire electronic air cleaner. I am pleased to have this opportunity to provide you with information. You asked how the RefreshAire works and specifically if it would remove pollen from the air. Yes, the RefreshAire removes pollen from the air—and smoke and dust as well. It then recirculates clean air. We think it makes offices, conference rooms, and cafeterias cleaner and healthier for everyone.

Closing Paragraph

27. The following concluding paragraph to a claim letter response suffers from faults in strategy, tone, and emphasis. Revise and improve.

According to your instructions, we are sending a replacement shipment of air conditioners by InterMountain Express. It should reach you by June 5. Once again, please accept our sincere apologies for the inconvenience and lost sales you have suffered as a result of this unfortunate incident.

CASE 7-1

Favorable Response to Claim

You are Peter Mosgrove, manager of WoodDoors, Inc., a firm that manufactures quality precut and custom-built doors and frames. You have received a letter dated March 21 from Geraldine Johnson, 38221 Evergreen Road, Lansing, Michigan 48909. Ms. Johnson is an interior designer, and she complains that the oak French doors she ordered for a client recently were made to the wrong dimensions.

Although they were the wrong size, she kept the doors and had them installed because her clients were without outside doors. However, her carpenter charged an extra $286.50 to install them. She claims that you should reimburse her for this amount, since your company was responsible for the error. You check her order and find that she is right. Instead of measuring a total of 11 feet $8\frac{1}{8}$ inches, the doors were made to measure 11 feet $4\frac{1}{8}$ inches. At the time her doors were being constructed, you had two new craftsmen in the factory; and they may have misread or mismeasured her order. Normally, your Quality Control Department carefully monitors custom jobs. You don't know how this job was missed. You resolve, however, to review personally the plant's custom product procedures.

Ms. Johnson is a successful interior designer and has provided WoodDoors with a number of orders. You value her business and decide to send her a check for the amount of her claim. You want to remind her that WoodDoors has earned a reputation as the manufacturer of the finest wood doors and frames on the market. Your doors feature prime woods, and the craftsmanship is meticulous. The design of your doors has won awards, and the engineering is ingenious. You have a new line of greenhouse windows that are available in three sizes. Include a brochure describing these windows.

Before you write your letter, answer the following questions.

1. What is the good news that should be revealed in the first sentence of this letter?

2. What item requires resale? How can you do that?

3. What can you say to regain the faith of this customer?

4. Should you include sales promotional items in this letter? How and where?

5. Should you apologize for the inconvenience your error caused?

6. How can you close this letter?

Review the writing plan for granting a claim. Use this letter for class discussion or write a response to Ms. Johnson on a separate sheet. Use block style.

CASE 7–2

Response to Information Request

Analyze the following poorly written message from an insurance company to one of its policyholders, Mrs. Helen Hindlin, Executive Vice President, Satellite Cable of Minnesota, 3980 East Fourth Street, St. Paul, Minnesota 55101. List its major faults. Outline a writing plan for a response to an information request. Then, on a separate sheet, rewrite the message rectifying the faults. Use block style.

Dear Helen:

SUBJECT: ACCIDENT LOSSES

Per your request by telephone on July 11, I have been thinking about your need for ways to make a reduction in your company's losses due to employee accidents. In response to your request, as I promised, I came up with some recommendations for things that I have found from our experience to be helpful in reducing company losses resulting from employee accidents.

One of the things you must do is ask your managers to complete an accident report whenever an accident occurs. It is also important that all employees be instructed in safe practices and safety requirements in their departments. In addition, we have found that a manager or supervisor must follow up any reported accident with an investigation. This investigation is necessary so that you can take corrective action in preventing a reoccurrence of the same kind of accident. Another recommendation regards the work site. Someone should inspect to be sure that employees are following safe procedures. Are they wearing required protective clothing? Are they using safety equipment as required? Most important, of course, is that all employees be first instructed in the safe practices and safety requirements of their departments.

We have found, Helen, that no loss-prevention program will be successful if the supervisors and management of the organization do not give their 100 percent cooperation. If you think that your managers and supervisors might have trouble implementing the suggestions made above, a seminar in loss prevention might be arranged for you. If I may be of further assistance, please do not hesitate to call upon me.

1. List at least five faults.

CASE 7–3

Order Response

Analyze the following poorly written message to Sam Stinson, McPherson Hardware, 4821 Shafter Avenue, Oakland, California 94609. List its major faults. Outline a writing plan for an order response. Then, on a separate sheet, rewrite the message rectifying its faults. Use block style.

Gentlemen:

Ineffective writing

We have your kind order under date of November 25. Permit me to say that most of the order will be shipped soon.

Only the Brown & Drecker heavy-duty contour sanders will be delayed. We've had quite a run on these sanders, and we just can't keep them in stock. Therefore, they will be sent separately from Buffalo, New York, and will probably arrive sometime around December 15. All the other items (the lightweight drill sets, saber saw blade assortments, and steel router tables) are being sent today by Rocky Mountain Express and will, in all probability, reach you by December 5.

We also have some new items that your hardware store might like. One item is especially interesting. It's a rotary/orbital-action sander that does the job with less fatigue. Attached please find a brochure describing some of our newer items.

If we can be of further service, do not hesitate to call upon us.

Sincerely,

1. List at least five faults.

2. Outline a writing plan for an order response.

Subject line:
   Opening:

     Body:

   Closing:

CASE 7–4

Response to Request for Information

A friend in a distant city is considering moving to your area for more education and training in your field. This individual wants to know about your program of study. Write a letter describing a program in your field (or any field you wish to describe). What courses must be taken? Toward what degree, certificate, or employment position does this program lead? Why did you choose it? Would you recommend this program to your friend? How long does it take? Add any information you feel would be helpful.

CASE 7–5

Favorable Response to Claim

Assume that you are a manager in the business where you now work (or one about which you have some knowledge). Imagine that a customer, colleague, or employee has made a legitimate claim against your organization. Write a letter granting the claim. Make the letter as realistic and factual as possible.

Additional Problems

1. As Rochelle Cornell, owner of Oregon High, producer of freeze-dried backpacking foods, answer the inquiry of Marc Vannault (described in Chapter 6, page 135, Additional Problem No. 1). You are eager to have Mr. Vannault sample your new all-natural line of products containing no preservatives, sugar, or additives. You want him to know that you started this company two years ago after you found yourself making custom meals for discerning backpackers who rejected typical camping fare. Some of your menu items are excellent for individuals on restricted diets. Some dinners are cholesterol- and salt-free, but he'll have to look at your list to see for himself. You will send him your complete list of dinner items and the suggested retail prices. You will also send him a sample "Saturday Night on the Trail," a four-course meal that comes with fruit candies and elegant appetizers. All your food products are made from choice ingredients in sanitary kitchens that you personally supervise. They are flash frozen in a new vacuum process that you patented. Although your dried foods are meant to last for years, you don't recommend that they be kept beyond 18 months because they may deteriorate. This could happen if a package were punctured or if the products became overheated. Your products are currently available at Pacific Camper, 2035 Redondo Avenue, Long Beach, CA 90804. Large orders may be placed directly with you. You offer a 5 percent discount on direct orders. Write a response to Marc Vannault, 3175 Fujita Street, Torrance, CA 90505.

2. Play the role of Clifford Bianchi, director, Employee Development Division, Pratt and Whitney (described in Chapter 6, page 135, Additional Problem No. 2). You are eager to respond to the request of Edith Sterling, assistant vice president, Bank of Virginia, 7943 Main Street, Alexandria, Virginia 22308. Send her a copy of an article you wrote for *Personnel Today* describing the employee suggestion program you implemented at Pratt and Whitney. In answer to her specific questions, you encourage employees to participate by publicizing the suggestion plan. You post notices on bulletin boards in all departments, you insert announcements into pay envelopes, and you place articles describing employees who have won awards for their suggestions in the company newsletter and local newspapers. As your article states, suggestions are first screened by department managers. The best

ones are then sent to an evaluation committee. You base your awards on the savings that result for the company. Employees receive a percentage of the actual savings. Your largest award was made to an engineer who suggested a way to discard fewer parts in jet engine inspections, saving Pratt and Whitney $9.7 million! You have found that an individual response to every suggestion is excellent for employee morale. You cover such problems as legal considerations and employee protests in your article. You have one important piece of advice for Ms. Sterling. She should enlist the support of top management immediately before working on the details of a program. You think that your results-oriented suggestion program has forged a stronger partnership between employees and management. Write a response to Ms. Sterling.

3. Respond to the order placed by Greg Fontecilla, manager, Datatronics, Inc., 2003 Maple Street, Litchfield, CT 06759 (described in Chapter 6, page 136, Additional Problem No. 3). Yes, all of the prices listed in your old catalog have increased. That's the bad news. The good news is that you have in stock nearly everything he ordered. The only item not immediately available is the desktop organizer, Item No. 23–K. That has to be shipped from the manufacturer in Pittsburgh, Pennsylvania. You've been having trouble with that supplier lately, perhaps because of heavy demand. However, you think that the organizer will be shipped no later than three weeks from the current date. You're pleased to have Datatronics' order. They might be interested in your new line of office supply products at discount prices. Send him a new catalog and call his attention to the low, low price on continuous form computer paper. It's just $39.95 for a box containing 2,700 sheets of 9½ by 11-inch, 20-pound printout paper. All the items he ordered, except the organizer, are on their way by UPS and should arrive in three days.

4. As the customer relations manager at Toys-R-Us, you are responding to a letter from Susan Lee (described in Chapter 6, page 136, Additional Problem No. 4). You think that the toy she has described is the "Wild Mantis," a battery-operated, four-wheel-drive toy racing car (your store No. 825990–2). It is remote controlled and climbs over most obstacles. Wild Mantis has operating headlights, forward/reverse gears, and controlled steering. It requires four "C" batteries, and it costs $24.97. It weighs 6 pounds and will cost $5.37 to ship to Maui, but it should arrive within her three-week deadline. The California sales tax is 6½ percent. Tell her that you are sending Wild Mantis and that you have charged the total amount (figure it out) to her Visa card. Write this order response to Susan Lee, 845 Wainee Street, Lahaina, Maui, HI 96761.

5. Assume that you are Mike Murphy, sales manager, Idaho Wood Products. It is your job to reply to customer claims, and today you must respond to Sandra Fenwick, president, Fenwick Consulting Services, 2248 26th Avenue West, Seattle, Washington 98199 (described in Chapter 6, page 136, Additional Problem No. 5). You are disappointed that she is returning the executive desk (Invoice No. 3499), but your policy is to comply with customer wishes. If she doesn't want to keep the desk, you will certainly return the purchase price plus shipping charges. On occasion, desks are

damaged in shipping, and this may explain the marred finish and the sticking drawers. You want her to give Idaho Wood Products another chance. After all, your office furniture and other wood products are made from the finest hand-selected woods by master artisans. Since she is apparently furnishing her office, send her another catalog and invite her to look at the traditional conference desk on page 10–E. This is available with a matching credenza, file cabinets, and accessories. She might be interested in your furniture-leasing plan, which can produce substantial savings. You promise that you will personally examine any furniture she may order in the future. Write her a letter granting her claim.

6. Assume the role of Marilyn Thatcher, customer service representative, Ever-Cool Manufacturing Company. You are responding to the claim of Paul Friedman, purchase manager, Datatronics, Inc., 2569 Missouri Street, Mesa, AZ 85016 (described in Chapter 6, page 136, Additional Problem No. 6). Tell Mr. Friedman that the Ever-Cool air conditioner can be taken to A–Z Appliance Repairs, 2320 Cactus Avenue, Phoenix, AZ 84290, for warrantied repair. Rarely do these heavy-duty room air conditioners need service. You are happy to honor the warranty. If Datatronics would like faster service, Ever-Cool has an agreement with Victory Mobile Service. For a nominal fee ($30), Victory will come to his office and, if possible, make the repair on the spot. This is sometimes more convenient than removing a heavy, mounted room air conditioner. He can make an appointment with Victory by calling (800) 574–8900. Write to Datatronics.

GRAMMAR/MECHANICS CHECKUP—7

Commas, 2

Review the Grammar/Mechanics Handbook Sections 2.05 to 2.09. Then study each of the following statements and insert necessary commas. In the space provided write the number of commas that you add; write *0* if no commas are needed. Also record the number of the G/M principle illustrated. When you finish, compare your responses with those shown below. If your answers differ, study carefully the principles shown in parentheses.

Example: When businesses encounter financial problems, they often reduce their administrative staffs.

      1   2.06a

1. As stated in the warranty this printer is guaranteed for one year.

2. Today's profits come from products currently on the market and tomorrow's profits come from products currently on the drawing boards.

3. Companies introduce new products in one part of the country and then watch how the product sells in that area.

4. One large automobile manufacturer which must remain nameless recognizes that buyer perception is behind the success of any new product.

_____   5. The imaginative promising agency opened its offices April 22 in Cambridge.

_____   6. The sales associate who earns the highest number of recognition points this year will be honored with a bonus vacation trip.

_____   7. Darren Wilson our sales manager in the Redwood City area will make a promotion presentation at the June meeting.

_____   8. Our new product has many attributes that should make it appealing to buyers but it also has one significant drawback.

_____   9. Although they have different technical characteristics and vary considerably in price and quality two or more of a firm's products may be perceived by shoppers as almost the same.

_____   10. To motivate prospective buyers we are offering a cash rebate of $2.

Review of Commas 1 and 2

_____   11. When you receive the application please fill it out and return it before Monday January 3.

_____   12. On the other hand we are very interested in hiring hard-working conscientious individuals.

_____   13. In March we expect to open a new branch in Concord which is an area of considerable growth.

_____   14. As we discussed on the telephone the ceremony is scheduled for Thursday June 9 at 3 p.m.

_____   15. Dr. Adams teaches the morning classes and Mrs. Wildey is responsible for evening sections.

---

1. (1) warranty, (2.06a)   3. 0   5. (1) imaginative, (2.08)   7. (2) Wilson, area, (2.09)
9. (1) quality, (2.06a)   11. (2) application, Monday, (2.06a, 2.04a)   13. (1) Concord, (2.06c)
15. (1) classes, (2.05)

Applying the Indirect Strategy

CHAPTER 8

Letters and Memos That Carry Negative News

In this chapter you will learn to do the following:

- Identify the need for indirectness in delivering bad news.
- Recognize six components in an effective indirect strategy.
- Apply skillful writing techniques in refusing requests.

- Retain goodwill while refusing claims.
- Demonstrate tact in refusing credit requests.

Analyzing the Message

As you have learned, the first step in writing a business letter or memo is analyzing your message and the effect you expect to have on the reader. If you think the message will antagonize, disappoint, upset, hurt, or anger the recipient, an indirect strategy may be more effective than the direct method you have been using up to now. Examples of letters that deliver disappointing news are those that deny requests, refuse claims, reveal price increases, decline invitations, announce shipping delays, turn down job applicants, discontinue services, or deny credit.

> If your message delivers bad news, use the indirect method.

Recipients of good news like to learn the news quickly. That's why the direct strategy is most effective. Directness, however, is not usually effective for bad news. Blurting out bad news at the beginning of a letter may upset the reader. He or she is in a poor frame of mind to receive the remainder of the letter. Or, worse yet, the bad news may cause the reader to stop reading altogether. Reasons for the refusal and explanations that follow may never be seen. The principal goal of the indirect strategy is this: we want the reader to read our reasons and explanations *before* we reveal the bad news.

> The indirect method allows the writer to explain before announcing the bad news.

The indirect strategy, which we will discuss shortly, is *generally* better for negative news—but not *always*. Some readers may prefer frankness and directness. If you know the reader well, the direct strategy may be appropriate even for negative messages. For example, assume that Dave Nelson, a good customer with whom you are friendly, must be told that his company's order can't be filled immediately. You know that Dave is a no-nonsense, up-front fellow who values candor. For him, the direct strategy may be appropriate. Further, if you have been unsuccessful in getting your message across by writing one or more messages using the indirect strategy, you may decide that bluntness is needed. The direct approach, for example, might be appropriate in responding to Sally Kelly. She has been told twice, in memos using an indirect strategy, that she does not qualify for a promotion because she lacks college training in her field. She applied for the promotion a third time and still had not enrolled in the necessary courses. This time her superior wrote a direct memo that spelled out the denial immediately and then explained the reasons for the denial.

Typically, though, we try to soften the blow of bad news by delaying it until after we have explained reasons justifying it. Delaying the bad news is just one part of an overall strategy that has proved effective in delivering messages with negative news. The indirect strategy includes six elements, which we will consider now.

Six components in the indirect strategy help shape a message that brings negative news.

Indirect Strategy

- Buffer
- Transition
- Explanation
- Bad news
- Alternative(s)
- Goodwill closing

Turn it around
Be --- careful, tactful & passive

Applying the Indirect Strategy

The indirect strategy gives you a general outline for presenting negative news. Before implementing it, however, you need to analyze each step and study illustrations that show how these steps are used in writing letters and memos. After you have examined the steps, you'll learn how to put them together in writing letters for common business situations that involve delivering negative news. By developing skill in using this strategy in the most common situations, you should be able to adapt it to similar business problems.

We'll discuss the indirect strategy in the order shown, but the thinking process actually follows a slightly different order. Skillful writers first decide whether their message will likely elicit a positive or negative reaction from the reader. If a request must be denied or a claim refused, they analyze their reasons for refusing. If they don't have good reasons, they can't write convincing letters. Thus, the explanation shapes the rest of the letter and determines the content and tone. Although the letter begins with a buffer, the thinking process begins with the reasons for delivering the bad news.

Developing a Good Buffer

A buffer is a device that reduces shock. In denying a request or delivering other bad news, we can reduce the shock a reader may suffer by opening with a buffer paragraph. This opening should put the reader in a receptive frame of mind. Our objective, remember, is to induce the recipient to read the entire letter. We want the reader to understand our reasons and explanations before we disclose the bad news.

An effective buffer generally possesses three characteristics: (1) it is *neutral*, (2) it is *upbeat*, and (3) it is *relevant*. A buffer is neutral when it does not signal the bad news that is to follow nor falsely suggest that good news will be forthcoming. A buffer is upbeat if it emphasizes something positive for the reader. The positive element could be resale material that relates to a product, a compliment or praise for the reader, or a statement that builds goodwill. A buffer is relevant if it refers to the situation at hand. A buffer statement that describes the unusually good weather may be neutral and upbeat, but it has no relation to the bad news.

Here are a number of buffer statements for negative letters. The first is the opening statement for a letter delivering the news that a candidate did not receive a job for which he was interviewed. The buffer refers to the interview positively but does not suggest that the candidate will be hired.

> I enjoyed talking with you last week about your background and the
> excellent business administration program at Louisiana Tech.

A letter denying a request for credit for merchandise that a customer wishes to return employs a resale buffer:

> Your selection of an Ambassador top-grain pigskin leather attaché case is
> a smart one, Mrs. Silva, because these cases combine fashionable styling
> with fine workmanship and peerless leathers.

A letter refusing an invitation to speak at an awards banquet begins with a compliment to the reader:

> You have done a splendid job of organizing the program for the
> October 5 awards banquet of Sigma Alpha.

A letter denying an adjustment to a customer's account opens with a warm statement regarding the customer's past payment record:

> We genuinely appreciate the prompt payments you have always made in
> response to our monthly billings.

Building a Smooth Transition

After the opening buffer statement, use a transition that guides the reader to the explanation that follows. Avoid red-flag words like *but, unfortunately,* and *however* because they are dead giveaways that bad news is to come.

Experienced writers try to plant a key word or idea in the buffer or transition that leads the reader naturally to the reasons for the refusal. In this next example, a business must refuse a request for campaign contributions for a city council candidate. Notice how the key words *candidate* and *contribution* form a link between the buffer and the explanation for refusing the request.

> Your efforts to build a campaign chest for city council candidate Jackie
> Ohlson are commendable. This candidate deserves the support of
> civic-minded businesses and individuals who are able to make
> *contributions.*

An effective buffer is neutral, upbeat, and relevant.

Try not to forecast bad news nor falsely imply good news.

Reference to a key word or idea builds a transition between the buffer and the following explanation.

Buffer

Transition

Explanation

Bad news

Alternative

Your *candidate*, if elected, will help administer funds to municipal departments and offices. As you may know, a significant portion of our business involves providing supplies for city offices. City council members who have accepted campaign contributions from vendors supplying city accounts may be accused of conflict of interest. Rather than place your candidate in this awkward position, our attorney advises us to avoid making financial contributions to the campaigns of city council candidates. Although we are unable to provide financial support, many of our employees will be contributing their time and efforts to work personally for the election of your candidate.

Goodwill closing

We hope that the participation of our staff will contribute to a successful campaign for Jackie Ohlson.

Presenting the Explanation Before the Bad News

The success of a negative letter depends upon how well the explanation is presented.

In the preceding example, key words in the buffer and transition lead the reader smoothly to the explanation. As you know, the explanation is the most important part of a negative letter. Without sound reasons for denying a request or refusing a claim, the letter will fail, no matter how cleverly it is written. The explanation is, after all, the principal reason for using the indirect method. We want to be able to explain before refusing.

In the explanation, as in the transition, don't let red-flag words (*but, however, unfortunately*) signal the refusal. Your explanation should show that you have analyzed the situation carefully. Tell clearly why a refusal is necessary. An item is no longer under warranty or was never warrantied in the first place, or a customer demands a cash refund for an item that cannot be resold, or a product fails because it was misused. In some instances, such as the denial of credit or the refusal to allow damaged goods to be returned, the explanation can emphasize reader benefits. The reader, along with other customers, benefits from lower prices if a business is able to avoid unnecessary credit costs and unfair returns.

Strive to project an unemotional, objective, and helpful tone. Don't lecture or patronize (*If you will read the operating instructions carefully . . .*), avoid sounding presumptuous (*I'm sure the salesman who demonstrated this unit explained that . . .*), and don't hide behind company policy (*Our company policy prevents us from granting your request*). Explain specifically why the company policy is necessary. If you have more than one reason for refusing, begin with the strongest reason. Present the bad news, and then continue with additional reasons for refusing.

Bad news should be clear but not overly emphasized.

DUFFY®   by BRUCE HAMMOND

Source: Duffy. Copyright 1988 Universal Press Syndicate. Reprinted with permission. All rights reserved.

Breaking the Bad News

In Chapter 4 you learned stylistic techniques for deemphasizing ideas. Now we will expand those techniques and apply them as you learn to break bad news.

You can soften the blow of bad news by using some of these seven techniques.

1. **Avoid the spotlight.** Don't put the bad news in a conspicuous position. The most emphatic positions in a letter are the first sentence and the last sentence. Other conspicuous spots are the beginnings and ends of sentences and paragraphs. The reader's attention is drawn to these positions and lingers there. Strategically, then, these are not good places for announcing bad news. To give the least emphasis to an idea, place it in the middle of a sentence or in the middle of a paragraph halfway through your letter.

2. **Use a long sentence.** Short sentences emphasize content. Since we want to deemphasize bad news, avoid short, simple sentences (*We cannot ship your goods*). Longer sentences diffuse the bad news and also give you a chance to explain the bad news or offer alternatives (see No. 7).

3. **Put the bad news in a subordinate clause.** Grammatical attention in a sentence is always focused on the independent clause. To deemphasize an idea, then, put it in a less conspicuous spot, like a subordinate clause; for example, *Although your credit application cannot be approved at this time, we welcome your cash business.* The bad news is subordinated in the dependent clause (*Although your credit application*) where the reader is less likely to dwell on it.

Be selective in applying these techniques whenever you break bad news.

4. **Use the passive voice.** The active voice, recommended for most business writing, is direct and identifies the subject of a sentence (*I cannot allow you to examine our personnel files*). To be less direct and to avoid drawing unnecessary attention to the writer, use the passive voice (*Examination of our personnel files cannot be permitted because . . .*). The passive voice focuses attention on actions rather than personalities; it helps you be impersonal and tactful.

5. **Be clear but not overly graphic.** Bad news is best received when it is clear but not painfully vivid. For example, the following refusal is unnecessarily harsh because it provides too many details:

   We cannot pay for your free-lance services in cash, as you request. Such payment is clearly illegal and violates federal law. All free-lance services that we authorize must be supported by check payments to individuals whose social security numbers are included in the record of the payment.

   This refusal would be more tactful if it were less direct and less graphic:

   Federal law requires that payments to free-lancers be made by check and be supported by social security numbers.

6. **Imply the refusal.** In certain instances, a refusal does not have to be stated directly. In the preceding example, the tactful revision does not actually

say *We cannot pay you in cash.* Instead, the refusal is implied. Recall the letter refusing campaign funds:

> Rather than place your candidate in this awkward position, our attorney advises us to avoid making financial contributions to the campaigns of city council candidates.

Instead of hammering home the bad news (*Therefore, we cannot contribute to this campaign*), the author spared the feelings of the reader by implying the refusal.

Here's another example of an implied refusal. Instead of refusing an invitation to speak at a campus job fair, a business executive writes:

> Although my appointment schedule is completely booked during the week of your employment fair, I wish you success with this beneficial event.

What is the danger of an implied refusal?

Implying a refusal is not quite as devastating as an explicit, spelled-out denial. Such subtleness saves the feelings of both the writer and the reader. Be very careful, however, in using this technique. It is imperative that the reader understand the refusal. Don't be so vague that additional correspondence is required to clarify the refusal.

7. **Offer an alternative.** If appropriate, suggest some recourse to the reader. You might offer a compromise, a substitute, or an alternative offer:

> For security reasons, visitors are never allowed inside Building J. It is possible, however, to tour our assembly facility in the fall during our Open House.

> My schedule prevents me from speaking to your group, but I have asked my colleague, Dr. George R. Duffy, to consider addressing your conference.

Closing with Goodwill

Provide a courteous, pleasant, and forward-looking closing that doesn't refer directly to the bad news.

After explaining the bad news clearly and tactfully, shift to an idea that renews good feelings between the writer and the reader. In our letter refusing to pay a free-lancer in cash, the closing regains his confidence:

> We hope that we may continue to use your services as a free-lancer again in the future.

If an alternative is presented, make it easy to accept:

> Dr. Duffy is an excellent speaker, and I'm sure your group would enjoy his presentation. I am including Dr. Duffy's address so that you may write him directly.

When writing to customers, encourage continued business relations. Resale or sales promotional material may be appropriate:

> I am enclosing a sample of a new imported fragrance and a coupon to save you $15 on your initial purchase. We look forward to serving you soon.

For the most effective closings, avoid these traps:

- **Don't refer to the bad news.** Focus on positive, friendly remarks. Don't needlessly revive the reader's emotions regarding the bad news.

- **Don't apologize.** You have valid reasons for refusing, and you've explained these reasons clearly. An apology at the end of your message undermines your explanation.

- **Don't conclude with clichés.** Remarks such as *If we may be of further service* or *Thank you for understanding our position* sound particularly insincere and ironic in messages delivering negative news.

- **Don't invite further correspondence.** Expressions such as *If you have any further questions* or *If you would like to discuss this further* suggest that the matter is still open for discussion. Don't encourage a pen-pal relationship. Your decision is fair and final.

> **Irony is the use of words to express something other than, and especially opposite of, the literal meaning.**

≈≈≈

Refusing Requests

When you must refuse a request and you feel that the refusal is likely to antagonize, upset, hurt, or anger the reader, use an indirect approach, such as the following writing plan illustrates:

Writing Plan for Refusing a Request or Claim

- **Buffer**—identifies previous correspondence incidentally or in a subject line and begins with neutral statement on which both the reader and the writer can agree.

- **Transition**—plants key idea or word that leads naturally to the explanation.

- **Explanation**—presents valid reasons for refusal, avoids red-flag words that forecast bad news, and includes resale or sales-promotion material if appropriate.

- **Bad news**—softens the blow by deemphasizing the refusal.

- **Alternative**—suggests a compromise, alternative, or substitute if possible.

- **Closing**—renews good feelings with a positive statement, avoids referring to the bad news, and doesn't apologize.

Expert and Faulty Letters That Refuse Requests

The letter shown in Figure 8.1 begins well enough. The opening sentence is neutral, although it contains unnecessary information that could be implied. The letter then deteriorates quickly with a blunt refusal of a magazine writer's request for information about employee salaries. It creates a harsh tone with such negative words as *sorry, must refuse, violate,* and *liable.* Since the refusal precedes the explanation, the reader probably will not be in a receptive frame of mind to accept the reasons for refusing. Notice, too, that the bad news is emphasized by appearing in a short sentence at the beginning of a paragraph. It stands out here and hurts the reader by its conspicuousness. The refusal explanation is overly

Ineffective writing

FIGURE 8.1   Blunt Refusal of Request

Dear Mrs. Marcus:

I have your letter of October 21 in which you request information about the salaries and commissions of our top young salespeople.

This refusal makes a poor impression because it sounds harsh, negative, and insincere.

I am sorry to inform you that we cannot reveal data of this kind. I must, therefore, refuse your request. To release this information would violate our private employee contracts. Such disclosure could make us liable for damages, should any employee seek legal recourse. I might say, however, that our salespeople are probably receiving the highest combined salary and commissions of any salespeople in this field.

If it were possible for us to help you with your fascinating research, we would certainly be happy to do so.

Sincerely yours,

---

graphic, containing references to possible litigation. Instead of offering constructive alternatives, this letter reveals only tiny bits of the desired data. Finally, the insincere-sounding closing does not build goodwill.

In Figure 8.2 the same request is refused more skillfully. Its opening reflects genuine interest in the request but does not indicate compliance. The second sentence acts as a transition by introducing the words *salespeople* and *salaries*, repeated in the following paragraph. Reasons for refusing this request are objectively presented in an explanation that precedes the refusal. Notice that the refusal (*Although specific salaries and commission rates cannot be released*) is a subordinate clause in a long sentence in the middle of a paragraph. To further soften the blow, the letter offers an alternative. The cordial closing refers to the alternative, avoids mention of the refusal, and looks to the future.

It's always easier to write refusals when alternatives can be offered to soften the bad news. But often no alternatives are possible. The refusal letter in Figure 8.3 involves a delicate situation in which a word processing manager has been asked by her superiors to violate a contract. Several of the attorneys for whom she works have privately asked her to make copies of a licensed software program for them. They apparently want this program for their personal computers. Making copies is forbidden by the terms of the software licensing agreement, and the manager refuses to do this. Rather than saying *no* to each attorney who asks her, she writes the following memo using the indirect strategy.

When you must refuse and you have no alternatives to suggest, the explanation and reasoning must be particularly logical.

The opening tactfully avoids suggesting that any attorney has actually asked to copy the software program. These professionals may prefer not to have their private requests made known. A transition takes the reader to the logical reasons

FIGURE 8.2   Skillful Request Refusal—Modified Block Style, Mixed Punctuation

CANON ELECTRONICS INTERNATIONAL

115 Fifth Avenue
New York, NY 10011–1010
(212) 593–1098

January 15, 19xx

Mrs. Sylvia Marcus
1305 Elmwood Avenue
Buffalo, NY 14222-2240

Dear Mrs. Marcus:

The article you are now researching for *Business Management Weekly* sounds fascinating, and we are flattered that you wish to include our organization. We do have many outstanding young salespeople, both male and female, who are commanding top salaries.

Buffer shows genuine interest, and transition sets up explanation.

Each of our salespeople operates under an individual salary contract. During salary negotiations several years ago, an agreement was reached in which both sales staff members and management agreed to keep the terms of these individual contracts confidential. Although specific salaries and commission rates cannot be released, we can provide you with a ranked list of our top salespeople for the past five years. Three of the current top salespeople are under the age of thirty-five.

Explanation gives good reasons for refusing request.

Refusal is softened by substitute.

Enclosed is a fact sheet regarding our top salespeople. We wish you every success with your article, and we hope to see our organization represented in it.

Closing is pleasant and forward looking.

Cordially,

Lloyd Kenniston

Lloyd Kenniston
Executive Vice President

je

Enclosure: Sales Fact Sheet

≈

FIGURE 8.3   Tactful Memo Refuses Request and Offers No Alternatives

---

TO: The Staff   July 8, 19xx

FROM: Barbara Stordevent, Manager, Word Processing *B.S.*

SUBJECT: DEPARTMENT USE OF LICENSED SOFTWARE

Opens with relevant but neutral buffer.	A number of computer users have expressed interest in the licensed word processing program <u>WordWrite</u>, which we recently acquired for the microcomputers in our Word Processing Center.
Transition picks up key word *licensed.* **Explanation neither preaches nor patronizes.**	This program, like many licensed programs, requires that each purchased copy be used only on a single machine. The agreement not only forbids that the program be copied for home use but also forbids making copies for additional machines within the office. One can easily understand why a software company must protect its programs from indiscriminate copying. If a business organization purchased one program and then allowed multiple copies to be made for other computers within the company or for employees to take home, the software company would find it impossible to earn enough profit to make the development of any future software program worthwhile.
Deemphasized refusal diverts attention to reader benefits.	When we purchased the <u>WordWrite</u> program, we agreed to limit its use to a single machine. Although this program must not be copied, we look forward to using it for many of your documents here in the Word Processing Center.
Closes with an off-the-subject but friendly remark.	Please drop by to see our new networking system and laser printer.

---

against copying. Notice that the tone is objective, neither preaching nor condemning. The refusal is softened by being linked with a positive statement. To divert attention from the refusal, the memo ends with a friendly, off-the-subject remark.

≈

Refusing Claims

All businesses offering products or services will receive occasional customer claims for adjustments. Claims may also arise from employees. Most of these claims are valid, and the customer or employee receives a positive response.

Even unwarranted claims are sometimes granted because businesses genuinely desire to create a good public image and to maintain friendly relations with employees.

Some claims, however, cannot be approved because the customer or employee is mistaken, misinformed, unreasonable, or possibly even dishonest. Letters responding to these claims deliver bad news. The indirect strategy breaks bad news with the least pain. It also allows the writer to explain why the claim must be refused before the reader realizes the bad news and begins resisting.

Effective Letters That Refuse Claims

In Figure 8.4 a customer wants a cash refund for a vacuum cleaner that she has used for three months. She claims that the vacuum doesn't do a good job of cleaning her shag carpeting. The machine, which was returned to catalog sales, shows heavy use and could not be resold. It has a warranty covering repair of defective parts, but apparently the customer is not claiming that anything needs to be repaired. She writes a letter demanding a refund of the full purchase price. The customer is understandably upset; she has invested in a vacuum that appears to be a poor choice for her needs. However, the store cannot accept the returned vacuum because it could not be sold as new merchandise.

The following letter opens with a neutral remark to which both the reader and the writer can agree. It includes the clause *for which it is designed*, skillfully leading to an explanation of the design and merit of the vacuum being returned. The explanation capitalizes upon resale information while at the same time describing a more appropriate model for the customer's shag carpeting. The gentle explanation does not blame the customer for making a poor choice; the tone is objective and constructive. Regarding the customer's request for a cash refund, the writer explains that the returned vacuum is used and could not be resold. Without actually saying *We will not give you your money back*, the writer implies this refusal by presenting convincing reasons explaining why such a refund is impossible. Two alternatives further deemphasize the bad news. A friendly invitation concludes the letter.

Even when the customer is wrong, the indirect strategy is useful to minimize customer discontent.

≋

Refusing Credit

Banks, other financial institutions, and businesses often deny credit by using impersonal form letters. These letters may list a number of possible reasons for the credit rejection, such as insufficient credit references, irregular employment, delinquent credit obligations, insufficient income, inadequate collateral, temporary residence, or inability to verify income.

Form letters are convenient for the writer, but they often antagonize the reader because they are unclear, inappropriate, or insensitive. Even when individuals are poor credit risks (and they probably know this), they may be hurt by tactless and blunt form letters. Form-letter refusals or poorly written letters not only hurt the feelings of the reader but also ignore an opportunity to build future business. An individual or business that is a poor credit risk today may become a good credit risk and a potential customer in the future.

Form letters announcing credit refusals are efficient for the sender but may displease the receiver.

An effective plan for writing a credit refusal follows the principles of the indirect strategy.

FIGURE 8.4   Tactful Claims Refusal—Block Style, Open Punctuation

home shopper services

12001 Southwest 49 Avenue
Portland, Oregon 97219-3200
(205) 783-8823

June 11, 19xx

Mrs. Vivian Vandermark
P.O. Box 33701
Bitter Lake Station
Seattle, WA 98133-0071

Dear Mrs. Vandermark

Subject line identifies customer's letter.

SUBJECT: YOUR JUNE 5 LETTER ABOUT YOUR DOVER CANISTER VACUUM

Buffer opens with remark to which everyone can agree.

You have every right to expect a newly purchased vacuum cleaner to do a good job of cleaning the type of carpeting for which it is designed.

Reasoning subtly suggests that reader purchased wrong model.

Your Dover 2-peak HP canister vac was designed as a powerful tool for cleaning plush carpeting, area rugs, wood and vinyl floors, and draperies. This model has deep-cleaning suction and quiet operation at an economy price. As our catalog states, this canister model does not contain the beater-bar construction of the more powerful but more expensive models. To properly clean deep shag carpets like yours, the best model is the 4.2-peak HP Dover Power-Mate beater-bar unit.

Implied refusal avoids saying "No" directly.

Alternatives soften the bad news.

Since your present canister vacuum has been used for three months and is no longer new, it cannot be reboxed and sold as a new unit. As you know, we sell only new merchandise through our catalog service. However, a considerable market for used units exists. If you believe the 2-peak HP canister model is inadequate for your present carpeting, you might consider selling it or keeping it for lighter cleaning. Then, examine in our fall catalog the beater-bar models recommended for deep shag carpets like yours. Most of these have adjustable height settings, allowing you to select the proper level for your shag carpet.

Sincere and friendly closing mixes sales promotion with invitation.

We are sending you an advance copy of the fall catalog showing our full line of fine Dover vacuums. If you would like a personal demonstration of the Power-Mate model, we would be happy to show you how it operates on shag carpeting at the display center in our retail store.

Sincerely

Melanie DeGraff

Melanie DeGraff
Service Consultant

tra

Writing Plan for a Credit Refusal

- **Buffer**—expresses appreciation for order or for credit application and includes resale information if appropriate.

- **Transition**—moves from buffer to explanation logically and repeats key idea or word if possible.

- **Explanation**—shows concern for the welfare of the reader, explains objectively why credit must be refused, and doesn't preach or hide behind company policy.

- **Bad news**—implies refusal or states it briefly, offers alternatives, and suggests possible extension of credit in the future.

- **Closing**—projects an optimistic look to the future and includes resale or sales-promotion material.

> Credit refusals use five-part strategy to break the bad news.

Tactful and Tactless Credit Refusals

Credit refusals can be separated into two groups: refusals to businesses and refusals to individuals. Although the same general strategy applies to both, some variations exist.

In Figure 8.5 the credit refusal to a business has several major faults. First, it offends the reader with insensitive, negative language (*we regret, unsatisfactory, your firm is considered a poor credit risk*). Second, the letter does not try to convert this order into a cash transaction. Third, it does not attempt to promote goodwill or build future business. Notice that the letter begins with the overused and mechanical *Thank you for your order*. Although this beginning is a little better

> Use similar techniques for refusing credit to individuals and to businesses.

FIGURE 8.5   Offensive Credit Refusal That Hurts Business

> Ineffective writing

Dear Mr. Sargema:

Thank you for your order of February 14 for 36 of our Unifax cordless phone systems.

Although we would like to do business with you, we regret to report that our credit investigation of your firm proved unsatisfactory. Because of excessive current credit obligations, your firm is considered a poor credit risk.

We hope that you will understand that, as a small business producing a quality product with a small profit margin, we have to be extremely careful to avoid credit losses.

Sincerely,

> Opening expresses appreciation mechanically.
>
> Bad news is blurted out before explanation.
>
> Explanation is factual but tactless.
>
> Closing offends reader by implying a credit loss.

UNIFAC COMMUNICATION SYSTEMS

3490 Franklin Street ◆ Auburn, NY 13902-0002 ◆ (212) 355-8792

February 19, 19xx

Mr. Greg Sargema
Federated Sound Suppliers
320 Orchard Park Boulevard
Buffalo, NY 14127-2110

Dear Mr. Sargema:

Opens confidently with resale.

You've come to the right place for cordless phone systems, Mr. Sargema, and we appreciate your February 14 order. The Nomad 400 model that you have ordered offers outstanding features, including two-way paging, pulse dialing, and intercom capabilities.

Moves from product discussion to credit investigation by means of effective transition.

Implies refusal without stating it directly.

Because we'd like to see this product distributed by your full-service dealership, we investigated your credit application. We found that you have current and long-term credit obligations that are nearly twice as great as your firm's total assets. This financial picture suggests that it would be unwise for your firm to incur further credit obligations at this time. When your firm's financial situation improves, however, we would sincerely like to serve you on a credit basis.

Suggests alternative plan for cash purchase.

Emphasizes reader benefits.

In the meantime, consider this plan. Order one dozen of the Nomad 400 units today. By paying for this reduced order with cash, you would receive a 2 percent cash discount. After you have sold these fast-moving units, place another cash order through our toll-free order number. We promise to deliver your items immediately so that your inventory is never depleted. In this way, you can obtain the units you want now, you can enjoy cash discounts, and you can replace your inventory almost instantaneously.

Looks forward optimistically to future business.

We're proud of our quality products and our competitive prices. If we can do business with you now or in the future, please call us at (800) 896-3320.

Yours truly,

Margaret Gormann

Margaret Gormann, Manager
Marketing Unit One

meg

than blurting out the bad news directly, it shows that the writer made no effort to individualize this letter. Throughout the letter the tone is destructive rather than constructive. The last paragraph places unseemly emphasis on the profit motive.

The letter shown in Figure 8.6 treats the same credit refusal in a totally different manner. It strives to retain the business represented by Mr. Sargema's order, providing a plan for reducing the order so that a cash purchase might be possible. The tone of the letter is cordial, and the alternative, constructive. The implied refusal shows concern for the reader but does not patronize.

When refusing credit to individuals, apply the same indirect strategy you learned in refusing credit for businesses. Be extremely careful, though, to avoid making the refusal sound like a personal attack on the individual's reputation. Instead, base the refusal on objective factors, such as the individual's income, expenses, and ability to repay.

Adapting the Indirect Strategy

In this chapter you learned how to use the indirect strategy for refusing requests, refusing claims, and denying credit. The same general principles of indirectness are appropriate whenever bad news must be delivered. For example, a company announcement reducing health coverage for employees would certainly represent bad news to the employees. The indirect strategy would be best for such an announcement. News that a supplier is out of a needed item or that a certain item is no longer manufactured or that the price of an item has risen—all these messages will be irritating to a customer. The indirect strategy is again most effective.

Application of the principles of indirectness is often successful in solving personal problems.

We have applied this strategy only to written business messages. The strategy is, however, also appropriate in oral communication and in interpersonal relations. If you must tell a friend that you can't fulfill a promise, a good explanation preceding the refusal may help you retain the friendship. If you must tell your brother that you dented the fender of his car, the indirect strategy described in this chapter will help you announce the bad news. Now that you've learned this strategy, you'll be able to adapt it to many situations beyond the letter and memo writing plans illustrated here.

How to Avoid Fifteen Dangerous Word Traps

Certain words are treacherous because they sound and look very much like other words. Test your knowledge of the following confusing words by circling the best choice for each sentence. Check your responses on page 195.

1. New employees must (adapt, adept, adopt) themselves to our policies.

2. He liked movies but was (adverse, averse) to standing in long lines.

3. Higher admission prices will certainly (affect, effect) our attendance.

4. The (biannual, biennial) meetings are held normally in March and October.

5. Despite the investment of much (capital, capitol), the venture failed.

6. We received (complementary, complimentary) passes to the vampire movie.

7. The speakers included three (eminent, imminent) chief executive officers.

8. From Ann's remarks I (imply, infer) that she is uninterested in this job.

9. Some of the company's (personal, personnel) must be transferred.

10. Before we can (precede, proceed), we must investigate your credit.

11. Her (principal, principle) means of income is her monthly salary.

12. We would rather promote from within (than, then) advertising publicly.

13. Please (disperse, disburse) this information to our dealers immediately.

14. Employees are concerned about (their, they're, there) insurance benefits.

15. We must decide (weather, whether) to increase vision care benefits.

APPLICATION AND PRACTICE—8

Discussion

1. Discuss at least five situations in which the indirect strategy would be appropriate for delivering a negative message.

2. The indirect strategy appears to be an effort to manipulate the reader. Discuss.

3. The organization and development of a message delivering negative news begins with the explanation. Discuss.

4. Analyze the effectiveness of the following opening statements for negative news letters:

   a. Unfortunately, we would like to approve your credit application but we cannot.
   b. I enjoyed talking with you last week when you came in to be interviewed for the position of assistant to the registrar.
   c. The weather recently has certainly been pleasant for this time of the year, hasn't it?

5. Analyze the effectiveness of the following closing statements for negative letters:

   a. Once again, please let me say that we would like to grant your request but we cannot allow outsiders to use our confidential company files even for such worthy research as you describe.
   b. If you have any further questions about this matter, please remember that I am available to serve you.
   c. Although we regret very much any inconvenience our shipping error has caused you, we trust that you will understand our position in this matter.

Short Answers

6. The indirect strategy should be used when you expect what kind of reader reaction?

7. List in proper sequence the six elements involved in organizing a negative message according to the indirect strategy.

8. What is a buffer and when should it be used?

9. What are three characteristics of a good buffer?

10. How can a writer develop a transition between the opening of a letter and an explanation that follows?

11. List seven ways to deemphasize bad news. Be prepared to discuss each.

12. List four ways that you should *not* close a negative message.

13. Name three red-flag words.

14. Write *passive* or *active* to indicate the voice of the verbs in the following sentences.

    a. We cannot refund the full purchase price.

    b. The full purchase price cannot be refunded.

    c. The shipment of your order has been delayed.

    d. Our delivery service has delayed shipment of your order.

15. Name four emphatic positions in a letter.

Writing Improvement Exercises

Subordinate Clauses.   You can soften the effect of bad news by placing it in a subordinate clause that begins with *although, since,* or *because.* The emphasis in a sentence is upon the independent clause. Instead of saying *We cannot serve you on* *a credit basis,* try *Since we cannot serve you on a credit basis, we invite you to take advantage of our cash discounts and sale prices.*

Revise the following refusals so that the bad news appears in a subordinate clause.

16. We no longer manufacture the Model SF–7. However, we now make a substitute, the Model SF–9, which we would like to send you.

17. We hope to have our plant remodeling completed by October. We cannot schedule tours of the bottling plant until after we finish remodeling.

18. Island Airways cannot accept responsibility for expenses incurred indirectly from flight delays. However, we do recognize that this delay inconvenienced you.

Passive-Voice Verbs.   Passive-voice verbs may be preferable in breaking bad news because they enable you to emphasize actions rather than personalities. Compare these two refusals:

Active Voice: I cannot authorize you to take three weeks of vacation in July.
Passive Voice: Three weeks of vacation in July cannot be authorized.

Revise the following refusals so that they use passive-voice instead of active-voice verbs.

19. We cannot refund cash for the items you purchased on credit.

20. I have already filled my schedule on the date you wish me to speak.

21. We do not examine patients until we have verified their insurance coverage.

Implied Refusals.   Bad news can be deemphasized by implying a refusal instead of stating it directly. Compare these refusals:

Direct Refusal: We cannot send you a price list nor can we sell our lawn mowers directly to customers. We sell only through dealers, and your dealer is HomeCo, Inc.

Implied Refusal: Our lawn mowers are sold only through dealers, and your dealer is HomeCo, Inc.

Revise the following refusals so that they are implied.

22. We cannot open a credit account for you because your application states that you have no regular employment. This allows us to serve you only as a cash customer.

23. I find it impossible to contribute to the fund-raising campaign this year. At present all the funds of my organization are needed to lease new equipment and offices for our new branch in Richmond. I hope to be able to support this fund in the future.

24. We cannot ship our fresh fruit baskets c.o.d. Your order was not accompanied by payment, so we are not shipping it. We have it ready, though, and will rush it to its destination as soon as you call us with your credit-card number.

CASE 8–1

Favor Refusal

Imagine that you are Ron Levin, manager of Datatech Computers. You have received a letter from Professor Lydia Keuser, at nearby San Jose City College, who wants to bring her class of 30 office automation students to your showroom to see the latest microcomputer hardware and software. You are eager to have 30 potential customers visit your showroom, where you carry a comprehensive line of microcomputers, compatible printers, and state-of-the-art software. But you can't possibly accommodate 30 people at once. Your workstations are arranged for demonstrations to only one or two viewers at a time. You must refuse Professor Keuser's request. However, since you hate to pass up this opportunity, suggest to her that you could bring a computer to her classroom for a demonstration, or she could divide her class into smaller groups for demos at the showroom.

Consider the refusal letter to Professor Keuser. Analyze the following options in relation to the indirect strategy. Circle the letters representing the most appropriate possibilities for the refusal letter.

1. To open this letter appropriately, you might

   a. Point out immediately that your showroom is too small to accommodate her entire class at once.

b. Express appreciation that Professor Keuser and her office automation class are interested in the microcomputers and software offered by Datatech Computers.

c. Explain that Datatech Computers carries only professional programs and that your stock does not include computer games, in which some college students may be interested.

d. Suggest that she divide her class into thirds and let you demonstrate your comprehensive line at three different times.

2. A logical transition for this letter might be for you to

a. Use sales promotion by describing the outstanding features of your best-selling computer and one of your software programs.

b. Warn Professor Keuser that 30 students gathered around one screen would create an impossible viewing situation.

c. Mention that you normally demonstrate your comprehensive line of microcomputers, printers, and software programs to individual customers.

d. Inquire regarding the level of computer expertise represented by the students in this class.

3. In explaining why you cannot accommodate the class, you might say that

a. Demonstrating to this large student group would interfere with sales to genuine customers in your showroom.

b. Customers usually come in singly or in pairs; hence you are prepared for demonstrations to small groups only.

c. You never demonstrate to large groups because individuals complain that they can't see what's on the screen or hear what's being said.

d. You would prefer not to demonstrate to students because many will not understand the complexities of computers; moreover, they are unlikely to make purchases in the near future.

4. Which of the following sentences softens the refusal most effectively?

a. Although your class cannot be accommodated in our showroom, we might be able to arrange a demonstration in your classroom.

b. We cannot accommodate your class in our showroom because your class is too large.

c. Although we might be able to arrange a demonstration in your classroom, we cannot accommodate your class in our showroom.

d. We sincerely regret that we cannot allow your class to come to Datatech Computers for a demonstration.

Use this problem for discussion. At the option of your instructor, write the entire letter (individually or as a class project) to Professor Lydia Keuser, San Jose City College, 2100 Moorpark Avenue, San Jose, California 95128–2799. You may wish to incorporate some of the sentences you selected here, but consider this a skeleton. Flesh out your letter with explanations, examples, appropriate connecting thoughts, and a goodwill closing. Use modified block style with indented paragraphs.

CASE 8–2

Request Refusal

Analyze the following poorly written message and list some of its major faults. Outline a writing plan for refusing a request. Then, on a separate sheet, rewrite the message, rectifying the faults.

TO: Anita Marcus, Records Manager   DATE: June 20, 19xx

FROM: Connie Clark, President

SUBJECT: CONFERENCE

Ineffective writing

Please be informed that I have taken under advisement your request to be allowed to attend the conference of the Association of Records Managers and Administrators, Inc., in New York. Unfortunately, this conference is six days long and comes in September, a very critical time for us.

I'm sorry to have to deny your request, because it looks like a worthwhile conference. It would afford an opportunity for records management personnel, like you, to learn more about current procedures and technologies. You've been doing an outstanding job of helping us begin the conversion of our files to microforms.

But to have you gone for a period of six days in September, when, as you know, we complete our budget requests for the following fiscal year is out of the question. We need you at our budget planning meetings, particularly since you have proposed the purchase of computer equipment that will generate micrographs directly. Another reason that you can't go in September, in spite of the fact that I would like to see you go, is that Cathy Watson, in your department, has requested the months of August through October for her maternity leave. Your absence, together with hers, would put us in a real bind.

For these reasons, I cannot allow you to leave in September. However, if there is a suitable conference at some other time in the year when your absence would be less critical, I would be happy to let you go. I'm sorry about this matter, Anita. This is certainly little thanks for the excellent progress you are making in the massive task of converting our filing system.

1. List at least five faults.

2. Outline a writing plan for a request refusal.

CASE 8–3

Credit Refusal

Analyze the following poorly written message and list its major faults. Outline a writing plan for refusing credit. Then, on a separate sheet, rewrite the message, rectifying its faults. Address the letter to Mr. John Rollins, 876 Avenue H, Winter Haven, Florida 33880. Use modified block style with indented paragraphs.

Dear Mr. Rollins:

Thank you very much for your April 23 order for computer paper, copy paper, and other supplies. We are delighted by your interest in our products and our company. Unfortunately, we cannot fill your order because of your poor credit rating.

Ineffective writing

Your application for credit indicates that your dealership now has a current-assets-to-liabilities ratio of only $1\frac{1}{2}$ to 1. Most financial authorities recommend that businesses of your size maintain a 2-to-1 ratio of current assets to liabilities. Our company policy prohibits us from issuing credit to any organization that does not meet this minimum requirement. We hope you will understand our desire to avoid any credit losses.

Since your dealership appears to be experiencing good sales, we're sure you will want to practice sound financial practices and avoid increasing your liabilities with additional credit purchases. For this reason, we invite you to let us fill your order on a cash basis.

At the present time we have in stock all the items that you requested. We can't send them, though, unless you have cash. If you would like these items rushed to you, call me personally at (213) 883-2980. If I can be of further service, don't hesitate to call upon me.

Sincerely,

Pamela Wright
Credit Manager

1. List at least five faults.

2. Outline a writing plan for refusing credit.

CASE 8–4

Claim Refusal

For class discussion analyze the following poorly written message. Discuss its major faults, and suggest a writing plan for refusing a claim. Then, at the option of your instructor, on a separate sheet rewrite the message, rectifying its faults. Address the letter to Mrs. Lois Sullivan, 422 Paramus Road, Paramus, New Jersey 97652. Use modified block style with indented paragraphs.

Dear Mrs. Sullivan:

Ineffective writing

We have your letter of May 23 demanding repair or replacement for your newly purchased BeautyTest mattress. You say that you enjoy sleeping on it; but in the morning when you and your husband get up, you claim that the mattress has body impressions that remain all day.

Unfortunately, Mrs. Sullivan, we can neither repair nor replace your mattress because those impressions are perfectly normal. If you will read your warranty carefully, you will find this statement: "Slight body impressions will appear with use and are not indicative of structural failure. The body-conforming coils and comfort cushioning materials are beginning to work for you and impressions are caused by the natural settling of these materials."

When you purchased your mattress, I'm sure your salesperson told you that the BeautyTest mattress has a unique, scientifically designed system of individually pocketed coils that provide separate support for each person occupying the bed. This unusual construction, with those hundreds of independently operating coils, reacts to every body contour, providing luxurious comfort. At the same time, this system provides firm support. It is this unique design that's causing the body impressions that you see when you get up in the morning.

Although we never repair or replace a mattress when it merely shows slight impressions, we will send our representative out to inspect your mattress, if it would make you feel better. Please call for an appointment at (800) 322-9800. Remember, on a BeautyTest mattress you get the best night's rest possible.

Cordially,

1. List at least five faults.

2. Outline a writing plan for a message that refuses a claim.

Additional Problems

1. As the sales manager of Wholesale Copier Exchange, you are faced with a difficult decision. The daughter of one of your best friends operates Eastland Escrow Services. For the past ten months, as a favor, you have allowed her to lease from you a full-featured Toshiba copier at a low rate of $200 per month. Now she wants to purchase the Toshiba, and she wants you to apply the lease payments against the purchase price. That means that she wants to deduct $2,000 from the basic purchase price of $7,695. Your quoted purchase price is already at rock bottom. You have been able to build business by selling a high volume of units while keeping your profit of margin quite low. Although you do have a limited leasing business, none of your leasing agreements include an option to apply the lease payments toward the purchase of a unit. Other companies may permit such an arrangement, but their purchase prices are probably much higher than yours. Even at $7,695, you will be earning a very slim profit. To allow a $2,000 discount would certainly mean a loss for you; and even for the daughter of a friend, you don't want to absorb a $2,000 loss. Eastland seems to like the performance they have received from this Toshiba, Model DC–3E. You have slightly cheaper models, but they have fewer features. If Eastland wants to give up the reduction and enlargement capability as well as the automatic paper selection device, you might be able to bring the purchase price down $1,500. Regardless of what Toshiba model Eastland purchases, you guarantee 6-hour emergency service and a 1-million-copy or 8-year warranty. Write a letter to Rachael Ramberg, Eastland Escrow Services, 4801 First Street North, Arlington, VA 22203, retaining her friendship and business but refusing her request.

2. Assume that you are plant operations manager for United Growers Association. You have received a letter from Reverend Donald T. Webster,

pastor of the First Church of Christ. Reverend Webster writes at the suggestion of Victor Cortez, whom you know well as the supervisor of your shipping fleet and one of your most valued employees. Mr. Cortez is a deacon at the First Church of Christ and has been instrumental in collecting food and clothing for poor families in Mexico. He has suggested to his pastor that United Growers might allow the church to borrow a small cargo truck over a weekend to pick up articles in the Oxnard and Ventura areas and deliver them to the church's mission in Ensenada, Mexico. You have sympathy with the plight of the poor and would like to encourage this worthwhile endeavor. However, company trucks cannot be loaned to outside organizations or individuals, even for worthy causes. Your liability insurance limits equipment coverage to specific deliveries, routes, and licensed drivers. You cannot allow any company truck to be borrowed officially (or unofficially), even by a trusted company employee for an admirable project. Write a refusal letter that recognizes the worth of this charitable project and acknowledges the high regard you hold for Mr. Cortez. Address the letter to Reverend Webster, First Church of Christ, 269 Anacapa View Drive, Ventura, CA 91076, and send a copy to Victor Cortez in the company mail.

3. As Lentax consumer affairs representative, you must refuse the claim of Gabriella Marconi, a professional photographer who purchased a Lentax macrofocusing teleconverter lens two years ago. Ms. Marconi wants the lens replaced, claiming that it no longer works properly, although it worked well for two years. Your service department has examined the returned teleconverter and determined that either it was improperly attached to another lens or it was dropped, causing a lack of synchronization with Ms. Marconi's aperture-priority camera. Lentax products are built to the highest quality standards and should provide years of satisfaction. The Lentax Limited 5-Year Warranty clearly states the following: "Malfunctions resulting from misuse, tampering, unauthorized repairs, modifications, or accident are not covered by this warranty." Refuse the request for replacement. Tell her, however, that since she purchased this lens from an authorized dealer, she may receive a 25 percent discount on repairs. Write to Ms. Gabriella Marconi, 120 Carlisle Street, Hanover, PA 17221.

✓ 4. As Richard Green, owner of Greenscapes, Inc., you must refuse the following request. Mr. and Mrs. John Nabor have asked that you replace the landscaping in the home they recently purchased in Kettering. You had landscaped that home nearly a year ago for the former owner, Mrs. Dryden, installing a sod lawn, and many shrubs, trees, and flowers. It looked beautiful when you finished, but six months later, Mrs. Dryden sold the property and moved to Dayton. Four months elapsed before the new owners moved in. After four months of neglect and a hot, dry summer, the newly installed landscaping suffered. You guarantee all your work and normally would replace any plants that do not survive. Under these circumstances, however, you do not feel justified in making any refund because your guarantee necessarily presumes proper maintenance on the part of the property owner. Moreover, your guarantee is made only to the individual who contracted with you—not to subsequent owners. You would like to retain the goodwill of the new owners, since this is an affluent neighborhood and you hope to attract additional work here. On the other hand, you can't afford to replace the materials invested in this job. You believe that the lawn could probably be rejuvenated with deep watering and fertilizer. You would be happy to inspect the property and offer suggestions to the Nabors. In reality, you wonder if the Nabors might not have a claim against the former owner or the escrow agency for failing to maintain the property. Clearly, however, the claim is not against you. Write to Mr. and Mrs. John Nabor, 4716 Highgate Drive, Kettering, Ohio 45429.

5. As manager of The Sports Connection, you must refuse the application of Geri Meyers for an extended membership in your athletic club. This is strictly a business decision. You liked Geri very much when she applied, and she seems genuinely interested in fitness and a healthful lifestyle. However, your "extended membership" plan qualifies the member for all your testing, exercise, aerobics, and recreation programs. This multiservice program is necessarily expensive and requires a solid credit rating. To your disappointment, however, you learn that Geri's credit rating is decidedly negative. She is reported to be delinquent in payments to four businesses, including Holiday Health Spa, your principal competitor. You do have other programs, including your "Drop In and Work Out" plan that offers use of available facilities on a cash basis. This plan enables a member to reserve space on the racquetball and handball courts; the member can also sign up for exercise and aerobics classes, space permitting. Since Geri is far in debt, you would feel guilty allowing her to plunge in any more deeply. Refuse her credit application, but encourage her cash business. Write to Geri Meyers, Stratford Apartments, No. 4, 15053 Sherman Way, Van Nuys, CA 91405.

6. As manager of Exbrook Restaurant Supply, you are sorry to have to refuse an order because of the poor credit rating of Mary Stephens. She is opening a new gourmet catering business in Fort Lauderdale called "The GodMother." You were delighted with her initial order for $1,430. However, when you checked her credit, you learned that she owed substantial sums for her catering truck and kitchen equipment. In fact, she seems to have no solid financial assets. You cannot allow a credit order. You know that every businessperson has to get started somehow, and you wish you could help her out in this fledgling business. You feel that her international menu (including unusual items like pasta primavera, moussaka, duck lasagna, and chicken fettuccine verde) will be quite successful, especially if she uses your quality ingredients. Write a sympathetic but firm credit refusal to Mary Stephens, The GodMother, 905 North Gulf Drive, Fort Lauderdale, FL 33334.

GRAMMAR/MECHANICS CHECKUP—8

Commas, 3

Review the Grammar/Mechanics Handbook Sections 2.10 to 2.15. Then study each of the following statements and insert necessary commas. In the space provided write the number of commas that you add; write *0* if no commas are needed. Also record the number of the G/M principles(s) illustrated. When you finish, compare your responses with those shown below. If your answers differ, study carefully the principles shown in parentheses.

2 _____ (2.21)   **Example:**   It was Ms. Jeffreys, not Mr. Simpson, who was assigned the Madison account.

_____   1. "The choice of a good name " said President Gordon "cannot be overestimated."

_____   2. Lois A. Wagner Ph.D. and Marilyn S. Smith M.B.A. were hired as consultants.

_____   3. Their August 15 order was shipped on Monday wasn't it?

_____   4. Brand names are important in advertising specialty goods such as refrigerators and television sets.

_____   5. The bigger the investment the greater the profit.

Review Commas 1, 2, and 3

_____   6. As you requested your order for ribbons file folders and envelopes will be sent immediately.

_____   7. We think however that you should reexamine your networking system and that you should consider electronic mail.

_____   8. Within the next eight-week period we hope to hire Sue Richards who is currently working in private industry.

_____   9. Our convention will attract more participants if it is held in a resort location such as San Diego Monterey or Las Vegas.

_____   10. If everyone who applied for the position were interviewed we would be overwhelmed.

_____   11. Our chief goal is to provide quality products backed by prompt efficient service.

_____   12. In the past ten years we have employed over 30 well-qualified individuals many of whom have selected banking as their career.

_____   13. Your shipment has been charged to your new account which we were pleased to open on the basis of your excellent credit.

_____   14. Steven Sims who spoke to our class last week is the author of a book entitled *Writing Winning Résumés*.

_____   15. Mrs. Hartung uses market research extensively and keeps a close watch on her own operations her competition and the market in order to identify the latest trends.

---

1. (2) name," Gordon, (*2.14a*)   3. (1) Monday, (*2.14b*)   5. (1) investment, (*2.12*)   7. (2) think, however, (*2.03*)   9. (2) Diego, Monterey, (*2.01, 2.15*)   11. (1) prompt, (*2.08, 2.15*)   13. (1) account, (*2.06c, 2.15*)   15. (2) operations, competition, (*2.01*)

*No comma precedes *and* because the words following are not an independent clause.

Word Trap Answers*

1. **adapt**, *v.*:   to make fit, adjust, or modify. [**adept** = skilled; **adopt** = borrow, to accept as one's own]

2. **averse**, *adj.*:   unwilling, disinclined. [**adverse** = unfavorable, hostile]

3. **affect**, *v.*:   influence, impress. [**effect**, *n.* = result, outcome; **effect**, *v.* = to produce a change]

4. **biannual**, *adj.*:   occurring twice a year. [**biennial** = occurring once every two years]

5. **capital**, *n.*:   assets, cash. [**Capitol** = building where Congress meets; **capitol** = building where state legislature meets]

6. **complimentary**, *adj.*:   free. [**complementary** = acting to complete or fill out]

7. **eminent**, *adj.*:   famous, distinguished. [**imminent** = impending]

8. **infer**, *v.*:   conclude, deduce. [**imply** = suggest indirectly, hint]

9. **personnel**, *n.*:   employees, staff. [**personal** = private]

10. **proceed**, *v.*:   continue, move forward. [**precede** = preface, come before]

11. **principal**, *adj.*:   chief, main. [**principle** = rule, belief, guideline]

12. **than**, *conj.*:   function word used in making a comparison. [**then** = next, at that time]

13. **disperse**, *v.*:   distribute, give, disseminate. [**disburse** = pay, apportion]

14. **their**, *adj.*, *pron.*:   plural possessive personal pronoun. [**they're** = they are; **there** = at that place or at that point]

15. **whether**, *conj.*:   function word introducing alternatives. [**weather** = atmospheric conditions]

*From page 182.

CHAPTER 9

Letters and Memos That Persuade

In this chapter you will learn to do the following:

- Use the indirect strategy to persuade.
- Write convincing claim request letters.
- Request favors persuasively.
- Present new ideas in persuasive memos.

- Analyze techniques used in sales letters.
- Compose carefully planned sales letters.

The ability to persuade is a key factor in the success you achieve in your business messages, in your career, and in your interpersonal relations. Persuasive individuals are those who present convincing arguments that influence or win over others. Because their ideas generally prevail, these individuals become decision makers—managers and executives. This chapter will examine the techniques for presenting ideas persuasively.

Being able to use persuasion skillfully is a primary factor in personal and business success.

Persuasive Requests

Persuasion is necessary when resistance is anticipated or when ideas require preparation before they can be presented effectively. For example, if Irene Ricketts purchased a new Ford and the transmission repeatedly required servicing, she might be forced to write to Ford's district office asking that the company install a new transmission in her car. Irene's claim letter should be persuasive; she must convince Ford that replacement, not repair, is needed. Routine claim letters, such as those you wrote in Chapter 6, are straightforward and direct. Persuasive requests, on the other hand, are generally more effective when they are indirect. Reasons and explanations should precede the big idea. To overcome possible resistance, the writer must lay a logical foundation before the big news is delivered. A writing plan for a persuasive request requires deliberate development.

Use persuasion when you must change attitudes or produce action.

Writing Plan for a Persuasive Request

- **Opening**—obtains the reader's attention and interest.

- **Persuasion**—explains logically and concisely the purpose of your request and proves the merit of your request.

- **Closing**—asks for a particular action and shows courtesy and respect.

Claim Request

The most important parts of a claim letter are the sections describing the desired action and the proof that such action is reasonable.

The organization of an effective persuasive claim centers on the closing and the persuasion. First, decide what action you want taken to satisfy the claim. Then, decide how you can prove the worth of your claim. Plan carefully the line of reasoning you will follow in convincing the reader to take the action you request. If the claim is addressed to a business, it is generally effective to appeal to the organization's pride in its products and its services. Refer to its reputation for integrity and your confidence in it. Show the validity of your claim and why the company will be doing the right thing in granting it. Most organizations are sincere in their efforts to produce quality products that gain consumer respect.

Anger and emotional threats against an organization do little to achieve the goal of claim letters. Claims are generally referred to a customer service department. The claims adjuster answering the claim probably bears no responsibility for the design, production, delivery, or servicing of the product. An abusive letter may serve only to offend the claims adjuster, thus making it difficult for the claim to be evaluated rationally.

Claim letters should avoid negative and emotional words and should not attempt to attribute blame.

The most effective claim captures the attention of the reader immediately in the opening and sets up the persuasion that follows. In the body of the claim, you should present convincing reasons to justify the claim. Try to argue without overusing negative words, without fixing blame for the problem, and without becoming emotional. To create the desired effect, arrange the reasons in a logical, orderly manner with appropriate transitions to guide the reader through the persuasion.

Following the persuasion, spell out clearly the desired action in the closing. Remember, the most successful claims are respectful and courteous.

Observe how the claim letter shown in Figure 9.1 illustrates the preceding suggestions. The opening statements secure the reader's attention and at the same time set up the description of events and persuasive arguments that follow. Notice the absence of rancor and harsh words, although the writer probably experienced angry feelings over these events. Notice, too, that the closing rounds out the letter by tying in a reference to the opening statement.

Favor Request

Asking for a favor implies that you want someone to do something for nothing—or for very little. Common examples are requests for the donation of time, money, energy, name, resources, talent, skills, or expertise. On occasion, everyone needs to ask a favor. Small favors, such as asking a coworker to lock up the office for you on Friday, can be straightforward and direct, since you anticipate little resistance. Larger favors require careful planning and an indirect strategy. Consider the appeal to a busy executive who is asked to serve on a committee to help

~~~

FIGURE 9.1   Claim Request—Block Style, Open Punctuation

A^MS ALBANY MOVING & STORAGE

Local   *
National   *
International   *

4950 Pretoria Avenue
Albany, Georgia 31705
(912) 883-3918

January 23, 19xx

G. Bendix, Inc.
3350 Peachtree Center
Suite 305
Atlanta, GA 35891

Ladies and Gentlemen

SUBJECT: BUTONE MODEL 150 HOT-WATER HEATING SYSTEM

Your Butone hot-water heating system appealed to my company for two
reasons. First, it promised high-efficiency heat with a 36 percent savings
in our heating oil costs. Second, your firm has been in the heating
business for forty years, and such a record must indicate a reputation of
concern for your customers.

Gains attention with favorable comments about the company.

We think that we were right about your heating system. Now we wonder if
we're right about your reputation.

Last September we purchased a Butone oil-fired Model 150 and had it
installed in our eight-room office building by your dealer, Pecan Heating
Contractors. For two weeks it heated our offices comfortably. One morning,
though, we arrived and found our rooms cold. We called Pecan Heating
Contractors, and their technician came out to inspect our system. He
reported that the automatic ignition device had failed. He replaced it, and
the system worked well for two days. Then, on the third day after this
repair, a fire developed in the combustion area of the heating unit,
destroying the circulating pump and its motor. Technicians from Pecan
Heating returned immediately and replaced the entire heating unit.

Explains events in orderly, logical fashion.

We assumed that this replacement was covered by the system's 5-year
warranty. That's why we were surprised two days ago to receive from
Pecan Heating Contractors a bill for $255.92 covering installation of the
new unit. In a telephone conversation, James Wilkins, of Pecan Heating,
said that the warranty covers only replacement of the unit. The cost of
installation is extra.

Argues convincingly that charge is unjustified.

We feel that this charge is unjustified. The fire that destroyed the unit resulted from either a defective unit or faulty servicing by Pecan Heating Contractors. Since we feel responsibility for neither of these conditions, we believe that we should bear no charges. Our insurance carrier shares this view.

Closes with action request that ties in with opening.

Please pay the attached bill or instruct Pecan Heating Contractors to cancel it. This would indicate to us that we were right both about your product and about your reputation.

Sincerely

Pamela Dougherty

Pamela Dougherty
Office Manager

rpw

Attachment

When you anticipate resistance to a favor request, use persuasive techniques.

handicapped children or the appeal to a florist who is asked to donate table arrangements for a charity fund-raiser or a request made to an eminent author to speak before a local library group. In each instance, persuasion is necessary to overcome natural resistance.

The letter shown in Figure 9.2 illustrates a poorly conceived favor request. An organization without funds hopes to entice a well-known authority to speak before its regional conference. Such a request surely requires indirectness and persuasion, but the following ineffective letter begins with a direct appeal. The reader is given an opportunity to refuse the request before the writer has a chance to present reasons for accepting. The second paragraph also provides an easy opportunity to refuse the request. Moreover, this letter contains little to convince Dr. Wickersham that she has anything to gain by speaking to this group. Finally, the closing suggests no specific action to help her accept, should she be so inclined.

A favor request is doomed to failure if the writer fails to consider its effect on the reader.

Notice, now, how the letter to Dr. Wickersham in Figure 9.3 applies the indirect strategy to achieve its goal. The opening catches her interest and makes her want to read more regarding the reaction to her article. By showing how Dr. Wickersham's interests are related to the organization's, the writer lays a groundwork of persuasion before presenting the request. The request is then followed by reasoning that shows Dr. Wickersham how she will benefit from accepting this invitation. This successful letter concludes with an action closing.

Persuasive Memo

Within an organization the indirect strategy is appropriate when persuasion is needed in presenting new ideas to management or to colleagues, in requesting action from employees, and in securing compliance with altered procedures.

FIGURE 9.2   Weak Favor Request

Ineffective writing

Dear Dr. Wickersham:

Would you be willing to speak to the American Personnel Managers Association's regional conference in Boston March 23?

Although we understand that your research, teaching, and consulting must keep you extremely busy, we hope that your schedule will allow you to be the featured speaker at our conference. We are particularly interested in the article you recently published in the *Harvard Business Review*. A number of our members indicated that your topic, "Cost/Benefit Analysis for Human Resources," is something we should learn more about. Perhaps you could select a topic that would be somewhat more practical and not so theoretical, since most of our members are personnel managers or personnel specialists.

We have no funds to pay you, but we would like to invite you and your spouse to be our guests at the banquet following the day's sessions.

We hope that you will be able to speak before our group.

Sincerely,

Direct opening is poor strategy in asking a favor. Provides easy excuse for reader to refuse.

Point of view is writer-centered instead of reader-centered.

Emphasizes negative statement through its placement. Fails to tell reader how to respond.

Whenever resistance is anticipated, a sound foundation of reasoning should precede the big idea so that the idea will not be rejected prematurely.

New ideas can be expected to generate resistance, whether they are moving downward as directives from management, moving upward as suggestions to management, or moving laterally among colleagues. It is natural to resist change. When asked to perform differently or to try something new, some individuals resist because they are lazy. Others resist because they fear failure. Still others resist because they feel threatened—the proposed changes may encroach on their status or threaten their security. Some individuals resist new ideas because they are jealous of the individual making the proposal.

Whatever the motivation, resistance to new ideas and altered procedures is natural. Prepare for this resistance by anticipating objections, offering counterarguments, and emphasizing benefits. Don't assume that the advantages of a new plan are obvious and therefore may go unmentioned. Use concrete examples and familiar illustrations in presenting arguments.

In the memo shown in Figure 9.4, Randy MacArthur, communications supervisor, argues for the purchase of an expensive new piece of equipment, an optical character reader (OCR). He expects his manager to resist this purchase because the manager knows little about OCRs and because the budget is already overextended. Randy's memo follows the writing plan for a persuasive request. It begins by describing a costly problem in which Randy knows the reader is interested. To convince the manager of the need for an OCR, Randy must first explain the operation of an OCR and how it could benefit the organization.

American Personnel Managers Association

P.O. Box 5893
Boston, Massachusetts 02148
(617) 543-8922

January 4, 19xx

Professor Beverly J. Wickersham
Central Texas College
Killeen, TX 76941

Dear Dr. Wickersham:

Grabs attention of reader by appealing to her interests.

Cost/benefit analysis applied to human resources is a unique concept. Your recent article on that topic in the *Harvard Business Review* ignited a lively discussion at the last meeting of the Boston chapter of the American Personnel Managers Association.

Many of the managers in our group are experiencing the changes you describe. Functions in the personnel area are now being expanded to include a wide range of salary, welfare, benefit, and training programs.

Persuades reader that her expertise is valued.

These new programs can be very expensive. Our members are fascinated by your cost/benefit analysis that sets up a formal comparison of the costs to design, develop, and implement a program idea against the costs the idea saves or avoids. We'd like to know more about how this can be done.

Softens negative aspects of request with reader's benefits.

The members of our association have asked me to invite you to be the featured speaker March 23 when we hold our annual East Coast regional conference in Boston. About 150 personnel management specialists will attend the all-day conference at the Park Plaza Hotel. We would like you to speak at 2 p.m. on the topic of "Applying Cost/Benefit Analysis in Personnel Today." Although we cannot offer you an honorarium, we can offer you an opportunity to help personnel managers apply your theories in solving some of their most perplexing problems. You will also be able to meet managers who might be able to supply you with data for future research into personnel functions. In addition, the conference includes two other sessions and a banquet, to which you and a guest are invited.

Ends confidently with specific action to be taken.

Please call me at (617) 543-8922 to allow me to add your name to the program as the featured speaker before the American Personnel Managers Association March 23 at 2 p.m.

Respectfully yours,

Joann Northen

Joann Northen
Executive Secretary

jjo

FIGURE 9.4   Persuasive Memo That Requests New Equipment

TO: George Romanoff   DATE: May 2, 19xx
                Director of Operations

FROM: Randy MacArthur   *R.M.*
                Communications Supervisor, Central Services

SUBJECT: REDUCING OVERTIME AND IMPROVING TURNAROUND
                TIME

Last month we paid nearly $7,500 in overtime to word processing specialists who were forced to work 50- and 60-hour weeks to keep up with the heavy demand for printed documents. Despite this overtime, the average turnaround time for documents submitted to Central Services is now 8 working days. | **Captures attention of reader with a problem that can be solved.**

Many of the documents submitted to us are already in print and must be rekeyed into our word processing system by our operators. For example, some of the engineers in Systems Design bring us rough-draft proposals that they have produced on their microcomputers, which are not compatible with ours. As a result we are forced to rekey the material. | **Explains background and rationale before making proposal.**

I estimate that we could eliminate at least 60 percent of our overtime and also reduce the turnaround time on documents by 5 days if we were to use an optical character reader (OCR) to read printed documents into our word processing system. OCRs look like photocopiers, but they read printed images and convert them to electronic images. | **Points out concrete examples of savings to be realized.**

OCRs are not perfect, of course. The medium-priced unit can now read only selected typefaces, and it is most accurate when reading from white paper only. However, most of the documents on which we would use the OCR are printed in standard typefaces and on white paper. | **Anticipates objections and answers them.**

Despite these limitations, I believe that 55 to 60 percent of the printed documents coming to us could be read by an OCR. By eliminating this tedious rekeying, we could save at least $4,500 in overtime each month. We could also reduce turnaround time in Central Services by as much as 60 percent. Moreover, by eliminating the rekeying of printed documents, fewer errors will be introduced; and, most importantly, our specialists will be much happier employees. | **Summarizes advantages of purchasing new equipment.**

For these reasons, I recommend that we purchase the TECH Turbofont Model 303 optical character reader. It can read print from six typestyles with 95 percent accuracy. Its purchase price of $12,300 will be recovered from the savings due to reduced overtime within three months. | **Delays mention of price until after convincing arguments have been presented.**

Enclosed is a specification sheet describing this model. Please give me authorization to submit a purchase order for this OCR by June 1 so that Central Services may improve turnaround time before we are asked to begin work on the fiscal reports in July. | **Ends with explicit request and provides end dating.**

Instead of using generalities, Randy cites specific examples of how the OCR would function in their company and how much savings it would produce. Randy also anticipates the limitations of the OCR and discusses their effect on the proposal. In the closing, Randy asks for a specific action and provides support documentation to speed his request. He also includes end dating, which prompts the manager to act by a certain date.

Sales Letters

Direct-mail selling is a rapidly growing, multibillion-dollar industry. The professionals who specialize in direct-mail marketing have made a science of analyzing a market, developing an appropriate mailing list, studying the product, preparing a comprehensive presentation that appeals to the needs of the target audience, and motivating the reader to act. This carefully orchestrated presentation typically culminates in a sales letter accompanied by a brochure, a sales list, illustrations of the product, testimonials, and so forth.

We are most concerned with the sales letter: its strategy, organization, and appeals. Because sales letters are nearly always written by professionals, you probably will never be called upon to write an authentic sales letter. Why, then, learn how to write one? In a sense, every letter that we write is a form of sales letter. We sell our ideas, ourselves, and our organizations. Learning the techniques of sales writing will help you be more effective in any communication that requires persuasion and promotion. Moreover, recognizing the techniques of selling will enable you to respond to such techniques more rationally. You'll be a better educated consumer of ideas, products, and services if you understand how sales appeals are made.

The following writing plan for a sales letter attempts to overcome anticipated reader resistance by creating a desire for the product and by motivating the reader to act.

> *Recognizing and applying the techniques of sales writing can be helpful even if you never write an actual sales letter.*

Writing Plan for a Sales Letter

- **Opening**—captures the attention of the reader.

- **Body**—emphasizes a central selling point, appeals to the needs of the reader, creates a desire for the product, and introduces price strategically.

- **Closing**—stimulates the reader to act.

Analyzing the Product and the Reader

> *Both the product and the reader require careful analysis before a successful sales letter can be written.*

Before implementing the writing plan, it's wise to study the product and the target audience so that you can emphasize features with reader appeal.

To sell a product effectively, learn as much as possible about its construction, including its design, raw materials, and manufacturing process. Study its performance, including ease of use, efficiency, durability, and applications. Consider warranties, service, price, and special appeals. Be knowledgeable not only about your product but also about the competitor's product so you can emphasize your product's strengths against the competitor's weaknesses.

The most effective sales letters are sent to a targeted audience. Mailing lists for selected groups can be purchased or compiled. For example, the manufacturer of computer supplies would find an appropriate audience for its products in the mailing list of subscribers to a computer magazine. By using a selected mailing list, a sales-letter writer is able to make certain assumptions about the readers. Readers may be expected to share certain characteristics, such as interests, abilities, needs, income, and so forth. The sales letter, then, can be adapted to appeal directly to this selected group. In working with a less selected audience, the letter writer can make only general assumptions and must use a shotgun approach, hoping to find some appeal that motivates the reader.

A target audience is one that is preselected for characteristics that make it a good market for a particular product.

Capturing the Reader's Attention

Gaining the attention of the reader is essential in unsolicited or uninvited sales letters. In solicited sales letters, individuals have requested information; thus, attention-getting devices are less important.

Attention-getting devices are especially important in unsolicited sales letters.

Provocative messages or unusual typographical arrangements can be used to attract attention in unsolicited sales letters. These messages may be found within the body of a letter, or in place of the inside address.

Offer:	Your free calculator is just the beginning!
Product feature:	Your vacations—this year and in the future—can be more rewarding thanks to an exciting new book from National Geographic.
Inside-address opening:	We Wonder, Mrs. Crain, If You Would Be Interested In Losing 5 Pounds This Week
Startling statement:	Extinction is forever. That's why we need your help in preserving many of the world's endangered species.
Story:	On a beautiful late spring afternoon, twenty-five years ago, two young men graduated from the same college. They were very much alike, these two young men . . . . Recently, these men returned to their college for their 25th reunion. They were still very much alike . . . . But there was a difference. One of the men was manager of a small department of [a manufacturing] company. The other was its president.

Other effective openings include a bargain, a proverb, a solution to a problem, a quote from a famous person, an anecdote, or a question.

Appealing to the Reader

Persuasive appeals fall into two broad groups: emotional appeals and rational appeals. Emotional appeals are those associated with the senses; they include how we feel, see, taste, smell, and hear. Strategies that arouse anger, fear, pride, love, and satisfaction are emotional. Rational strategies are those associated with reason and intellect; they appeal to the mind. Rational appeals include references to making money, saving money, being more efficient, and making the best use of resources. In general, use rational appeals when a product is expensive, long-lasting, or important to health and security. Use emotional appeals when a product is inexpensive, short-lived, and nonessential.

Emotional appeals relate to the senses; rational appeals relate to reasoning and intellect.

Banks selling checking and savings services frequently use rational appeals. They emphasize saving money in checking fees, earning interest on accounts, receiving free personalized checks, and saving time in opening the account. A travel agency selling a student tour to the Mexican Riviera uses an emotional strategy by describing the "sun, fun, rockin' and partying" to be enjoyed. Many successful selling campaigns combine appeals, emphasizing perhaps a rational appeal while also including an emotional appeal in a subordinated position.

Emphasizing Central Selling Points

In your sales letters develop one or two central selling points and stress them.

Although a product may have a number of features, concentrate on just one or two of those features. Don't bewilder the reader with too much information. Analyze the reader's needs and fit your appeal directly to the reader. The letter selling a student tour to the Mexican Riviera emphasized two points:

1. **We see to it that you have a great time.** Let's face it. By the end of the semester, you've earned your vacation. The books and jobs and stress can all be shelved for a while.

2. **We keep our trips cheap.** Mazatlan 1A is again the lowest-priced adventure trip in the entire United States.

The writer analyzed the student audience and elected to concentrate on two appeals: (1) an emotional appeal to the senses (having a good time), and (2) a rational appeal to saving money (paying a low price).

Creating a Desire for the Product

In convincing readers to purchase a product or service, you may use a number of techniques:

THE WALL STREET JOURNAL

"It doesn't matter if the salesman convinced you — you just don't put aluminum siding on a castle, and that's that."

Source: From *The Wall Street Journal*. Reprinted with permission of the Cartoon Features Syndicate, Inc.

■ **Reader benefit.** Discuss product features from the reader's point of view. Show how the reader will benefit from the product.

> You will be able to extend your swimming season by using our new solar pool cover.

■ **Concrete language.** Use concrete words instead of general or abstract language.

> Our Mexican tour provides more than just a party. Maybe you've never set eyes on a giant 60-foot saguaro cactus . . . or parasailed 1,000 feet above the Pacific Ocean . . . or watched a majestic golden sunset from your own private island.

■ **Objective language.** Avoid language that sounds unreasonable. Overstatements using words like *fantastic, without fail, foolproof, amazing, astounding,* and so forth do not ring true. Overblown language and preposterous claims may cause readers to reject the entire sales message.

■ **Product confidence.** Build confidence in your product or service by assuring customer satisfaction. You can do this by offering a free trial, a money-back guarantee, a free sample, or by providing a guarantee or warranty. Another way to build confidence is to associate your product with respected references or authorities.

> Our concept of economical group travel has been accepted and sponsored by five city recreation departments. In addition, our program has been featured in *Sunset Magazine,* the *Los Angeles Times,* the *San Francisco Chronicle,* and the *Oakland Tribune.*

■ **Testimonials.** The statements of satisfied customers are effective in creating a desire for the product or service.

> A student returning from Mazatlan's cruise last year said, "I've just been to paradise."

Introducing Price Strategically

If product price is a significant sales feature, use it early in your sales letter. Otherwise, don't mention price until after you have created the reader's desire for the product. Some sales letters include no mention of price; instead, an enclosed order form shows the price. Other techniques for deemphasizing price include the following:

Introduce price early if it is a sales feature; otherwise, delay mentioning it.

1. **Show the price in small units.** Instead of stating the total cost of a year's subscription, state the magazine's price in terms of each issue. Describe insurance premiums in terms of their cost per day.

Price can be deemphasized by using one of these five techniques.

2. **Show how the reader is saving money by purchasing the product.** In selling solar heating units, for example, explain how much the reader will save on heating-fuel bills.

3. **Compare your prices with competitors'.** Describe the savings to be realized when your product is purchased.

4. **Make your price a bargain.** A special introductory offer is one third off the regular price, or the price includes a special discount if the reader acts immediately.

5. **Associate the price with reader benefits.** For example, "For as little as $3 a month, you'll enjoy emergency road and towing protection, accident insurance, emergency trip-interruption protection, and nine other benefits."

Stimulating Action

You can encourage the reader to act by applying one or more of these methods.

The closing of a sales letter has one very important goal: stimulating the reader to act. A number of techniques help motivate action:

- **Make the action clear.** Use specific language to tell exactly what is to be done.

  Fill out the enclosed postage-paid card.
  Call this toll-free number.
  Send the enclosed reservation card along with your check.

- **Make the action easy.**

  Just use the enclosed pencil to indicate the amount of your gift. Drop the postage-paid card in the mail, and we'll handle the details.

- **Offer an inducement.** Encourage the reader to act while low prices remain in effect. Offer a gift or a rebate for action.

  Now is a great time to join the Chevron Travel Club. By joining now, you'll receive a handsome black and gold-tone electronic calculator and a quartz pen-watch.

- **Limit the offer.** Set a specific date by which the reader must act in order to receive a gift, a rebate, benefits, low prices, or a special offer.

  Act quickly, because I'm authorized to make this special price on solar greenhouses available only until May 1.

- **Make payment easy.** Encourage the reader to send a credit-card number or to return a card and be billed later.

Examining Sales Letters

The letter shown in Figure 9.5 illustrates many of the sales techniques suggested here. It attracts the reader's attention by showing how much money can be saved on a checking account. This central selling feature is then developed throughout the letter, although other selling points are also mentioned. The bank's services are described with emphasis upon reader benefits. Finally, the reader is motivated to respond with a special incentive that requires immediate action.

The sales letter shown in Figure 9.6 fails to achieve its purpose for a number of reasons: it lacks a central selling point, it fails to develop reader benefits, and its language is vague. The cigars being sold obviously require an emotional appeal with a vivid description of the pleasures to be experienced from the pur-

---

Century Federal Bank

3200 East 30th Avenue, Eugene, OR 97405–3201

Marg Taylor
AVP & Manager
Personal Financial Center

April 3, 19xx

Mr. Frank Lawrence
1045 Redwood Drive
Eugene, OR 97431

Dear Mr. Lawrence:

Why pay $50, $100, or even $150 a year in checking account service charges when Century Federal has the right price for checking--FREE!

At Century Federal we want your business. That's why we're offering "Totally Free Checking." Compare the cost of your present checking account. We know you'll like the difference. We also have six other personalized checking plans, one of which is certain to be right for you.

In addition to the best price on checking accounts, we provide a variety of investment opportunities and two hassle-free credit-line programs. Once you qualify, you can use your credit line at any time without applying for a new loan each time you need money. With one of our credit-line programs, you can write a check for just about anything, including a vacation, home improvements, major purchases, unexpected medical bills, or investment opportunities.

If you have not yet heard about Century Federal, you'll find that we have eight convenient locations to serve you.

Check out the details of our services described in the enclosed pamphlets. Then check us out by stopping in to open your free checking account at one of our eight convenient locations. You can also open your account by simply filling out the enclosed postage-paid card and returning it to us.

If you open your Century Federal checking account before June 15, we'll give you 200 free checks and we'll buy back any unused checks you have from your present checking account. Act now to start saving money. We look forward to serving you.

Sincerely yours,

Marg Taylor

Marg Taylor
Accounts Vice President

mt:egh
Enclosures

Startling statement captures attention and sets up central selling point.

Emphasizes central selling point but also introduces other services.

Focuses on rational appeals.

Suggests specific reader benefits.

Makes it easy for reader to open account.

Offers incentive for action before given date.

Ineffective writing

FIGURE 9.6   Poor Sales Letter

Dear Sir:

Lackluster opening doesn't motivate reader to continue.

We have a cigar offer you can't refuse. If you enjoy a good cigar, read on.

We all remember when Cuba produced the only really good cigars. Since an embargo was placed on Cuban cigars, most of us genuine cigar-lovers have done without the traditional Cuban style of tobacco and cigar culture.

Fails to develop a central selling point.

Describes product in general language with few concrete references.

Well, now we're able to change all that. We'd like to send you our fine cigars that we think compare favorably with the finest cigars ever produced in Cuba. Our sampler contains an assortment of 42 unique cigars. Our factory-to-you distribution plan eliminates middleman delays, and you get your cigars when they are fresh.

Try them out. If you don't agree that these cigars are among the finest you've ever had the pleasure of smoking, we'll be happy to refund your money. You will, of course, have to return whatever cigars are left in your sampler to receive your refund.

Reader doesn't know how to respond.

Our sampler awaits your trial. Give these cigars a chance. One of our Corona Chicos will convince you that these are the finest cigars this side of Havana.

Sincerely,

---

chase of this product. However, this letter stresses the money-back guarantee for a sampler offer that is only partially explained. The letter also fails to develop confidence in the product and doesn't tell the reader how to respond to the sampler offer.

An improved version of this sales letter shown in Figure 9.7 illustrates considerable planning on the part of the writer. This letter is organized around the action to be taken (returning a card to receive a special sampler offer). It also concentrates on a central selling point (the unique Cuban-seed leaf tobacco), but it mentions other product features as well. The concrete language helps the reader envision the taste, feel, and smell of a fine cigar. The description of the raw materials and the production process builds confidence in the product, as does the money-back guarantee. The effective closing tells the reader how to respond easily and painlessly. An added stimulus to immediate action is the reference to a limited product supply in the last sentence.

〜

FIGURE 9.7   Sales Letter That Appeals to the Senses—Modified Block Style, Mixed Punctuation

The
GREAT SOUTHERN
TOBACCO COMPANY
Fine tobacco specialists

4439 Reynolds Boulevard ● Richmond, Virginia 23252 ● (212) 320-8711

July 11, 19xx

Mr. M. Sebastian Landon
3350 Bonsall Canyon
Malibu, CA 90265

Dear Mr. Landon:

You can enjoy a box of 42 custom-blended Cuban-seed leaf cigars--cigars that you can't buy in any store anywhere--by simply returning the mailing label on this letter.

I've taken the liberty of reserving in your name, Mr. Landon, one of our Sterling Sampler boxes of 42 fine cigars, including 8 Plaza, 8 Panetela Extras, 12 Juniors, 6 Directors, 4 Churchills, and 4 Corona Chicos. Try them out. Put them to your own test. Unless you're 100 percent satisfied, return the partially empty box for a <u>full</u> refund--and no questions will be asked!

We can make this remarkable offer because we have complete confidence in these unique cigars. Our peerless cigars are made from Pinar del Rio tobacco, formerly available only in Cuba. Smuggled out of Cuba, this priceless leaf tobacco is now grown to perfection in the Honduras by Cuban experts.

Our custom-blended cigars are made from tobacco crops that have enjoyed as much as four years of tender loving care from seed to cigar. When your sampler box arrives, break the seal and open it. Choose a cigar. Unwrap it. Smell it. Roll it gently between your thumb and forefinger, and feel the soft crinkle of expertly cured tobaccos.

Then light it up, savor the mellow aroma, and see how slowly, smoothly, and evenly it burns. Notice the silver-white ash, and see how long the ash grows before it drops--both signs of truly fine cigars.

The cigars that will fill your sampler box now reside in our temperature- and humidity-controlled humidor. Once we hear from you,

Attracts attention with special offer.

Plants reference to desired action early in letter.

Makes reader feel special with personalized reference.

Builds confidence in product with guarantee.

Emphasizes central selling point: the Cuban-seed leaf tobacco.

Concrete language appeals to senses of smell, touch, and sight.

Continues to build product interest with additional sensory appeals.

we'll remove them and ship them to you immediately. They'll arrive factory-fresh, in peak smoking condition, rather than spending four to six months in the distribution pipeline, as mass-produced cigars do.

Deemphasizes price and encourages immediate response.

Send no money now. Just return your mailing label in the postage-paid reply envelope. We'll send your Sterling Sampler of custom-blended Cuban-seed leaf cigars and bill you only $10.90, a savings of $3.63 on the regular per-cigar price. To avoid disappointment, return your mailing label today. Remember that there's a strict limit to the amount of top-quality tobacco produced; this offer can't be extended indefinitely.

Cordially yours,

Kendall J. Masters

Kendall J. Masters, President

Enclosures

The ability to persuade is a powerful and versatile communication tool. In this chapter you learned to apply the indirect strategy in writing claim letters, making requests, writing sales letters, and overcoming resistance to new ideas. The techniques suggested here will be useful in many other contexts beyond the writing of these business documents. You will find that logical organization of arguments is also extremely effective in expressing ideas orally.

In coming chapters you will learn how to modify and generalize the techniques of direct and indirect strategies in preparing goodwill messages as well as writing short and long reports.

APPLICATION AND PRACTICE—9

Discussion

1. Why is the ability to persuade a significant trait in both business and personal relations?

2. The organization of a successful persuasive claim centers upon the reasons and the closing. Why?

3. Should favor requests be written directly or indirectly? Discuss.

4. Why do individuals resist change?

5. Some individuals will never write an actual sales letter. Why is it important for them to learn the techniques for doing so?

6. How is a sales letter like a persuasive claim letter? How are they different?

Short Answers

7. In the indirect strategy, what should precede the big idea?

8. List at least four examples of favor requests.

9. Name at least eight items a salesperson should know about a product before attempting to sell it.

10. The most effective sales letters are sent to what kind of audience?

11. What is an unsolicited sales letter? Give an example.

12. What is a solicited sales letter? Give an example.

13. List at least five ways to gain a reader's attention in the opening of a sales letter.

14. In selling a product, when are rational appeals most effective?

   When are emotional appeals most effective?

15. Name six writing techniques that stimulate desire for a product.

Writing Improvement Exercises

Strategies.   For each of the following situations, check the appropriate writing strategy.

	Direct Strategy	Indirect Strategy
16. An appeal for a contribution to Children's World, a charity	_____	_____
17. An announcement that henceforth all dental, health, and life insurance benefits for employees will be reduced	_____	_____
18. A request to another company for personnel information regarding a job applicant	_____	_____
19. A letter to a painting contractor demanding payment for replacing ceramic floor tiles damaged by sloppy painters	_____	_____
20. A request for information about an oak desk and computer workstation	_____	_____
21. A letter to a grocery store asking for permission to display posters advertising a school fund-raising car wash	_____	_____

22. A request for a refund of the cost of a computer
    program that does not perform the functions it was
    expected to do   _____ _____

23. A request for a refund of the cost of a hair dryer
    that stopped working after a month's use (the hair
    dryer carries a one-year warranty)   _____ _____

24. An invitation to a prominent author to speak
    before a student rally   _____ _____

25. A memo to employees describing the schedule and
    selections of a new mobile catering service   _____ _____

CASE 9–1

Persuasive Request Letter

Analyze the following poorly written persuasive claim and list its major faults.
Outline an appropriate writing plan for a persuasive claim. After class
discussion, your instructor may ask you to rewrite this message, rectifying its
faults. Address your letter to International Copy Services, 1506 West Thomas
Road, Phoenix, Arizona 85013. Assume that you are writing on your company's
letterhead. Use block style.

Gentlemen:

   Our Regal compact system copier SP-270F has caused us nothing but
trouble since it was installed. It was purchased in September, and repairs
have been needed no less than five times since September. This means that
we have been without our copier at times when we desperately needed it.
Therefore, we want you to replace this copier that won't work and bring us
a new unit--or you can refund the amount that it cost when it was
purchased.

   Just after it was installed, the automatic document feeder jammed.
Your technician, after our telephone call, came out to promptly fix it. But
we still lost almost a day of copier use. It wasn't long before another repair
was needed. In October the document feeder jammed again, and our copies
were looking light in appearance. On October 12 your technician made a
replacement of parts in the document assembly; the toner apparatus was
also cleaned by him. This worked fine for five days. Next the collator
jammed. We tried different paper, as recommended by your technician, but
it still doesn't work well. In just four months of ownership, that copier
has required five repair calls. That means that we have been without a
copier a lot of the time. And we are very angry about the time and energy
required to have it serviced.

   We selected the Regal SP-270F copier because it promised automatic
document feeding, that two-sided copies could be made at once and it had
automatic collation and fast speed.

Ineffective writing

Attached please find a copy of our service record with this SP-270F copier. We believed your advertisement that said that Regal made "tough copiers for tough customers." Now I'm getting tough. Call me at 469-2900 immediately because I want action by February 1.

Angrily,

1. List at least five faults.

2. Outline a writing plan for a persuasive request.

CASE 9–2

Persuasive Request Memo

Imagine that you are Dan McMasters, president of Jelly Belly, Inc. The sales of your company's jelly beans have skyrocketed since Kevin King, star of a popular TV show, featured Jelly Bellies on his show. The big problem now is that you can't keep track of your inventories. You need to know how long your jelly beans have been on the shelves of your retailers so that you can replace the candy with fresh inventories when needed. Initially, you kept track of inventories by hand; then you moved to keypunched cards. However, sales are now so great that you can no longer keep adequate records. Your company cannot expand until you solve these inventory control and distribution problems. You believe that a computer-controlled system could be the answer.

However, Jane Braverton, manager of your Marketing Division, considers herself a people-oriented person, not a machine-oriented person. She's not keen on computers. Jane has been with the company since its inception. She's an excellent manager, and you want to keep her. You must convince her that automating inventory and distribution is essential if the business is to compete today and to grow in the future.

You want her to meet with you and Herman Goltz to begin the process of selecting and implementing a computer hardware and software package to help solve your problems. Since her division is greatly affected, you must have her cooperation. You will give her released time to learn about computer systems. You will work with her, and you will also hire consultants to help. You expect her department to run more efficiently after the system is installed. The overall workload for Jane and her staff should decrease.

Write a memo to Jane discussing your concerns. To get you started, answer these questions.

1. What is the big idea in this message?

2. What action do you want Jane to take?

3. What strategy should your memo follow?

4. What are some benefits that Jane will experience as a result of automating her division?

5. What objections do you expect Jane to have to your proposal?

6. What counterarguments can you offer to offset her anticipated objections?

CASE 9–3

Personal Persuasive Request

In your own work or organization experience, identify a situation where persuasion is necessary. Should a procedure be altered to improve performance? Would a new or different piece of equipment help you perform your work more efficiently? Do you want to work other hours or perform other tasks? Do you deserve a promotion?

Once you have identified a situation requiring persuasion, write a memo to your boss or organization head. Use actual names and facts. Employ the concepts and techniques in this chapter to help you convince your boss that your idea should prevail. Include concrete examples, anticipate objections, emphasize reader benefits, and end with a specific action to be taken.

CASE 9–4

Sales Letter Analysis

Select a one-page sales letter that you or a friend has received. (If you are unable to find one, your instructor may be able to help.) Read the letter carefully. Then answer the following questions.

1. At what audience is the letter aimed?

2. Is the appeal emotional or rational? Is the appeal effective? Explain.

3. What techniques capture the reader's attention?

4. Is the opening effective? Explain.

5. Is a central selling point emphasized? Explain.

6. Does the letter emphasize reader benefits? Explain.

7. List examples of concrete language.

8. How is confidence in the product or service developed?

9. How is price introduced?

10. What action is to be taken, and how is the reader motivated to take that action?

After class discussion, your instructor may ask you to write an improved version of this letter. Implement suggestions from this chapter.

CASE 9–5

Personal Sales Letter

Identify a situation in your own job or a previous job where a sales letter is needed. Using suggestions from this chapter, write an appropriate sales letter. Promote a product or service. Use actual names, information, and examples. Make your sales letter as realistic as possible.

Additional Problems

1. Assume you are office manager for First Federal Savings. You have noticed lately that employees are selling things in the office—one person is a cosmetics representative, another shows catalogs of shoes, and one is a part-time Tupperware distributor. You have observed that employees can get very involved in these transactions—on First Fed's time. What policy should the office adopt towards such salesmanship? Should you allow this selling? If so, when? Write a persuasive memo to the staff describing your position. Remember that you need their cooperation; you don't want to sound like a dictator.

2. Prepare a form letter (see Figure 10.12) that you will send to several local or national companies. Address it to the personnel director (by name, if possible). Persuade that individual to send you one or more sample copies of résumés that are typical in this field. Encourage the personnel director to mask any confidential information. Explain that you are interested in the format and content of the résumés since you will be applying for employment shortly. Mail the letters. Share with the class any responses you receive.

3. You are the business manager for Rudolpho's, a producer of gourmet ice cream. Rudolpho's has 12 ice cream parlors in the San Francisco area and a reputation for excellent ice cream. Your firm was approached by an independent ice cream vendor who wanted to use Rudolpho's name and

recipes for ice cream to be distributed through grocery stores and drugstores. As business manager, you worked with a law firm, Lancomb, Pereigni, and Associates, to draw up contracts regarding the use of Rudolpho's name and quality standards for the product. When you received the bill from Louis Lancomb, you couldn't believe it. The bill itemized 38 hours of attorney preparation, at $200 per hour, and 55 hours of paralegal assistance, at $50 per hour. The bill also showed $415 for telephone calls, which might be accurate because Mr. Lancomb had to converse with the Rudolpho's owners, who were living in Manila at the time. Write a persuasive letter to Mr. Lancomb. You doubt that an experienced attorney would require 38 hours to draw up the contracts in question. Perhaps some error was made in calculating the total hours. Moreover, you have checked with other businesses and found that excellent legal advice can be obtained for $150 per hour. Rudolpho's would like to continue using the services of Lancomb, Pereigni, and Associates for future legal business. Such future business is unlikely if an adjustment is not made on this bill. Write a persuasive request to Louis Lancomb, Attorney-at-Law, Lancomb, Pereigni, and Associates, 2690 Mission Street, San Francisco, CA 94103.

4. As Michelle Garcia, you are unhappy with the printer you recently purchased for your secretarial service. The salesperson promised that the Suki Multiwriter II could produce proportional spacing at near letter quality. The printer does produce 10- and 12-pitch spacing, but not proportional spacing. You particularly need proportional spacing for use on grant proposals that you prepare for a number of your clients. You have read the manual and can find no reference to proportional spacing. You have consulted a friend who is a programmer; he says that this printer is incapable of producing proportional printing. You are very angry because this product has been misrepresented and you have wasted so much time and energy trying to make it work. You decide to control your anger and write to the manufacturer explaining your complaint without being too harsh. You want your money back or a replacement printer that will work with your computer and your WordStar software program to generate proportional printing. Include your salesperson's name and a copy of the invoice. Write to Suki, Inc., Office Products Division, 15 Gardner Road, Fairfield, NJ 07006.

5. Your school has no internship program in your field. You realize that work experience is invaluable both to acquaint you with the field and to help you find employment. You write to Marvin Clarkson, personnel manager of The Selby Company, asking him to hire you as an intern. Although you're taking a full load of courses, you feel you could work 12 to 15 hours per week for one semester. You would have to arrange the internship hours around your existing class schedule. Describe your desire to function in a specific capacity, but express your willingness to serve wherever the company can accommodate you. Of course, you expect no remuneration, but you will be receiving up to 3 units of credit if Selby can take you for one semester. Write a persuasive letter to Marvin Clarkson, Personnel Manager, The Selby Company, 1901 San Antonio Avenue, Houston, TX 77027.

6. As employee relations manager of Blue Cross of California, one of your tasks is to promote Project H.E.L.P. (Higher Education Learning Program), an on-the-job learning opportunity. Project H.E.L.P. is a combined effort of major corporations and the Los Angeles Unified School District. You must find 12 employees who will volunteer as instructors for 50 or more students. The students will spend four hours a week at the Blue Cross Encino facility earning an average of five units of credit a semester. This semester the students will be serving in Medical Review Claims, Word Processing, Corporate Media Services, Library, and Administrative Support departments. Your task is to write a memo to the employees in these departments to encourage them to volunteer. They will be expected to supervise and instruct the students. Employees will receive two hours of released time per week to work with the students. The program has been very successful thus far. School officials, students, and employees alike express satisfaction with the experience and the outcomes. Write a persuasive memo with convincing appeals that will bring you 12 volunteers to work with Project H.E.L.P.

7. You are corresponding secretary of Alpha Psi Omega, your campus business honorary organization. For your installation banquet you have been instructed to invite Donald T. Brannock, personnel director, RWR Corporation, to speak. RWR is a large computer manufacturer in your city, and some graduates from your school are hired by RWR each year. Alpha Psi Omega members are interested in the changes that technology is creating in employment at RWR. They're also eager for advice on the kinds of entry-level jobs at RWR and the skills required for these positions. You know Mr. Brannock is busy, so you want to think of some way to make this invitation appealing. Because RWR encourages its executives to participate in community affairs, you might appeal to his organization's excellent record of civic involvement. By the way, you would also include Mrs. Brannock in this invitation. Provide details of the event. Write a favor request to Donald T. Brannock, Director, Personnel Services, RWR Corporation, 2931 Crosby Street, Stamford, CT 06926.

GRAMMAR/MECHANICS CHECKUP—9

Semicolon and Colon Use

Review Sections 2.16 through 2.19 in the Grammar/Mechanics Handbook. Then study each of the following statements. Insert any necessary punctuation. Use the delete sign (⌀) to omit unnecessary punctuation. In the space provided for each line, indicate the number of changes you made and record the number of the G/M principle(s) illustrated. (When you replace one punctuation mark with another, count it as one change.) If you make no changes, write 0. This exercise concentrates on semicolon and colon use, but you will also be responsible for correct comma use. When you finish, compare your responses with those shown below. If your responses differ, study carefully the specific principles shown in parentheses.

Example: The job of Mr. Wellworth is to make sure that his company   2   (2.16a)
has enough cash to meet its obligations; moreover, he is
responsible for locating credit when needed.

1. Short-term financing refers to a period of under one year long-term   _____
   financing on the other hand refers to a period of ten years or more.

2. Cash resulting from product sales does not come in until December   _____
   therefore our cash flow becomes critical in October and November.

3. We must negotiate short-term financing during the following months   _____
   September October and November.

4. Some of the large American corporations that offer huge amounts of   _____
   trade credit are: Ford Motor Company, General Electric Company,
   Gulf Oil Company, and USX Corp.

5. Although some firms rarely, if ever, need to borrow short-term   _____
   money; many businesses find that they require significant credit to
   pay for current production and sales costs.

6. A supermarket probably requires no short-term credit, a greeting card   _____
   manufacturer however typically would need considerable short-term
   credit.

7. We offer three basic types of credit open-book accounts promissory   _____
   notes and trade acceptances.

8. Speakers at the conference on credit include the following   _____
   businesspeople Sheridan Black financial manager Lytton Industries
   Miriam Minkoff comptroller Citibank and Mark Kendall legal
   counsel Security Federal Bank.

9. The prime interest rate is set by one or more of the nation's largest   _____
   banks and this rate goes up or down as the cost of money to the
   bank itself fluctuates.

10. Most banks are in business to lend money to commercial customers   _____
    for example retailers service companies manufacturers and
    construction firms.

11. Avionics, Inc. which is a small electronics firm with a solid credit   _____
    rating recently applied for a loan but First Federal refused the loan
    application because the bank was short on cash.

12. When Avionics, Inc., was refused by First Federal its financial   _____
    managers submitted applications to: Fidelity Trust, Farmers Mutual,
    and Mountain Federal.

13. The cost of financing capital investments at the present time is very   _____
    high therefore Avionics' managers may elect to postpone certain
    expansion projects.

_____ 14. If interest rates reach as high as 18 percent the cost of borrowing becomes prohibitive and many businesses are forced to reconsider or abandon projects that require financing.

_____ 15. Several investors decided to pool their resources then they could find attractive investments.

1. (3) year; financing, hand, (*2.03, 2.16b*)   3. (3) months: September, October, (*2.10, 2.17a*)
5. (1) money, (*2.06a, 2.16b*)   7. (3) credit: accounts, notes, (*2.01, 2.17a*)   9. (1) banks, (*2.05*)
11. (3) Inc., rating, loan; (*2.06c, 2.16c*)   13. (2) high; therefore, (*2.16*)   15. (1) resources; (*2.16b*)

CHAPTER 10

Special Messages

In this chapter you will learn to do the following:

- Recognize opportunities for writing goodwill messages.
- Appreciate how special messages can build goodwill.

- Write letters of appreciation, congratulations, and sympathy.
- Write letters of recommendation and introduction.

This chapter includes a diverse group of special messages that require you to adapt the strategies and writing techniques you have learned in previous chapters. Some of the messages convey personal goodwill, and others carry business information of a special nature. None of them has a specific writing plan. You will find, as you progress in your development of the craft of writing, that you are less dependent on writing plans to guide you. Although you will not be provided with detailed writing plans, we will point out similarities between situations and make suggestions regarding appropriate strategies. This chapter will be helpful not only for its opportunities to adapt strategies but also for the models provided.

Goodwill Letters

Goodwill letters carry good wishes, warm feelings, and sincere thoughts to friends, customers, and employees. These are letters that do not *have* to be written—and often are not written for a number of reasons. Because these letters are not urgent and because words do not come readily to mind, it's easy for writers to procrastinate. Writers may feel an urge to express thanks or congratulations or sympathy, but they put it off until the moment passes. Then it's too late. Yet, there's hardly an individual who doesn't appreciate receiving sincere thanks or words of congratulations. It is human nature to desire social approval: we want to be accepted, remembered, consoled, appreciated, and valued. Although busy or unsure business writers may avoid writing goodwill letters, these messages are worth the effort because they gratify both senders and receivers and because they fulfill important human needs.

Greeting cards and commercial thank-you notes provide ready-made words, but they fail to express personal thoughts. When you receive a card, what do you read first—the printed words of the card maker or the penned-in remarks of the

Letters that convey social approval satisfy deep human needs for both the sender and the receiver.

sender? The personal sentiments of the sender are always more expressive and more meaningful to the reader than is the printed message.

Goodwill messages are most effective when they are immediate, spontaneous, sincere, and personal. They should follow a direct strategy.

1. Identify the situation.

2. Include specific detail and personal thoughts.

3. Close with a forward-looking thought or a concluding remark.

Letters of Appreciation

Extend thanks and show appreciation when someone has done you a favor or whenever an action merits praise. Letters of appreciation may be written to cus-

Source: *The Wall Street Journal*. Reprinted with permission of the Cartoon Features Syndicate, Inc.

FIGURE 10.1 Appreciation for a Customer's Business

Dear Mrs. Panko:

Staffing your organization with temporary office workers for the past six years has been our pleasure, and we are grateful for your business.

Holidays are excellent opportunities for goodwill greetings.

As we begin the new year, I want you to know, Mrs. Panko, that you may continue to count on us for temporaries who are as productive as your permanent personnel. As a regular user of our services, you know how cost-effective it is to keep a lean staff, calling on us to help you fill in with temporaries during peak periods and for special projects.

Thank you for allowing us to send you our qualified temporaries. We appreciate the confidence you have shown in our agency for these past six years, and we look forward to at least six more years of mutually profitable dealings.

Sincerely,

tomers for their business, to hosts and hostesses for their hospitality, to colleagues for jobs well done, and to individuals for kindnesses performed. (See Figures 10.1, 10.2, and 10.3.)

Letters of Congratulations

Letters of congratulations deliver recognition for special events, such as a promotion, appointment, award, graduation, or significant honor, and also mark personal events, such as an engagement, marriage, anniversary, or birth. These messages contain warmth, approval, and praise. Avoid mechanical phrases like "Congratulations on your promotion. You certainly deserve it." Try to include personal references and specific details that make your thoughts different from the bland and generalized expressions in greeting cards. Often brief and conver-

Personalized references and details about the individual distinguish good congratulatory messages from commercial cards.

~~~

FIGURE 10.2   Letter of Appreciation for Favor

Dear Ms. Blankenship:

Your excellent guided tour of the Communications Services Center at Warner Labs was the highlight of the semester for our class.

This thank-you letter goes to the employee but a photocopy goes to her supervisor.

Your lucid description of the Center's operations and equipment enabled our business communications class to better understand some of the technical applications in this field. We very much appreciated, Ms. Blankenship, learning how authors originate letters and reports using your Dextran central dictation system. Equally interesting was the flow of these documents through the entire production cycle. Your careful preparation for our group and your painstaking organization of the tour schedule allowed our class to see numerous operations in a short time. Many students commented on your enthusiastic and knowledgeable presentation.

Give the reader the spotlight by concentrating on his or her accomplishments.

Our trip to Warner was entertaining and instructive. We enjoyed the modern interior design, the "urban Eden" of indoor plants and trees, the colorful artwork and furniture, and the lovely employee lounges. Most importantly, though, we appreciated your tour because it helped bridge the gap between classroom information and real-world applications in the field of communications.

Sincerely,

pc* Mrs. Carmen Sevelas
    Manager, Communication Services

---

*pc means "photocopy" and replaces the carbon copy notation (cc).

≈

FIGURE 10.3   Letter of Appreciation for Hospitality

Dear Professor and Mrs. Shelton:

Thank-you letters generally refer to the fine food, warm hospitality, and good company provided.

Thanks for inviting me and the other members of our business club to your home for dinner last Saturday.

The warm reception you gave us made the evening very special. Your gracious hospitality, the delicious dinner served in a lovely setting, and the lively discussion following dinner all served to create an enjoyable evening that I will long remember.

We appreciate the opportunity you provided for us students to become better acquainted with each other and with you.

Sincerely,

sational, congratulatory letters may be handwritten or typed. If a news clipping announced the good news, it's a nice touch to attach the article to your congratulatory letter.

Successful administrators build cordial employee relations by writing personal letters of appreciation and congratulations (see Figure 10.4).

≈

FIGURE 10.4   Letter Congratulating Employee on Promotion

Dear Pam:

I am delighted to hear of your promotion to the position of supervisor of Reprographics. It seems only yesterday that you were an inexperienced part-time assistant who came to my office with excellent skills, bubbling enthusiasm, and a desire to succeed.

We missed you when you left our department, but we take great pride in your accomplishments and wish you every success in your new position.

Sincerely,

Letters of Sympathy

Grief is easier to bear when we know others care. Whatever the misfortune, show your concern with sympathetic words. Depending upon the situation, express the loss that you feel, console the reader, and extend your willingness to help in any way possible. Recognize virtues in the loved one and assure the reader that he or she is not alone in this unhappy moment. If you need ideas regarding what to say in a message of sympathy, examine the model here. Inspiration can also be gleaned from the thoughts expressed in commercially prepared cards. Study the cards, adapt some of the ideas, and then write your own individual message.

Figure 10.5 shows a letter written by a manager to a division secretary who lost her husband.

Probably the hardest of all letters to write are those of sympathy; here are suggestions on what to include.

~~

Special Information Letters

Another group of special letters employing the direct strategy includes messages that introduce individuals, ask for recommendations, and offer recommendations.

Letter of Introduction

On occasion, a letter of introduction, such as the one in Figure 10.6, is helpful to expedite social or business activities or to reduce red tape, especially when an individual is far from home. Such letters establish a person's character or status and are supported by the writer's character or status. They may be written for friends, employees, or business acquaintances. In a letter of introduction, (1) identify your relationship, (2) explain why you are writing, (3) request help, and (4) express appreciation.

A letter of introduction should do four things: (1) identify the writer's relationship with the subject, (2) explain the reason for writing, (3) ask for assistance, and (4) convey thanks.

~~

FIGURE 10.5 Letter of Sympathy

Dear Jane,

We were deeply saddened to learn of your loss. Although words are seldom adequate to express sympathy, I want you to know that I count myself among your many friends who share your grief and understand the profound loss that you are experiencing.

Henry's kind nature, his patience, and his devotion to you were apparent to all. He will be missed. If there is any way that we may ease your sorrow, you know that we are here.

Sincerely,

≈

FIGURE 10.6   Letter of Introduction

Dear Fred:

Miss Natalie Kienzler, the daughter of one of my closest friends, will soon be moving to Hartford. Natalie just graduated from Lane Community College in Eugene, Oregon, and she seeks employment in a law firm.

As an attorney in Hartford, Fred, you may have some suggestions for her when she arrives and begins her job search. I've given her your telephone number and encouraged her to call you.

You have my sincere appreciation for any assistance you can extend to Natalie.

Cordially,

Letter Requesting Recommendation

When individuals apply for employment, for admission to special programs, or for acceptance into some social organizations, recommendations may be requested. For example, if Ron Twersky were applying for a job, he might be asked to supply the names of individuals who could provide information about his work experience, skills, and character. These individuals might then be sent forms to fill out regarding Ron. Some organizations might request that they write letters in support of Ron's application.

When you ask for a letter of recommendation, provide a "brag sheet."

Before listing individuals as references, always ask their permission. This is not only courteous but also prudent. By offering an opportunity to accept or refuse, applicants can find individuals who will write favorable recommendations. A word of encouragement to applicants: don't hesitate to request recommendations from instructors. Part of their duty involves helping students find employment. You can help by providing information about yourself: a résumé, data sheet, or "brag sheet." Indicate what characteristics or facts you think are important.

Figure 10.7 shows a letter asking for permission to list an instructor as a reference.

Letter of Recommendation

As you progress in your career, you may be asked to write letters of recommendation. Such letters typically fall into two categories: general recommendations and employment recommendations.

General recommendations may be written to nominate individuals for awards, to support applications for memberships in societies, or to admit indi-

~~~

FIGURE 10.7   Letter Requesting Recommendation Permission

Dear Professor Earle:

I am now completing my course work at Heald Business College, and I plan to begin looking for employment in the merchandising field.

Your course in retail merchandising was my introduction to the field, and your instruction provided an excellent background in this career area. Because you know this field well and because you also know my work as a student, may I use your name as a reference when I apply for employment? I am enclosing a fact sheet that lists information that may be helpful to you when you write about me.

I am grateful to you both for the excellent foundation you provided in merchandising and for any help you can provide in my job search. I have enclosed a postage-paid card on which you can indicate your willingness to serve as a reference.

Sincerely,

Never list an individual as a reference unless you ask permission first.

---

viduals to special programs. Employment recommendations are written to support applications for employment.

Writers of recommendations, of course, must be truthful. Even though recommendations are expected to show an applicant in the best light, they should not be false or deceptive. If you are asked to write a recommendation, do so only for individuals about whom you can speak positively. If you have doubts about an individual's personal or professional qualifications or if you feel that you do not know the applicant well enough to write convincingly, refuse to complete a recommendation. Encourage the applicant to find a reference who can write knowledgeably and enthusiastically.

Write letters of recommendation only for individuals you can truthfully support.

Once you accept an invitation to write a recommendation, ask the applicant to supply you with personal and professional data. Request a data sheet or a resume, and ask what information the applicant wants emphasized.

In a general letter of recommendation, consider the following suggestions:

1. Identify the reason for writing.
2. Suggest the confidentiality of the recommendation.
3. Establish your relationship with the applicant.
4. Describe the applicant's professional and personal qualities.
5. Describe the applicant's relations with others.

To write a complete letter of recommendation, include these ten topics.

6. Include specific details and examples that illustrate the applicant's personality and performance.

7. Compare the applicant with others in his or her field.

8. Offer an overall rating of the applicant.

9. Summarize the significant attributes of the applicant.

10. Draw a conclusion regarding the recommendation.

~~~

FIGURE 10.8   General Letter of Recommendation

TO: Awards Selection Committee   DATE: April 12, 19xx

FROM: Cinda Skelton, Manager *C.S.*
            Information Services

SUBJECT: RECOMMENDATION OF KELLY MCKINLEY

Identifies reason for writing.

It is with great pleasure that I recommend Kelly McKinley for the Employee of the Year award.

Establishes relationship with applicant.

Kelly has been employed by First National Bank in the Word Processing Division for nearly five years. For the past three years, I have been able to observe her performance carefully when she worked first as Senior Correspondence Secretary and later as Lead Correspondence Secretary in my division.

Describes candidate's skills and professional accomplishments with specific details.

Kelly's excellent language skills and keyboarding ability enable her to turn out documents rapidly and accurately. Because of her superior skills in transcribing dictated material, she is in great demand. Kelly also demonstrates genuine interest in and aptitude for the many kinds of equipment she has been required to operate. She is so knowledgeable that I asked her to serve on the selection committee when a new word processing system was reviewed recently. While serving on this committee, Kelly suggested a new method for coding and distributing work to our correspondence secretaries. Using Kelly's plan, the secretaries now enjoy greater variety in their work tasks and the supervisor can track the distributed tasks more efficiently.

Describes personal attributes.

In addition to her keyboarding, transcribing, and problem-solving skills, Kelly interacts well with her superiors and with her fellow workers. Her sunny disposition, flexible attitude, and cheerful outlook make her a very pleasant person with whom to work.

Compares candidate with others in her field and offers an overall rating.

I rank Kelly among the top 2 percent of all the employees I've ever supervised. Her skills are outstanding; her work, excellent; and her attitude, exemplary. Few employees have ever deserved to be named Employee of the Year more than Kelly McKinley.

The letter in Figure 10.8 was written to recommend an employee for an award. This letter implements all of the preceding suggestions except one: it does not mention confidentiality. In this instance, the writer did not consider her comments to be private or personal; she would not object if her letter were shown to others or published.

Letters of recommendation regarding employment are similar to general letters of recommendation. They not only cover the ten topics described earlier but also may include information relating to length of employment, job duties, and career potential.

Writers of letters of recommendation, particularly those letters that affect employment and future careers, should be aware of privacy rights legislation passed in the 1970s. Written to protect individuals' rights of access to their records, these laws and subsequent court interpretations open files that were once confidential. Job applicants may now read letters written about themselves, unless they choose to waive their rights.

Despite the restrictions that writers may feel, letters of recommendation are still useful in the employment process. Because such letters describe a candidate's experience and qualifications, they help personnel officers match capable candidates with positions appropriate to their abilities.

Letters of recommendation must be specific to be helpful. The letter shown in Figure 10.9 is ineffective because it presents little more than generalities. It describes the candidate as "responsible, creative, industrious, and cooperative." Such abstract words create a positive attitude toward the candidate, but they do not help a personnel officer place this candidate in a position suited to his skills and talents.

> **Letters of recommendation are most helpful when they illustrate a candidate's abilities and experience.**

An improved version of this recommendation for Christopher Davis, shown in Figure 10.10, gives specific information. The letter illustrates the candidate's sense of responsibility by describing his willingness to work overtime when necessary. The writer also uses actual examples to show how the candidate is creative, industrious, and cooperative. In addition to using specific incidents and details, notice how this effective letter illustrates the suggestions given earlier regarding appropriate content in a letter of recommendation.

〜〜〜

FIGURE 10.9   Letter of Recommendation That Lacks Specifics

Ineffective writing

Dear Mr. Winfield:

I am happy to recommend Mr. Christopher Davis. In his work for us, he was an able technician. He was responsible, creative, industrious, and cooperative. Once in a while he was late, but we understood why.

If I may be of further service, please call upon me.

Sincerely,

≈

FIGURE 10.10   Effective Employment Letter of Recommendation—Modified Block Style, Mixed Punctuation

◁ ZANTROL, INC.

◀ 3410 Pocahontas Parkway · Richmond, Virginia
23260-2420   (237) 593-4391

June 4, 19xx

Mr. James Winfield
Personnel Manager
Colonial Investment Corp.
P.O. Box 3450
Petersburg, VA 23260-3410

Dear Mr. Winfield:

Establishes reason for writing and confidentiality of message.   Mr. Christopher Davis, whom your organization is considering for a systems programmer position, asked me to submit confidential information on his behalf.

Reveals relationship of writer to applicant.   I supervised Mr. Davis for the past two years when he worked as a part-time microcomputer technician in the Computer Users Center of our executive headquarters. In assisting employees learn to operate microcomputers and solve their problems, he demonstrated computer expertise and creativity.

Includes specific examples of applicant's work to illustrate work habits and capabilities.

Attempts to present a fair picture of the applicant's qualities but deemphasizes negative traits.   His knowledge of computers and computer systems enabled him to work with our systems engineer in developing a local area network to link computers and share resources. Our programmers, systems engineers, and users alike considered Mr. Davis to be helpful, reliable, knowledgeable, and responsible. Although he sometimes had difficulty getting to our offices on time because of his classes at John Tyler Community College, he was always willing to work overtime whenever we needed him to complete a project.

Compares applicant with others in his field, offers an overall rating, and summarizes significant attributes.   Mr. Davis accepted direction easily but could also work independently when necessary. For example, when I asked him to organize our software storage, he did a good job without supervision. Of all the microcomputer technicians we have employed, I consider Mr. Davis to be among the top third. In his work for us, he demonstrated computer proficiency and a cooperative attitude. We admired his perseverance and work ethic, for it's not always easy to maintain a job while attending college.

It is a pleasure to recommend Mr. Davis, and I feel certain that he will be successful as a systems programmer.

Sincerely,

Maynard C. Young

Maynard C. Young
Operations Manager

rtt

When you leave a job, ask for a letter of recommendation. Even if you are not immediately applying for other employment, solicit a recommendation from your supervisor so that you will have references available when you need them. Too often, supervisors change jobs or businesses relocate, leaving former employees without contacts. An undirected letter of recommendation, as shown in Figure 10.11, begins with a general salutation.

FIGURE 10.11   Undirected Letter of Recommendation

To Prospective Employers:

Tammy DuPre was employed as a sales representative on our staff from June 1985 through June 1987. When she completed her bachelor's degree in 1987, she left our company to seek full-time employment in the Chicago area.

Ms. DuPre developed fine selling skills in the two years she sold our full line of Rave cosmetics. Twice she received bonuses for sales exceeding her assigned goal. She exercised initiative in organizing her territory, using her computer to maintain a data base of customers. Ms. DuPre was particularly effective in selling our line of makeup during holiday periods and over the summer.

She was reliable, honest, and hardworking, rarely missing a sales meeting or a report deadline. Of all the sales representatives we have employed, I would rank Ms. DuPre among the top 15 percent. We would be happy to hire her again, were she to apply.

Sincerely,

Draws conclusion regarding applicant's potential.

Ask for an undirected letter of recommendation when you leave a job.

≈

Form and Guide Letters

Form letters are prewritten, printed messages used to deliver repetitious and routine information. To save the expense of composing, transcribing, and printing individual letters, many organizations prepare standardized form letters for recurring situations. Form letters contain blanks for such variables as names and addresses, dates, balances, and other specific data. Form letters are efficient for sales messages, personnel policy announcements, procedural explanations for customers and suppliers, order acknowledgments, and other repetitive information.

Guide letters are individually typed, but they are composed of prewritten sentences and paragraphs.

Guide letters use prewritten sentences and paragraphs but, unlike form letters, are individually typed. Although somewhat more personalized, guide letters serve the same functions as form letters. Insurance companies, for example, send thousands of guide letters to policyholders to answer routine questions regarding their coverage. Rather than compose individual responses, company representatives select appropriate paragraphs from a book of ready-made answers and instruct a transcriptionist to use these paragraphs in preparing a letter on word processing equipment.

When used properly, form and guide letters are efficient and cost-effective.

Form and guide letters unquestionably save time and money. Well-written, repetitive messages used appropriately are expedient and accepted by readers. Poorly written or misused letters, on the other hand, are doubly offensive. Readers' feelings are hurt because they are treated mechanically, and they are also confused because a letter did not apply to them or did not answer their questions.

Word processing equipment makes the preparation and processing of form and guide letters simple. If you decide to use this means of delivering messages, follow these guidelines:

- Be certain that your form and guide letters are appropriate to the situation for which they will be used.

- Compose your letters so that they are responsive and yet require insertion of a minimum number of variables.

- Test your form and guide letters over a long period to see if they are effective.

- Revise your letters based on reader reactions.

The guide letter in Figure 10.12 shows how repetitive messages can be tailored to individual circumstances by inserting variable data in the places provided. Word processing equipment merges a shell document with variable data to produce personalized letters quickly and economically.

~~~

FIGURE 10.12   Repetitive Letter With Variables

(Name) _____

(Address) _____

_____

Dear _____ :

We appreciate your interest in our English/American study program offered to Japanese students. The enclosed pamphlet describes the program in detail and shows pictures of students who have participated in the past.

In brief, our organization, Connections International, supplies transportation, tours, and cultural/social programs for Japanese students coming to California to study the English language and American culture.

Our next group is scheduled to arrive _____ , and the tentative cost is _____ per student per week. This payment covers transportation, travel, and entertainment as outlined in the enclosed pamphlet. An advance payment of _____ at least three weeks in advance of departure is required. This payment is necessary in order to set the program in operation, retain the proper vehicles, and make necessary hotel and lodging reservations. This deposit will be deducted from the total payment for the group.

Thank you very much for considering the cultural immersion programs of Connections International. We look forward to providing warm and rewarding experiences for your students.

Sincerely,

APPLICATION AND PRACTICE—10

Discussion

1. Why do we frequently put off writing goodwill letters?

2. Why write a letter of sympathy or congratulations when a greeting card will accomplish the same end?

3. Under what circumstances would a letter of introduction be appropriate?

4. Why should an applicant ask permission before listing an individual's name as a reference?

5. As a means of screening candidates, are letters of recommendation a valid source of information?

Short Answers

6. In goodwill messages the writer typically covers what three areas?

7. Name three instances when letters of appreciation are appropriate.

8. Why should a copy of a letter of appreciation be sent to an employee's supervisor?

9. What four kinds of information or topics can you include in a letter of sympathy?

10. Name three instances when letters of recommendation, other than for employment, might be written.

11. What is a "brag sheet"?

12. List ten suggestions regarding information to be included in a letter of recommendation.

1. Identify reason for writing

2. Suggest the confidentiality of it.

3. ESTABLISH RELATIONSHIP w/ employee

4. Employees personal & professional qualifications. [specific areas of focus requested?]

5. Describe applicant's relations w/ others.

6. Include specifics, examples, incidents to illustrate #4 & 5

7. Compare employee to others w/ others — scale

8. Overall RATING — summary & significant attributes

#9.

9D. Final conclusion regarding applicant — hirability. How highly recommended.

13. In addition to the preceding topics, letters of recommendation for employment should include what extra information?

14. How can the writer of a letter of recommendation avoid generalities?

15. Most goodwill letters would follow which strategy, direct or indirect?

CASE 10–1

Employment Recommendation

Assume that you are Ross Neil, manager of Builder's City. Alan B. Khory, one of your favorite department managers, has now completed his college education and will be leaving the store. Mr. Khory asks you to write a recommendation for him to enter a management trainee program for a large retailer. You know that he is a quiet, unassertive individual; but he has been an excellent hardware manager for you these past three years.

You ask Mr. Khory to refresh your memory about his performance at Builder's City. He reminds you that he started as a clerk and became department manager at the Winnetka store within six months, while at the same time working toward a college degree. His department has five employees. Within his department he tried to streamline operations. He reduced crowded displays so that the store wasn't so cluttered. He tried to increase inventory turnarounds so that fewer duplicate items were stored in the retail display area. He solved some problems that increased sales and, of course, increased profits. When the new computerized inventory system was introduced, he was very interested in it; his department was operational long before some others.

You feel that Mr. Khory has been one of your most enterprising and responsible department managers. You hate to lose him, but you can understand his desire to achieve his long-term goal in administrative management. In your letter you want to show that he has those traits that are necessary to be a good manager. Your opinion is that he will be an excellent management trainee. Instead of saying that Mr. Khory is able to solve problems and possesses initiative, you want to show how he demonstrates these qualities. You also want to present a fair picture. You feel that you should mention that Mr. Khory is quiet, though he gets along well both with customers and with those employees that he supervises. He was, after all, responsible for training all new employees hired for the hardware department. He was also responsible for planning a work schedule that kept the employees happy and provided adequate sales coverage.

Before you begin writing this letter of recommendation, outline a plan. The information presented here is unorganized and poorly expressed. Improve it. Add any realistic data necessary to create a good letter. Conclude your letter with a statement regarding the potential success of Mr. Khory. Use block style. Address your letter to Ms. Jane Bennett, Personnel Director, Federated Stores, Inc., 3900 East Carson Street, Long Beach, CA 90808.

CASE 10-2

Letter of Appreciation

You are genuinely appreciative of the care shown by Eleanore Chu, R.N., for your bedridden mother over the past two years. You decide to send her a box of chocolates and the following note.

Dear Eleanore:

Thanks for everything you have done for Mother. We really appreciate your visits over the past two years. You helped us through some very difficult times. Thanks again for your help.

Most sincerely,

Then you reconsider. You decide to write a longer letter that expresses your gratitude and also lets her employer know what an outstanding employee she is. Here are some facts you should include in your letter. Nurse Chu not only took care of your mother's medical needs but also taught you how to care for your mother. She was enthusiastic and always had lots of cheerful conversation; everyone felt better when she visited. She made suggestions and even gave you demonstrations of professional techniques for easing your mother's discomfort. The entire family appreciated Ms. Chu's compassion and concern for your mother. She visited for two years. During that time your mother's condition improved, and now it has stabilized. You feel that she is an extraordinary nurse and an excellent representative of her employer, HomeCare, Inc.

Write the letter to Eleanore Chu, R.N., HomeCare, Inc., 2105 East Henrietta Road, Rochester, NY 14620. Use a modified block style. Add any necessary information. Be sure that her employer, Dr. Chandler H. Alexander, President, HomeCare, Inc., is informed of your praise.

CASE 10–3

Letter of Sympathy

Assume that the spouse of a colleague or friend has died. Write a letter of sympathy. Include enough detail to make your letter significantly different from greeting card messages.

CASE 10–4

Letter of Appreciation

Write a letter of appreciation to your boss (supervisor, manager, vice president, president, or chief executive officer) and his or her spouse. Assume that you and other members of your immediate staff were entertained at an elegant dinner during the winter holiday season. Include specific details that make your letter personal, sincere, and concrete.

CASE 10–5

Request for Recommendation

Write to an instructor or a previous employer asking for permission to use that individual as a reference.

CASE 10–6

Letter of Recommendation

Assume that you are the manager of a department where you now work (or previously worked). Write a letter of recommendation for an employee of your choice. Assume that this individual is leaving the company and wants to take a letter of recommendation. Use as much factual data as possible, but fill in from your imagination if necessary. If you are not working at present, interview a fellow student. Assume that you are the student's instructor; write a letter of recommendation for the student.

Additional Problems

1. As corresponding secretary of Alpha Psi Omega, campus business honorary organization, write to Donald T. Brannock, thanking him for the informative and entertaining talk he presented at the installation banquet (see Chapter 9, page 220, Additional Problem No. 7). Provide details. Send to the RWR employee newsletter a copy of your letter and a photograph of Mr. Brannock delivering his speech before your group.

2. Dirk Sondberg, a part-time worker in your department for the past three years, has just completed the requirements for a B.S. in accounting. Although he will probably be leaving, you are very happy for him. Write a letter of congratulations.

3. The mother of one of your coworkers died after a lengthy illness. Death was inevitable, but your friend was devastated. Write a letter of condolence.

4. One of your instructors has been nominated for a teaching award. Selected students have been asked to write letters in support of the nomination. Write a letter recommending an instructor of your choice to Professor Thomas Watkins, Teaching Award Committee, School of Business.

5. As office manager of the law firm of Ernst, Katz, and Ernst, you have been asked to write a letter describing the service of Wendy White, who is moving to another city with her husband. Wendy has been a fine legal secretary, and you are happy to accommodate her. Since she has not asked you to address the letter to a specific individual, write an undirected letter of recommendation.

6. After finishing the course of instruction at your school, you have taken a job in your field. One of your instructors was especially helpful to you when you were a student. This instructor also wrote an effective letter that was instrumental in helping you obtain your job. Write a letter thanking your instructor.

7. Write a form or guide letter to selected students at your college. These students have filled out applications to graduate, but a computer search of their records indicates that they are missing some requirement. Leave a blank space to fill in the missing requirement(s). Tell these students that a mistake may have been made; perhaps their records have an error or are not up to date. Regardless, the students must come in for a conference with a records officer. Since time is limited, the conferences have already been scheduled. Leave a blank space for the date of the conference to be filled in for each student.

GRAMMAR/MECHANICS CHECKUP—10

Possessives

Review Sections 2.20 to 2.22 in the Grammar/Mechanics Handbook. Then study each of the following statements. Underscore any inappropriate form. Write a correction in the space provided and record the number of the G/M principle illustrated. If a sentence is correct, write *C*. When you finish, compare your responses with those provided below. If your answers differ, study carefully the principles shown in parentheses.

Example: In just two <u>years</u> time, the accountants and managers devised   years' _____
an entirely new system.

1. Two supervisors said that Mr. Wilsons work was excellent.   _____

2. In less than a years time, the offices of both attorneys were moved.   _____

———————————— 3. None of the employees in our Electronics Department had taken more than two weeks vacation.

———————————— 4. All the secretaries agreed that Ms. Lanhams suggestions were practicable.

———————————— 5. After you obtain your boss approval, send the application to Personnel.

———————————— 6. We tried to sit at our favorite waitress station, but all her tables were filled.

———————————— 7. Despite Harold grumbling, his wife selected two bonds and three stocks for her investments.

———————————— 8. The apartment owner requires two months rent in advance from all applicants.

———————————— 9. Four companies buildings were damaged in the fire.

———————————— 10. In one months time we hope to be able to complete all the address files.

———————————— 11. Only one ladies car had its engine running.

———————————— 12. One secretaries desk will have to be moved to make way for the computer.

———————————— 13. Several sellers permits were issued for two years.

———————————— 14. Marks salary was somewhat higher than David.

———————————— 15. Lisas job in accounts receivable ends in two months.

---

1. Mr. Wilson's (*2.20a, 2.21*)   3. weeks' (*2.20b*)   5. boss's (*2.20b*)   7. Harold's (*2.22*)
9. companies' (*2.20b*)   11. lady's (*2.20a*)   13. sellers' (*2.20b*)   15. Lisa's (*2.20a*)

Expanding Communication Skills

CHAPTER 11

Informal Reports

In this chapter you will learn to do the following:

- Gather data from four primary sources to write informal business reports.
- Organize report data deductively or inductively.
- Present data objectively to gain credibility.
- Write information and recommendation reports.
- Write justification and progress reports.
- Write proposals and minutes of meetings.
- Write summaries and to-file reports.

In addition to letters and memos, reports play a significant role in delivering information within and among organizations. You can learn to write good reports by examining basic techniques and by analyzing appropriate models. In this chapter we'll concentrate on informal reports. These reports tend to be short (usually under ten pages), they use memo or letter format, and they are personal in tone.

Informal reports are relatively short (under ten pages) and are usually written in memo or letter format.

Eight Kinds of Informal Reports

In this chapter we'll consider eight categories of informal reports frequently written in business. In many instances the boundaries of the categories overlap; distinctions are not always clear-cut. Individual situations, goals, and needs may make one report take on some characteristics of a report in another category. Still, these general categories help beginning writers get started. They are presented here in a brief overview. Later in the chapter they will be illustrated and discussed in more detail.

- **Information reports.** Reports that collect and organize information are informative or investigative. They may record routine activities, such as daily, weekly, and monthly reports of sales or profits. They may investigate options, performance, or equipment. Although they provide information, they do not analyze that information.

- **Recommendation reports.** Recommendation reports are similar to informative reports in that they present information. However, they offer analysis in addition to data. They attempt to solve problems by evaluating options and offering recommendations. These reports are solicited; that is, the writer has been asked to investigate and report.

- **Justification reports.** Like recommendation reports, justification reports attempt to solve problems. However, they are unsolicited; that is, the writer generates the report on his or her own. He or she observes a problem, analyzes alternatives, and describes a plan to solve the problem.

- **Progress reports.** Progress reports monitor the headway of unusual or nonroutine activities. For example, progress reports would keep management informed about a committee's preparations for a trade fair 14 months from now. Such reports usually answer three questions: (1) Is the project on schedule? (2) Are corrective measures needed? (3) What activities are next?

Reports that provide data are informational; reports that draw conclusions and make recommendations are analytical.

- **Proposals.** A proposal is an offer to perform a service, sell a product, investigate a subject, or solve a problem. Proposals attempt to convince an audience that the writer is the best person to perform the task. For example, Coca-Cola seeks help in appealing to a younger market. It solicits proposals from market research companies, who then submit bids detailing their qualifications and their plans for solving the problem.

- **Minutes of meetings.** A record of the proceedings of a meeting is called "the minutes." This record is generally kept by a secretary. Minutes may be kept for groups that convene regularly, such as the monthly meeting of a club; or minutes may be kept for groups that meet irregularly, such as committees.

- **Summaries.** A summary condenses the primary ideas, conclusions, and recommendations of a longer report or publication. Employees may be asked to write summaries of technical reports. Students may be asked to write summaries of periodical articles or books to sharpen their writing skills.

- **To-file reports.** Reports prepared to document an idea or action are called "to-file" reports. These useful reports provide a written record of conversations, directives, and decisions. In today's often litigious business world, such reports are becoming increasingly important.

Report Formats

Informal reports may appear in four formats: memo form, letter form, report form, or on prepared forms.

How should a report look? The following four formats are frequently used. (1) **Letter format** is appropriate for informal reports prepared by one organization for another. These reports are much like letters except that they are more carefully organized, using headings and lists where appropriate. (2) **Memo format** is appropriate for informal reports written for circulation within an organization. They follow the conventions of memos that you learned in Chapter 5—with the addition of headings. (3) **Report format** is used for longer and somewhat more formal reports. Printed on plain paper (instead of letterhead or memo forms), these reports begin with a title followed by carefully displayed headings and subheadings. (See an illustration of report format in Figure 11.8, formal minutes of a meeting.) (4) **Prepared forms** are useful in reporting routine activities, such as police arrest reports or merchandise inventories. Standardized headings on these forms save time for the writer; forms also make similar information easy to locate.

Guidelines for Writing Informal Reports

Define Project

Begin the process of report writing by defining your project. This definition should include a statement of purpose. Ask yourself questions like these: Am I writing this report to inform, to analyze, to solve a problem, or to persuade? The answer to this question should be a clear, accurate statement identifying your purpose. In informal reports the statement of purpose may be only one sentence; that sentence usually becomes part of the introduction. Notice how the following introductory statement describes the purpose of the report:

> This report presents data regarding in-service training activities coordinated and supervised by the Personnel Service Department between the first of the year and the present.

After writing a statement of purpose, analyze who will read your report. If your report is intended for your immediate supervisors and they are supportive of your project, you need not include extensive details, historical development, definition of terms, or persuasion. Other readers, however, may require background data and persuasive strategies.

The expected audience for your report influences your writing style, your research method, your vocabulary, your areas of emphasis, and your communication strategy. Remember, too, that your audience may consist of more than one set of readers. Reports are often distributed to secondary readers who may need more details than the primary reader.

Begin a report by formulating a statement of purpose. Why are you writing this report?

Gather Data

A good report is based on solid, accurate, verifiable facts. Where do you get these facts?

Company records.   Many business-related reports begin with analysis of company records and files. From these records you can observe past performance and methods used to solve previous problems. You can collect pertinent facts that will help determine a course of action.

The facts for reports are often obtained from company records, observation, interviews, and research.

Observation.   Another logical source of data for many problems lies in personal observation and experience. For example, if you were writing a report on the need for additional word processing equipment, you might observe how much the current equipment is being used and for what purpose.

Interviews.   Talking with individuals directly concerned with the problem produces excellent first-hand information. Interviews also allow for one-on-one

"Then I can assume, Sir, that you didn't find
my report to be particularly useful! . . ."

Source: *Business As Usual*, Jerry Van Amerongen. Reprinted with permission of Simon & Schuster. Copyright 1986 by Cowles Syndicate, Inc.

communication, thus giving you an opportunity to explain your questions and ideas in eliciting the most accurate information.

Research.   Reading brochures and company literature can provide significant data. In addition, the library can be an unlimited source of current and historical information. For short, informal reports the most usable data will probably be found in periodicals. The *Business Periodicals Index* is the best source for business magazines and short publications. More detailed suggestions about library research will be found in Chapter 12.

Determine Organization

Like correspondence, reports may be organized inductively (indirectly) or deductively (directly). Placement of the big idea (recommendations or conclusions) is delayed in the inductive approach. Figures 11.1 and 11.2 show the same material for a report organized two different ways.

In Figures 11.1 and 11.2, you see only the skeleton of facts representing a complex problem. However, you can see the effects of organization. The inductive approach brings the reader through the entire process of analyzing a problem. It mirrors our method of thinking: problem, facts, analysis, recommendation. As you learned earlier, this strategy is successful when persuasion is necessary. It's also useful when the reader lacks knowledge and must be informed. However, busy executives or readers already familiar with the problem may want to get to the point more quickly.

The deductive approach is more direct; recommendations and conclusions are presented first so that readers have a frame of reference for reading the following discussion and analysis. Business reports are commonly organized deductively. Analyze your audience and purpose to determine the best overall strategy.

~~~

FIGURE 11.1 Inductive Organization

<u>Inductive Organization</u>

Problem/ Introduction:	Inadequate student parking on campus during prime class times.
Facts:	10,000 permits sold for 3,000 parking spaces; some parking lots unusable in bad weather; large numbers of visitors without permits fill parking spaces; no land for new lots.
Discussion:	Carpool? Try shuttles from distant parking lots? Enforce current regulations more strictly? Charge premium for parking in prime locations or during prime times? Build double-deck parking structures? Restrict visitors?
Recommendations:	Short-term: begin shuttle program. Long-term: solicit funds for improving current lots and building new multistory structures.

The difference between inductive and deductive strategy is the placement of conclusions and recommendations.

~~~

FIGURE 11.2 Deductive Organization

<u>Deductive Organization</u>

Problem/ Introduction:	Inadequate student parking on campus during prime class times.
Recommendations:	Short-term: begin shuttle program. Long-term: solicit funds for improving current lots and building new multistory structures.
Facts:	10,000 permits sold for 3,000 parking spaces; some lots unusable in bad weather; large numbers of visitors without permits fill spaces; no land for new lots.
Discussion:	Carpool? Try shuttles from distant parking lots? Enforce current regulations more strictly? Charge premium for parking in prime locations or during prime times? Build double-deck parking structures? Restrict visitors?

Be Objective

Reports are convincing only when the facts are believable and the writer is credible. You can build credibility in a number of ways.

Reports are more believable if the author is impartial, separates fact from opinion, uses moderate language, and cites sources.

1. **Present both sides of an issue.** Even if you favor one possibility, discuss both sides and show through logical reasoning why your position is superior. Remain impartial, letting the facts prove your point.

2. **Separate fact from opinion.** Suppose a supervisor wrote, *Our department works harder and gets less credit than any other department in the company.* This opinion is difficult to prove, and it damages the credibility of the writer. A more convincing statement might be, *Our productivity has increased 6 percent over the past year, and I'm proud of the extra effort my employees are making.* After you've made a claim or presented an important statement in a report, ask yourself, *Is this a verifiable fact?* If the answer is no, rephrase your statement to make it sound more reasonable.

3. **Be sensitive and moderate in your choice of language.** Don't exaggerate. Instead of saying *most people think . . .* , it might be more accurate to say *some people think . . . .* Obviously, avoid using labels and slanted expressions. Calling someone a *bozo,* an *egghead,* or an *elitist* demonstrates bias. If readers suspect that a writer is prejudiced, they may discount the entire argument.

4. **Cite sources.** Tell your readers where the information came from. For example, *In a telephone interview with Thomas Boswell, director of transportation, October 15, he said . . . .* Or *The Wall Street Journal (August 10, p. 40) reports that . . . .* By referring to respected sources, you lend authority and credibility to your statements. Your words become more believable and your argument, more convincing.

Use Effective Headings

Good headings are helpful to both the report reader and the writer. For the reader, they serve as an outline of the text, highlighting major ideas and categories. They also act as guides for locating facts and in pointing the way through the text. Moreover, headings provide resting points for the mind and for the eye, breaking up large chunks of text into manageable and inviting segments. For the writer, headings force organization of the data into meaningful blocks.

Functional headings show the outline of a report; talking heads provide more information.

Functional heads (like *Problem, Summary, and Recommendations*) help the writer outline a report. But talking heads (like *Students Perplexed by Shortage of Parking* or *Short-Term Parking Solutions*) provide more information to the reader. Many of the examples in this chapter use functional heads for the purpose of instruction. It's sometimes possible to make headings both functional and descriptive, such as *Recommendations: Shuttle and New Structures.* Whether your heads are talking or functional, keep them brief and clear.

Most informal reports are simple, requiring only one level of heading. Longer, more formal reports demand subdividing the topic into levels of headings (see page 284, Chapter 12).

Here are general tips on displaying headings effectively:

- Strive for parallel construction. Use balanced expressions such as *Visible Costs* and *Invisible Costs* rather than *Visible Costs* and *Costs That Don't Show.*

- Don't enclose headings in quotation marks.

- Don't use headings as antecedents for pronouns. For example, if the heading reads *Laser Printers*, don't begin the next sentence with *These are often used with desktop publishing software.*

Information Reports

Information reports provide information without drawing conclusions or making recommendations. Some information reports are highly standardized, such as police reports, hospital admittance reports, monthly sales reports, or government regulatory reports. Essentially, these are fill-in reports using prepared forms for recurring data. Other information reports are more personalized, as illustrated in Figure 11.3. They often include these sections:

> **Information reports usually contain three parts: introduction, findings, and summary.**

- **Introduction.** This part may also be called *Background*. In this section do the following: (1) explain why you are writing; (2) describe what methods and sources were used to gather information and why they are credible; (3) provide any special background information that may be necessary; (4) give the purpose of the report, if known; (5) offer a preview of your findings.

- **Findings.** This section may also be called *Observations*, *Facts*, *Results*, or *Discussion*. Important points to consider in this section are organization and display. Since information reports generally do not include conclusions or recommendations, inductive or deductive organization may be less appropriate. Instead, consider one of these methods of organization: (1) chronological, (2) alphabetical, (3) topical, or (4) most important to least important.

    To display the findings effectively, number the paragraphs, underline or boldface the key words, or indent the paragraphs. Be sure that words used as headings are parallel in structure. If the findings require elaboration, include this discussion with each segment of the findings or set aside a separate section entitled *Discussion*.

- **Summary.** This section is optional. If it is included, use it to summarize your findings objectively and impartially.

Recommendation Reports

Recommendation reports present information and analysis intended to solve a problem. They are usually written in response to requests by superiors. The writer is expected to analyze data, draw conclusions, and make recommendations. The report may be arranged inductively or deductively, depending on the problem,

> **Unlike information reports, recommendation reports include conclusions and recommendations.**

~~~

FIGURE 11.3   Information Report—Letter Format

J A G E R   S E R V I C E S,   I N C.

3920 Santa Monica Boulevard
Los Angeles, California 90066-0120
(213) 478-3201

August 4, 19xx

Ms. Karen Butts, Promotions Manager
Universal Records, Inc.
5890 Hollywood Boulevard
Hollywood, CA 90382

Dear Ms. Butts

SUBJECT: AVAILABILITY OF NAMES FOR NEW RECORDING SERIES

Here is the report you requested regarding the availability of names for
use in a new recording series within the Universal Records label.

Introduction

The following information is based on trademark searches of the U.S.
Patent and Trademark Office, the Copyright Office, several other sources of
patent data within the music industry, and the services of our attorneys.
My staff conducted a full search of the five names you submitted. Of this
group we find that two names are possible for your use.

*The findings may
also be entitled
Observations, Facts,
Results, or
Discussion.*

Discussion of Findings

1. Gold Label. Our research disclosed one recording company using the
   "Gold Label" name, and this causes us some concern. However, our
   outside counsel advises us that the name "Gold Label" is available for
   Universal's use in light of the trademark registrations for "Gold Note"
   currently owned by your affiliated companies.

Ms. Karen Butts   Page 2   August 4, 19xx

2. <u>The Master Series</u>. Several registrations containing the word "Master" appear in the Patent and Trademark Office. Since many registrations exist, no one can assert exclusive rights to that word. Therefore, Universal's use of the name "The Master Series" is not precluded.

3. <u>Heavenly Voices.</u> Our search of copyright records disclosed that approximately seven songs were recorded in 1990 on the "Heavenly Voices" record label, with an address in Sausalito, California. Repeated attempts to reach this business have been unsuccessful.

4. <u>Celestial Sounds.</u> A record label using this name produced 12 titles in 1987. Apparently the recording company is now defunct, but the trademark registration, No. 1,909,233, persists.

5. <u>Cherubim.</u> This name has at least one currently operating outstanding trademark, Trademark Registration No. 2,109,900 for "Cherubim Music."

<u>Summary</u>

Of the five names discussed here, the first two appear to be open to you: "Gold Label" and "The Master Series." The names "Heavenly Voices" and "Celestial Sounds" require additional research. Since "Cherubim" is trademarked, it is unavailable for your consideration.

Should you have any other names you would like us to check, please call me at 978-8990. It's always a pleasure to serve you.

Sincerely

Robert Jager

Robert Jager
President

era

---

audience, and purpose. To arrange a report inductively, place the conclusions and recommendations near the beginning. For deductive arrangement, place them toward the end. Figure 11.4 shows a short recommendation report arranged in a memo format.

~~~

FIGURE 11.4   Recommendation Report—Memo Format

DataCom, Inc.

Internal Memorandum

TO:	Thomas A. Varner, Director Personnel Services	DATE:	June 3, 19xx

FROM: Judy Gray, Manager *Judy*
         Information Services

SUBJECT: DEVELOPING PROCEDURES FOR USING TEMPORARY
            EMPLOYEES

At your request I am submitting this report detailing my
recommendations for improving the use of temporary employees in all
departments within DataCom. My recommendations are based on my own
experience with hundreds of temporary employees in my department and
on my interviews with other department managers.

Background

DataCom has increased its number of service accounts from 58 to 97
over the past three years. During that same period the number of
permanent employees has increased only 12 percent. Because we have not
been able to find qualified individuals to hire as full-time employees, we
have been forced to rely on temporary employees more heavily than ever
before. During the past year DataCom has required the services of
189 temporary employees, an increase of 76 over the previous year.

Joe Hernandez in Personnel reports that he does not expect the
employment picture to improve in the future. He feels that DataCom will
probably continue to hire large numbers of temporary employees for at
least the next two years.

Problem

Temporary employees are hired by department managers who have
little experience in acquiring temps, planning their work, or supervising
them. As a result, the productivity of the temps is not always as great as it
could be. Moreover, we sometimes hire expensive, highly skilled
individuals for routine tasks. These workers are bored with their assigned
tasks and dissatisfied with their experience at DataCom; hence they refuse
to return.

Thomas A. Varner   Page 2   June 3, 19xx

Conclusions

DataCom could improve the productivity, effectiveness, and morale of its temporary employees by instituting changes in three areas: (1) establishing standardized procedures to be followed by all departments requesting temps, (2) introducing techniques for department managers to follow when temps first arrive, and (3) providing suggestions for adequate supervision after temps are on the job.

Recommendations

System for Requesting Temps. I recommend that Personnel prepare a form that supervisors complete when they need temporary employees. The form will require department managers to indicate precisely what skills are required for the tasks to be completed. We should not request a secretary for a task that a typist could perform. Requests for temps should then be channeled through one office, such as Personnel.

Is this report arranged inductively or deductively?

Procedures for Introducing Temps to Workforce. When temps are hired, department managers can improve the productivity of these new employees by following these suggestions:

1. Lay out and organize the work to be completed.

2. Simplify the tasks as much as possible.

3. Ensure that supplies and operating equipment are available.

4. Provide ample directions.

5. Encourage the temp to ask questions clarifying tasks.

Follow-up Supervision. Probably the most important suggestion involves supervision. As soon as a temp starts on the job, assign a nearby supervisor. Spot-check the temp an hour after work is begun and at intervals throughout the entire task. Don't wait until a task is completed to discover a misunderstood direction.

Limitations

The success of these recommendations is limited by two factors. First, the Personnel Division must agree to assume the task of regulating the hiring of all temporary employees. Second, department managers must be supportive of the new procedures. To secure their cooperation, an in-service training workshop should be provided to instruct managers in working with temps.

Here are possible sections for a recommendation report:

Introduction	Analysis of Facts
Background	Options
Problem	Rejected Alternatives
Method of Collecting Data	Limitations
Findings	Conclusions
Presentation of Facts	Recommendations

Justification Reports

Justification reports are unsolicited; that is, the idea orginates with the writer.

Justification reports include information, analysis, and recommendations. Unlike recommendation reports, however, they are unsolicited—that is, the idea for a justification report starts with the writer instead of with a superior. The writer may wish to purchase equipment, change a procedure, or revise existing policy. Typically, the desired change will be obvious to the reader. Therefore, persuasion should not be a primary factor. Start directly with the proposal or problem. Follow this with some or all of the following topics: Present System, Proposed System, Advantages, Cost and Savings, Methods or Procedures, Conclusion, and Discussion. Figure 11.5 shows a justification report within Hershey Chocolate Company.

Progress Reports

Progress reports generally answer three questions: (1) Is the project on schedule? (2) Are corrective measures needed? (3) What activities are next?

Progress reports describe the headway of unusual or nonroutine projects. Most progress reports include these four parts: (1) the purpose and nature of the project, (2) a complete summary of the work already completed, (3) a thorough description of work currently in progress, including personnel, methods, obstacles, and attempts to remedy obstacles; and (4) a forecast of future activities in relation to the scheduled completion date, including recommendations and requests. In Figure 11.6 Gail Desler explains the construction of a realty company branch office. She begins with a statement summarizing the construction progress in relation to the expected completion date. She then updates the reader with a brief recap of past progress. She emphasizes the present status of construction and concludes by describing the next steps to be taken.

Proposals

A proposal is an offer or a bid to sell a product, provide a service, explore a topic, or solve a problem. As such, it must persuade or sell the reader on a plan

~~~

FIGURE 11.5   Justification Report—Memo Format

MEMORANDUM

TO: Orene Harder, Vice President   DATE: June 11, 19xx
           Operations Division

FROM: Jack Harris, Office Manager
           Accounting Department

SUBJECT: INSTALLATION OF FLAT, UNDERCARPET WIRING TO
           UPDATE CURRENT ELECTRICAL, DATA PROCESSING, AND
           COMMUNICATION WIRING SYSTEM

Proposal

Because the Accounting Department of Hershey Chocolate Company needs
a flexible, economical wiring system that can accommodate our
ever-changing electrical, communication, and data-processing needs, I
propose that we install a flat, undercarpet wiring system.

Present System

At present our department has an outdated system of floor ducts and
power poles and a network of surface wiring that is overwhelmed by the
demands we are now placing upon it. The operation of 27 pieces of
electrical equipment and 34 telephones requires extensive electrical
circuits and cabling. In addition, our overhead lighting, consisting of
fluorescent fixtures in a suspended egg-crate structure, has resulted in
excessive wiring above the drop ceiling.

We have outgrown our present wiring system, and future growth is
contingent upon the availability of power. Since Hershey's goal is to have a
computer terminal at every workstation, we must find a better way to
serve our power needs than through conventional methods.

Advantages of Proposed System

Power, telephone, and data cables are now available in a flat form only
.043 inches thick. This flat, flexible cable can be installed underneath
existing carpeting, thus preventing costly and disruptive renovation
necessary for installing additional round cables. Because flat cables can

**Functional headings,
like these, help the
reader understand
the overall
organization of the
report but offer
little specific data.**

be moved easily, an undercarpet system would provide great flexibility. Whenever we move a computer terminal or add a printer, we can easily make necessary changes in the wiring.

Undercarpet wiring would allow us to eliminate all power poles. These poles break up the office landscaping and create distracting shadows about which employees complain.

Installation of an undercarpet wiring system in the Accounting Department would enable Hershey to evaluate the system's effectiveness before considering it for other areas, such as sales, customer services, and field warehousing.

Cost and Savings

The AMP Products Corporation of Harrisburg estimates that undercarpet wiring for the Accounting Department would cost about $29,000. If we were to use conventional methods to install round wiring, we would have to renovate our entire department, costing over $200,000. Undercarpet wiring, then, saves Hershey over $170,000. Equally important, however, is the savings in terms of productivity and employee satisfaction, which would deteriorate if renovation were required.

---

of attack for solving the problem or performing the service. Typically, informal proposals include these topics:

- **Introduction**—description of problem or proposal
- **Proposed solution**—steps or procedures to solve problem or provide service
- **Staffing**—those who will solve the problem and their qualifications
- **Schedule**—timetable of procedures
- **Cost**—budget of expected expenditures
- **Authorization**—request for approval to begin project

Figure 11.7 shows the major portion of a proposal by Computer Assistance, Inc., to install hardware and software for an accounting firm.

Minutes

Minutes provide a summary of the proceedings of meetings. Minutes may be formal or informal, according to the group and the purpose of the minutes.

FIGURE 11.6 Progress Report

MEMORANDUM

TO: Jeanne Dostourian, President   DATE: April 20, 19xx

FROM: Gail Desler *G.D.*
             Development Officer

SUBJECT: **CONSTRUCTION PROGRESS OF MALIBU BRANCH OFFICE**

<u>Summary</u>

Construction of Dostourian Realty's Malibu branch office has entered Phase 3. Although we are one week behind the contractor's original schedule, the building should be ready for occupancy August 15.

<u>Past Progress</u>

Phase 1 involved development of the architect's plans; this process was completed February 5. Phase 2 involved submission of the plans for county building department approval. The plans were then given to four contractors for estimates. The lowest bidder was Holst Brothers Contractors. This firm began construction on March 25.

This report was written for an audience familiar with the project; therefore, it needn't be as thorough as some reports might be.

<u>Present Status</u>

Phase 3 includes initial construction procedures. The following steps have been completed as of April 20:

1. Demolition of existing building at 27590 Pacific Coast Highway.

2. Excavation of foundation footings for the building and for the surrounding wall.

3. Installation of steel reinforcing rods in building pad and wall.

4. Pouring of concrete foundation.

The contractor indicated that he was one week behind schedule for the following reasons. The building inspectors required additional steel reinforcement not shown on the architect's blueprints. Further, excavation of the footings required more time than the contractor anticipated because the 18-inch footings were all below grade.

<u>Future Schedule</u>

Despite some time lost in Phase 3, we are substantially on target for the completion of this office building by August 1. Phase 4 includes framing, dry walling, and plumbing.

FIGURE 11.7   Proposal—Letter Style

COMPUTER ASSISTANCE, INC.

2390 Marshall Avenue
Arlington, West Virginia 23403

May 15, 19xx

Ms. Nedra K. Lowe, CPA
Lowe & Associates Accountancy
5492 Lavalette Boulevard
Huntington, West Virginia 25705

Dear Ms. Lowe:

As you requested, we have prepared a proposal for assisting Lowe &
Associates Accountancy in computerizing its accounting data.

Introduction

We understand that Lowe & Associates wishes to install hardware and
software that will enable it to operate each of its four regional offices with
separate, single-user computers and software. Each regional office needs
to automate its general ledger and accounts payable functions. The
Huntington office wishes to combine the information generated by the
regional offices on monthly basis for reporting purposes.

Our organization was formed in 1985 to assist businesses like yours
select and implement PC-based accounting systems. Since then we have
successfully installed a multitude of systems, serving customers from
accounting firms to restaurants to wholesale distributors.

Proposal

**Since they are
legally binding, sales
proposals must be
prepared very
carefully.**

We propose that you allow us to demonstrate two software packages
appropriate for your firm: MAS90 and ACCPAC Plus. Both of these
software packages provide customizable financial statements, and they
support departmentalization and company consolidation. We will
highlight the features of each program, but you will be allowed to choose
the one you prefer. We will install the program you select and provide

Ms. Nedra K. Lowe   Page 2   May 15, 19xx

training on-site or in our training room. If you engage us, we would divide the project into three phases:

1. <u>System Design and Setup</u>.   The tasks to be performed in this phase include the following:

   * Determine the computer and peripheral equipment to be used in each office

   * Establish the procedure for transporting data to home office (by modem or mail)

   •
   •
   •

Staffing

Beverley Husak, our talented software consultant trained at Huntington University, will demonstrate the two packages. Hardware hookup and installation of software will be done by our veteran technician, William Andrews, who has installed dozens of systems over the past five years. Training and follow-up support will be provided by Ms. Husak.

Schedule

We expect to complete a substantial portion of the project within four to five weeks after starting. Implementation follow-up will occur in the weeks immediately following the initial phase. Technical and accounting support is available as needed after the installation. We will require a meeting with the management staff involved in this project to clarify the specific installation and training requirements as described in this proposal prior to beginning the actual installation.

Some proposals include a detailed daily, weekly, or monthly schedule of activities.

Cost

Our fees are based on the number of hours spent on the job by our staff multiplied by their respective billing rates. Our current rates are as follows:

Technicians	$ 60/hr
Software consultant	70/hr
President	200/hr

Ms. Nedra K. Lowe   Page 3   May 15, 19xx

See Attachment 1 for a detailed listing of the projected costs for consulting, software, installation, and training.

Authorization

If this information correctly anticipates your needs and meets your expectations, please sign the enclosed duplicate copy and return it to us. In addition, include a retainer for the amount of the software plus $5,000 as authorization for us to begin the project.

Sincerely,

Linda Wilkinson

Linda Wilkinson
President

psf

Enclosures

Traditional minutes, as illustrated in Figure 11.8, are written for large groups and legislative bodies. The following items are usually included in this order:

1. Name of group, date, time, place, name of meeting
2. Names of people present; names of absentees, if appropriate
3. Disposition of previous minutes
4. Old business
5. Announcements, reports
6. Summary of discussions
7. Motions presented in exact wording, vote, action taken
8. Name and signature of individual recording minutes

Informal minutes, illustrated in Figure 11.9, are shorter and easier to read. They place less emphasis upon the conventions of reporting and who said what. Informal minutes concentrate on decisions, action, and responsibility. For these reasons, the minutes of smaller organizations and business meetings may follow this format.

FIGURE 11.8   Minutes of Meeting, Traditional—Report Format

P$_S$A PROFESSIONAL
         SECRETARIES
         ASSOCIATION

**19xx International Convention
Planning Committee Meeting**

October 23, 19xx, 10 a.m.
Conference Room A, Century Towers

Present: Marilyn Andrews, Melody Franklin, June Gonzales,
           Brenda Miller, Margaret Zappa, Martha Zebulski

Absent: Amy Costello

The meeting was called to order by Chair Margaret Zappa at
10:05 a.m. Minutes from the June 22 meeting were read and approved.

Announcements

1. The chair announced that the time and location of the committee's
   next meeting have been changed to January 4 at the Kansas City
   Marriott Hotel, Sunset Room.

2. Melody Franklin encouraged committee members to attend a PSA
   leadership conference scheduled for February 10.

Reports—Seminars/Workshops

June Gonzales reported that she was working on the development of
five professional workshops for the convention. These major workshops
would be conducted by leaders in office automation, personnel
management, and personal development. By the next meeting June
expects to have specific individuals committed to presentations.

Conference Hotel Options

Brenda Miller and Martha Zebulske said that they hoped the
committee members had had time to study the information distributed
earlier regarding the three hotels being considered for the Houston

**Large organizations
and legislative
bodies require
traditional or formal
minutes to record
their proceedings.**

conference: Sheraton Plaza, Hilton Regency, and Embassy Suites Houston. Brenda reported that the Hilton has superior banquet facilities, ample conference rooms, and recently remodeled interiors. However, the best rate we can secure for rooms is $95 per night. Martha said that the Embassy Suites Houston also has excellent banquet facilities, adequate meeting rooms, and will offer us rooms at $82 per night. No one spoke in favor of the Sheraton Plaza. Following considerable discussion, Melody Franklin moved that we hold the 19xx PSA International Convention at the Embassy Suites Houston. Brenda Miller seconded the motion. The motion passed 5–1.

Conference Theme

The chair reviewed themes of three previous conventions, all of which focused on technology and the changing role of the secretary.
June Gonzales suggested the following possibility: "The New, The Tried and True, and The Unusual." Martha Zebulski suggested a communication theme but had no specific ideas. Several other possibilities were discussed. The chair appointed a subcommittee of June and Martha to bring to the next committee meeting two or three concrete theme ideas.

Exhibits

Brenda Miller suggested that the number of exhibits be expanded at the Houston convention. At past conventions, exhibits of office equipment, furniture, software, and publications were adequate. For this convention, however, Brenda felt that we should try to involve more companies and products. Discussion followed regarding how this might be accomplished. Brenda Miller moved that the PSA office staff develop a list of possible exhibitors. These potential exhibitors should be sent flyers promoting the convention and encouraging them to be represented. Marilyn Andrews seconded the motion. It passed 6–0.

The meeting was adjourned at 11:45 by Margaret Zappa.

Respectfully submitted,

Melody Franklin

Melody Franklin, Secretary

FIGURE 11.9 Minutes of Meeting, Informal — Report Format

Malibu Beach Homeowners' Association

Board of Directors Meeting
April 12, 19xx

MINUTES

Directors Present: J. Weinstein, A. McGraw, J. Carson, C. Stefanko,
                     A. Pettus
Directors Absent: P. Hook

Summary of Topics Discussed

1. Report from Architectural Review Committee. Copy attached.

2. Landscaping of center divider on Paseo Canyon. Three options considered: hiring private landscape designer, seeking volunteers from community, assigning association handyman to complete work.

3. Collection of outstanding assessments. Discussion of delinquent accounts and possible actions.

4. Use of beach club by film companies. Pros: considerable income. Cons: damage to furnishings, loss of facility to homeowners.

5. Nomination of directors to replace those with two-year appointments.

Smaller, less formal organizations may use streamlined, more efficient minutes like these.

Decisions Reached

1. Hire private landscaper to renovate and plant center divider on Paseo Canyon.

2. Attach liens to homes of members with delinquent assessments.

3. Submit to general membership vote the question of renting the beach club to film companies.

Action Items

Item	Responsibility	Due Date
1. Landscaping bid	J. Carson	May 1
2. Attorney for liens	P. Hook	April 20
3. Creation of nominating committee	A. Pettus	May 1

≈≈

FIGURE 11.10   Summary of Article—Memo Format

TO: Professor Valerie Evans   DATE: November 18, 19xx

FROM: Edwin Hwang, Student *E.H.*

SUBJECT: ANALYSIS OF COMPUTER MAINTENANCE ARTICLE

In response to your request, here is an analysis of "Taking the Sting Out of Computer Repair," which appeared in the July, 1990, issue of Office Administration and Automation.

A summary includes primary ideas, conclusions, and recommendations but usually omits examples, illustrations, and references.

Major Points

The author, Michael B. Chamberlain, discusses four alternatives available to users of computer equipment regarding service. Each has advantages and disadvantages.

1. Factory service. The user sends the equipment back to the factory for repairs. Expert service is provided, but generally the time required is impossibly long.

2. Dealer service. A few dealers maintain service departments where computers that they have sold can be brought for repair. However, such departments are expensive to operate; hence few dealers provide them. Too, their location may be inconvenient for users.

3. Customer self-service. Large companies may maintain in-house repair departments, but their technicians find it difficult to keep abreast of changing hardware and software.

4. Third-party service. Independent computer maintenance organizations offer convenience, but they can't always handle multivendor systems.

The author favors the fourth option and provides many tips on how to work with third-party maintenance companies. Before choosing such an organization, he warns, make sure that it has experts who can work with your particular computer configuration.

<u>Strengths and Weaknesses</u>

The strength of this article lies in the discussion on how to choose a service organization. The author also gives a helpful preventive maintenance checklist for microcomputer owners.

This article had two weaknesses. First, the author failed to support his choice of third-party maintenance companies effectively. Second, the article is poorly organized. It was difficult to read because it was not developed around major ideas. It contains excellent information, but better organization and headings would have helped the reader recognize groups of significant data.

Summaries

A summary compresses essential information from a longer publication. Employees are sometimes asked to write summaries that condense technical reports, periodical articles, or books so that their staffs or superiors may grasp the main ideas quickly. Students are often asked to write summaries of articles, chapters, or books to sharpen their writing skills and to confirm their knowledge of reading assignments (see Figure 11.10). A summary includes primary ideas, conclusions, and recommendations. It usually omits examples, illustrations, and references. Organized for readability, a summary often includes headings and enumerations. It may include the reactions of the reader.

A summary condenses the primary ideas, conclusions, and recommendations of a longer publication.

To-File Reports

To-file reports document oral decisions, directives, and discussions. They create a concise, permanent record that may be important for future reference. Because individuals may forget, alter, or retract oral commitments, a written record should often be established. However, to-file reports should not be made for minor events.

To-file reports provide a record of conversations for future reference.

To-file reports typically include the names and titles of involved individuals, along with a summary of the decision. A copy of the report is sent to involved individuals so that corrections or amendments may be made before the report is filed. Figure 11.11 shows a to-file report in memo format.

The eight types of reports discussed and illustrated in this chapter are representative of commonly seen reports in business transactions. All of the examples in this chapter are considered relatively informal. Longer, more formal reports are necessary for major investigations and research. These reports, along with suggestions for research methods, are presented in Chapter 12.

~~~

FIGURE 11.11   To-File Report—Memo Format

DataCom, Inc.

Internal Memo

TO: Wayne McEachern   DATE: **February 4, 19xx**
           Chief Counsel

FROM: Jean Taylor
           Business Manager

SUBJECT: DISPOSITION OF UNORDERED MERCHANDISE

This confirms our telephone conversation today in which you advised me
regarding the disposition of unordered merchandise sent to my office by
vendors. It is my understanding that I am under no obligation to return
this merchandise since its delivery was unauthorized. I further
understand that after a reasonable time has elapsed, we may use this
merchandise or dispose of it as we see fit.

Please let me hear from you if this record of our conversation is
inaccurate.

APPLICATION AND PRACTICE—11

Discussion

1. How are business reports different from business letters?

2. Of the reports presented in this chapter, discuss those that require inductive development versus those that require deductive development.

3. How are the reports that you write for your courses similar to those presented here? How are they different?

4. Compare and contrast traditional and informal minutes of meetings. Why would some organizations require traditional minutes?

5. Compare and contrast justification reports and proposals.

Short Answers

6. List eight kinds of short reports. Be prepared to describe each.

7. List four formats suitable for reports. Be prepared to discuss each format.

8. From the lists that you made above, select a report category and appropriate format for each of the following situations.

   a. Your supervisor asks you to read a long technical report and tell him or her the important points.

   b. You want to tell management about an idea you have for improving a procedure that you think will increase productivity.

   c. You just completed a telephone conversation with a union representative detailing your rights in a disagreement you had with your supervisor.

   d. You are asked to record the proceedings of a meeting of your school's student association.

   e. You want to describe how the products of your company, Pacific Tile, can be used by Del Webb Company in its new housing project.

f. As Engineering Department office manager, you have been asked to describe your highly regarded computer system for another department.

g. As a police officer, you are writing a report of an arrest.

h. You write a report describing how 5 acres of empty beachfront could be developed into luxury condominiums.

9. What is the primary distinction between a recommendation report and a justification report?

10. Name four or more sources of information for reports.

11. If you were about to write the following reports, where would you gather information? Be prepared to discuss the specifics of each choice.

a. You are a student representative on a curriculum committee. You are asked to study the course requirements in your major and make recommendations.

b. As department manager, you must write job descriptions for several new positions you wish to establish in your department.

c. You are proposing to management the replacement of a copier in your department.

d. You must document the progress of a 12-month campaign to alter the image of Levi-Strauss jeans.

12. What three questions do progress reports typically address?

13. What one factor distinguishes reports developed inductively from those developed deductively?

14. List six items that the writer of a proposal should include.

15. What is the purpose of a to-file report?

16. Information reports that are not organized inductively or deductively may be arranged by what four methods?

17. Why are informal minutes easier to read than traditional minutes?

18. An article summary that your employer asks you to write should include what items?

19. Proposals offer to do what?

20. In formal minutes how are motions treated?

CASE 11–1

Information Report

Your instructor wants to learn about your employment. Select a position you now hold or one that you have held in the past. (If you have not been employed, select an organization to which you belong.) Write an information report describing your employment. As an introduction, describe the company and its products or services, its ownership, and its location. As the main part of the report, describe your position, including its tasks and the skills required to perform these tasks. Summarize by describing the experience you gained. Your report should be 1-1/2 to 2 pages, single-spaced, and should follow memo format.

CASE 11–2

Information Report

Gather information about a position for which you might be interested in applying. Learn about the nature of the job. Discover whether certification, licenses, or experience is required. Describe the working conditions in this field. Collect information regarding typical entry-level salaries and potential for advancement.

If your instructor wishes to make this an extended report, collect information about two companies where you might apply. Investigate each company's history, products and/or services, size, earnings, reputation, and number of employees. Describe the functions of an employee working in the position you have investigated. To do this, interview one or more individuals who are working in that position. Devote several sections of your report to the specific tasks, functions, duties, and opinions of these individuals. You can make this into a recommendation report by drawing conclusions and making recommendations. One conclusion that you could draw relates to success in this career area. Who might be successful in this field?

CASE 11–3

Recommendation Report

An employer for whom you worked last year regarded you highly. Although you are no longer employed there, this individual called to ask your candid opinion on how to retain employees. He is concerned about the high rate of turnover. What advice can you offer? How do similar businesses recruit and retain their employees? Using actual experiences, write a letter report responding to this request.

CASE 11–4

Justification Report

You have been serving as a student member of a college curriculum advisement committee. Examine the course requirements for a degree or certificate in your major. Are the requirements realistic and practical? What improvements can you suggest? Interview other students and faculty members for their suggestions. Write to the dean of your college proposing your suggestions.

CASE 11–5

Justification Report

In your work or your training, identify equipment that needs to be purchased or replaced (computer, printer, VCR, copier, camera, etc.). Write a justification report comparing two or more brands.

CASE 11–6

Progress Report

You made an agreement with your parents (or spouse, relative, or significant friend) that you would submit a progress report at this time describing headway toward your educational goal (employment, certificate, degree). Write that report in memo format.

CASE 11–7

Proposal

You want to start your own business (fast food franchise, secretarial service, pet-grooming service, photocopy store, etc.) and you need financial backing. Write a convincing proposal to your parents, rich uncle, or philanthropist friend that will get you the capital you need. Do research to learn how much investment is required.

CASE 11–8

Minutes

Attend an open meeting of an organization at your school or elsewhere. Record the proceedings in formal or informal minutes.

CASE 11–9

Summary

Your boss, Russell M. Silver, is worried about computer viruses (or a topic your instructor approves). He asks you to find a good article (at least 1,000 words long) in a magazine that suggests ways to avoid the problem in his company. Look in *Datamation*, *Personal Computing*, *Byte*, or some other magazine to find an appropriate article. Write a two-page summary for him.

CASE 11–10

To-File Report

You just saw your office manager in the hall, and she told you that you could take a three-week vacation in August. You know she has a bad memory, and you don't want her to forget or renege on her promise. Write her a to-file report.

CASE 11–11

Longer Report

Identify a problem in a business or organization with which you are familiar, such as sloppy workmanship, indifferent service, poor attendance at organization meetings, uninspired cafeteria food, antique office equipment, arrogant management, lack of communication, underappreciated employees, wasteful procedures, and so forth. Describe the problem in detail. Assume you are to report to management (or to the leadership of an organization) about the nature and scope of the problem. Decide which kind of report to prepare (information, recommendation, justification), and decide on the format. How would you gather data to lend authority to your conclusions and recommendations? Determine the exact topic and report length after consultation with your instructor.

GRAMMAR/MECHANICS CHECKUP—11

Other Punctuation

Although this checkup concentrates on Sections 2.23 through 2.29 in the Grammar/Mechanics Handbook, you may also refer to other punctuation principles. Insert any necessary punctuation in the following statements. Use the delete sign ( ) to omit unnecessary punctuation. In the space provided for each line, indicate the number of changes you make. Count each mark separately; for example, a set of parentheses counts as 2. If you make no changes, write 0. When you finish, compare your responses with those shown below. If your responses differ, study carefully the specific principles shown in parentheses.

2 _____ (2.27)   **Example:** (Deemphasize.) The consumption of Mexican food products is highest in certain states (California, Arizona, New Mexico, and Texas), but this food trend is spreading to other parts of the country.

_____   1. (Emphasize.) The convention planning committee has invited three managers Jim Lowey, Frank Beyer, and Carolyn Wong to make presentations.

_____   2. Would you please Miss Sanchez use your computer to recalculate these totals?

_____   3. (Deemphasize.) A second set of demographic variables see Figure 13–9 on page 432 includes nationality, religion, and race.

_____   4. Because the word recommendation is frequently misspelled we are adding it to our company style book.

_____   5. Recruiting, hiring, and training: these are three important functions of a personnel officer.

_____   6. The office manager said, "Who placed an order for 15 dozen ribbon cartridges

_____   7. Have any of the research assistants been able to locate the article entitled How Tax Reform Will Affect You

_____   8. (Emphasize.) The biggest oil-producing states Texas, California, and Alaska are experiencing severe budget deficits.

9. Have you sent invitations to Mr Ronald E Harris, Miss Michelle Hale, and Ms Sylvia Mason   _____

10. Dr. Y. W. Yellin wrote the chapter entitled Trading on the Options Market that appeared in a book called Securities Markets.   _____

11. James said, "I'll be right over" however he has not appeared yet.   _____

12. In business the word liability may be defined as any legal obligation requiring payment in the future.   _____

13. Because the work was scheduled to be completed June 10; we found it necessary to hire temporary workers to work June 8 and 9.   _____

14. Did any c o d shipments arrive today   _____

15. Hooray I have finished this checkup haven't I   _____

---

1. (2) managers— Wong— (2.26a, 2.27)   3. (2) (see page 432) (2.27)
5. (1) training— (2.26c)   7. (3) "How You"? (2.28e, 2.28f)
9. (4) Mr. E. Ms. Mason? (2.23b, 2.24)   11. (2) over"; however, (2.16, 2.28f)
13. (1) June 10, (2.06)   15. (3) Hooray! checkup, I? (2.24, 2.25)

CHAPTER 12

Formal Reports

In this chapter you will learn to do the following:

- Write a meaningful statement of purpose for a formal report.
- Collect data from both primary and secondary sources.
- Research topics from books, periodicals, and computer databases.
- Recognize three methods for documenting data sources.

- Distinguish among five organizational strategies.
- Outline topics and use appropriate heading format.
- Illustrate data, using tables, charts, and graphs.
- Sequence 13 parts of a long report.

Formal reports, whether they offer only information or whether they also analyze that information and make recommendations, typically have three characteristics: formal tone, traditional structure, and length. Although formal reports in business are infrequently seen, they serve a very important function. They provide management with vital data for decision making. In this chapter we will consider the entire process of writing a formal report: preparing to write, collecting data, documenting data, organizing data, illustrating data, and presenting the final report.

The primary differences between formal and informal reports are tone, structure, and length.

Preparing to Write

Like informal reports, formal reports begin with a definition of the project. Probably the most difficult part of this definition is limiting the scope of the report. Every project has limitations. Decide at the outset what constraints influence the range of your project and the methods you use in achieving your purpose. How much time do you have for completing your report? How much space will you be allowed for reporting on your topic? How accessible are the data you need? How thorough should your research be? If you are writing about low morale among swing-shift employees, how many of your 475 employees should you interview? Should you limit your research to company-related morale factors, or should you consider external factors over which the company has no control? In investigating variable-rate mortgages, should you focus on a particular group, such as first-time homeowners in a specific area, or should you consider all mortgage holders? The first step in writing a report, then, is determining the precise boundaries of the topic.

Once you have defined the project and limited its scope, write a statement of purpose. The statement of purpose should describe the goal, significance, and limitations of the report. Notice how the following statement pinpoints the research and report:

> The purpose of this report is to explore employment possibilities for entry-level paralegal workers in the city of San Francisco. It will consider typical salaries, skills required, opportunities, and working conditions. This research is significant because of the increasing number of job openings in the paralegal field. This report will not consider legal secretarial employment, which represents a different employment focus.

The planning of every report begins with a statement of purpose explaining the goal, significance, and limitations of the project.

Collecting Data

Effective reports, whether formal or informal, are founded on accurate data. Data collected for a report may be grouped into two categories, primary and secondary. Primary information is obtained from first-hand observation and experience. Secondary information comes from reading what others have observed or experienced.

Primary Sources

Five logical sources of information for a report are company records, observation, interviews, surveys, and experiments.

Primary data are facts that have not already been collected and recorded by someone else.

Company Records.   Information for reports regarding company operations often originates in company records. Accounting and marketing reports would necessarily include data of previous performance taken from existing records.

Observation.   In business reports personal observation often provides essential data. For example, if Sam Erwin, a marketing manager, were writing a report recommending changes in sales territories, he would probably begin by carefully observing the current territories and analyzing sales coverage. If Samantha Jones, a student, were reporting on employment possibilities, she might begin by observing classified ads in a local newspaper.

Interviews.   Collecting information by talking with individuals gives the researcher immediate feedback and provides a chance for explanation of questions if necessary. If the information collected is to be used scientifically or systematically, the interviewer should follow an interview schedule—that is, the same questions, stated identically, should be addressed to all interviewees.

Surveys.   If many questions need to be asked of a large group of individuals and if costs must be kept down, then surveys may be used to collect data. Good surveys, however, cannot be conducted casually. Questions should be carefully written and tested on sample groups before actually being administered. Thought should be given to how the results will be tabulated and interpreted.

Experiments.   Although experimentation is more common to the physical and social sciences, decision makers in business may also use this technique to gather information. In promoting a new product, for example, a business might experiment with an ad in two different newspapers and compare the results.

Secondary Sources

Secondary data for business reports usually come from library resources. Many formal reports begin with extensive library research to provide an overview of the problem being investigated. In fact, for any problem about which you are unfamiliar, your school or public library is the place to begin seeking information. Nearly always you will find that someone else has studied the same or a similar problem and has written something helpful. If you are an infrequent library user, begin your research by talking with the reference librarian about your project. Most libraries also provide brochures or other printed material to help you locate reference materials on their shelves and in other libraries. Here are four major sources of library information for you to consult.

Many formal business reports require library research to provide background data.

Card Catalog.   Libraries in the past indexed all their books on 3-by-5 cards alphabetized by author and/or by subject. Many libraries today, however, have computerized their card catalogs. Some systems are fully automated, showing the user not only whether a book is located in the library but also whether it is currently available. Librarians are usually happy to show readers how to find information in the catalogs and how then to locate the books on shelves. Books provide excellent historical, in-depth data on a subject. However, more current information is generally available in magazines listed in periodical guides.

Guide to Periodicals.   Periodicals are magazines, journals, and pamphlets. They often provide the most up-to-date information on a topic. To locate articles in general-interest magazines, such as *Time, Reader's Digest, The New Yorker, Better Homes and Gardens*, and *U.S. News & World Report*, consult the *Readers' Guide to Periodical Literature*. To locate articles in business, industrial, and trade publications, consult the *Business Periodicals Index*. Other indexes include the *Education Index, The Applied Science and Technology Index*, and *The Public Affairs Information Service Bulletin*.

Encyclopedias, Dictionaries, Handbooks.   The reference section of a library holds special collections of helpful material. General encyclopedias include *Americana, Columbia*, and *Britannica*. Specialized encyclopedias include *Encyclopedia of Social Science, Encyclopedia of Science and Technology, Exporter's Encyclopedia*, and *Accountant's Encyclopedia*. The reference section may also house excellent dictionaries that function as encyclopedias, such as Prentice-Hall's *Encyclopedic Dictionary of Business*. Handbooks provide current data in specialized fields. For employment information consult the *Occupational Outlook Handbook* (U.S. Department of Labor). Other handbooks include the *HOW 6: Handbook for Office Workers* (published by PWS-KENT and coordinated with this book), *Handbook of Auditing Methods, Handbook of Business Administration, Management Handbook, Sales Executives' Handbook*, and *Real Estate Handbook*.

Newspapers.   Newspapers from around the country and the world not only are fascinating to read but also supply current information. Locating articles on your topic, however, is difficult unless you limit yourself to the newspapers that index their articles. Some indexes to consider are *Barron's Index*, *Index of the Christian Science Monitor*, *Los Angeles Times Index*, *National Observer Index*, *The New York Times Index*, and *The Wall Street Journal Index*.

Computer Data Bases.   Data bases are computerized collections of information. Instead of looking at printed documents, you locate data by using a computer. Businesses or private subscribers typically pay for data-base services by the minutes of use. These services provide information regarding weather, catalog shopping, travel arrangements, stock market reports, sports scores, current affairs, movie reviews, and many other topics. Most libraries today provide computer bibliography search help at little or no cost. Research librarians will help you decide on appropriate data bases and key words to describe your topic.

Documenting Data

To give formal reports credibility and authority, researchers generally rely upon a certain amount of secondary data obtained at a library.

Library Research

Here are tips for conducting library research.

- Take a good supply of coins with you to the library so that you can make photocopies of promising pages.

- Before you begin working with listings of periodicals, find out what magazines your library has on-shelf. It's most disappointing to find fascinating titles for articles in magazines that your library doesn't carry.

- Don't allow yourself to become a victim of information overload. You can't read everything that's been written about your subject. Look up only *relevant* and *current* references. Be selective.

- Be resourceful and persevering when searching for data. For example, if you're looking for information about speaking skills for businesspeople, you might look under such descriptors as *speech, communication, language, public relations,* and *conversation.*

- Take excellent notes. Place each reference on a separate card or sheet of paper. Record the author's name, title of the article or book, and complete publication information, in addition to your notes regarding the content of the references.

- Use only a few quotations in your report. Good writers use direct quotes only (1) to emphasize opinions because of the author's status as an expert, (2) to duplicate the exact wording before criticizing, or (3) to repeat identical phrasing because of its precision, clarity, or aptness.

Footnoting.   If you use data from secondary sources, the data must be acknowledged; that is, you must indicate where the data originated. Even if you paraphrase (put the information in your own words), the ideas must be documented.

> **To document a formal report with secondary sources, you must take good library notes, include source notes in the report, and list all references in a bibliography.**

In Appendix 3, page 379, you will find three methods of documentation: (1) the footnote method, (2) the endnote method, and (3) the parenthetic or MLA method.

Bibliography.   A bibliography is an alphabetic list of all books, articles, and other sources of data cited or consulted in preparing a formal report. This list is useful to readers and a necessary component in a long, formal report. Instructions for preparing a bibliography are also given in Appendix 3, page 384.

Organizing Data

The readability of a report is greatly enhanced by skillful organization of the facts presented. You have already studied numerous strategies or plans of organization for shorter documents.

Organizational Strategies

Here is a brief overview of possible plans for the organization of formal reports.

- **Deductive Organization.** As you recall from earlier instruction, the deductive strategy presents big ideas first. In formal reports that would mean beginning with proposals, recommendations, or findings. For example, if you were studying five possible locations for a proposed shopping center, you would begin with the recommendation of the best site and follow with discussion of other sites. Use this strategy when the reader is supportive and knowledgeable.

- **Inductive Organization.** Inductive reasoning presents facts and discussion first, followed by conclusions and recommendations. Since formal reports generally seek to educate the reader, this order of presentation is often most effective. Following this sequence, a study of possible locations for a shopping center would begin with data regarding all proposed sites followed by analysis of the information and conclusions drawn from that analysis. *persuasive*

- **Chronological Organization.** Information sequenced along a time frame is arranged chronologically. This plan is effective for presenting historical data or for describing a procedure. A description of the development of a multinational company, for example, would be chronological. A report explaining how to obtain federal funding for a project might be organized chronologically. Often topics are arranged in a past-to-present or present-to-past sequence.

- **Geographical or Spatial.** Information arranged geographically or spatially is organized by physical location. For instance, a report analyzing a company's national sales might be divided into sections representing different geographical areas such as the East, South, Midwest, West, and Northwest.

- **Topical or Functional.** Some subjects lend themselves to arrangement by topic or function. A report analyzing changes in the management hierarchy of an organization might be arranged in this manner. First, the report would consider the duties of the CEO followed by the functions of the general manager, business manager, marketing manager, and so forth.

In organizing a long, formal report, you may find that you combine some of the preceding plans. However it's done, you must break your topic into major divisions, usually three to six. These major divisions then must be partitioned into smaller subdivisions. To identify these divisions, you may use functional heads (such as *introduction, findings, discussion, conclusions, recommendations*) or talking heads that explain the contents of the text. You may wish to review the suggestions for writing effective headings that appeared in Chapter 11, page 250.

> The overall presentation of a topic may be inductive or deductive, while parts of the report are chronological (such as the background) or topical (such as discussion of findings).

Outlining.   The best way to organize a report is by recording its divisions in an outline. This outline is a tool of the writer; it is not part of the final report. The purpose of an outline is to show at a glance the overall plan of the report. Figure 12.1 shows an abbreviated outline of a report about forms of business ownership.

Figure 12.2 illustrates the format for levels of headings in reports. Notice that the title represents a first-degree heading and appears in all caps centered on a line. Other headings reveal their importance and their relevance to the outline by their position and their format. Second-degree headings are centered and underscored. Third-degree headings start at the left margin and are underscored. Fourth-degree headings (sometimes called *paragraph headings*) are indented; text immediately follows the heading.

Illustrating Data

Tables, charts, graphs, illustrations, and other visual aids can play an important role in clarifying, summarizing, and emphasizing information. Numerical data become meaningful, complex ideas are simplified, and visual interest is provided by the appropriate use of graphics. Here are general tips for making the most effective use of visual aids.

> The tips presented here for generating and implementing graphics in formal reports are useful in other presentations as well.

General Guidelines

- Clearly identify the contents of the visual aid with meaningful titles and headings.

- Refer the reader to the visual aid by discussing it in the text and mentioning its location and figure number.

- Locate the table close to its reference in the text.

- Strive for vertical placement of visual aids. Readers are disoriented by horizontal pages in reports.

- Give credit to the source if appropriate.

Tables

Probably the most frequently used visual aid in reports is the table. A table presents quantitative information in a systematic order of columns and rows. Be sure to identify columns and rows clearly. In Figure 12.3 *Years of Schooling Required* represents the row heading; *Current Jobs* and *New Jobs* represent column headings.

FIGURE 12.1   Outline Format

FORMS OF BUSINESS OWNERSHIP

I. Sole proprietorship (*first main topic*)

   A. Advantages of sole proprietorship (*first subdivision of Topic I*)

      1. Minimal capital requirements (*first subdivision of Topic A*)

      2. Control by owner (*second subdivision of Topic A*)

      3. Tax savings (*third subdivision of Topic A*)

   B. Disadvantages of sole proprietorship (*second subdivision of Topic I*)

      1. Unlimited liability (*first subdivision of Topic B*)

      2. Limited management talent (*second subdivision of Topic B*)

      3. Credit availability (*third subdivision of Topic B*)

II. Partnership (*second main topic*)

   A. Advantages of partnership (*first subdivision of Topic II*)

      1. Access of capital (*first subdivision of Topic A*)

      2. Management talent (*second subdivision of Topic A*)

      3. Ease of formation (*third subdivision of Topic A*)

   B. Disadvantages of partnership (*second subdivision of Topic II*)

      1. Unlimited liability (*first subdivision of Topic B*)

      2. Personality conflicts (*second subdivision of Topic B*)

FIGURE 12.2   Format of Headings

↓ 13 lines

First-degree heading   FORMS OF BUSINESS OWNERSHIP

↓ 2 lines

Second-degree heading   Sole Proprietorships

↓ 3 lines

Third-degree heading   Advantages of Sole Proprietorships

↓ 2 lines

Fourth-degree heading   Minimal capital requirements . _____

_____ .

Control by owner . _____

_____ .

Tax savings . _____

_____ .

↓ 3 lines

Disadvantages of Sole Proprietorships

↓ 2 lines

Unlimited liability . _____

_____ .

Limited management talent . _____

_____ .

Credit availability . _____

_____

↓ 3 lines

Partnerships

↓ 2 lines

Advantages of Partnerships

↓ 2 lines

Access to capital . _____

_____

Management talent . _____

_____ .

Ease of formation . _____

_____

↓ 3 lines

Disadvantages of Partnerships

↓ 2 lines

Unlimited liability . _____

_____

Personality conflicts . _____

_____

FIGURE 12.3   Table

Table 1

SCHOOLING REQUIRED FOR CURRENT AND FUTURE EMPLOYMENT

Years of Education Now and in Year 2000

Years of Schooling Required	Current Jobs	New Jobs
8 years or less	6%	4%
1 to 3 years of high school	12%	10%
4 years of high school	40%	34%
1 to 3 years of college	20%	22%
4 years of college or more	22%	30%

Source: Bureau of Labor Statistics, Hudson Institute

Charts and Graphs

A chart or graph clarifies data by showing the relationship between one variable and another.

Pie charts.   Pie, or circle, charts help readers visualize a whole and the proportions of its components, as shown in Figure 12.4. Pie charts are particularly useful in showing percentages. In preparing pie charts, begin dividing the pie at the 12 o'clock position. It's helpful to include both a description and the actual percent of the total with each segment. Group a number of small components into one segment. All segments should total 100 percent. Labels are easiest to read when typed horizontally outside the segments.

Line Charts.   Line charts are useful in showing changes in quantitative data over time. Like many visual aids, line charts cannot show precise data; instead,

FIGURE 12.4   Pie Chart

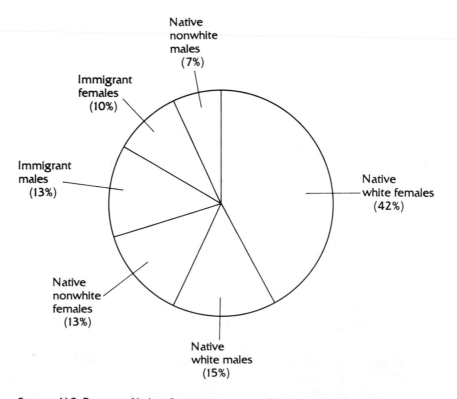

NEW ENTRANTS TO U.S. LABOR FORCE BY YEAR 2000

Distributed by Sex and Citizenship

Native nonwhite males (7%)

Immigrant females (10%)

Immigrant males (13%)

Native white females (42%)

Native nonwhite females (13%)

Native white males (15%)

Source: U.S. Bureau of Labor Statistics.

they give an impression of a trend or movement. Notice in Figure 12.5 that the time variable (years) is shown horizontally and the quantitative variable (pounds of production) is shown vertically. A solid line indicates one item; a broken line represents another.

Bar Charts.   A bar chart uses horizontal bars or vertical columns to compare information. Figure 12.6 shows fast-growing occupations projected to the year 2000. Could this information have been meaningfully expressed in a pie chart?

Organization Chart.   An organizational chart shows management structure and line of authority. The chart in Figure 12.7 defines the hierarchy of authority from the board of directors to individual managers.

Other Visual Aids

In addition to tables, charts, and graphs, you can produce other graphics even if you have little artistic or graphics skill. An extensive selection of stick-on lettering, borders, and designs makes graphic illustration much easier than ever before. Visit a stationery center, office-supply house, art-supply center, or bookstore to see the large assortment of aids for amateur and professional graphics designers. Inexpensive books are also available with "clip-art," a collection of pictures, designs, and printed expressions. You can clip the design or expression

Professional graphics effects can be created with readily available commercial products.

FIGURE 12.5   Line Chart

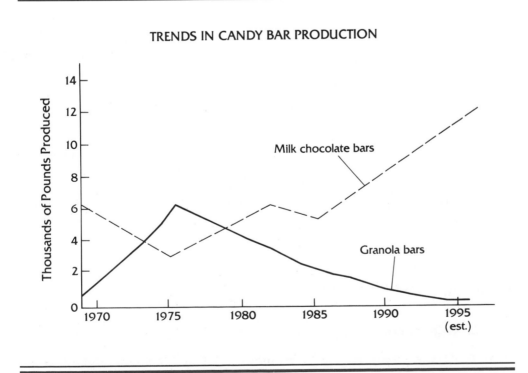

~~

FIGURE 12.6　Bar Chart

Why does this chart use horizontal bars instead of vertical columns?

In making bar charts, start with graph paper or draw your own grid marking off even segments before you make the first column.

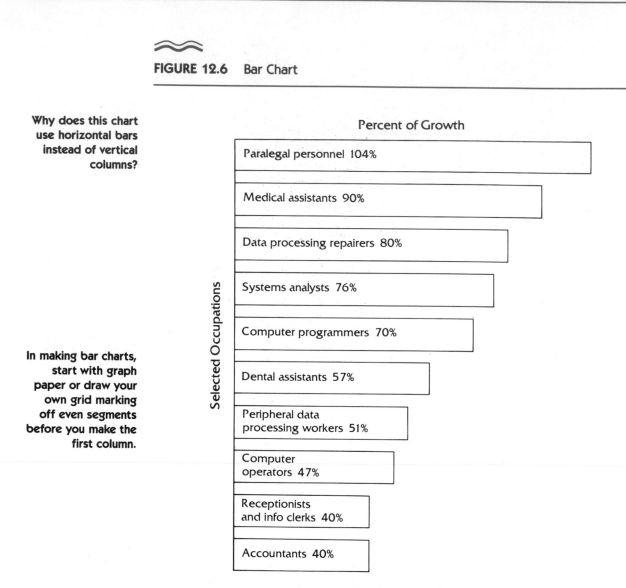

Percent of Growth

Selected Occupations

- Paralegal personnel 104%
- Medical assistants 90%
- Data processing repairers 80%
- Systems analysts 76%
- Computer programmers 70%
- Dental assistants 57%
- Peripheral data processing workers 51%
- Computer operators 47%
- Receptionists and info clerks 40%
- Accountants 40%

Figure 3.　Fast-Growing Occupations, 1990–2000
Source: Bureau of Labor Statistics

you want, paste it on your page, and make a photocopy for a slick-looking final copy.

~~

Presenting the Final Report

Overall Organization

Long reports generally are organized into three major divisions and a number of subdivisions. The order of three divisions in a formal report is outlined here.

FIGURE 12.7   Organization Chart

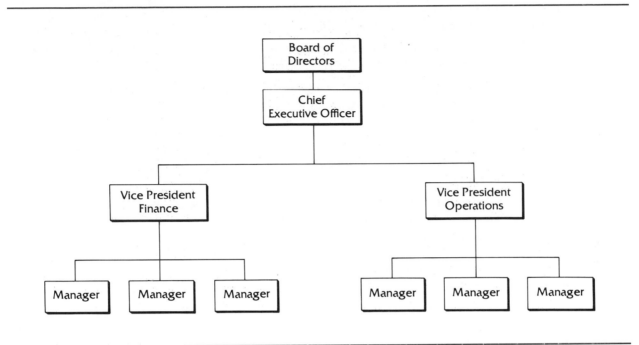

Prefatory Parts (parts preceding the body)

Title fly*

Title page

Letter of authorization*

Letter of transmittal

Table of contents

Abstract, synopsis, or executive summary

Body

Introduction or background

Discussion of findings

Summary, conclusions, recommendations

Supplementary Parts

Endnotes or Works Cited

Bibliography

Appendix*

*Not illustrated in our model formal report.

Long, formal reports contain three major sections: prefatory parts, body, and supplementary parts.

Parts

Now let's look more carefully at the individual parts of a long, formal report. Refer to Figure 12.8 for illustration of most of these parts.

- **Title Fly.** A single page with the title begins a formal report. In less formal reports, the title fly is omitted. Compose the title of your report carefully so that it shows immediately what the report covers and what it does not cover.

- **Title Page.** In addition to the title, the title page shows the author, the individual or organization who authorized the report, the recipient of the report, and the date.

- **Letter of Authorization.** If a letter or memo authorizes the report, it may be included in the prefatory material. This optional part is omitted from the model in Figure 12.8.

- **Letter of Transmittal.** This is the first impression the reader receives of the report; as such, it should be given serious consideration. Use the direct strategy and include some or all of the suggestions here:

1. Deliver the report ("Here is the report you authorized").
2. Present an overview of the report.
3. Suggest how to read or interpret it.
4. Describe limitations, if they exist.
5. Acknowledge those who assisted you.
6. Suggest follow-up studies, if appropriate.
7. Express appreciation for the assignment.
8. Offer to discuss the report personally.

- **Table of Contents.** Identify the name and location of every part of the report except the title fly, title page, and table of contents itself. Use spaced periods (leaders) to join the part with its page number.

- **Abstract, Synopsis, Epitome, or Executive Summary.** A summary condensing the entire report may carry any of these names. This time-saving device, which should be kept under one page, summarizes the purpose, findings, and conclusions.

- **Introduction or Background.** After the prefatory parts, begin the body of the report with an introduction that includes any or all of the following items:

1. Explanation of how the report originated and why it was authorized.
2. Description of the problem that prompted the report and the specific research questions to be answered.
3. Purpose of the report.
4. Scope (boundaries) and limitations or restrictions of the research.
5. Sources and methods of collecting data.
6. Summary of findings, if the report is written deductively.
7. Preview of the major sections of the report to follow, thus providing coherence and transition for the reader.

* If you want to

FIGURE 12.8 Model Long Report

[Letter of Transmittal]

MONROE, DEL RIO INDUSTRIAL CONSULTANTS

588 Park Avenue
Boston, Massachusetts 02116

January 12, 19xx

City Council
City of Boston
Boston, MA 02290

Ladies and Gentlemen:

The attached report, requested by the Boston City Council in a letter to Goldman-Lyon & Associates dated May 20, describes the economic impact of Roxbury Industrial Park on the city of Boston. We believe you will find the results of this study useful in evaluating future development of industrial parks within the city limits.

This study was designed to examine economic impact in three areas:

(1) Current and projected tax and other revenues accruing to the city from Roxbury Industrial Park

(2) Current and projected employment generated by the park

(3) Indirect effects on local employment, income, and economic growth

Primary research consisted of interviews with 15 Roxbury Industrial Park tenants and managers, in addition to a 1990 survey of over 5,000 RIP employees. Secondary research sources included the Annual Budget of the City of Boston, county and state tax records, government publications, professional periodicals, and relevant books.

Our research indicates that Roxbury Industrial Park exerts a significant

---

beneficial influence on the Boston metropolitan economy. We would be pleased to discuss this report and its conclusions with you at your request.

Sincerely,

Diana Del Rio
Senior Research
Consultant

DDR:mef
Attachment

ECONOMIC IMPACT
OF ROXBURY INDUSTRIAL PARK

ON THE CITY OF BOSTON

Prepared for

The Boston City Council
Boston, Massachusetts

Prepared by

Diana Del Rio
Senior Research Consultant
Monroe, Del Rio Research Consultants

January 10, 19xx

FIGURE 12.8 Continued

[Contents]

TABLE OF CONTENTS

iii

iv

ABSTRACT

The city of Boston can benefit from the development of industrial parks like the Roxbury Industrial Park. Both direct and indirect economic benefits result, as shown by this in-depth study conducted by Monroe-Del Rio Research Associates. The study was authorized by the Boston City Council when Goldman-Lyon & Associates sought the City Council's approval for the proposed construction of a G-L industrial park. The City Council requested evidence demonstrating that an existing development could actually benefit the city.

The conclusion that the city of Boston benefits from industrial parks is based on data supplied by a survey of 5,000 Roxbury Industrial Park employees, personal interviews with managers

v

and tenants of RIP, city and state documents, and professional literature.

Analysis of the data revealed benefits in three areas:

(1) Revenues. The city of Boston earned nearly $1 million in tax and other revenues from the Roxbury Industrial Park in 1988. By 1995 this income is expected to reach $1.7 million (in constant 1988 dollars).

(2) Employment. In 1988 RIP businesses employed a total of 7,035 workers, who earned an average wage of $24,920. By 1995 RIP businesses are expected to employ directly nearly 15,000 employees who will earn salaries totaling over $450 million.

(3) Indirect benefits. Because of the multiplier effect, by 1995 Roxbury Industrial

vi

Note: This report is shown in double spacing. Some business writers prefer single spacing to conserve paper and filing space.

FIGURE 12.8 Continued

Park will directly and indirectly generate a total of 38,362 jobs in the Boston metropolitan area.

On the basis of these findings, it is recommended that development of additional industrial parks be encouraged to stimulate local economic growth.

vii

ECONOMIC IMPACT OF ROXBURY INDUSTRIAL PARK

Problem

This study was designed to analyze the direct and indirect economic impact of Roxbury Industrial Park on the city of Boston. Specifically, the study seeks answers to these questions:

(1) What current tax and other revenues result directly from this park? What tax and other revenues may be expected in the future?

(2) How many and what kind of jobs are directly attributable to the park? What is the employment picture for the future?

(3) What indirect effects has Roxbury Industrial Park had on local employment, incomes, and economic growth?

2

Background

The development firm of Goldman-Lyon & Associates commissioned this study of Roxbury Industrial Park at the request of the Boston City Council. Before authorizing the development of a proposed Goldman-Lyon industrial park, the City Council requested a study examining the economic effects of an existing park. Members of the City Council wanted to determine to what extent industrial parks benefit the local community, and they chose Roxbury Industrial Park as an example.

For those who are unfamiliar with it, Roxbury Industrial Park is a 400-acre industrial park located in the city of Boston about four miles from the center of the city. Most of the area lies within a specially designated area known as

3

Redevelopment Project No. 2, which is under the jurisdiction of the Boston Redevelopment Agency. Planning for the park began in 1975; construction started in 1977.

The park now contains 14 building complexes with over 1.25 million square feet of completed building space. The majority of the buildings are used for office, research and development, marketing and distribution, or manufacturing uses. Approximately 50 acres of the original area are yet to be developed.

Data for this report came from a 1990 survey of over 5,000 Roxbury Industrial Park employees, interviews with 15 RIP tenants and managers, the Annual Budget of the City of Boston, county and state tax records, current books, and articles from professional journals. Projections for future revenues resulted from

FIGURE 12.8 Continued

4

analysis of past trends and "Estimates of Revenues for Debt Service Coverage, Redevelopment Project Area 2." The results of this research indicate that major direct and indirect benefits have accrued to the city of Boston and surrounding metropolitan areas as a result of the development of Roxbury Industrial Park. The research findings presented here fall into three categories: (1) revenues, (2) employment, and (3) indirect effects.

Discussion of Findings

Revenues

Roxbury Industrial Park contributes a variety of tax and other revenues to the city of Boston. Figure 1 summarizes these revenues.

5

Figure 1

REVENUES RECEIVED BY THE CITY OF BOSTON FROM ROXBURY INDUSTRIAL PARK

Current Revenues and Projections to 1995

	1990	1995
Sales and use taxes	$604,140	$1,035,390
Revenues from alcohol licenses, motor vehicle in lieu fees, and trailer coach licenses	126,265	216,396
Franchise taxes	75,518	129,424
State gas tax receipts	53,768	92,134

6

Licenses and permits	48,331	82,831
Fines and forfeitures	47,727	81,795
Other revenues	16,312	30,192
Total	$972,061	$1,668,162

Projections, based on constant 1990 dollars, were calculated at an annual growth rate of 8 percent. Source of current revenues: Massachusetts State Board of Equalization, Bulletin. Boston: State Printing Office, 1990, p. 103.

Sales and use revenues. The city's largest source of revenue from RIP is the sales and use tax. Revenue from this source totaled $604,140 in 1990, according to figures provided by the Massachusetts State Board of Equalization.[1]

7

Sales and use taxes accounted for more than half of the park's total contribution to the city of $972,062.

Other revenues. Other major sources of city revenues from RIP in 1988 include alcohol licenses, motor vehicle in lieu fees, and trailer coach licenses ($126,265), franchise taxes ($75,518), and state gas tax receipts ($53,768).

Projections. Total city revenues from RIP will nearly double by 1995, producing an income of $1.7 million. This projection is based on an annual growth rate in sales of 8 percent in constant 1990 dollars. Inflation, of course, may increase this figure.

Employment

Distribution. A total of 7,035 employees work in various industry groups at Roxbury

FIGURE 12.8 Continued

8

Industrial Park, as shown in Figure 2. The largest number of workers (58 percent) is employed in manufacturing and assembly operations. In the next largest category, the computer and electronics industry employs 24 percent of the workers. Some overlap between the manufacturing and computer categories probably exists because electronics assembly could be included in either group. Employees also work in publishing (9 percent), warehousing and storage (5 percent), and other industries (4 percent).

Wages. In 1990 employees at RIP earned a total of $181.5 million in wages, as shown in Figure 3. The average employee in that year earned $24,920. The highest average wages were paid to employees in white-collar fields, such as computer and electronics ($32,800) and

9

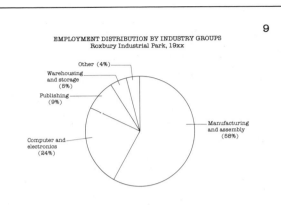

Figure 2. EMPLOYMENT DISTRIBUTION BY INDUSTRY GROUPS
Source: 19xx survey of RIP employees.

publishing ($26,300). Average wages for workers in blue-collar fields ranged from $23,400 in manufacturing and assembly to $20,200 in warehousing and storage.

Projections. By 1995 Roxbury Industrial Park is expected to more than double its number of

10

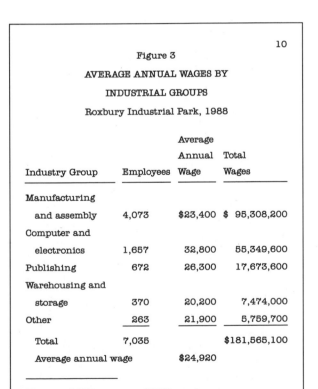

Figure 3

AVERAGE ANNUAL WAGES BY
INDUSTRIAL GROUPS

Roxbury Industrial Park, 1988

Industry Group	Employees	Average Annual Wage	Total Wages
Manufacturing and assembly	4,073	$23,400	$ 95,308,200
Computer and electronics	1,657	32,800	55,349,600
Publishing	672	26,300	17,673,600
Warehousing and storage	370	20,200	7,474,000
Other	263	21,900	5,759,700
Total	7,035		$181,565,100
Average annual wage		$24,920	

Source: 1990 survey of RIP employees.

11

employees, bringing the total to over 15,000 workers. The total payroll in 1995 will also more than double, producing over $450 million (using constant 1990 dollars) in salaries to RIP employees. These projections are based on an 8 percent growth rate[2], along with anticipated increased employment as the park reaches its capacity.

Future development in the park will influence employment and payrolls. One RIP project manager stated in an interview that much of the remaining 50 acres is planned for medium-rise office buildings, garden offices, and other structures for commercial, professional, and personal services.[3] Average wages for employees are expected to increase because of an anticipated shift to higher paying white-collar jobs.

Industrial parks often follow a similar pattern

12

of evolution.[4] Like many industrial parks, RIP evolved from a warehousing center to a manufacturing assembly center and is entering final stages of its development, where the focus centers on office functions. Already marketing and other commercial activities have taken over many of the buildings that were originally designed for warehousing. The trend toward white-collar employment is expected to escalate as more computer software producers, financial data analysts, and electronics firms enter the park.

Indirect Effects

In addition to the direct effects represented by tax revenues and employment salaries, Roxbury Industrial Park has affected the immediate local community and the greater Boston metropolitan area in a number of indirect ways.

13

As industries in RIP expand, they create a demand for more goods and services from other industries, resulting in increased employment in these industries. Similarly, expenditures by RIP employees increase the demand for consumer goods and services, again creating new jobs. Thus, the growth of RIP has a multiplier effect, creating still greater growth in employment and incomes in the larger economic community. . . .

.
.
.

Conclusions and Recommendations

Analysis of tax revenues, employment data, personal interviews, and professional literature leads to the following conclusions and recommendations regarding the economic impact of Roxbury Industrial Park on the city of Boston:

14

(1) Sales tax and other revenues produced nearly $1 million in income to the city of Boston in 1990.

(2) By 1995 sales tax and other revenues are expected to produce $1.7 million in city income.

(3) RIP currently employs 7,035 employees, the majority of whom are working in manufacturing and assembly. The average employee in 1990 earned $24,920.

(4) By 1995 RIP is expected to employ more than 15,000 workers producing a total payroll of over $450 million.

(5) Employment trends indicate that by 1995 more RIP employees will be engaged in higher-paying white-collar positions.

(6) Because of the multiplier effect, RIP employees create further growth in the local

15

economy through their expenditures for goods and services.

(7) Predictions indicate that by 1995 RIP will directly and indirectly generate a total of 38,362 new jobs in the Boston metropolitan area.

On the basis of these findings, we recommend that the City Council of Boston authorize the development of additional industrial parks to stimulate local economic growth.

.
.
.

~~~
FIGURE 12.8 Continued

16

NOTES

1. Massachusetts State Board of Equalization, Bulletin (Boston: State Printing Office, 1990) p. 26.

2. Arthur M. Miller, "Estimates of Revenues for Debt Service Coverage, Redevelopment Project Area No. 2," Miller and Schroeder Municipals (New York: Rincon Press, 1989) pp. 78–79.

3. Ivan M. Novack, personal interview, 30 September 1990.

4. Deborah Law and Wayne Barry, Industrial Development in a Healthy Economy (New York: Dryden Press, 1987) p. 320.

5. Mark T. Conway, "Site Selection, Plant Locations, and Local Communities," Industrial Development, May 1985, Vol. 120, p. 79.

6. Conway, p. 81.

17

7. Allen P. Cohen, "Industrial Parks Invade Suburbia," New York Times, 10 December 1990, Sec. IV, p. 1, cols. 4–5.

18

BIBLIOGRAPHY

Avila, Mario. Personal interview. 2 June 1989.

City of Boston. Annual Budget. Boston: Municipal Printing Office, 1989.

Cohen, Allen P. "Industrial Parks Invade Suburbia." New York Times, 10 December 1990, Sec. IV, p. 1, cols. 4–5.

Conway, Mark T. "Site Selections, Plant Locations, and Local Communities." Industrial Development, May 1985, pp. 71–85.

Kupczek, Mitchell. Personal interview. 15 July 1987.

Law, Deborah, and Wayne Barry. Industrial Development in a Healthy Economy. New York: Dryden Press, 1987.

Massachusetts State Board of Equalization. Bulletin. Boston: State Printing Office, 1990.

Miller, Arthur M. "Estimates of Revenues for Debt Service Coverage, Redevelopment Project Area No. 2." Miller and Schroeder Municipals. New York: Rincon Press, 1989.

Murphy, Ronald D. "Strategy and Structure: Chapters in the History of the Industrial

---

19

Enterprise," Harvard Business Review, December 1989, pp. 78–93.

Novack, Ivan M. Personal interview. 30 September 1990.

Suffolk County Auditor-Controller. Prospectus for Tax Allocated Bonds. Boston: County Printing Office, 1989.

Taylor, Barbara A. Trends in Industrial Real Estate. New York: Charles Scribner's Sons, 1988.

■ **Discussion of Findings.** This is the main section of the report and contains numerous headings and subheadings. It is unnecessary to use the title *Discussion of Findings*; many business report writers prefer to begin immediately with the major headings into which the body of the report is divided. Like short reports, you may organize the body deductively, inductively, chronologically, geographically, or topically. Present your findings objectively, avoiding the use of first-person pronouns (*I, we*). Include tables, charts, and graphs if necessary to illustrate findings. Analytic and scientific reports may include another section entitled *Implications of Findings*, in which the findings are analyzed and related to the problem. Less formal reports contain the author's analysis of the research findings within the *Discussion* section.

■ **Summary, Conclusions, Recommendations.** If the report has been largely informational, it ends with a summary of the data presented. If the report analyzes research findings, then the report ends with conclusions drawn from the analyses. An analytic report frequently poses research questions. The conclusion to such a report reviews the major findings and answers the research questions.

If a report seeks to determine a course of action, it may end with conclusions and recommendations. The recommendations regarding a course of action may be placed in a separate section or incorporated with the conclusions.

■ **Footnotes, Endnotes, or Works Cited.** See Appendix 3, Documentation, page 379, for details on how to document sources. In the footnote method the source notes appear at the foot of each page. In the endnote method they are displayed immediately after the text on a page called *Notes*. In the parenthetic or MLA method of documentation, the notes are listed on a page called *Works Cited* or *Works Consulted*.

■ **Bibliography.** Most formal reports will include a bibliography that lists all sources consulted in the report research—whether they were actually cited in notes or not. See Appendix 3, page 384, regarding the bibliography.

■ **Appendix.** The appendix contains any supplementary information needed to clarify the report. Charts and graphs illustrating significant data are generally part of the report proper. However, extra information that might be included in an appendix are such items as a sample questionnaire, a questionnaire cover letter, correspondence relating to the report, maps, other reports, and optional tables.

APPLICATION AND PRACTICE—12

Discussion

1. If formal reports are seldom written in business, why study them?

2. How is the process of writing a formal report similar to that of writing an informal report?

3. How could a report be organized inductively and topically at the same time?

4. Should every long, formal report have graphic aids? Explain.

5. Distinguish between primary and secondary data. Which are more likely to be useful in a business report?

Short Answers

6. Name five plans for organizing data in a formal report. Be prepared to explain each.

7. What is the first step in writing a formal report?

8. If you were writing a formal report on computerizing your company's accounting functions, what primary sources of data would you seek? Be prepared to explain.

9. List four sources of secondary information, and be prepared to discuss how each might be useful in writing a formal report on computerizing your company's accounting functions.

10. List four degrees of headings, and explain how they are different.

11. Pie charts are most helpful in showing what?

12. Line graphs are most effective in showing what?

13. If you've never used a library before, where should you probably begin?

14. List the parts of a formal report. Be prepared to discuss each.

15. Should business reports be single- or double-spaced?

Writing Improvement Exercises

Outlining

16. Construct an outline using the following data gathered initially to write a report. Include a title. Assume that you would collect more data later. After you complete the outline, indicate what level of heading each line of the outline would require.

The operation of a business would be very risky without some form of property insurance. Most fire insurance policies protect against loss to buildings and their contents. Wooden buildings, of course, would cost more than brick buildings to insure. The contents of buildings are valued separately. Insurance experts believe that nearly one third of all business-related fires may be caused by arson. Another form of property insurance is marine insurance. Ocean marine insurance is the oldest form of insurance in the country. It protects the ship and its cargo. Inland marine insurance, strangely enough, protects against damage to property being transported in three areas: goods transported by ship, truck, or train, that is, goods being moved by any of these three means may be covered with inland marine insurance.

Nearly 30 million automobile accidents occur each year in the U.S. Automobile insurance is a form of property insurance. It covers many areas, including body injury, medical payment coverage (to protect policyholders, their family members, and any passengers in the car), and uninsured motorist coverage. Auto insurance also includes property damage. This pays the cost of damage to other people's property (such as buildings and cars). Collision insurance is different. It pays for damage to the policyholder's car. You can have full coverage or deductible ($100 to $500).

Organizing.   Assume that you are a research consultant with Search, Inc. Your firm has been asked to find a sales and distribution site in the Denver area for Farrell Electrical Components, 3450 Overland Avenue, Los Angeles, CA 90034. Farrell seeks suitable office space, including a reception area (where three office employees could work), one private office, and a conference/display area. Farrell also wants 3,000 square feet of heated warehouse space. It should be equipped with a sprinkler system and have 18-foot ceilings. If sales are successful, Farrell may need an additional 2,000 square feet of warehouse space in the future. Farrell needs to locate near Stapleton International Airport; moreover, it must be close to trucking terminals and main thoroughfares in an area zoned for light industry. It also seeks an impressive-looking building with a modern executive image. Farrell wants to lease for at least two years with possible renewal. It needs to make a decision within three weeks. If no space is available, it will delay until next year.

You have been assigned the task of researching this assignment and then writing a report that includes a recommendation for Farrell based upon your findings.

17. Who is the audience for this long report? Should you include extensive background data explaining why the report is being written? Explain.

18. Would you rely on primary or secondary research? How would you gather data for this report?

19. What constraints will limit your research?

20. What visual aids would enhance this report?

21. On a separate sheet write a statement of purpose that could become part of the introduction to your report. Include Farrell's requirements.

22. You have narrowed the choices to five locations near Stapleton International Airport. On a separate sheet make a table from the following rough notes. Include a title and subtitle, as well as appropriate columnar headings.

23. Compose a lead-in sentence that introduces the preceding table in your report.

24. What strategy would you follow in organizing this report? Why?

Activities

25. **Visual aids.** From *U.S. News & World Report, U.S.A. Today, Business Week,* a textbook, or some other publication, locate one example of a table, a pie chart, a line chart, a bar chart, and an organization chart. Bring copies of these visual aids to class. How effectively could the data have been expressed in words, without the graphics? Is the appropriate graphic form used? How is the graphic introduced in the text? Your instructor may wish you to submit a memo discussing visual aids.

26. **Library.** Assume that you have been asked to recommend a library to fellow students who have little library experience. Visit your school or public library. Observe its resources, method of operation, shelf lists, and personnel. Write a one-page memo report describing your findings.

27. **Bibliography.** Select a topic that interests you. Prepare a bibliography of at least five current magazine articles, three books, and five other references that contain relevant information regarding the topic. Your instructor may ask you to divide your bibliography into sections: *Books, Periodicals, Other Resources.* You may also be asked to annotate your bibliography; that is, compose a brief description of each reference, such as this:

Rash, Wayne, Jr. "Dawn of the Dead Disk." *Byte*, July 1989, 137–140. This article discusses the need for timely, complete backups of data stored on hard disks so that when a hard disk crashes, a business may continue with the least interruption.

28. **Computer databases.** Compose a list of computer information sources available through a library in your area. What are the charges for receiving data? What is the procedure for using the services? Write a memo describing your findings. Include one or more visual aids to illustrate your data.

29. **Interview report.** Collect information regarding communication skills used by individuals in a particular career field (accounting, management, marketing, office administration, paralegal, and so forth). Interview three or more individuals in a specific occupation in that field. Determine how much and what kind of writing they do. Do they make oral presentations? How much time do they spend in telephone communication? What recommendations do they have for training for this position? What conclusions can you draw from your research? What recommendations would you make for individuals entering this field? Write a report of about five single-spaced or ten double-spaced pages. Include at least one visual aid. Your instructor may wish you to include a section requiring library

research into the perception of businesspeople over the past ten years regarding the communication skills of employees.

GRAMMAR/MECHANICS CHECKUP—12

Capitalization

Review Sections 3.01 through 3.16 in the Grammar/Mechanics Handbook. Then study each of the following statements. Circle any lowercase letter that should be capitalized. Draw a slash (/) through any capital letter that you wish to change to lowercase. Indicate in the space provided the number of changes you made in each sentence and record the number of the G/M principle illustrated.* If you made no changes, write *0.* When you finish, compare your responses with those shown below. If your responses differ, study carefully the principle in parentheses.

Example: After consulting our Attorneys for Legal advice, Vice President Mills signed the Contract.   4   (3.01, 3.06a)

1. All american passengers from Flight 402 must pass through Customs Inspection at Gate 17 upon arrival at Baltimore international airport.   _____

2. Personal tax rates for japanese citizens are low by International standards; rates for japanese corporations are high, according to Iwao Nakatani, an Economics Professor at Osaka university.   _____

3. In the end, Business passes on most of the burden to the Consumer: What looks like a tax on Business is really a tax on Consumption.   _____

4. Lisa enrolled in courses in History, Sociology, Spanish, and Computer Science.   _____

5. Did you see the *Forbes* article entitled "Careers in horticulture are nothing to sneeze at"?   _____

6. Although I recommend the Minex Diskettes sold under the brandname Maxidisk, you may purchase any Diskettes you choose.   _____

7. According to a Federal Government report, any regulation of State and County banking must receive local approval.   _____

8. The vice president of the united states said, "this country continues to encourage Foreign investments."   _____

9. The Comptroller of Ramjet International reported to the President and the Board of Directors that the internal revenue service was beginning an investigation of their Company.   _____

*G/M principles are listed in ascending order.

10. My Mother, who lives near St. Petersburg, reports that protection from the Sun's rays is particularly important in the South.

11. Our Managing Editor met with Leslie Hawkins, Manager of the Advertising Sales Department, to plan an Ad Campaign for our special issue.

12. In the fall, Editor in Chief Porter plans an article detailing the astounding performance of the austrian, West german, and italian currencies.

13. To reach Belle Isle park, which is located on an Island in the Detroit river, tourists pass over the Douglas MacArthur bridge.

14. On page 6 of the catalog you will see that the computer science department is offering a number of courses in programming.

15. Please consult figure 3.2 in chapter 5 for U.S. census bureau figures regarding non-english-speaking residents.

---

1. (5) American, customs inspection, International Airport (*3.01, 3.02, 3.07*)   3. (4) business, consumer, business, consumption (*3.01, 3.13*)   5. (5) Horticulture, Are, Nothing, Sneeze, At (*3.12*)
7. (4) federal government, state, county (*3.10*)   9. (6) comptroller, president, Internal Revenue Service, company (*3.01, 3.04, 3.06e*)   11. (5) managing editor, manager, ad campaign (*3.01, 3.06d, 3.06e, 3.09*)
13. (4) Park, island, River, Bridge (*3.01, 3.03*)   15. (5) Figure, Chapter, Census Bureau, English (*3.02, 3.04, 3.07*)

CHAPTER 13

Communication for Employment

~~~~~~

In this chapter you will learn to do the following:

- Locate job market information.
- Analyze your employment qualifications.
- Write an effective résumé.
- Compose solicited and unsolicited letters of application.
- Write other employment documents.
- Answer job interview questions skillfully.

Regarding your future career, the most important document you may ever write is your résumé. In this chapter you will learn to write an effective résumé, as well as an application letter and other messages related to employment. To be able to create documents that will help you win the best position, begin by analyzing the job market and your qualifications.

Your résumé may be the most important document you ever write.

~~~~

Preparation for Employment

Analyzing the Job Market

Whether you are applying for your first permanent position, competing for promotion, or changing careers, you need to gather employment information and analyze the job market. A résumé and application letter will be most successful if they are written to respond to the employment requirements and expectations in your field. To learn about employment specifications in your field, consider these sources of information.

How to Get Job Information

- **Want Ads.** Most newspapers feature employment opportunities in the Sunday edition. Study the ads for job descriptions, salaries, and qualifications.
- **Reference Librarian.** Ask your school or local public library reference librarian for employment information in your field. Learn about newsletters, journals, and magazines in your field.

- **Government Publications.** Look specifically at the latest editions of the *Dictionary of Occupational Titles* and the *Occupational Outlook Handbook* published by the U.S. Department of Labor.

- **Interviews.** Talk with someone in your field. Ask questions about qualifications and preparation for the position in which you are interested.

- **School Placement Service.** Consult job listing and bulletin board notices. Ask about positions in your field.

- **Part-time Job.** Seek a summer or part-time job in your career area.

- **Organizations.** Join a professional organization in your field. Subscribe to its publications. Many organizations encourage student membership status with reduced rates. Learn about your field and make valuable contacts.

- **Instructors.** Ask for advice from teachers in your field, especially those who work with employers through advisory committees or consulting.

Part-time employment in your field is probably the best way to gather information, make contacts, and get started in a career.

Analyzing Your Qualifications

The composition of your résumé begins with a thorough analysis of your background, experience, and qualifications.

You, like many students writing their first résumé, may think that you have little experience that will qualify you for a permanent or professional position. To help you analyze and organize data for your résumé, take stock of your experience and achievements by filling out inventory lists. Focus on employment, course work, special training and skills, and relevant extracurricular activities. Your lists should look like this:

Employment Inventory

Employer _____ Dates _____

Job title _____

Duties, responsibilities (list three to five):

_____

_____

Special Skills Inventory

List three to five special aptitudes or skills:

_____

_____

The verbs and adjectives you use to describe your accomplishments should be precise and vivid. Using action words and providing sufficient information will make your résumé come alive. Which of the following résumé statements is more helpful: *Kept books for Sunset Avionics,* or *Performed all bookkeeping functions including quarterly inventory count and valuation?* Here are some words to help you describe yourself.

Effective Adjectives for Successful Résumés

adaptable	efficient	painstaking
aggressive	enthusiastic	proficient
alert	flexible	reliable
ambitious	hardworking	resourceful
competent	logical	responsible
conscientious	loyal	serious
creative	objective	thoughtful

Effective Action Verbs for Successful Résumés

analyzed	discovered	organized
arranged	distributed	orginated
assembled	edited	oversaw
assisted	evaluated	participated
calculated	expedited	planned
charted	formulated	prepared
composed	generated	presented
consolidated	hired	provided
coordinated	identified	recorded
created	instituted	reorganized
delegated	learned	researched
demonstrated	maintained	revised
designed	managed	solved
developed	obtained	streamlined
directed	operated	

Ideas for Using Action Verbs

Reduced delivery delays.

Improved inventory procedures.

Devised streamlined stocking techniques.

Ordered medical supplies for Surgery, Cardiac Surgery, and Nursing.

Supervised mailing of monthly statements.

Collected payments from 125 accounts.

Oversaw installation of automated record-keeping.

Expedited repairs on company-owned vehicles.

Followed up overdue shipments.

Trained and supervised counter clerks.

Advised supervisor regarding purchase of microcomputer.

Increased productivity in word processing center.

Scheduled use of conference rooms.

Saved money on supplies through comparative shopping.

Identified key factors in sales decline.

Arranged travel accommodations for four executives.

≋

Résumé

The résumé is a summary of your experience, skills, and qualifications. The principal purpose of the résumé is to win an interview. The résumé also serves as a reminder of your qualifications after the interview.

Your goal in sending a résumé is securing an interview.

For an impressive résumé that wins you an interview, pay attention to its appearance. Use good-quality white bond paper (20- to 24-pound with 25 percent rag content) and sharp, black type. Leave ample white space in the margins and between headings.

The best way to prepare a résumé is by using a word processing program on a computer. Word processing allows you to experiment with headings, placement, and spacing to fit everything on the page attractively. You can revise the wording so that items are parallel and precisely stated. Moreover, you can update your résumé easily in the future. No document is better suited to word processing than the résumé.

If you don't have access to a computer with a good printer, it makes sense to have your résumé professionally typed. However, don't rely on someone else to write it. No one knows you better than yourself. For extra copies, use a good-quality photocopy machine.

Your résumé is your substitute, so make sure that it looks good. Robert Half, who runs a national recruiting firm, says that he reads résumés in this way: "I always begin by gaining a general impression of the résumé. Is it neat and obviously prepared with care? Typos? Sloppy sentences, bad grammar? Job applicants who turn out a sloppy, careless résumé for themselves (they've had all the time they need to do it right) can pretty much be counted on to do the same in their job."[1]

Personnel officers prefer one-page résumés.

Try to fit your résumé on one page. One personnel officer who receives hundreds of résumés said that he rarely reads those longer than one page. He doesn't have time. Most individuals can fit all their data on one page by planning carefully, by writing concisely, and by experimenting with different formats. If, however, you've had much experience and you're applying for a high-level position, a two-page résumé may be appropriate.

The use of novel form, paper, and typeface in a résumé is acceptable only if you are a graphic designer or you're applying in a field where evidence of creativity is valued.

Don't be tempted to capture attention by using humorous cartoons (no wanted posters with your picture inside), colored paper, flashy borders, odd-sized paper, or script typeface. Such novelties detract from your credentials.

[1]Robert Half, "Managing Your Career: How Do You Read a Resume?" *Management Accounting* (May 1988): 20.

What Do Big Businesses Look for in Résumés?

In a survey of Fortune 500 companies, 152 personnel directors indicated the items they considered most important and least important. Excluding obviously important items like name, address, previous employment, and college education, here's how they ranked other résumé items in order of importance.

Most Important Résumé Items	Least Important Résumé Items
Special skills, aptitudes	Religion
Awards, honors, college achievements	Race
Grade-point average	Gender
Willingness to relocate	High school grades
Achievements—work experience	Photograph
Professional organizations	Marital status
College extracurricular activities	Birthplace
Scholarships, college achievements	Height/weight
Career objective	Church involvement
References, previous employers	High school activities

Personnel officers for large national corporations appear to be less interested in personal items, perhaps for legal reasons, and more interested in college and job-related data, grade-point average, and willingness to relocate. A new résumé category that 70 percent of these busy personnel directors said they liked to see is a summary of qualifications.

Source: Harcourt and Krizan, *Journal of Business Communication* (Spring 1988) 177.

Résumés usually begin with a main heading and a career objective. The remaining categories—education, work experience, activities and achievements, and personal data—should be arranged in order of effectiveness in getting you the job. Put your most important qualifications first. Deemphasize any weaknesses. For example, if you have obvious gaps in your work record, avoid putting employment dates in a conspicuous position.

A winning résumé contains some or all of the following categories: main heading, career objective, education, work experience, special skills or achievements, and references.

Main Heading

Keep the main heading uncluttered and simple. List your name, address, and telephone number. If at all possible, include a number where messages may be left for you. (Prospective employers tend to call the next applicant when no one answers.) You may omit the word *Résumé*, particularly if you have little extra space. If you must show a temporary address, place it on one side of the heading and your permanent address on the other.

One personnel officer said that the heading Résumé is as unnecessary as the word Letter on a letter.

DONNA H. JENKINS

Address Until 6/15:   Permanent Address:

1717 North Green Street   1762 Lerado Drive
Bowling Green, Ohio 46403   Toledo, Ohio 43623
(419) 372-3944   (419) 555-3290
(419) 368-8922 (messages)

An alternate, creative heading may make your résumé stand out from the others but may limit its usefulness and visual impact. Consider the following headings:

QUALIFICATIONS OF JEREMY VELASQUEZ FOR MANAGEMENT TRAINEE

KIMBERLY ANN DUNN'S PREPARATION FOR WORK AS A LEGAL SECRETARY

Sales Training and Background of Solomon M. (Sol) Salinsky

Profile of Robert J. Woodrum
for the Position of Systems Analyst
for General Dynamics Corporation

Career Objective

Most personnel directors prefer résumés that include a career or employment objective. Such a statement shows that a candidate has considered short- and long-term goals and has made a commitment to a career. Decide whether you prefer a narrow career objective aimed at a specific job or a general objective that will make you employable in a number of job categories. Compare the following specific and general objectives:

Specific employment objectives.

To obtain a position as an administrative secretary in a large insurance organization that offers career paths leading to a management position in administrative support.

To become a junior paralegal in an urban law firm specializing in litigation, with the long-range goal of attending law school and becoming an attorney.

General employment objectives.

Entry-level position with a progressive firm that provides an opportunity to work with people as well as products in developing and selling effective information systems. Long-range goal is to become a product development manager.

To begin a career in personnel with exposure to recruiting, training, benefit administration, and contract negotiation. Eventually hope to become a personnel manager.

If you have two separate employment areas in which you plan to apply, make separate résumés with different objectives. For example, Linda Danforth should write two résumés if she expects to seek employment as a secretary or as a cosmetics representative. It's easy to produce different résumés using similar data if you use word processing equipment.

Education

Place your education next if it is more impressive than your work experience. Begin with the school you attended most recently. Employers are most interested in postsecondary schooling, but your high school may be listed if you have not completed an associate's or bachelor's degree. In this section include the name and location of the school, dates of attendance, major and minor fields of study, and degrees or diplomas received. Your grade-point average is important to prospective employers. One way to enhance your GPA is to calculate it in your major courses only (e.g., 3.6 GPA in major). A list of completed courses makes dull reading; use such a list only if you can relate the courses to the position sought. Include certificates earned, seminars attended, and workshops completed. Indicate the percentage of your education that you financed, if appropriate. If your education is incomplete, include such statements as *A.A. degree expected 9/93* or *72 units completed in 120-unit program*. Entitle this section *Education, Academic Preparation*, or *Professional Training*.

> **Emphasize your education if it's more impressive than your experience.**

Work Experience

Put this section first if your work experience is significant and relevant to the position you are seeking. List your most recent employment first and work backwards, including only those jobs that you think will help you win this position. Include the following data:

1. Employer's name and address (city and state)

2. Dates of employment (month and year)

3. Job title (most important position)

4. Significant duties, activities, accomplishments, and promotions

> **Your résumé does not require a complete history of your previous employment. Some job applications may ask for a full employment history, but your résumé may be selective.**

Describe your employment accomplishments concisely but concretely. Avoid generalities, such as *Interacted with customers*. Be more specific, such as *Greeted customers cheerfully, Successfully resolved problems regarding custom drapery orders*, or *Acted as intermediary between customers and drapery workroom*. Include forceful verbs, omit the personal pronoun *I*, and use balanced, parallel constructions.

In listing your work experience, you can achieve emphasis through the format you choose for presenting your data. Notice how the following examples emphasize the information shown first.

> **Select and emphasize work experiences that qualify you for the particular job in which you are interested.**

Emphasizes Job Title

Secretary Teletech Controls, Inc., Dearborn, MI, June, 1989–August 1991 (half-time).

> Accurately transcribed dictated letters, memos, and software documentation.
>
> Used word processing and data-base programs on IBM PC.
>
> Was promoted from typist to secretary after 9 months.
>
> Received praise from manager for ability to work under pressure.

Don't be modest about selling yourself.

Emphasizes Employer

First Atlantic Savings—Teller, August, 1987 to January, 1989.

> Recorded accurately over $100,000 worth of deposits and withdrawals daily.
>
> Reconciled day's cash and check totals consistently with computer journal scan.
>
> Handled customer inquiries and complaints resourcefully and cheerfully.

Emphasizes Dates

6/87 to 12/89   The R. T. French Company, Rochester, NY. Supervisor of Inventory Control.

> Promoted from accounting assistant in cost control to assistant supervisor after nine months.
>
> Became supervisor after eighteen months, overseeing the work of nine employees and a budget of $430,000.
>
> Devised and introduced new inventory-tracking procedures that saved over $25,000 annually.

Strive to illustrate and quantify examples of your strong character traits.

Try to select work experiences and achievements that illustrate your initiative, dependability, responsibility, resourcefulness, economy, and interpersonal skills. If possible, quantify them: *Keyboarded all the production models for a 215-*

page employee procedures manual; Handled over $2,000 in counter sales daily; or *Missed only two days of work in the past twenty-four months.* Employers are interested in concrete examples of your qualifications.

Special Skills, Achievements, and Characteristics

Your work experience and education may not portray a complete picture of you or your potential for employment. Evaluate your special attributes, skills, extracurricular activities. Select characteristics or accomplishments that demonstrate writing and speaking skills, leadership, organizational skills, and cooperation. Include awards, scholarships, honors, recognition, commendations, certificates, and licenses. Show special skills, such as your ability to use specific computer programs, office equipment, sign language, or foreign languages. Highlight exceptional aptitudes, such as learning computer programs quickly without instruction and working well under stress.

Provide a picture of a well-rounded individual.

Emphasize items in this category, particularly if you have little work experience. You may list your special skills or use action statements to demonstrate them. Strive for parallel (balanced) constructions in these statements.

Knowledge of Lotus 1-2-3 and WordPerfect.

Excellent grammar, language, and writing skills developed in business English and business communication courses.

Tutored Houghton College students by helping them revise term papers and reports.

Collected dues, kept financial records, and paid bills while serving as treasurer of 35-member Chevron Riding Club.

Awarded Roanoke Trust Company's $200 prize as outstanding student in finance.

Served as member of championship soccer team.

Promoted from typist to secretary after 9 months.

Received praise from manager for ability to work under pressure.

Personal Data

The trend in résumés today is to omit personal data, such as birth date, marital status, height, weight, and religious affiliation. This information is being omitted because it doesn't relate to genuine occupational questions. However, willingness to relocate is important.

A survey of employers revealed that one in four would select a nonsmoker in competition with an equally qualified smoker.

References

Opinion is divided about listing the names and addresses of references on a résumé. Such a list takes up valuable space and generally is not instrumental in securing an interview. After an interview, however, a list of individuals willing to discuss your qualifications becomes important. A prospective employer may at that time want to check your background by calling those individuals you suggest.

~~~~~~~~

Double-Edged Praise

One professor developed a Lexicon of Inconspicuously Ambiguous Recommendations (LIAR) to be used when he was reluctant to offer praise. Here are some of his suggestions:

"I most enthusiastically recommend this candidate with no qualifications whatsoever."

"In my opinion you will be very fortunate to get this person to work for you."

"I would urge you to waste no time in making this candidate an offer of employment."

"I can assure you that no person would be better for this job."

"I'm happy to say that this candidate is a former employee."

Whether or not you decide to include references on your résumé, you should have their names available when you begin your job search. Ask three to five instructors or previous employers if they would be willing to answer inquiries regarding your qualifications for employment. Be sure to provide them with an opportunity to refuse. No reference is better than a negative one. Do not include personal or character references, such as friends or neighbors, because personnel officers rarely consult them.[2] Interviewers are more interested in the opinions of individuals who are considered objective. Moreover, personnel officers see little reason for including the statement *References furnished upon request* if the names do not appear on the résumé.[3]

Traditional (Chronological) Résumé

Traditional chronological résumés include the headings *Education, Work Experience,* and so forth.

A résumé that includes categories for education, work experience, activities, personal data, and references is considered a traditional résumé. Education and experience are listed chronologically. The form and order of the traditional résumé represent the style that most candidates use and that many organizations expect. This résumé style, however, may not be the best style for you. The traditional résumé spotlights job titles, company names, and dates of employment. This format is excellent for individuals who have experience in their field of employment and who show steady career growth. (See Figures 13.1, 13.2, 13.3, and 13.4 for examples of model traditional résumés.)

---

[2]Kevin L. Hutchinson, "Personnel Administrators' Preferences for Resume Content: A Survey and Review of Empirically Based Conclusions," *The Journal of Business Communication* (Fall 1984): 10.
[3]*Ibid.*

FIGURE 13.1 Résumé in Traditional (Chronological) Format

KEVIN JAMES BECKER
3340 Craycroft Drive
Dayton, OH 45424   (513) 438-8871

OBJECTIVE

Responsible management trainee position in the retail field with long-range goal of becoming senior retail manager.

SUMMARY OF QUALIFICATIONS

Education: Associate's degree, marketing/management major.
Experience: Sales, management experience, Rike's Department Store
Strengths: Outgoing personality, microcomputer skills, communication and organizational skills.

EDUCATION

Sinclair Community College, Dayton, Ohio. Associate of Arts degree expected June, 1991. Acquired theoretical and practical knowledge of management, marketing, and merchandising by successfully completing courses in small business management, human relations, principles of selling, sales management, and retail merchandising. Developed communication skills in Public Speaking I and Business Writing 32.

Grade-point average in major: 3.6 (4 = A).
Financed 100 percent of college expenses.

EMPLOYMENT

Rike's Department Store, 9/88 to present.
Promoted from salesperson to assistant sales manager after 6 months; designed and arranged point-of-purchase displays; assembled toys and children's furniture; maintained a clean and safe sales floor; trained new salespeople, teaching them merchandise, sales techniques, and customer courtesy; completed inventories needed for maintaining correct stock levels.

Summers, 1985-88. Managed own gardening and landscaping service.

ACTIVITIES, ACHIEVEMENTS

Learned to operate data-base, word processing, and other programs on my computer.
Served as regular Red Cross blood donor.
Participated as an active member of Tipp City Four Wheelers Club.
Completed Safety Training/Fire Prevention Supervision course.

REFERENCES

Professor Nancy Moody, Department of English, Sinclair Community College, Dayton, OH 45429 (513) 710-3592
Professor John Shah, Department of Business Administration, Sinclair Community College, Dayton, OH 45429 (513) 710-3597
Edward Hopper, Manager, Toy Department, Rike's Department Store, Second and Main Streets, Dayton, OH 45420 (513) 225-8796

SARAH H. JOHNSON
5529 Meeting House Road
Elkins Park, PA 19117
(215) 340-1190

Career Objective

To be employed as a paralegal in a law office where I may assist attorneys specializing in probate or family law.

Employment Experience

Administrative Assistant   Hirshfield, Cohen, & Yellin
June, 1989, to present   Philadelphia, PA

- Promoted from file clerk to calendaring position after 7 months.
- Scheduled court reporters for 28 busy attorneys.
- Mastered the *Barrister* computer program in 25 hours with little instruction.

Area office clerk   Visiting Nurse Association
May, 1986, to June, 1988   Philadelphia, PA

- Admitted and discharged patients in absence of R.N.
- Typed and mailed doctors' orders.
- Answered all incoming telephone calls on Horizon telephone system.
- Learned Burroughs computer system with only 20 hours of training.

Secretary   Maynard, Rothman, & Farrell
June, 1984, to May, 1985   Upper Darby, PA

- Typed 50 to 70 financial statements and other legal documents weekly.
- Composed selected letters from attorney's dictated outline.
- Answered clients' questions on busy telephone system.

Education

Community College of Philadelphia, Associate of Arts degree, 1984.
Secretarial science major. Dean's List, two semesters.
Temple University. Now attending evening classes in paralegal training.

Skills

Typing: 85 wpm   Shorthand: 70–80 wpm
Dictaphone skills   10–key by touch
Microcomputer MS DOS skills   Horizon telephone system
Ability to learn computer programs quickly.

References

Provided on request.

FIGURE 13.3 Résumé in Traditional (Chronological) Format

CONFIDENTIAL RÉSUMÉ

JAMIE WILKE	17536 Strathern Street Northridge, CA 91325	(818) 345-1901 Available immediately

OBJECTIVE Responsible and challenging position in accounting department of large corporation in Los Angeles area.

EXPERIENCE

Staff Accountant
1988 to present

MICOM SYSTEMS, INC., SIMI VALLEY, CA 93063

Responsibilities

Reviewed and analyzed journal entries, labor records, and material and cost reports; estimated departmental revenue and expenses totaling approximately $225,000 annually; interpreted contracts and related state and federal regulations to determine accounting treatment.

Accomplishments

Devised and implemented improved system for estimating material costs; promoted from tax assistant to staff accountant after six months; received commendation for superior service to company.

Bookkeeper
1984 to 1988

GENERAL MOTOR INNS, INC., DES MOINES, IA 50309

Responsibilities

Processed invoices for data entry; reconciled daily income and expense reports from 12 Holiday Inns; assisted in preparing payroll for over 60 employees.

Accomplishments

Compiled departmental manual containing detailed job descriptions for all employees; administered office in absence of manager; received 110 percent salary increase in four years.

Bookkeeper
1984 to 1985

FEDERAL RESERVE BANK OF CHICAGO, DES MOINES, IA 50304

Responsibilities

Operated check sorter; reconciled computer printouts to incoming statements.

Accomplishments

Became fastest and most accurate operator of check sorter.

EDUCATION

Los Angeles Valley College. Working toward bachelor's degree in
   accounting. 86 of 120 units completed.
Des Moines Area Community College. Certificate in bookkeeping and
   accounting.

FIGURE 13.4   Traditional Résumé Prepared With Desktop Publishing Software

BEVERLEY A. HUDAK
1877 South Union Blvd.
Lakewood, CO 80228
(303) 969-0432

OBJECTIVE	Provide microcomputer accounting software installation and support for small- to medium-sized businesses.

SUMMARY OF QUALIFICATIONS

Education: A.A. in Accounting, Los Angeles Pierce College

Experience: Accounting Software Consultant, Office Manager, F/C Bookkeeper

Skills: General

· Bookkeeping through financial statements
· Communications and technical writing
· Office administration and management
· Microcomputer skills, MS-DOS

Software

· MAS90 Accounting	· WordPerfect & PageMaker
· ACCPAC Plus	· Lotus 1-2-3 & Excel
· Solomon III	· Many others

EDUCATION

Los Angeles Pierce College, Los Angeles, California   1989

A.A. in Accounting, Dean's Honor List

Computer Associates, Los Angeles, California   1988

Certificate of Completion
Seminars in Consulting Ethics and Marketing and ACCPAC accounting software

State of the Art, Costa Mesa, California   1987–1988

Certificate of Completion
Seminars in MAS90 accounting software including Sales Orders and Inventory Control

EXPERIENCE

Accounting Software Consultant   1/87–Present

Financial Forecasting Group, Los Angeles, California
Perform microcomputer accounting systems consultation, installation, implementation, and technical support for a wide range of businesses. Provide administrative assistance to company president and in-house accounting supervision, computer maintenance, and technical support. Duties include writing proposals, manuals, and correspondence.

Office Manager   9/85–1/87

Post Premiums, Inc., Studio City, California
Established order processing procedures and filing system. Administered computerized accounting system and implemented a local area network.

Full-Charge Bookkeeper   9/84–9/85

Sunset Avionics, Van Nuys, California
Performed all bookkeeping functions including quarterly inventory internal audit.

References available upon request.

Functional Résumé

The functional résumé format focuses attention upon a candidate's skills rather than upon the candidate's past employment. Like the traditional résumé, the functional résumé includes the candidate's name, address, telephone number, job objective, and education. Instead of listing jobs, however, the functional résumé shows skills and accomplishments. The skills section is the largest, typically including two or three headings, such as *Communication Skills, Supervisory and Management Skills,* or *Retailing and Marketing Experience.*

> **A functional résumé may emphasize skills and potential rather than experience and job titles.**

The functional résumé format is effective both for highlighting accomplishments and for deemphasizing a negative employment history. People who have changed jobs frequently or who have gaps in their employment record may prefer the functional résumé. Students who have little employment experience and individuals who are changing career areas, such as military retirees, also appreciate the functional résumé format.

One of the disadvantages of the functional résumé format is that it takes longer to write. It is also more difficult to read. In addition, prospective employers are more accustomed to seeing the traditional résumé. They might reject the newer functional approach simply because it is different.

To be safe, you should include a short employment history in a functional résumé. This job list will satisfy employers who are accustomed to seeing it. Examine the functional résumé shown in Figure 13.5.

> **Even on a functional résumé, it's wise to include a short employment history.**

Application Letter

Written to introduce the résumé and to secure an interview, the letter of application (or cover letter) follows the persuasive strategy discussed in Chapter 9. The letter should include three parts: (1) an opening that obtains the interest of the reader, (2) a body that explains and convinces, and (3) a closing that asks for a particular action.

Obtaining Interest

The first step in gaining the interest of your reader is addressing that individual by name. Rather than sending your letter to the "Personnel Manager" or "Personnel Department," make an effort to identify the name of the appropriate individual. If necessary, call the organization for the correct spelling and for the complete address. This personal touch distinguishes your letter and demonstrates your serious interest in employment.

> **Learn the name of the personnel director so that you can address that individual personally.**

The opening of a cover letter depends on whether the application is solicited or unsolicited. If an employment position has been announced and applicants are being solicited, then the beginning of your letter of application may be more direct. If you do not know whether a position is open and you are prospecting for a job, use an indirect approach. Whether direct or indirect, the opening should attract the attention of the reader. Avoid overworked and unimaginative openings such as *Please consider this letter an application for the position of . . .* or *This is an application for . . . .*

> **Use a direct strategy for solicited applications; use the indirect approach for unsolicited applications.**

≈≈≈

FIGURE 13.5   Résumé in Functional Format

TAMMY R. MCKAY

Address until June 1992:   Permanent address:

   590 West Florida Avenue   3690 South Elm Street
   Urbana, IL 61801   Peoria, IL 61096
   (217) 608-8555   (309) 455-3202

CAREER OBJECTIVE

   Entry-level position in sales with progressive firm. Desire opportunity for advancement into management. Willing to travel.

EDUCATION

   University of Illinois, Urbana, Illinois. B.A., 1992
     Major: Political science. Minor: Psychology.

COMMUNICATION SKILLS

- Demonstrated barbecue products and accessories in central and northern Illinois retail outlets, achieving sales amounting to 120 percent of forecast.
- Conducted telephone survey of selected businesses in two counties to determine users of farm equipment and to promote company services.
- Participated in President's task force to solicit contributions to Illini Foundation.
- Personally generated over $15,000 in telephone subscriptions to Illini Foundation.
- Helped conduct survey, analyzed results, and wrote a 20-page report regarding the need for developing a cultural events program at the University of Illinois.
- Presented talks before selected campus classes and organizations encouraging students to vote in coming elections.

ORGANIZATIONAL AND MANAGEMENT SKILLS

- Helped organize highly successful campus campaign to register student voters.
- Set up schedule of events and made arrangements for Newman Club weekend student retreat.
- Trained and supervised two counter employees at Pizza Bob's.
- Organized my courses, extracurricular activities, and part-time employment to graduate in seven semesters. Earned 3.2 point average (A = 4.0) while financing 70 percent of my education.

EMPLOYMENT

   1991–92 Pizza Bob's, Champaign, Illinois.
   1990   Bovay & Associates Manufacturers' Representatives, Chicago, Illinois.
   1989   Market Research, Inc., Chicago, Illinois.

For solicited jobs, consider the following techniques and examples for opening your letter:

1. Refer to the name of an employee in the company where you are applying.

> Ms. Helen Lynn of your staff has informed me that your organization is seeking a data communications specialist. The attached summary of my qualifications demonstrates my preparation for this position.

> At the suggestion of Mr. William L. Nelson of your Personnel Department, I submit my qualifications for the job of personnel assistant.

2. Refer to the source of your information precisely. If you are answering an advertisement, include the exact position advertised and the name and date of the publication. For large organizations, it's also smart to mention the section of the newspaper where the ad appeared.

If you are answering an ad, include the exact position advertised, along with the name and date of the publication.

> Your advertisement in Section C-2 of the May 10 *Washington Post* for an entry-level technical writer greatly appeals to me. With my computer experience and college training in technical writing, I believe I could serve Excellon Industries well.

> The May 15 issue of the *Herald Examiner* reports that you are seeking a mature, organized, and reliable administrative assistant.

3. Refer to the job title and describe how your qualifications fit the requirements.

> Will an honor graduate with a degree in recreation and two years of part-time experience organizing social activities for a convalescent hospital qualify for your position of activity director?

> Because of my specialized training in computerized accounting at North Texas State University, I feel confident that I have the qualifications you described in your advertisement for an accountant.

If your letter of application is unsolicited, try one of these techniques in your opening:

1. Demonstrate interest in and knowledge of the reader's business.

Do research in *Standard & Poor's Corporation Records* and other publications to learn about a company before you apply.

> Since American Medical Corporation is organizing a new information management team for its recently established group insurance division, could you use the services of a well-trained business administration graduate who seeks to become a data processing professional?

2. Show how your special talents and experience will benefit the company.

> When was the last time you interviewed a college-trained individual with excellent communication skills, self-starting personality, and recent experience in word processing?

> Do you have an opening for an energetic, aggressive individual with successful sales experience?

3. Use a catchy phrase or quote, particularly if you are seeking a position in an industry that values creativity.

> "Out, out bright candle" may be exclaimed on the stage, but your production lighting need never be in jeopardy. As an experienced theatrical technician with a strong background in analog/digital electronics, I would be able to provide lighting and sound to meet the exact specifications of both your local and your traveling productions.

Explaining and Convincing

Use persuasive techniques to convince the reader that you are qualified.

Once you have captured the attention of the reader, use the body of the letter to explain your purpose and to present convincing evidence of your qualifications.

If you are responding to an advertisement, show how your preparation and experience fill the stated requirements. If you are prospecting for a job, you may not know the exact requirements. Your employment research and knowledge of your field, however, should give you a reasonably good idea of what is expected for this position.

Emphasize reader benefits. Describe your strong points in relation to the needs of the employer.

Instead of	Try This
I have completed courses in business communications, report writing, and technical writing.	Courses in business communications, report writing, and technical writing have helped me develop the research and writing skills required of your technical writers.

Show how your strongest qualifications fulfill the requirements of the position.

Use the application letter to explain, amplify, and interpret selected facts from the three sections of your data sheet: education, experience, and personal qualities. Choose your strongest qualifications and show how they fit this job. Students with little experience will probably spotlight their education and its practical applications, as this candidate did:

> Because you need an architect's apprentice with proven ability, I submit a drawing of mine that won second place in the Montclair College drafting contest last year.

Include illustrations of your ability to work well with others.

In this part of your letter, discuss relevant personal traits. Employers are looking for candidates who get along well with others, take responsibility, show initiative, and learn easily. Notice how the following paragraph treats interpersonal skills.

> In addition to developing technical and academic skills at Ohio University, I have not neglected personal qualities. As vice president of the business students' organization, Alpha Gamma Sigma, I organized and supervised two successful fund-raising events. These activities involved coordinating the efforts of 35 students. To your company I offer these same organizational and interpersonal skills.

Use this section or the next to refer the reader to your résumé. Do so incidentally as part of another statement or directly. Here are two examples:

As you will notice from my résumé, I will graduate in June with a bachelor's degree in business administration.

Please refer to the attached résumé for additional information regarding my education, experience, and references.

In writing the body of your letter of application, keep these points in mind:

Here are tips for writing a successful letter of application.

1. Emphasize only those skills, accomplishments, and qualities that are related directly to the job. If you try to cover everything, your letter will be too long and too general.

2. Use concrete examples in place of generalities. Instead of *I have supervisory experience*, write *I supervised five employees*. Instead of *I am responsible*, write *I was responsible for scheduling all conventions*.

3. Be confident. Instead of *It is my belief that I could be an effective manager*, write *I can be an effective manager*. Follow such assertions with evidence of your potential.

4. Suggest reader benefits. Instead of *I have developed good interpersonal skills*, write *Being able to work well with others will help me serve your clients effectively*.

5. Avoid obvious flattery, such as *I am extremely interested in your fine company*.

6. Don't mention specifics regarding salary. It's better to save this subject for the interview.

Asking for Action

After presenting your case, drive for action in your last paragraph. Ask for an interview. If you live in a distant city, you may ask for an employment application or an opportunity to be interviewed by the organization's nearest representative. Never ask for the job. To do so would be presumptuous and naive. In requesting an interview, try to suggest reader benefits. Sound sincere and appreciative. Make it easy for the reader to agree—supply your telephone number and optimum times to call you. Observe these examples:

Conclude your letter by asking for an interview—not for a job.

> I hope that this brief description of my qualifications and the additional information on my résumé indicate to you my genuine desire to put my skills as an architect's apprentice to work for you. Please call me at (212) 388-9012 before 10 a.m. or after 3 p.m. to arrange an interview.

> If you need an industrious, well-trained word processing specialist with proven communication skills, call me at (415) 228-3221 to arrange an interview. I can meet with you at any time convenient to your schedule.

Putting It All Together

In Figure 13.6 a recent graduate writes a solicited letter of application in response to a newspaper advertisement. Notice how the letter puts together the three parts of the application letter to produce a convincing selling tool. The goal here is to obtain an interview.

In Figure 13.7 a young applicant seeks a job where none is known to be available. The writer emphasizes his work experience because it is directly related to

FIGURE 13.6   Solicited Letter of Application

3420 Altoona Drive
Urbandale, IA 50312
June 2, 19xx

Ms. Maria S. Morales
Office Manager
Granger Insurance Company
1003 West Norwalk Avenue
Des Moines, IA 50422

Dear Ms. Morales:

Begins strongly by showing how the writer's background matches the job description.

> With two years of part-time office experience and a soon-to-be-completed associate's degree in office administration, I feel that I could be the "well-trained" administrative assistant for which you advertised in the April 26 issue of the Des Moines Register.

Highlights information from the three most important parts of the résumé: education, experience, and personal activities.

> Fifty units of course work in office administration have provided me with excellent training on microcomputer-based word processing and data-base programs, such as those used in your office. Composing and revising business letters and reports in my business communications class, as well as transcribing over 100 dictated letters and memorandums in my transcription class, helped me perfect my communication skills.

> Two years of part-time employment in the office of James D. Turner, attorney-at-law, taught me how to work under pressure and how to organize my activities for maximum productivity. I enjoyed the team effort required by big projects, and I was commended for my professional attitude.

> As you will see from my résumé, I have actively participated in campus activities, providing me with interpersonal and leadership experiences that should enhance my effectiveness as an employee in your business.

Closes confidently by connecting the request for an interview with a statement of reader benefit.

> If you want a well-prepared administrative assistant who could be immediately productive in your office, Ms. Morales, please leave a message for me at (515) 630-2204 so that I may return your call and arrange an interview.

Sincerely,

Kayce Hook

Kayce Hook

Enclosure

FIGURE 13.7   Unsolicited Letter of Application

2901 Miramar Avenue, #202
Hallandale, FL 33231
May 25, 19xx

Mr. John R. Simpson
Vice President, Personnel
Resorts International, Inc.
Orlando, FL 32455

Dear Mr. Simpson:

Is there an opening in your junior management trainee program for an energetic individual with both practical experience and formal training in hotel/restaurant management?

Gains attention by spotlighting the applicant's qualifications for the position.

For the past two years I have worked as part-time clerk and now as desk manager of a 100-unit resort complex in Boca Raton. In this position I am responsible for custodial and room service staff scheduling, convention planning, and customer relations. The supervisory, organizational, and communication skills that I have developed in this capacity will enable me to function successfully as a trainee at one of your resort centers.

As a result of this job and others where I worked with the public, I have realized that I enjoy serving customers and meeting the challenges that public service demands. I decided to enter the hospitality field, and in June I will be receiving an associate's degree in hotel management from Miami Metropolitan College.

Relates applicant's experiences directly to the position being sought.

Complementing my work experience and studies are personal qualities that will make me a successful manager. In supervising six employees, I learned to make decisions, to take responsibility for those decisions, and to work harmoniously with others. In supporting myself while completing my degree, I learned to manage my time and to persevere despite adversity. Most importantly, I discovered a career that is perfectly suited to my talents and goals.

Uses concrete examples to demonstrate personal qualities.

Professor Jerome Mitchell, chairman of the hotel/restaurant management program at Miami Metropolitan College, as well as other individuals listed as references on the enclosed résumé, will confirm my potential as a management trainee in your program.

Calls attention to résumé and to references.

At a time convenient for you, I would appreciate the opportunity to discuss my qualifications for beginning a career with your company. I will call you early next Monday to see if we can arrange a meeting.

Because the writer cannot be reached by telephone, he takes the initiative for making contact.

Sincerely,

Michael W. Weston

Michael W. Weston

Enclosure

the position he wants. Notice how often he uses specific examples to illustrate his qualifications.

~~~

Other Employment Documents

Application Request Letter

For some organizations you must request a job application form.

Some organizations consider candidates only when they submit a completed application form. To secure a form, write a routine request but provide enough information about yourself to assure the business that you are a serious applicant, as shown in Figure 13.8.

Application Follow-up Letter

A follow-up letter reminds the prospective employer of your sincere interest and enables you to emphasize your strongest qualifications or to add new information.

If your letter or your application generates no response within a reasonable time, you may decide to send a short follow-up letter like the one shown in Figure 13.9. Doing so (1) jogs the memory of the personnel officer, (2) demonstrates your serious interest, and (3) allows you to emphasize your significant qualifications or to add new information.

Interview Follow-up Letter

After you have been interviewed, send a brief letter of thanks. This courteous gesture will distinguish you from other applicants (most will not bother), and it will remind the interviewer of your visit.

Send a follow-up letter immediately after the interview.

Follow-up letters are most effective if sent immediately following the interview. In your letter refer to specific topics discussed in the interview. Avoid worn-out phrases, such as *Thank you for taking the time to interview me* or *I ap-*

~~~

FIGURE 13.8   Application Request Letter

Dear Mr. Stevens:

Please send me an application form for work in your Personnel Department. In June I will be completing my studies in communications at Northeastern University in Boston. My program included courses in management, public relations, and communications.

I look forward to moving to your city in June and beginning a career in personnel management.

Sincerely,

FIGURE 13.9   Application Follow-up Letter

Dear Ms. Morales:

Please be assured that I am still interested in becoming an administrative assistant with your organization.

Since I wrote to you in May, I have completed my schooling and have been employed as a summer replacement for office workers in several downtown offices. This experience has honed my word processing and communication skills; it has also introduced me to a wide range of office procedures.

Please keep my application in your active file and let me know when I may put my formal training, technical skills, and practical experience to work for you.

Sincerely,

preciate the time that you took from your busy schedule to interview me. Notice in the follow-up letter in Figure 13.10 how the writer expresses appreciation without using stereotyped expressions.

FIGURE 13.10   Interview Follow-up Letter

Dear Ms. Marquardt:

In our conversation last week, I appreciated learning about the products and the departmental operations of Datatech.

Thanks for providing a tour of your information processing center and introducing me to the supervisor and the trainer. After meeting them and observing the equipment and procedures used to turn out documents in the center, I remain confident that I could be a productive member of your staff. To give me an opportunity to prove my abilities, call me at 322-4891.

Sincerely,

> The writer expresses thanks while at the same time reinforcing the application.

Application Form

Many organizations require that applicants complete an application form in place of or in addition to submitting a résumé. An application form permits them to gather and store standard data about each applicant. Here are some tips on filling out such forms:

Job application forms require detailed information. Be prepared by following these suggestions.

1. Carry a card summarizing those vital statistics not included on your résumé. If you are asked to fill out an application form in an employer's office, you will need a handy reference to the following data: social security number; graduation dates; beginning and ending dates of all employment; salary history; full names, titles, and present work addresses of former supervisors; full names, occupational titles, occupational addresses, and telephone numbers of persons who have agreed to serve as references; and your present telephone number (if you have a new one and may forget it).

2. Fill out the form neatly. Look over all the questions before starting. Print your answers if your handwriting is poor.

3. Answer all questions. Write *Not Applicable* if appropriate.

4. Be prepared for a salary question. Unless you know what comparable employees are earning in this company, the best strategy is to suggest a salary range or to write in *Negotiable* or *Open*.

5. Ask if you may submit your résumé in addition to the application form.

How to Respond to Ten Frequently Asked Interview Questions

1. **Why do you want to work for us?** Questions like this illustrate the need for you to research an organization thoroughly before the interview. Do library research, ask friends, and read the company's advertisements and other printed materials to gather data. Describe your desire to work for them not only from your perspective but also from their point of view. What have you to offer them?

2. **Why should we hire you?** Here is an opportunity for you to sell your strong points in relation to this specific position. Describe your skills, academic preparation, and relevant experience. If you have little experience, don't apologize—the interviewer has read your résumé. Emphasize strengths as demonstrated in your education, such as initiative and persistence in completing assignments, ability to learn quickly, self-sufficiency, and excellent attendance.

3. **What can you tell me about yourself?** Use this chance to promote yourself. Stick to professional or business-related strengths; avoid personal or humorous references. Be ready with at least three success stories illustrating characteristics important to this job. Demonstrate responsibility you have been given; describe how you contributed as a team player.

4. **What are your strongest (or weakest) personal qualities?** Stress your strengths, such as "I believe I am conscientious, reliable, tolerant, patient, and thorough." Add examples that illustrate these qualities: "My supervisor said that my research was exceptionally thorough." If pressed for a weakness, give a strength disguised as a weakness: "Perhaps my greatest fault is being too painstaking with details." Or, "I am impatient when tasks are not completed on time." Don't admit weaknesses, not even to sound human. You'll be hired for your strengths, not your weaknesses.

5. **What do you expect to be doing ten years from now?** Formulate a realistic plan with respect to your present age and situation. The important thing is to be prepared for this question.

6. **Do you prefer working with others or by yourself?** This question can be tricky. Provide a middle-of-the-road answer that not only suggests your interpersonal qualities but also reflects an ability to make independent decisions and work without supervision.

7. **Have you ever changed your major field of interest during your education? Why?** Another tricky question. Don't admit weaknesses or failures. In explaining changes, suggest career potential and

new aspirations awakened by your expanding education, experience, or maturity.

8. **What have been your most rewarding or disappointing work (or school) experiences?** If possible, concentrate on positive experiences such as technical and interpersonal skills you acquired. Avoid dwelling on negative or unhappy topics. Never criticize former employers. If you worked for an ungrateful, penny-pinching, slave driver in a dead-end position, say that you learned all you could from that job. Move the conversation to the prospective position and what attracts you to it.

9. **Have you established any new goals lately?** Watch out here. If you reveal new goals, you may inadvertently admit deficiencies. Instead of "I've resolved to finally learn how to operate a computer," try "Although I'm familiar with basic computer applications, I'm now reading and studying more about computer applications in . . . ."

10. **What are your long- and short-term goals?** Suggest realistic goals that you have consciously worked out before the interview. Know what you want to do with your future. To admit to an interviewer that you're not sure what you want to do is a sign of immaturity, weakness, and indecision.

APPLICATION AND PRACTICE

Discussion

1. Why is the résumé the most important document you may ever write?

2. How can inventory lists help you write a résumé?

3. On your résumé is it better to state a narrow career objective or a general career objective that will make you employable in a number of job categories? Why?

4. Should you include the names of references on your résumé? Discuss.

5. If prospective employers are most interested in the résumé, why bother to write a letter of application?

6. Discuss four or more personal characteristics that employers are seeking in applicants.

Short Answers

7. Name six sources of job information.

8. List six headings you might use in your résumé.

9. How is a traditional résumé different from a functional résumé?

10. What are the advantages of using the traditional résumé format?

11. What are the advantages of using the functional résumé format?

12. What are two functions of the letter of application?

13. Describe the three parts of the letter of application.

14. List three techniques for opening a solicited letter of application.

15. List three techniques for opening an unsolicited letter of application.

16. Name at least five things to avoid in a letter of application.

17. List three reasons for sending a follow-up letter if you have had no response to an application letter or an employment application.

18. If an application form requests a salary figure, how should you respond?

Writing Improvement Exercise

Application Letter

19. Analyze each section of the following letter of application.

Dear Personnel Manager:
(1)   Please consider this letter as an application for the position of staff accountant that I saw advertised in the *Houston Post* on April 27. Accounting has been my major in college, and although I have had no paid work experience in this field, I believe that I could be an asset to Meyers & Jacoby.

(2) For four years I have studied accounting, and I am fully trained for full-charge bookkeeping as well as computer accounting. I have taken 36 units of college accounting and courses in electronic data processing. I have also taken other courses that may help me in business, including business communications, human relations, report writing, and economics.

(3) In addition to my course work, during the tax season I have been a student volunteer for VITA. This is a project to help individuals in the community prepare their income tax returns, and I learned a lot from this experience. I have also received some experience in office work and working with figures when I was employed as an office assistant for Copy Quick, Inc.

(4) I am a competent and responsible person who gets along pretty well with others. I have been a member of some college and social organizations and have even held elective office.

(5) I feel that I have a strong foundation in accounting as a result of my course work and my experience. Along with my personal qualities and my desire to succeed, I hope that you will agree that I qualify for the position of staff accountant with Meyers & Jacoby.

Sincerely,

Make specific suggestions to the writer of this letter for improving each of the five paragraphs.

Activities

20. Learn about employment in your field. Visit your school or local library. Photocopy a page from the *Dictionary of Occupational Titles* that describes a position for which you could apply in two to five years. Photocopy pages from the *Occupational Outlook Handbook* that describe employment in the area in which you are interested. Save these copies to attach to your letter of application.

21. Clip a job advertisement from the classified section of a local or national newspaper. Select an ad describing the kind of employment you will seek in two to five years. (If you can find no advertisement, write one. Construct an advertisement for a legitimate position that could possibly have appeared in an advertisement.) Save this advertisement to attach to your résumé when you submit it.

22. Using information you have gathered from your research and from other sources, describe the successful candidate for the position in Activity

No. 21. What education will this individual have? Experience? Skills? Personal qualities? Physical abilities? Appearance?

23. In preparation for writing your résumé, write two career objectives for yourself. Write one that is broad, encompassing both short- and long-term goals. Write another that is narrow and aimed at a specific job.

24. Make inventory lists for these areas: course work achievements, employment and internships, activities and achievements, and personal qualities. Use active verbs. Review the examples and résumés in this chapter.

   - **Course work achievements.** List degrees, certificates, and training accomplishments. List courses, seminars, or skills that are relevant to the job you seek.

   - **Employment and internships.** Begin with your most recent job. For each position, list the following information: employer; your job title; dates of employment; and three to five duties, activities, or accomplishments. Emphasize activities related to the job you seek.

   - **Activities and achievements.** List three to five personal activities that you enjoy, and any extracurricular achievements. Analyze your items. Do any of them demonstrate personal and character traits that employers value? Write action statements using these items.

   - **Personal qualities.** List three to five of your strongest personal characteristics relevant to employment. Write statements that demonstrate these characteristics.

25. Using the data you have just developed, write your résumé. Use a word processor if possible. Revise until it is perfect. Attach a copy of the advertisement from Activity No. 21.

26. Write a letter of application delivering your résumé. Attach the photocopies from Activity No. 20.

27. Assume that you were interviewed for this position. Write a follow-up letter.

28. Write an unsolicited letter seeking a part-time or summer position with an actual firm in your area.

29. Fill in the sample application blank shown in Figure 13.11. Take the time to find all the necessary information. This filled-in form can then be removed and carried with you to serve as a reference when applying for employment.

30. Practice employment interviewing. Choose a partner in your class. Make a list of five employment questions from those shown on pages 329–330. Prepare answers to those questions. Before the class you and your partner will role-play an actual interview. One acts as interviewer; the other is the candidate. Prior to the interview, the candidate tells the interviewer what job and company he/she is applying to. For the interview, the interviewer and candidate should dress appropriately and sit in chairs facing each other before the class. The interviewer greets the candidate and makes

FIGURE 13.11   Sample Employment Application

TO OUR APPLICANTS: Please answer all questions completely. If you need help in completing this application, please request assistance from a member of this office. We will be pleased to serve you.

NAME: Last	First	Middle	TODAY'S DATE

PRESENT ADDRESS: No. Street	City	State	Zip Code

HOME TELEPHONE: ( )	WORK TELEPHONE: ( )	SOCIAL SECURITY NUMBER:

POSITION APPLIED FOR:	SALARY EXPECTED	DATE OPEN FOR HIRE

WOULD YOU WORK – ☐ Full-time?   ☐ Part-time?   REFERRED BY:

WERE YOU PREVIOUSLY EMPLOYED BY US?   ☐ Yes   ☐ No   IF "YES", WHEN?

DO YOU HAVE THE LEGAL RIGHT TO BE EMPLOYED IN THE U.S.?   ☐ Yes   ☐ No   VISA NUMBER (if any)   EXPIRATION DATE:

PERSON TO BE NOTIFIED IN CASE OF ACCIDENT OR EMERGENCY: NAME

ADDRESS: TELEPHONE NUMBER: ( )

HAVE YOU SERVED IN THE ARMED SERVICES?   ☐ Yes   ☐ No   IF "YES", WHEN?

HAVE YOU EVER BEEN CONVICTED OF A FELONY?   ☐ Yes   ☐ No

ON THE LINES BELOW, PLEASE LIST ANY FRIENDS OR RELATIVES WHO ARE STUDENTS HERE OR ARE WORKING FOR US.
        Name   Relationship

1.

2.

EDUCATION

NAME AND LOCATION OF HIGH SCHOOL: DID YOU GRADUATE?   ☐ Yes   ☐ No

Name of College, University, Trade or Vocational School	Location	Major Subjects	Degrees or Certificates

SKILLS/ABILITIES

Please list any skills or abilities you have which you think may be used in your employment here. Any craft, trade, office, clerical, professional or administrative skills or abilities may be included. Also list any skills or abilities you gained doing volunteer work, household duties or while pursuing a hobby.

Skill/Ability	Duration of Training	Length of Experience

TYPING SPEED: Manual   Electric   SHORTHAND SPEED: WORD PROCESSING OR DATA ENTRY?   NAME MACHINES OPERATED:

OTHER OFFICE MACHINES OPERATED:

FIGURE 13.11 Continued

EMPLOYMENT/EXPERIENCE

Please list all jobs and activities for the past ten years or since attending school as a full-time student. Include part-time employment and self-employment. Include experience gained doing volunteer work or community service work. Begin with the most recent employment and activities first.

NAME OF EMPLOYER	YOUR JOB TITLE
ADDRESS OF EMPLOYER	DESCRIBE WORK YOU PERFORMED
SUPERVISOR'S NAME, JOB TITLE AND TELEPHONE NUMBER	

DATE STARTED	DATE ENDED	DURATION	PAY	REASON FOR LEAVING

NAME OF EMPLOYER	YOUR JOB TITLE
ADDRESS OF EMPLOYER	DESCRIBE WORK YOU PERFORMED
SUPERVISOR'S NAME, JOB TITLE AND TELEPHONE NUMBER	

DATE STARTED	DATE ENDED	DURATION	PAY	REASON FOR LEAVING

NAME OF EMPLOYER	YOUR JOB TITLE
ADDRESS OF EMPLOYER	DESCRIBE WORK YOU PERFORMED
SUPERVISOR'S NAME, JOB TITLE AND TELEPHONE NUMBER	

DATE STARTED	DATE ENDED	DURATION	PAY	REASON FOR LEAVING

NAME OF EMPLOYER	YOUR JOB TITLE
ADDRESS OF EMPLOYER	DESCRIBE WORK YOU PERFORMED
SUPERVISOR'S NAME, JOB TITLE AND TELEPHONE NUMBER	

DATE STARTED	DATE ENDED	DURATION	PAY	REASON FOR LEAVING

REFERENCE CHECKS

MAY WE ASK YOUR PRESENT OR PREVIOUS EMPLOYERS ABOUT YOU? ☐ Yes ☐ No	NOT UNTIL I GIVE NOTICE ON (date):

DRIVER'S LICENSE NUMBER:	CLASS *(circle one)* I II III	STATE WHERE ISSUED:

SIGNATURE:

X   DATE:

By my signature above, I certify that all answers and statements on this application are true and complete to the best of my knowledge. I understand that should an investigation disclose untruthful of misleading answers, my application may be rejected, my name removed from consideration, or my employment terminated.

him/her comfortable. The candidate gives the interviewer a copy of his/her résumé. The interviewer asks two (or more depending upon your instructor's time schedule) questions from the candidate's list. The interviewer may also ask follow-up questions if appropriate. When finished, the interviewer ends the meeting graciously. After one interview, reverse roles and repeat.

GRAMMAR/MECHANICS — 13

Number Style

Review Sections 4.01 through 4.13 in the Grammar/Mechanics Handbook. Then study each of the following pairs. Assume that these expressions appear in the context of letters, reports, or memos. Write (a) or (b) in the space provided to indicate the preferred number style and record the number of the G/M principle illustrated. When you finish, compare your responses with the following. If your responses differ, study carefully the principles in parentheses.

Example: (a) six investments (b) 6 investments   a _____ (4.01a)

1. (a) sixteen credit cards (b) 16 credit cards _____

2. (a) Fifth Avenue (b) 5th Avenue _____

3. (a) 34 newspapers (b) thirty-four newspapers _____

4. (a) July eighth (b) July 8 _____

5. (a) twenty dollars (b) $20 _____

6. (a) on the 15th of June (b) on the fifteenth of June _____

7. (a) at 4:00 p.m. (b) at 4 p.m. _____

8. (a) 8 sixty-four page books (b) eight 64-page books _____

9. (a) over 18 years ago (b) over eighteen years ago _____

10. (a) 2,000,000 residents (b) 2 million residents _____

11. (a) fifteen cents (b) 15 cents _____

12. (a) a thirty-day warranty (b) a 30-day warranty _____

13. (a) 2/3 of the books (b) two thirds of the books _____

14. (a) two telephones for 15 employees (b) 2 telephones for 15 employees _____

15. (a) 6 of the 130 letters (b) six of the 130 letters _____

---

1. b (4.01a)   3. a (4.01a)   5. b (4.02)   7. b (4.04)   9. b (4.08)   11. b (4.02)
13. b (4.12)   15. a (4.06)

CHAPTER 14

Listening and Speaking

〰〰〰

In this chapter you will learn to do the following:

- Identify barriers to effective listening.
- Suggest techniques for becoming an active and effective listener.
- Analyze the audience, organize the content, and prepare visual aids for an oral presentation.
- Select the best method for delivering an oral report.
- Discuss techniques for reducing stage fright.
- Implement techniques of effective speaking.
- Participate in productive and enjoyable meetings.
- Use the telephone as an efficient business tool.
- Recognize efficient dictation techniques.

Successful people, in both their business and their private lives, require a variety of communication skills. Some estimates suggest that adults spend 45 percent of their communicating time listening; 30 percent, speaking; 16 percent, reading; and 9 percent writing. Writing skills demand the most attention because they are most difficult to develop and because written documents record the most significant events in our lives. However, you should also develop other communication skills that are often taken for granted, such as listening and speaking. Like writing, listening and speaking are talents that can be improved through awareness, study, and practice.

Adults spend 45 percent of their communicating time listening and 30 percent speaking.

〰

Improving Listening Skills

Do you ever pretend to be listening when you're not? Do you know how to look attentive in class when your mind wanders far away? Do you ever "tune out" people when their ideas are boring or complex? Do you find it difficult to concentrate on ideas when a speaker's appearance or mannerisms are strange?

Most of us would answer "yes" to one or more of these questions because we have developed poor listening habits. In fact, some researchers suggest that we listen at only 25 percent efficiency. Such poor listening habits are costly in business. Letters must be retyped; shipments, reshipped; appointments, rescheduled; directions, restated. One large corporation postulated that if each of America's 100 million workers made a simple $10 listening mistake, the total loss would be $1 billion. Some business organizations decided that they could not af-

Most individuals listen at only 25 percent efficiency.

ford to pay the price of poor listening. These companies instituted programs to improve listening habits among their personnel.

For most of us, listening is a passive, unconscious activity. We don't require our minds to work very hard at receiving sounds, and we don't give much thought to whether or not we're really listening. Only when a message is urgent do we perk up and try to listen more carefully. Then we become more involved in the communication process. We reduce competing environmental sounds; we concentrate on the speaker's words; we anticipate what's coming; we ask questions. Good listeners are active listeners.

Passive listeners don't get involved; active listeners make a physical and mental effort to hear.

To improve listening skills, we first need to recognize barriers that prevent effective listening. Then we need to focus on specific techniques that are effective in improving listening skills.

Barriers to Effective Listening

Barriers to listening may be physical, psychological, verbal, or nonverbal.

As we learned in Chapter 1, barriers can interfere with the communication process. Some of the barriers and distractions that prevent good listening are discussed here.

- **Physical Barriers.** You cannot listen if you cannot hear what is being said. Physical impediments include hearing disabilities, poor acoustics, and noisy surroundings. It's also difficult to listen if you're ill, tired, uncomfortable, or worried.

- **Psychological Barriers.** As noted in Chapter 1, every person brings to the communication process a different set of cultural, ethical, and personal values. Each of us has an idea of what is right and what is important. If other ideas run counter to our preconceived thoughts, we tend to "tune out" the speaker and thus fail to hear. For example, if Carolyn Dee thinks that her work is satisfactory, she might filter out criticism from her supervisor. Such selective listening results in poor communication and is unproductive both for the listener and for the speaker.

- **Language Problems.** We've already learned that jargon and unfamiliar words can destroy the communication process because such words lack meaning for the receiver. In addition, emotion-laden or "charged" words can adversely affect listening. If the mention of words like *abortion* or *overdose* had an intense emotional impact, a listener may be unable to concentrate on the words that follow.

- **Nonverbal Distractions.** Many of us find it difficult to listen if the speaker is different from what we consider normal. Unusual clothing, speech mannerisms, body twitches, or a nonconformist hairstyle could cause sufficient distraction to prevent us from hearing what the speaker has to say.

Most Americans speak at about 125 words per minute. The human brain can process information at least three times as fast.

- **Thought Speed.** Because thought speed is over three times as great as speech speed, listener concentration flags. Our minds are able to process thoughts much faster than speakers can enunciate them. Therefore, we become bored and our minds wander.

- **Faking Attention.** Most of us have learned to look as if we are listening even when we're not. Such behavior was perhaps necessary as part of our socialization. Faked attention, however, seriously threatens effective listening because it encourages the mind to flights of uncontrolled fancy. Those who practice faked attention often find it difficult to concentrate even when they want to.

- **Grandstanding.** Would you rather talk or would you rather listen? Naturally, most of us would rather talk. Since our own experiences and thoughts are most important to us, we grab the limelight in conversations. We sometimes fail to listen carefully because we're just waiting politely for the next pause so that we can have our turn to speak.

How to Become an Active Listener

You can reverse the harmful effects of poor listening habits by making a conscious effort to become an active listener. Listening actively means becoming involved. You can't sit back and hear whatever a lazy mind happens to receive. These techniques will help you become an active and effective listener.

- **Stop talking.** The first step in becoming a good listener is to stop talking. Let others explain their views. Learn to concentrate on what the speaker is saying, not on what your next comment will be.

- **Control your surroundings.** Whenever possible, remove competing sounds. Turn off radios, close windows or doors, turn off noisy appliances, or move away from loud people or engines. Choose a quiet time and place for listening.

To become a good listener, control your surroundings and your mind-set.

- **Establish a receptive mind-set.** Expect to learn something by listening. Develop a positive and receptive frame of mind. If the message is complex, consider it mental gymnastics. It's hard work but good exercise for the mind to stretch and expand its limits.

- **Keep an open mind.** We all sift and filter information through our own prejudices and values. For improved listening, discipline yourself to listen objectively. Be fair to the speaker. Hear what is really being said, not what you want to hear.

- **Listen for main points.** Concentration is enhanced and satisfaction is heightened when you look for and recognize the speaker's central themes.

- **Capitalize on lag time.** Make use of the quickness of your mind by reviewing the speaker's points. Anticipate what's coming next. Evaluate evidence the speaker has presented. Don't allow yourself to daydream.

- **Listen between the lines.** Focus on both what is spoken and what is unspoken. Listen for feelings as well as for facts.

- **Judge ideas, not appearances.** Concentrate on the content of the message, not on its delivery. Avoid being distracted by the speaker's appearance, voice, or mannerisms.

- **Hold your fire.** Force yourself to listen to the speaker's entire argument or message before reacting. Such restraint may enable you to understand the speaker's reasons and logic before you jump to unwarranted conclusions.

Listening actively may mean taking notes and providing feedback.

- **Take selective notes.** For some situations, thoughtful note-taking may be necessary to record important facts that must be recalled later. Select only the most important points so that the note-taking process does not interfere with your concentration on the speaker's total message.

- **Provide feedback.** Let the speaker know that you are listening. Nod your head; maintain eye contact. Ask relevant questions at appropriate times. Getting involved improves the communication process for both the speaker and the listener.

Improving Speaking Skills

Listening and speaking make up a large part of the time you spend communicating. How much time you devote to speaking—and, more particularly, to making speeches and oral presentations—depends on your occupation and on the level you reach in your career. Few businesspeople regularly deliver formal speeches. Instead, most of us communicate orally in informal conversations and small-group discussions.

Yet, every college-educated individual aspiring to a business career is well-advised to develop speaking skills. A computer equipment sales representative may have to sell his or her products before a group of potential customers. An accountant must explain the financial position of an organization to management. A travel agent describes an excursion package to a single client or to a group. An office manager clarifies new office procedures, and a structural engineer explains load bearing to a land developer. Just as the need for writing skills increases as you rise in your profession, so does the need for speaking skills. It is no coincidence that most individuals promoted to executive-level positions are effective writers and speakers.

As you advance in your career, the ability to express your ideas orally takes on greater significance.

Preparing an Oral Report

One of the most common speaking functions for businesspeople is the presentation of ideas in an oral report. Such a presentation is most frequently made informally to a superior or to a small group of colleagues. Only occasionally do businesspeople make formal speeches before large groups.

Planning an oral report is similar in many ways to preparing for a written report. You need to analyze the audience, organize the content, and plan visual aids.

Before you make an oral presentation, you should (1) analyze the audience, (2) organize your topic, and (3) plan visual aids, if appropriate.

Analyzing the Audience

Knowing about your audience will help you decide how to structure your report. The size of the audience influences the formality of your presentation: a large audience generally requires a more formal and less personalized approach. Other factors, such as age, sex, education, experience, and attitude toward the subject, also affect your presentation. Analyze these factors to determine your strategy, vocabulary, illustrations, and level of detail. Your answers to specific questions will guide you in adapting the topic to your audience:

- How will this topic appeal to this audience?
- What do I want the audience to believe?

- What action do I want the audience to take?

- What aspects of the topic will be most interesting to the audience?

- Which of the following will be most effective in making my point: Statistics? Graphic illustrations? Demonstrations? Case histories? Analogies? Cost figures?

Organizing Content

Begin to organize your oral report by defining its purpose. Is your goal to inform? To persuade? To recommend? In describing your goal, write a statement of purpose by completing the following sentence: The goal of this report is

A precise statement of purpose helps you organize the content of your presentation.

- To inform all staff members of the benefits and options in the new health care program.

- To persuade the sales vice president that a consolidation of the Ohio and Michigan territories would reduce costs and increase efficiency.

- To recommend to the Board of Directors the establishment of a members' advisory committee that would encourage input from the rank and file of the organization.

After you have a firm statement of purpose, organize your report to reach your goal. Like business letters and written reports, oral reports may follow either a direct or an indirect strategy. It seems most logical, though, to organize a report indirectly. Since listeners are generally unfamiliar with a problem, they typically need some explanation or introductory comment to ease them into the topic.

Whether you use a direct or indirect approach, make an outline to guide the organization of your report. Concentrate on two to four main points only. Follow an outline form such as that shown in Chapter 12 for a long report.

Most presentations should focus on only two to four principal points.

Like long reports, oral presentations often contain three parts: introduction, body, and conclusion. One old-timer explains the organization of speeches as follows: *(1) tell them what you're going to tell them, (2) tell them what you have to say, and then (3) tell them what you've just told them.* Such redundancy may seem deadly, but repetition helps the audience retain information.

The audience for oral reports, unlike readers, cannot control the rate of presentation or reread main points. Therefore, knowledgeable speakers help their listeners recognize the organization and main points in an oral report by emphasizing and reiterating them. Good speakers also keep the audience on track by including helpful transitions, reviews, and previews.

Help the listener follow your presentation by describing its organization (introduction, body, and conclusion).

- **Introduction.** At the beginning of your report, identify yourself (if necessary) and your topic. Describe the goal of your report, how it is organized, and what main points you will cover. Also in your introduction make an effort to capture the attention of the audience with a question, startling fact, joke, story, quotation, or some other device. Make sure, of course, that your attention-getter is relevant to your topic.

- **Body.** Follow your outline in presenting the two to four main points of your topic. Develop each with adequate, but not excessive, support and detail. Keep your presentation simple and logical—listeners have no pages to leaf back through if they should become confused.

Include verbal signposts so that listeners know where you've been and where you're heading in your presentation.

The best devices you can use to ensure comprehension are verbal signposts that tell where you've been and point where you're going. Summarize a segment of your report with a summary statement like

We see, then, that the two major problems facing management are raw material and labor costs.

or combine a review with a preview, such as

Now that we've learned how sole proprietorships are different from partnerships, let's turn to corporations.

I've described two good reasons for consolidating sales territories, but the final reason is most important.

Repeat main ideas as you progress. Indicate new topics or shifts in direction with helpful transitional expressions, such as *first, second, next, then, therefore, moreover, on the other hand, on the contrary, in conclusion*, and *and so forth*.

Conclude your presentation by emphasizing the information that you want your listeners to remember.

- **Conclusion.** You may end a presentation by reviewing the main themes of the talk, or you may round out the presentation by referring to your opening. Concentrate on the information that achieves your purpose. What do you want your listeners to believe? What action do you want them to take? When you finish, ask if audience members have any questions. If silence ensues, remark that you'll be happy to answer questions individually after the program is completed.

Planning Visual Aids

Oral reports are most successful when they show and tell.

Show-and-tell is effective not only for grade-schoolers but also for adults. Some authorities suggest that we learn and remember 85 percent of all our knowledge visually. The oral report that incorporates visual aids is twice as likely to be understood and retained as a report lacking visual supplements. By appealing to both the senses of sight and sound, a message can double its impact.

When you incorporate visual aids into an oral report, keep a few points in mind:

1. Use visual aids only for major points or for information that requires clarification.

2. Keep the visual aids simple.

3. Make sure the necessary equipment works properly. Have a backup ready.

4. Ensure that everyone can see the visual aid.

Visual aids are particularly useful for inexperienced speakers because the audience concentrates on the aids rather than on the speaker and because visual aids can jog the memory of the speaker.

5. Talk to the audience, not to the visual aid.

In selecting ways to illustrate your oral report, you have a number of options, each with its particular uses, advantages, and disadvantages.

- **Transparencies.** Easy and inexpensive, transparencies can be used to project a message on a screen in a lighted or unlighted room. They are popular in business and education because the masters can be typed or written on plain paper. The masters are transferred onto transparent film by means of a thermograph or photocopy machine. The transparency is then placed onto an overhead projector, which projects the image onto a screen.

Typed transparencies are especially useful because they can be made in advance, and they are easy to read when prepared with a large-format typewriter or computer printer. They emphasize points for the viewers and can serve to prompt the speaker.

- **Flip Charts.** Like a giant pad of paper, a flip chart consists of large sheets attached at the top. You may prepare the sheets in advance, or write on them as you speak and flip through the pad. Flip charts are usually less visible than transparencies because they are propped on an easel on a level with the speaker and because the sheets are smaller than the images projected on a screen. However, flip charts require no special equipment, and they can be quite colorful if you use felt-tip markers.

- **Slides.** For picturesque, nonverbal messages, slides can be colorful and entertaining. Verbal messages on slides are more difficult to achieve unless you use a graphic-design service. Slides, of course, require a slide projector and a screen, as well as an operator. When you project slides in a darkened room, you lose eye contact with the audience and you run the risk of putting the audience to sleep.

- **Handouts.** Speakers often use handouts, such as a sheet of paper or a packet, to supplement the presentation. Handouts may consist of an outline, list of selected main points, illustration, flow chart, table, or any other material that helps clarify the report. Members of the audience appreciate handouts because they have ready-made notes to take with them to remind them of the report. The major disadvantage of handouts is that audience members may read the handouts instead of listening to the speaker. For this reason, some speakers distribute handouts only at the end of their presentations.

  Experienced speakers distribute handouts when they conclude their presentations.

- **Opaque Projections.** An opaque projector can project any typed or printed page on a screen. If you wished to show a page from a book, you could do so with an opaque projector. However, these projectors are seldom used in business today.

Delivering the Oral Report

Delivery Methods

Once you have prepared your report, how will you present it? If you are like most speakers, you will use one of four delivery methods: (1) memorized delivery, (2) reading delivery, (3) extemporaneous delivery, or (4) impromptu delivery.

- **Memorized Delivery.** Inexperienced speakers often feel that they must memorize an entire report to be effective. Actually, unless you're a trained actor, a memorized delivery sounds wooden and unnatural. Also, forgetting your place can be disastrous. Therefore, memorizing an entire oral presentation is not recommended. However, memorizing significant

  Don't try to memorize an entire oral presentation. It sounds artificial and is a catastrophe if you become confused.

parts—the introduction, the conclusion, or a significant quotation—can be dramatic and impressive.

If you read an oral presentation, you may put your audience to sleep.

- **Reading Delivery.** Reading a report to an audience creates a negative impression. It suggests that you don't know your topic very well, so that the audience loses confidence in your expertise. Reading also prevents you from maintaining eye contact with the audience. If you can't see their reactions, you can't benefit from feedback. Worst of all, reading is simply boring. If you must read your report, practice it enough so that you can look up occasionally as you present familiar sections.

Write out complete sentences for the key ideas in your talk.

- **Extemporaneous Delivery.** The most effective method for presenting oral reports is the extemporaneous delivery. In this method you plan the report carefully and talk from notes containing key sentences. By practicing with your notes, you can talk to your audience in a conversational manner. Your notes should not consist of entire paragraphs, nor should they be single words. Instead, use complete sentences based on the major ideas in your outline. These key ideas will keep you on track and will jog your memory, but only if you have thoroughly practiced the presentation.

- **Impromptu Delivery.** An impromptu, or off-the-cuff, delivery is necessary if you are asked to give a spur-of-the-moment report. For example, you might be asked to report on the progress of a March of Dimes collection drive of which you are chairperson. Many activities in business require impromptu oral reports. Usually, you are very familiar with your topic, but you have little time to prepare your thoughts. Presenting accurate, coherent, persuasive, and well-organized information without adequate preparation is very difficult for even the most professional speaker. If you are asked to give an impromptu report, take a few moments to compose your thoughts and to jot down your main points.

Delivery Techniques

Nearly everyone experiences some degree of stage fright when speaking before a group. Such fears are quite natural. You can learn to control and reduce stage fright, as well as to incorporate techniques of effective speaking in your presentations, by studying suggestions from experts. Successful speakers use these techniques before, during, and after their reports.

Here are techniques that experts use before, during, and after delivering oral presentations.

Before You Speak:

- **Prepare thoroughly.** One of the most effective devices to reduce stage fright is the confidence that you know your topic well. Research your topic diligently and prepare a careful sentence outline. Those who try to "wing it" usually suffer the worst butterflies.

- **Rehearse repeatedly.** Practice your entire presentation, not just the first half. Place your outline sentences on separate cards. You may also wish to include transitional sentences to help you move to the next topic. Use these cards as you practice, and include your visual aids in your rehearsal. Record your rehearsal on tape so that you can hear how you sound.

- **Time yourself.** Try to make your presentation in no more than twenty minutes. Most audiences tend to get restless during longer talks. Set a timer during your rehearsal to measure your speaking time.

- **Demand a lectern.** Every beginning speaker needs the security of a high desk or lectern from which to deliver a presentation. It serves as a note holder and a convenient place to rest awkward hands and arms.

- **Check the room.** Before you talk, make sure that a lectern has been provided. If you are using sound equipment or a projector, make sure they are operational. Check electrical outlets and the position of the viewing screen. Ensure that the seating arrangement is appropriate to your needs.

- **Practice stress reduction.** If you feel tension and fear while you are waiting your turn to speak, use stress reduction techniques. Take very deep breaths. Inhale to a count of ten; hold this breath to a count of ten; exhale to a count of ten. Concentrate on your breathing, not on the audience awaiting you.

  Deep-breathing exercises can significantly reduce stress.

During Your Presentation:

- **Begin with a pause.** When you first approach the audience, take a moment to adjust your notes and make yourself comfortable. Establish your control of the situation.

- **Present your first sentence from memory.** By memorizing your opening, you can immediately establish rapport with the audience through eye contact. You'll also sound confident and knowledgeable.

- **Maintain eye contact.** Look at your audience. If the size of the audience frightens you, pick out two individuals on the right and two on the left. Talk directly to these people.

- **Control your voice and vocabulary.** Speak in moderated tones but loudly enough to be heard. Eliminate verbal static, such as *ah, er,* and *uh.* Silence is preferable to meaningless fillers when you are thinking of your next idea.

- **Put the brakes on.** Many novice speakers talk too rapidly, displaying their nervousness and making it very difficult for audience members to understand their ideas. Slow down and listen to what you're saying.

- **Move naturally.** Use the lectern to hold your notes so that you are free to move about casually and naturally. Avoid fidgeting with your notes, your clothing, or items in your pockets. Learn to use your body to express a point.

- **Use visual aids effectively.** Discuss and interpret each visual aid for the audience. Move aside as you describe it so that it can be seen fully. Use a pointer if necessary.

- **Avoid digressions.** Stick to your outline and notes. Don't suddenly include clever little anecdotes or digressions that occur to you as you speak. If it's not part of your rehearsed material, leave it out so that you can finish on time. Remember, too, that your audience may not be as enthralled with your topic as you are.

  Avoid digressions that occur to you as you speak.

- **Summarize your main points.** Conclude your presentation by reiterating your main points or by emphasizing what you want the audience to think or do. Once you have announced your conclusion, proceed to it directly. Don't irritate the audience by talking for five or ten more minutes.

After Your Presentation:

- **Distribute handouts.** If you prepared handouts with data the audience will need to have after the presentation, pass them out when you finish.

- **Encourage questions.** If the situation permits a question-and-answer period, announce it at the beginning of your presentation. Then, when you finish, ask for questions. Set a time limit for questions and answers.

- **Repeat questions.** Although the speaker may hear the question, some people in the audience often do not. Begin each answer with a repetition of the question. This also gives you thinking time.

- **Answer questions directly.** Avoid becoming defensive or debating the questioner.

- **Keep control.** Don't allow one individual to take over. Keep the entire audience involved.

- **End gracefully.** To signal the end of the session before you take the last question, say something like "We have time for just one more question." After you answer the last question, express appreciation to the audience for the opportunity to talk with them.

> Don't let a question-and-answer period dissolve into numerous individual conversations. Keep control by repeating questions for the entire audience to hear.

Evaluating Presentations

The oral report evaluation form shown in Figure 14.1 should be useful to speakers preparing a presentation. It's also helpful to students who will evaluate oral reports in a classroom situation.

Developing Successful Meetings and Conferences

Whether you like attending them or not, meetings and conferences are a necessary part of business today. These meetings can be more successful—and even enjoyable—if leaders and participants sharpen their listening and speaking skills.

Meetings and conferences consist of three or more individuals who meet for discussion. Meetings are called to gather information, clarify policy, seek consensus, and solve problems. Meetings are different from speeches, where one individual talks *at* an audience. In meetings individuals *exchange* ideas.

Meetings differ from conferences in that they are smaller and less formal. We'll concentrate on meetings in this discussion, although most of the advice holds for conferences as well. Meetings can be occasions for successful exchange of information, or they be boring failures and time wasters.

≈

FIGURE 14.1 Oral Report Evaluation Form

SPEAKER'S NAME _____

Oral Report Evaluation

Excellent	10 points
Above average	8–9
Average	5–7
Needs improvement	4 or below

                                                                    Points
                                                                    _____

1. Were the opening and closing clear and well
   planned?   _____

2. Did the speaker help you remember two to four
   main points?   _____

3. Were the speaker's movements and eye contact
   natural?   _____

4. Was the visual aid handled appropriately?   _____

5. Was the report well organized, coherent, and
   obviously practiced before presentation?   _____

TOTAL POINTS   _____

On the back add a statement of praise and suggest one pointer for
improvement.

Why Meetings Fail

Many failed meetings are the result of poor planning. Perhaps the meeting was unnecessary. Alternatives—such as personal conversation, memos, or telephone calls—might have served the purpose as well.

Poor leadership dooms some meetings. The leader fails to keep the group discussing target items. The discussion digresses or flounders on trivia, and no resolution is reached. Then the group must meet again, and no one enjoys additional meetings.

Poor meetings are usually the result of poor planning or ineffective leadership.

Planning Meetings

Successful meetings begin with planning. Decide first on a goal or an objective, and then determine whether a meeting is the best way to achieve the goal. If the goal is to announce a new policy regarding the scheduling of vacations, is a meeting the best way to inform employees? Perhaps a memo would be better.

Agendas help prepare participants for meetings.

If a meeting is necessary, prepare an agenda of items to be discussed. The best agendas list topics, an estimate of time for each item, and an ending time. They also include the names of individuals who are responsible for presenting topics or for performing some action. Send the agenda (and perhaps the minutes of the last meeting) at least two days prior to the meeting. Notify only those people directly concerned with the business of this meeting. Plan to serve refreshments if you think the participants need them.

THE WALL STREET JOURNAL

"Jenkins, is there something I should know?"

Source: From *The Wall Street Journal*. Reprinted with permission of the Cartoon Features Syndicate.

Conducting Meetings

Some experts say that the most important part of a meeting is the first five to ten minutes when the leader introduces the topic and sets the tone.

Conducting good meetings requires real skill, which not every leader immediately has. Such skill comes with practice and with knowledge of the following pointers. To avoid wasting time and irritating the attendees, always start meetings on time—even if some participants are missing. Delaying sets a poor example. Individuals who came on time resent waiting for latecomers. Moreover, latecomers may fail to be on time for future meetings, knowing that the leader doesn't always start punctually.

Begin with a 3- to 5-minute introduction that includes the following: (1) goal and length of the meeting, (2) background of the problem, (3) possible solutions and constraints, (4) tentative agenda, and (5) procedures to be followed. At this point ask if participants agree with you thus far.

Then assign one attendee to take minutes. It's impossible for the leader to direct a meeting and record its proceedings at the same time. Open the discussion, and from that point forward, say as little as possible. Adhere to the agenda and the time schedule. Keep the discussion on the topic by tactfully guiding speakers back to the main idea. You might say, "Well, gosh, Jeff, I'm afraid I don't understand exactly how your new motorcycle relates to our vacation policy. Can you explain?" Encourage all individuals to participate. You can do this by occasionally asking for the opinions of the smart but silent participants. Try not to let one or two people monopolize the discussion. When the group seems to have reached a consensus, summarize it in your own words and look to see if everyone agrees. Finally, end the meeting at the agreed time. Announce that a report of the proceedings will be sent to all.

Participating in Meetings

As a participant, you can get the most out of a meeting and contribute to its success by coming prepared. Read the agenda and gather any information necessary for your knowledgeable participation. One way to make yourself visible in an organization is to shine at meetings. Know the problem, its causes, possible solutions, alternatives, and how others have dealt with it. Careful preparation and wise participation at meetings often cause management to recognize upwardly mobile employees.

Employees looking for ways to recommend themselves to their superiors consider meetings to be opportunities for showing their stuff.

Arrive at the meeting on time. Be ready to speak on an issue, but consider your timing. It may be smart to wait for others to speak first so that you can shape your remarks to best advantage. You can help the leader keep the discussion on target with remarks such as, "Sure, I love a bargain, too, Lisa, but right now I'm very concerned about how to solve this problem. Has anyone considered . . . ?"

Productive, enjoyable meetings result from good planning, skillful leadership, and active participation.

Improving Telephone Techniques

Telephones can be used to increase productivity and generate goodwill. Most of us, however, give little conscious attention to the impression our telephone personality conveys or to how we could transform the telephone into a valuable business tool. Let's first take a look at techniques for typical telephone users; then we'll discuss tips for individuals who make heavy use of the telephone.[1]

Tips for Typical Telephone Users

Before making a telephone call, decide whether the call is really necessary. Perhaps the information could be delivered by memo more efficiently. One West Coast company found that telephone interruptions consumed about 18 percent of staff members' workdays. With the staff's approval, a new policy was implemented. If any matter could wait three hours, a special interoffice memo was recommended. Receivers of the memos had to answer immediately. This memo system resulted in a 30 percent reduction of time lost by in-house phone interruptions.

Frequent telephone calls interrupt workers and reduce productivity. Consider writing a memo instead of calling.

[1]Based on "Chats," Day-Timers, Inc., Allentown, PA.

If a telephone call must be made, follow these suggestions to make it most productive.

Making Telephone Calls

1. **Prepare a mini agenda.** Jot down notes regarding all the topics you need to discuss. You know how embarrassing it is when you must call a second time because you forgot an important item the first time.

2. **Use a three-point intro.** When placing a call, immediately give (a) your name, (b) your affiliation, and (c) a brief explanation of your reason for calling. For example, "May I speak to Sara Price? This is Jeff Moss of Datatech, and I'm seeking information about the March convention in Hawaii." This three-point intro enables the other individual to respond immediately without asking further questions.

3. **Be cheerful and responsive.** Let your voice show the same kind of animation that you radiate when you greet people in person. In your mind try to envision the individual answering the telephone. Smile at that person. Some companies urge employees to use a mirror to ensure that they smile. A smile affects the tone of voice.

4. **Bring it to a close.** When your business is transacted, it is the caller's responsibility to end the call. This is sometimes difficult to do if the other individual wants to ramble on and on. Use closing language, such as "I've certainly enjoyed talking with you," "I've learned what I needed to know, and now I can proceed with my work," "Thanks for your help," "I must go now, but may I call you again in the future if I need . . . ?"

> **The three-point intro consists of your name, your business, and a brief description of the subject of your call.**

Source: Reprinted with special permission of North America Syndicate, Inc.

5. **Avoid telephone tag.** If you call someone who's not in, ask when it would be best for you to call again. Leave word that you will call at a specific time—and do it. If you ask an individual to call you, give a time when you can be reached—and be in.

Receiving Telephone Calls

1. **Identify yourself immediately.** In answering your telephone or someone else's, provide your name and other identification, if appropriate.

Remember that the caller may not be familiar with your name or your department. Say it clearly and slowly, so that you can be understood.

2. **In answering calls for others, be courteous and helpful.** Don't, however, give out confidential information. It's better to say, "She's away from her desk" or "He's out of the office" than to report a colleague's exact whereabouts.

3. **Take messages carefully.** Repeat the spelling of names and verify telephone numbers. Write the message legibly and record the time and date.

4. **In transferring calls, explain what you're doing.** Explain why you are transferring, and identify the extension to which you are transferring the call in case the caller is disconnected.

Tips for Heavy Telephone Use

The preceding advice is helpful for individuals who make a normal number of calls each workday—perhaps five to ten calls. Some individuals, however, make many more calls each day. They rely on the telephone so heavily that additional techniques are necessary for them to work efficiently.

1. **Set up a hot line.** Set aside one telephone line, with an answering machine, for top priority calls. Give the number of your hot line to selected staff and associates who want to be sure to reach you. Leave a message that the machine will be checked frequently. Pick up your messages every hour or at regular intervals.

   If you use a telephone answering machine, check its messages frequently.

2. **Delegate authority.** Ask an intermediary (your secretary or administrative assistant) to screen calls. Prepare your callers by telling them that your assistant has been briefed and has background information on most matters. An assistant can often expedite action and prevent unnecessary callbacks.

3. **Plan phone-free periods.** Many busy managers set aside a period of time when they accept no telephone calls. Uninterrupted work time is necessary for optimum performance in many tasks. In answering calls during this time, your assistant can say, "Ms. Atkins is dictating just now. May I have her call you back between 4 and 5 p.m.?"

4. **Designate telephone hours.** To reduce work interruptions, allocate a specific daily time for making and taking calls. By placing all your calls at once, you develop an efficient routine. Too, it's good policy to be available personally to callers at some time each day. Some executives use 8 to 9 a.m. for taking calls and 4 to 5 p.m. for making calls.

5. **Confirm in writing.** Jot down the highlights of an agreement or details of a discussion during important calls. Read your notes back to the other person; then send a quick handwritten or typed to-file report to confirm the conversation. Keep a copy for your files.

One-Minute Manager

Short telephone calls are effective tools in an imaginative manager's arsenal of management techniques. One-minute telephone calls can be used to do the following:

- Monitor the progress of a project
- Deliver a compliment
- Express concern about an employee's health or family situation
- Announce schedule changes
- Reveal important data to key customers ahead of published announcements
- Gather immediate feedback
- Ensure that deadlines are understood and agreed on in advance

Employers today are looking for individuals who have developed good communication skills. Active listeners and confident speakers have a competitive edge in the business world, not only for entry-level positions but especially for higher-level management positions.

How to Dictate like an Executive

As businesses continue to automate, many employees are called on to dictate their ideas into machines for transcription by secretaries or word processing specialists. Dictating is the composition of business documents—but it's done orally instead of manually. With a little practice and a few pointers, you can dictate like a seasoned executive.

- **Learning the Equipment.** Become familiar with your dictation equipment before you need to produce real documents. Read the instructions or documentation; know how to operate the equipment. Understand its capabilities. Practice composing sample messages and playing back your words. Recognize that you will improve with practice.

- **Organizing Your Materials.** Always gather the necessary supporting documents and data for each message before you begin. If you need to check on the price of a printer or the date of a meeting, do so before you start. Make notes in the margin of the document you are answering. Don't write out the entire message.

- **Getting Off to a Good Start.** Set aside a period of time when you won't be disturbed. Then dictate the most urgent message first. Identify yourself and your department. Describe your dictation. "This is a letter (or memo) to be printed on letterhead with two copies. Use the current date."

- **Speaking Clearly.** It's surprising how easy it is to confuse dictated words—*p*'s sound like *b*'s or *d*'s; *f*'s sound like *s*'s. To improve the chances of accurate transcription, enunciate clearly. Clarify difficult sounds by using names to identify letters, such as *d* as in *Don*, *s* as in *Sam*, *p* as in *Paul*. Spell out words that sound alike, such as *residents* and *residence*.

- **Dictating Punctuation.** Although it's hard at first, you can train yourself to end sentences with spoken periods. In time you'll learn to dictate commas, semicolons, and other punctuation, as well as capitalization. Such thoughtfulness is helpful to the transcriptionist and greatly reduces the need for returning documents for correction.

- **Reading Minds.** Transcriptionists, like other mere mortals, are usually poor mind readers. Therefore, you must dictate paragraphs, indentions, underlining, and any unusual spelling or formatting.

- **Correcting Errors.** As soon as you make an error, stop dictating, back up the tape, and rerecord the correction. If you don't recognize the error until you finish, most systems have a method for you to leave messages regarding special instructions or error notations.

- **Avoiding Distractions.** Don't eat, chew gum, smoke, or make bothersome sounds when dictating. Also, don't leave blank spaces on the tape. Use the pause device when you stop to collect your thoughts.

- **Being Considerate.** The mark of a real professional is the courtesy with which he or she treats the transcriptionist. Address the transcriptionist by name, if possible. Throughout the dictation, remember that you are not speaking to a machine; you are working with a person. When you finish, thank the transcriptionist.

Activity

Your instructor may allow you to practice developing your skills by dictating a message slowly to a classmate.

APPLICATION AND PRACTICE—14

Discussion

1. If most of our communicating time is spent listening, speaking, and reading, why is a disproportionate amount of time spent learning writing skills?

2. Discuss seven barriers to effective listening and give an example of each from the business world.

3. Discuss the advantages and disadvantages of taking notes while you are listening. When would note-taking be most effective?

4. Compare and contrast the development of oral and written reports.

5. Why is it necessary to keep the audience informed of the organization of an oral report?

6. Discuss the duties of a leader and the functions of a participant at business meetings and conferences.

Short Answers

7. According to some estimates, adults spent what percent of their communicating time

   a. listening
   b. speaking
   c. reading
   d. writing

8. How fast does the average American speak?

9. List 11 ways to improve your listening skills. Be prepared to discuss each.

10. Name five characteristics that you should identify about your audience before preparing an oral report.

11. On how many main points should an oral report concentrate?

12. What is the first step in developing an oral report?

13. List the three parts of an oral report. Be prepared to discuss what goes in each part.

14. List five kinds of visual aids for oral reports. Be prepared to discuss each.

15. List five techniques that are helpful in overcoming stage fright.

16. Notes for an oral report should consist of what?

17. What is an agenda, and what should it include?

18. Who takes the minutes of a meeting, and what are done with them?

19. Give an example of an efficient three-point opening to a telephone call. Use your own name and data.

20. What is telephone tag, and how can it be avoided?

21. List five ways an individual who uses the telephone frequently could improve productivity. Be prepared to discuss each way.

Activities

22. Observe the listening habits in one of your classes for a week. Write a memo report to your instructor describing your observations.

23. Analyze your own listening habits. What are your strengths and weaknesses? Decide on a plan for improving your listening skills. Write a memo to your instructor including your analysis and your improvement plan.

24. You are a student in a business management or other class. Your instructor notices that you have good listening habits. Disturbed by the poor listening skills of some other class members, your instructor asks you to do research and to present a program (for extra credit) to help students improve their listening skills. For this presentation:

    a. Write a specific statement of purpose.
    b. Prepare a complete outline.
    c. Write the introduction.
    d. List visual aids that would be appropriate. Describe their content.

25. If you are now employed or have been employed, adapt the assignment in Activity No. 24 to your work. Assume that your supervisor has asked you to present an in-service training workshop that helps employees improve listening skills. Respond to the instructions in Items (a) through (d).

26. Visit your library and select a speech from *Vital Speeches of Our Day*. Write a memo report to your instructor in which you analyze the speech in terms of the following items:

    a. Effectiveness of the introduction, body, conclusion
    b. Evidence of effective overall organization
    c. Use of verbal signposts to create coherence
    d. Emphasis of two to four main points
    e. Effectiveness of supporting facts (use of examples, statistics, quotations, and so forth)

27. Adapt a newspaper or magazine article to an oral report format. Assume that you are to present this report before your business communications class. Submit the outline, introduction, and conclusion to your instructor, or present the report to your class.

28. Write a memo to your instructor describing the fears or anxieties that you have experienced when presenting a speech. Suggest ways to reduce your fears.

29. Interview two or three individuals in your professional field. How is oral communication important in this profession? Does the need for oral skills change as one advances? What suggestions can this individual make for developing proficient oral communication skills among newcomers to the field? Discuss your findings with your class.

30. Present an impromptu report. Submit to your instructor a list of three to four business or nonbusiness topics you know well. These topics may include a range of interests, from "How to Choose a Used Car" to "The U.S. Trade Deficit." Your instructor will select one topic from this list. Take ten minutes in class to organize an oral presentation that concentrates on an aspect of your topic that can be covered in three minutes. Make notes that include an introduction, body, and conclusion. Your instructor will divide your class into groups of four to six students. Present your report before your group. (All groups will be reporting simultaneously.) As a listening exercise, evaluate each student's report and delivery. Make note of at least three facts you learned from each report. Your instructor may ask you to prepare a short evaluation form for the impromptu reports.

31. If you prepared a business report in Chapter 11, deliver it as an extemporaneous report before your class. Your instructor will determine how much time you have. Use visual aids, if appropriate, and be sure to leave enough time for questions and answers. Class members will evaluate the report using the oral report evaluation form (Figure 14.1).

32. Plan a meeting. Assume that the next meeting of your associated students' organization will discuss preparations for a careers day in the spring. The group will hear reports from committees working on speakers, business recruiters, publicity, reservations of campus space, setup of booths, and any other matters you can think of. As president of your ASO, prepare an agenda for the meeting. Compose your introductory remarks to open the meeting. Your instructor may ask you to submit these two documents or use them in staging an actual meeting in class.

33. Dictate a letter or memo in class. Your instructor will divide the class into sets of partners, each set with Partner 1 and Partner 2. Your instructor will select a memo or letter from an earlier chapter for Partner 1 and another for Partner 2. Study your problem and prepare notes, but do not write out complete sentences. Review the pointers on how to dictate. Then, dictate the document slowly to your partner, who will write in longhand. For homework each partner will transcribe the dictated document. Return the transcribed document to your partner and discuss your experience.

34. Listen for instructions. Your instructor will "talk" or explain the facts from one of the letter or memo assignments in an earlier exercise. The instructor may add extraneous information or omit something vital. Take notes from your instructor's presentation. Ask questions, if necessary. Do not look at a written version of the data. Then write the document prescribed.

35. Practice making and taking telephone calls. Your instructor will divide the class into pairs. Read the scenario for (a), which follows. Take a moment

to rehearse your role silently. Then play the role with your partner. If there is time, repeat the scenarios, changing roles.

Partner 1	Partner 2
a. Use your own name. You are the personnel manager of Datatronics, Inc. Call Elizabeth Franklin, office manager at Whispering Pines Resort. Inquire about a job applicant, Lisa Lee, who listed Ms. Franklin as a reference. Place the call.	You are the receptionist for Whispering Pines. The caller asks for Elizabeth Franklin, who is having a root canal at her dentist's today. Answer the call appropriately.
b. Call Ms. Franklin again the following day to inquire about the same job applicant, Lisa Lee. Ms. Franklin answers today, but she talks on and on, describing the applicant in great detail. Tactfully close the conversation.	Play the role of Ms. Franklin, office manager. Describe Lisa Lee, an imaginary employee (think of someone with whom you've worked). Include many details, such as how well she worked with others, her appearance, her smoking habit, etc.
c. Play the role of receptionist for Frank Morris, of Morris Enterprises. Answer a call for Mr. Morris, who is working in another office, at Ext. 245, where he will accept calls.	Use your own name as legal assistant for Bernard Silverstein. Call Frank Morris to verify a meeting date Mr. Silverstein has with Mr. Morris.
d. You are now Frank Morris, president of Morris Enterprises. Call your attorney, Bernard Silverstein about a legal problem.	You are the receptionist for the attorney, Bernard Silverstein. Mr. Silverstein is skiing in Aspen and will return in two days, but he doesn't want his clients to know where he is. Take a message.
e. Call Mr. Silverstein again.	Take a message again.
f. Call Mr. Silverstein again, but this time leave a message that will ensure communication.	Take a message.

36. Make a five-minute oral presentation. Select a challenging business-related magazine article of at least 1,000 words. Prepare a well-organized presentation that includes the following: (a) an attention-getting opening plus an introduction to the major ideas, (b) three to four main points that are easy for the audience to identify, and (c) a conclusion that reviews the main points and ends by asking for questions. Avoid self-conscious remarks such as "My report is about . . ." or "The article says . . ." or "I guess that ends it." Use one visual aid. Allow no more than three minutes for questions and answers. Your instructor may ask you to distribute copies of your article to the class one or two days prior to your presentation so that they may ask informed questions. Turn in an outline to your instructor before your presentation.

37. Prepare a five- to ten-minute oral report. Use one of the following topics or a topic that you and your instructor agree on. You are an expert who has been called in to explain some aspect of the topic before a group of interested individuals. Since your time is limited, prepare a concise yet forceful report with effectual visual aids.

a. How and why are some companies (like Apple Computer) building recreation and parties into the corporate culture?
b. What kinds of employment advertisements are legal, and what kinds are potentially illegal?
c. Would Japanese management techniques work in this country?
d. Should smoking be allowed in public places?
e. How should one dress for an employment interview?
f. What is the economic outlook for a given product (shoes, women's apparel, domestic cars, TV sets, etc.) this year?
g. What franchise would offer the best opportunities for investment for an entrepreneur in your area?
h. What brand and model of computer and printer represent the best buys for home use today?
i. What is the current employment outlook in three career areas of interest to you?
j. Why should you be hired for a position that you have applied for?
k. For its sales personnel, should your company rent automobiles, own them, or pay mileage costs on employee-owned vehicles?
l. Where should your professional organization hold its next convention?
m. What local plant or animal is endangered, and how can it be protected?
n. What evidence supports the view that VDTs are dangerous to users?
o. How can your school (or company) improve its image?
p. Why should individuals invest in a company or scheme of your choice?
q. What are some common and uncommon ways in which fax messages are being used today?

GRAMMAR/MECHANICS CHECKUP—14

Punctuation Review

Review Sections 1.17 and 2.01 to 2.29 in the Grammar/Mechanics Handbook. Study each of the following statements and insert any necessary punctuation. In the space provided, indicate the number of marks that you added. When you finish, compare your responses with those shown below. If your responses differ, study carefully the specific principles shown in parentheses.

1 _____ (2.05)   **Example:**   The District of Columbia has never been much of a financial mecca, but suddenly it has attracted some big names in banking.

_____   1. A Cleveland based law firm Sanders & Dempsey has been promoting D.C. banking.

2. D.C. banking may have fewer restrictions therefore many large banks   _____
   are rushing to apply for full service and limited service privileges.

3. By April the following four New York banks had applied to open D.C.   _____
   branches Chase Manhattan, Morgan, Chemical, and Bankers Trust.

4. What the bankers seem to be hoping is that the Districts liberal   _____
   banking laws will permit their limited service banks to offer financial
   services forbidden elsewhere.

5. George Hancock who is now an attorney with Sanders & Dempsey   _____
   formerly worked in the Comptrollers office.

6. During his time with the agency Mr. Hancock interpreted local state   _____
   and federal banking laws and regulations.

7. He was as a matter of fact aware of additional banking opportunities   _____
   not just those in the District.

8. When interviewed recently he said "No one really knows how far a   _____
   bank can go because the law has never been fully utilized"

9. A limited service bank can acquire other institutions more easily than   _____
   a full service bank its purchases need no approval by the Federal
   Reserve.

10. (Emphasize.) Three major banks Chase, Morgan, and Bankers   _____
    Trust now have branches in the nations capital.

11. When the bank rush began local officials became concerned but they   _____
    did not act until April.

12. An article entitled Banks Rush to Set Up Shop in District appeared   _____
    in the Washington Post

13. The District Council on the other hand hopes to establish permanent   _____
    far reaching regulations.

14. Acting on behalf of the Council Councilwoman Reese said that the   _____
    District may have to examine banks applications more carefully.

15. Banks must now meet new requirements for example they must offer   _____
    $50 million in the form of loans to local businesses.

---

1. (3) Cleveland-based firm, Dempsey, (*1.17e, 2.09*)   3. (1) branches: (*2.17*)   5. (3) Hancock, Dempsey, Comptroller's (*2.09, 2.20a*)   7. (3) was, fact, opportunities, (*2.03, 2.12*)   9. (3) limited-service full-service bank; (*1.17e, 2.16b*)   11. (2) began, concerned; (*2.06a, 2.16c*)   13. (4) Council, hand, permanent, far-reaching (*1.17e, 2.03, 2.08*)   15. (2) requirements; example, (*2.16*)

Formatting Letters and Memorandums

The first impression a letter or memo makes on its reader often determines whether that document will actually be read. The appearance of a document also affects the reader's reaction to its contents. A neatly typed letter on good paper, arranged in proper form and centered, is inviting to read. It carries a nonverbal message indicating that the writer cares about this document and its effect on the reader. An attractive letter or memo suggests that the writer is a caring and careful individual. It suggests that the business he or she represents is successful and well managed.

To send a positive, nonverbal message along with the words of your letters and memos, pay attention to form and appearance. Make your documents neat, correct, and inviting. So that you may become familiar with customary format and placement, here is a description of the parts and styles for business letters and memorandums.

Letter Parts

Letterhead. Most business organizations use $8\frac{1}{2}$-by-11-inch paper printed with a letterhead displaying their official name, address, and telephone number (see Figure A1.1). Sometimes the letterhead also includes a logo and an advertising message (such as *Great Western Banking: A new brand of banking*).

Return Address. If you type a letter on paper without a printed letterhead, place your address immediately above the date (see Figure A1.2, Letter 4). Do not include your name here; you will type your name at the end of your letter. In typing your return address, avoid abbreviations except for the two-letter state abbreviation (see Table A1.1).

Dateline. On letterhead paper, type the date two carrier returns below the last line of the letterhead or 2 inches from the top edge of the paper (line 13). On plain paper place the date immediately below your return address. Since the date goes on line 13, start the return address an appropriate number of lines above it. The most common dateline format is as follows:

June 9, 1989

Letterhead # PACIFIC GENERAL BELL

. . . .

Serving all your communication needs

. . . .

13590 Victory Boulevard
Reseda, CA 91335-1430

↓ line 13

Dateline   September 22, 19xx

↓ 3 to 10 lines

Inside Address   Software Services, Inc.
Attention Telecommunications Manager
19533 Burbank Boulevard
Woodland Hills, CA 91371-1299

↓ 2 lines

Salutation   Ladies and Gentlemen:

↓ 2 lines

SUBJECT: CHANGES IN TELEPHONE SERVICE

↓ 2 lines

Body   As part of our plan to expand and improve telephone service provided to California customers, we will be making some changes in the central office equipment serving your area. This will enable us to offer you a variety of new services.

The new equipment we are installing may affect some customers' telephone equipment. Please contact your dealer prior to December 1, which is our change date. We plan to have our new equipment in operation approximately January 1.

Your equipment dealer will need to know these facts:

1. Pacific Bell is installing DMS-100 equipment in the Reseda 01 Central Office.

2. Installation is planned for December 15.

The new switching equipment will offer many electronic services such as Call Waiting, Call Forwarding, Speed Calling, and other features. Enclosed is a brochure describing these services. Requests for changes or additions to your existing telephone service should be directed to your Pacific General Bell business office representative at (818)883-1902.

↓ 2 lines

Complimentary   Sincerely,
Close
↓ 2 lines

Organization Name   PACIFIC GENERAL BELL

↓ 4 lines

Author   Jerry C. Tuffeland
Vice President, Services

Reference Initials   JCT:meg

Enclosure Notation   Enclosure

Copy Notation   c J. R. Ralston

Letter 1

Rodeo Drive Graphics Designers | 5210 Rodeo Drive, Beverly Hills, California 90024

November, 17, 19xx

Mr. Mark S. Stevenson
Office Manager
Galaxy Enterprises
17690 Ventura Boulevard
Sherman Oaks, CA 91436

Dear Mr. Stevenson

SUBJECT: BLOCK LETTER FORMAT

This letter illustrates full block style. All typed lines begin at the left margin. The date is usually typed two inches from the top or two lines below the last line of the letterhead, whichever is lower.

This letter also shows open punctuation. No colon follows the salutation, and no comma follows the complimentary close. Although this punctuation style is quite efficient, we find that most of our customers prefer to include punctuation after the salutation and the complimentary close.

If a subject line is included, it is typed two lines below the salutation. The word *SUBJECT* is optional. Most readers will recognize a statement in this position as the subject without an identifying label.

The complimentary close appears two lines below the end of the last paragraph. Four lines below the complimentary close appear the typed name and identification of the letter author.

The full block style is quite popular among word processing specialists because it requires fewer keystrokes than other letter styles.

Sincerely

Rochelle Davis

Rochelle Davis
Graphics Designer

wts

Letter 1
Block Letter Style, Open Punctuation

Letter 2

PACIFIC
WESTERN
COLLEGE
*885 Redwood Highway
Crescent City, CA 95531*

May 12, 19xx

First Federal Banking Services
Attention Office Manager
220 Oceanview Avenue
Eureka, CA 95421

Ladies and Gentlemen:

Here is the information you requested regarding modified block letter style.

The modified block style letter is different from the full block style in two respects: (1) the date may be centered or may appear flush with the right margin, as shown here, and (2) the closing lines begin five spaces to the left of the page center.

In the modified block style letter, paragraphs may be indented five spaces or blocked at the left margin. Either style is acceptable in business offices.

If a letter contains an attention line, it may appear in one of two positions: on the second line of the inside address (as shown here) or two lines below the last line of the inside address block. We recommend that it appear as shown in this letter because it may be copied to the envelope easily with word processing equipment.

Many business organizations prefer the modified block letter style because of its traditional appearance. Enclosed is additional information regarding letter styles.

Cordially yours,

Darlene McClure

Darlene McClure, Professor
Office Technologies Department

trt

Enclosure

Letter 2
Modified Block Style, Mixed Punctuation

Letter 3

◆ **Unified Insurance Services**
2560 Fifth Street Albany, NY 14144-0125
Commercial   Residential   Life

November 12, 19xx

Professor Karen Butts
Department of Business
Tompkins-Cortland Community College
Dryden, NY 13053-3102

SIMPLIFIED LETTER FORMAT

This letter, Professor Butts, illustrates the simplified letter format that our office prefers. This format has the following distinctive features:

1. All lines begin at the left margin.

2. The salutation and complimentary close are omitted.

3. A subject line in all caps appears three lines below the inside address and three lines above the first paragraph.

4. The author's name and identification appear five lines below the last paragraph.

We enjoy this letter style because it's efficient. It's also useful because we no longer must worry about the propriety of salutations, complimentary closes, and individuals' titles. Moreover, this letter style is effective in writing to businesses when we have no individual to address.

James D. Clark
JAMES D. CLARK, VICE PRESIDENT

wer

c Victoria Munoz

Letter 3
Simplified Letter Style

Letter 4

3420 Concordia Lane
Moorhead, MN 56560
March 30, 19xx

Ms. Marilyn Theissman, President
Rochester Health Care Specialists
1045 Blue Lake Drive
Rochester, MN 54201

Dear Ms. Theissman:

At your request I am sending you this message in illustration of the personal business letter style.

This letter style is appropriate for people writing letters as individuals instead of writing as representatives of business organizations.

The heading includes the writer's street and city address, along with the date. These lines begin on line 11 at the center of the page, or they may be blocked to end at the right margin. The inside address appears about four to eight lines below the date, depending upon the length of the letter.

The letter may be typed in block or modified block style with open or mixed punctuation. The paragraphs may be indented or blocked.

The writer signs the letter between the complimentary close and the typed signature. Normally no reference initials are included since the writer has prepared the letter.

Sincerely,

Melanie Grable

Melanie Grable

Letter 4
Personal Business Letter Style

TABLE A1.1   Two-letter State Abbreviations

State	Zip	State	Zip	State	Zip	State	Zip
Alabama	AL	Illinois	IL	Montana	MT	Puerto Rico	PR
Alaska	AK	Indiana	IN	Nebraska	NE	Rhode Island	RI
Arizona	AZ	Iowa	IA	Nevada	NV	South Carolina	SC
Arkansas	AR	Kansas	KS	New Hampshire	NH	South Dakota	SD
California	CA	Kentucky	KY	New Jersey	NJ	Tennessee	TN
Colorado	CO	Louisiana	LA	New Mexico	NM	Texas	TX
Connecticut	CT	Maine	ME	New York	NY	Utah	UT
Delaware	DE	Maryland	MD	North Carolina	NC	Vermont	VT
District of Columbia	DC	Massachusetts	MA	North Dakota	ND	Virginia	VA
Florida	FL	Michigan	MI	Ohio	OH	Washington	WA
Georgia	GA	Minnesota	MN	Oklahoma	OK	Wisconsin	WI
Hawaii	HI	Mississippi	MS	Oregon	OR	Wyoming	WY
Idaho	ID	Missouri	MO	Pennsylvania	PA		

For European or military correspondence, use the following dateline format:

9 June 1989

Inside Address.   Type the inside address—that is, the address of the organization receiving the letter—single-spaced, starting at the left margin. The number of lines between the dateline and the inside address depends on the size of the body of the letter, the size of type (the pitch) used, and the length of the typing lines. Generally, 2 to 10 lines are appropriate.

Be careful to duplicate the exact wording and spelling of the recipient's name and address on your documents. Copy this information from the letterhead of the correspondence you are answering. If, for example, you are responding to *Jackson & Perkins Co.*, don't address your letter to *Jackson and Perkins Corp.*

For inside (letter and envelope) addresses, use a courtesy title, such as *Mr.*, *Ms.*, *Mrs.*, *Dr.*, *Professor*, or *Reverend*, whenever possible. If you are unsure of a woman's title, *Ms.* is appropriate. If an individual's name does not indicate gender (for example, *Leslie* or *Pat*), omit the title.

Remember, the inside address is there not for readers who already know who and where they are, but for the writers so that they may accurately file a copy.

In general, avoid abbreviations unless they appear in the printed letterhead of the document being answered.

Letters may be addressed to an organization, to an individual within an organization, or to the attention of an individual within an organization. Study the following examples and the salutations appropriate for each.

Letter Addressed to an Organization	Letter Addressed to an Individual Within an Organization
American Metals, Inc. 23690 Sunset Avenue Monterey Park, CA 91754 Gentlemen:	Mr. Arnold M. Hansen American Metals, Inc. 23690 Sunset Avenue Monterey Park, CA 91754 Dear Mr. Hansen:

Letter Addressed to the Attention of an Individual Within an Organization

American Metals, Inc.		American Metals, Inc.
Attention Mr. Arnold M. Hansen	or	23690 Sunset Avenue
23690 Sunset Avenue		Monterey Park, CA 91754
Monterey Park, CA 91754		
		Attention Mr. Harold M. Hansen
Gentlemen:		
		Gentlemen:

Attention Line.   An attention line, as shown in the preceding example as well as in Figure A1.2, Letter 2, allows you to send your message officially to an organization but for the attention of a specific individual, officer, or department. Notice that the appropriate salutation for a letter addressed to an organization (despite its attention line) is *Gentlemen* or *Ladies and Gentlemen*.

Attention lines are useful because your message can be directed to a specific individual. However, if the addressed individual is no longer with the organization, your letter will be processed by an appropriate successor. It would not be forwarded as a private letter to the individual addressed on the envelope.

Place the attention line two lines below the inside address, or type it immediately below the organization name within the inside address (see Figure A1.2, Letter 2). The latter position is preferable for word processing equipment since the address can then be automatically copied to the envelope and the attention line will not interfere with the last-line placement of the zip code. (Mail can be sorted automatically by optical character scanners at the post office if the zip code appears in the last line of a typed address.) A colon following the word *Attention* is optional.

Salutation.   Place the letter greeting, or salutation, two lines below the last line of the inside address or the attention line (if used). The letter may be addressed to an individual (*Dear Scott* or *Dear Mr. Waters*) or to an organization (*Gentlemen*). If women are part of management, use *Ladies and Gentlemen*. Even if you are on a first-name basis, the appropriate punctuation following the salutation is a colon, not a comma. Do not use an individual's full name in the salutation (not *Dear Mr. Scott Waters*) unless you are unsure of gender. If you do not know whether to use *Mr.* or *Ms.*, then you may include both the given and surnames without a courtesy title: *Dear Leslie Jones*.

Subject Line.   A brief indication of the subject of the document may be typed two lines below the salutation (see Figure A1.1). The subject line is often entirely in capitals with a colon following the word *SUBJECT*.

Body.   Most business letters are typed single-spaced, with double spacing between paragraphs.

Complimentary Close.   Typed two lines below the last line of the letter, the complimentary close may be formal (*Very truly yours*) or informal (*Sincerely yours* or *Cordially*).

Author, Title, Department.   Three to four blank lines should be left after the complimentary close so that the author has space to sign. The author's name should be typed, in addition to the signature, so that it's legible. The title, department, or division identification may be included if desired.

Reference Initials.   If used, the initials of the typist and author are typed two lines below the author's name and title.

Enclosure Notation.   When an enclosure or attachment accompanies the letter, a notation to that effect is typed two lines below the reference initials. This notation reminds the typist to insert the enclosure in the envelope, and it reminds the recipient to look for the enclosure or attachment. The notation may be spelled out (*Enclosure, Attachment*), or it may be abbreviated (*Enc., Att.*). It may indicate the number of enclosures or attachments, and it may also identify an enclosure specifically (*Enclosure: Brochure No. 213*).

Copy Notation.   If you make copies of correspondence for other individuals, you may use *cc* to indicate carbon copy, *pc* to indicate photocopy, or merely *c* for any kind of copy (see Figure A1.2, Letter 3). A colon following the initial(s) is optional.

Letter Styles

You should be familiar with at least four letter styles.

Block Style.   The letter shown in Figure A1.2, Letter 1, is arranged in block style. This means that all lines begin at the left margin. Since this style is easy to format, it's quite popular.

Modified Block Style.   The letters shown in Figure A1.1 and A1.2, Letter 2, illustrate modified block style. The date may be centered, begun at the center of the page, or backspaced from the right margin. The closing lines—including the complimentary close, author's name, and author's title—begin at the center. The first line of each paragraph may begin at the left margin or may be indented five or ten spaces. All other lines begin at the left margin.

Simplified Style.   The American Management Society recommends the simplified letter style shown in A1.2, Letter 3. All lines begin at the left margin. A subject line appears in all caps four blank lines below the inside address. The salutation and complimentary close are omitted. The signer's name and identification appear in all caps four blank lines below the last paragraph. Although seldom seen in business, this letter style is efficient and avoids the problem of appropriate salutations and courtesy titles.

Personal Business Style.   Individuals preparing their own personal letters on plain paper should follow the style shown in Figure A1.2, Letter 4. The writer's street and city address appear on lines 11 and 12. The date immediately follows on line 13. The writer may choose block or modified block formatting.

Memorandum Parts

Printed Forms.   For intraoffice correspondence, many offices use memorandum forms imprinted with the organization name. This stationery is different from letterhead paper intended for external correspondence. Memorandum stationery generally displays only the company name, division, or department; it does not include the company address or descriptive advertising.

Headings.   Memorandum forms typically have the following printed guide words: *To, From, Date*, and *Subject*. The position of the guide word for *Date* may vary. In filling in data following the guide words, align the bottom of the print with the bottom of the guide words. Leave two spaces after the guide words before beginning the text.

Body.   The message of a memo begins three lines beneath the last guide word. Leave $1\frac{1}{4}$-inch side margins, and single-space the body of a memo.

Signature.   Unlike business letters, memos are not signed. Instead, authors may sign their initials after their typed names following *From* in the heading.

Memorandum Styles

Memorandums are generally typed on printed memo stationery. However, if no printed forms are available, memos may be typed on plain paper or on paper printed with the company letterhead. On a full sheet of paper, start on line 7. Double-space and type in all capitals the guide words: TO:, FROM:, DATE:, SUBJECT:. Align all the fill-in information two spaces after the longest guide word (SUBJECT:). Leave three lines after the last line of the heading and begin typing the body of the memo. Like business letters, memos are single-spaced.

Memos are generally formatted with side margins of $1\frac{1}{4}$ inches, or they may conform to the printed memo form, as shown in Figure A1.3.

Formatting and Spacing

Business letters should be typed so that they are framed by white space. By setting proper margins and by controlling the number of carrier returns between the date and the inside address, you can arrange your letters so that they are attractively balanced on the page. Here are typical settings for 10- or 12-pitch machines. Reduce the number of lines following the date if your letter has special parts such as a subject line, attention line, or company name in the closing.

	Letters with 150 Words or Fewer in the Body	Letters with 150 to 250 Words in the Body	Letters with 250 to 350 Words in the Body
Side margins:	2 inches	$1\frac{1}{2}$ inches	$1\frac{1}{4}$ inches
Lines after the date:	7 to 11 (12 pitch)	5 to 9 (12 pitch)	3 to 5 (12 pitch)
	6 to 8 (10 pitch)	4 to 6 (10 pitch)	3 to 4 (10 pitch)

In preparing documents on a typewriter or computer, follow accepted spacing conventions. Space twice after a period, question mark, or exclamation point

≈

FIGURE A1.3   Memorandum

↓ line 7

TO: Almeda Wilmarth, Supervisor   DATE: January 24, 19xx
           Legal Division

FROM: Judy Leusink, Director *J·L·*
           Personnel Services

SUBJECT: HEALTH CARE BENEFITS SEMINAR

↓ 3 lines

Please plan to attend a seminar February 5 at 4 p.m. in the Main
Conference Room to learn about options in our new health care plan.

At that meeting a representative from Massachusetts Mutual will describe
the "Managed Care" program. This plan is designed to provide the most
cost-effective form of treatment for major illnesses or injury. If you or one
of your dependents suffers an illness or injury that requires long-term
care, you will probably be counseled by a nurse or physician from Mass
Mutual to discuss the options available. At this meeting you will learn
more about the following:

1. How "Managed Care" works for Data General employees

2. Options for major illness coverage

3. Your responsibilities

4. Our contract benefits

If you are unable to attend, please call Sherri Jones at Ext. 255.

---

at the end of a sentence. Generally space once after periods following abbreviations (such as *Mr. J. A. Jones*). Space twice after a colon, except in the expression of time (3:15 p.m.). Space once after semicolons.

Correction Symbols

Here is a set of symbols that your instructor may use in grading your written documents. Study the symbols and the examples illustrating them. Then complete the two exercises following the list. Exercise No. 1 emphasizes the first half of the list; Exercise No. 2, the second half. When you finish, compare your responses with those provided.

Agr   **Agreement error**
A wide range of opportunities *are* available.
Every one of the new employees must pick up *their* orientation packet.

Awk   **Awkward**
In the future no office will be complete without computer systems, nor home.

Cap   **Capitalization**
In our company the *Office Manager* must be able to speak *spanish* as well as *english*.

Chop   **Choppy**
There are many types of dictation systems. One system is endless loop. Nonremovable tape flows in a circle. Then there is the centralized system.

Cl   **Clarity**
The decline in interest rates has lessened the demand for funds, and it may improve even more in the next several months.

Coh   **Coherence**
My background is in systems analysis, but I would be happy to move to Portland.

CS   **Comma splice**
In early days humans drew on walls, they later put information on stone tablets.

Emp   **Emphasis**
The winter conference is scheduled for Palm Springs, and the weather is usually balmy then.

Exp   **Expletive**
There was an announcement by Occidental that it had sold its geothermal energy operations.

Frag   **Fragment**
Which explains why the airline was unable to provide service between London and New York.

Jarg   **Jargon**
If producer prices stay *soft*, the *Fed* may take action that prevents further easing.

Log   **Logic**
Computer prices are falling steadily; therefore, the quality of the product must be declining also.

MM   **Misplaced or dangling modifier**
Sealed in an airtight crock, the Davises savored the aroma of the imported cheese.

Neg   **Negative tone**
Your order *cannot* be shipped because you *neglected* to include your shirt size.

Org   **Organization**
In delivering our product, we must first trace out a route. Then we must consider follow-up, dispatching, corrective action, and scheduling.

Par   **Parallel construction**
Business letters should be written concisely, clearly, and *with accuracy.*

Pas   **Passive voice**
Three separate sets of tax information must be kept.

Pn   **Punctuation**
Consumer profiles are hard to pin down; except in rather general terms.

RB   **Reader benefit**
I am referring your letter requesting insurance information to our local agent. (Improved: So that he may answer your questions personally, I am sending your request to our local agent.)

Rdn   **Redundant**
In its *final conclusions*, the committee outlined the *basic essentials* for a plan of action.

Ref   **Reference unclear**
The consultant suggested improving our telephone system, our lines of communication, and our communication delivery system, *which* immediately won management approval.

Rep   **Repetitious**
The *accident* victim may recover damages as a result of injuries suffered in the *accident.*

Run-on   **Run-together sentence**
We must seek ways to reduce expenses then we can attempt to develop an overall operating budget.

Sp   **Spelling**
The Accounting and Payroll departments turned in *there* reports late.

Spec	**Lacks specificity**	
	A lot of people think it's a good idea.	
Syx	**Syntax**	
	Printer ribbon on the table is sitting.	
Tone	**Tone**	
	We know that you will want our salesman to drop by and enliven your showroom with his fantastic demonstration.	
TR	**Transition**	
	First on the agenda is Mr. Richards, who will discuss the four-day work plan. Mrs. Carroll is concerned about the photocopier.	
Var	**Sentence variety**	
	Mr. Lopez was interested in operating a franchise. He made inquiries. He learned about investment requirements. He attended training sessions.	
W	**Wordy**	
	At this point in time your account shows a balance in the neighborhood of $120.	
WW	**Wrong or inappropriate word**	
	Word processing *shortens* the number of times a document must be retyped.	
X	**Obvious error**	
	Greater competition in the financial field far-reaching changes in savings and banking institutions.	
?	**Do you really mean this?**	
	Policeman are not there to create disorder; they are there to preserve disorder.	

≈

Correction Symbol Exercise No. 1

The following sentences all have composition faults. Using the first half of the correction symbol list, mark each fault with the appropriate symbol in the spaces provided. Sentence faults may be described by more than one symbol. Check your responses when you finish. If you have questions, consult your instructor.

Example: To be successful in business, good financial judgment must be exercised. *MM*

1. There are purchase requisitions that must be turned in by the purchasing agent or buyer before June 10. _____

2. The list of approved suppliers appear to be nearly finished. _____

3. The purchase order describes the goods requested, and he can often obtain quantity discounts by ordering large amounts. _____

4. Miss Johnson is responsible for coding, computing, recording, and the storage of purchase data. _____

5. Employees turn in purchase requisitions. The purchasing agent conducts a systematic appraisal. The idea is to find the lowest cost. A formal purchase order is completed.

_____

6. General Electric spent $1 billion automating its manufacturing plants, it expects to install 1,000 computer-controlled robots.

_____

7. Manufacturing plants that produce such varied products as dishwashers, jet engines, locomotives, and toaster ovens.

_____

8. We're sorry to hear of your complaint about our Model SX–10 copier. Apparently you did not read the instruction manual.

_____

9. Being an experienced attorney, the contract was expertly prepared.

_____

10. The consumer price index is rising each year, which is causing inflation.

_____

11. Employees may not want to get mentally involved, thus giving their mind maximum opportunity to wander.

_____

12. Most foremen's jobs are time-consuming, and they are always under pressure.

_____

13. The security ramifications of computer networks and indirect access potential provided by modems and telephone lines overshadow all other considerations.

_____

14. We hope that there will be improved writing as a result of these exercises.

_____

15. Growth and change in today's office has created an explosion of paperwork.

---

1. Exp   2. Agr (*appears*)   3. Coh   4. Par   5. Chop or Var   6. CS   7. Frag   8. Neg
9. MM   10. Log   11. Agr (their *minds*)   12. CI or Coh or Ref   13. Jarg   14. Exp (*there*)
15. Agr (*have* created)

≋

Correction Symbol Exercise No. 2

The following sentences all have composition faults. Using the second half of the correction symbol list, mark each fault with the appropriate symbol in the spaces provided. Sentence faults may be described by more than one symbol. Check your responses when you finish. If you have questions, consult your instructor.

W_____   **Example:**   We deem it advisable to inform you that your account is now four months past due.

_____

1. President Goldfield commended the office staff and it's efficiency in completing the massive task.

_____

2. We think that something is needed to improve our jobs.

_____

3. The report was submitted on March 15 by Mr. Thompson.

_____

4. The solution that she proposed made perfectly good sense.

5. Jim and Kevin both volunteered to work this weekend. Later he changed his mind.

6. I have many years of experience as a life underwriter, and I can plan a comprehensive insurance plan for you.

7. The sales manager announced several changes in sales territory assignments in his monthly sales announcement.

8. One of the things we offer our customers is group life insurance.

9. Microfilm is a wonderful product we use it to store active records.

10. The union gives up nine paid days. The company agrees to profit sharing. The union gives up a pay increase. The company establishes a prepaid legal-services plan.

11. Health care costs are raising because employees have begun to place greater emphasis on contract benefit programs.

12. In relation to the above-referenced claim, my client is willing to settle for the sum of $1,000.

13. Businesses produce more paper than ever before, and the price of staring it climbs every day.

14. Our fabulous new workstation will allow you to breeze through your day's work in record time and enjoy many extra happy hours at your favorite bar.

15. More agreements are reached by arbitration then by strike action.

---

1. Sp (*its*)   2. Spec   3. Pas   4. Rdn (*perfectly good*)   5. Ref or Cl   6. RB   7. Rep
8. WW (*things*)   9. Run-on   10. Var   11. WW (*rising*)   12. W   13. ? (*storing*)
14. Tone   15. Sp (*than*)

Documenting Data

Long reports typically include information from other sources. You can quote this information directly, using the exact words of the original author, or you can paraphrase, putting the author's ideas into your own words. In both cases credit must be given to the original author. To do this, use the conventions of documentation—that is, follow accepted procedures for showing where information originated. Although many methods of documenting reports are currently in practice, we will discuss only three: (1) the footnote method, (2) the endnote method, and (3) the parenthetic, or MLA, method. The footnote method was commonly used for research papers because readers could easily see references. However, it was difficult for typists to judge the position of these references at the bottoms of pages. For that reason, some writers began using endnotes. The parenthetic method simplifies the documentation process even further. But we may see a return to footnote and endnote use, now that many word processing indexing programs make the process so easy.

In this discussion we will be concerned only with suggestions for the writers of long business reports. We will not try to present a comprehensive treatment of documentation, including all the exceptions and procedures appropriate for authors of books, doctoral dissertations, and masters' theses. For more detailed treatments of documentation techniques, see *The Chicago Manual of Style*, Thirteenth Edition, University of Chicago Press; *The MLA Handbook for Writers of Research Papers*, Third Edition, Modern Language Association of America; *A Manual for Writers of Term Papers, Theses, and Dissertations* by Kate L. Turabian; or *HOW 6: Handbook for Office Workers*, Sixth Edition, by Clark and Clark.

Footnote Method

The traditional method for citing sources is footnoting. As the name suggests, references appear at the foot or bottom of each page. Refer to Figure A3.1 for illustration of some of the following suggestions regarding footnotes in a long report.

1. Place a superscript (raised number) at the *end* of the sentence that contains information to be acknowledged, regardless of where the quoted or paraphrased data appears in the sentence.

2. Number footnotes consecutively throughout the report.

3. Indent and single-space quoted material of four or more typewritten lines as shown in Footnote 2 of Figure A3.1.

4. At the bottom of the page, use a 1 1/2-inch line to separate the footnotes from the text.

5. Single-space footnote entries and double-space between them.

6. For book entries include author (first name first), name of book in all caps or underscored, edition, publishing information in parenthesis (city, state abbreviation if city is not commonly recognizable, name of publisher, date), and page or pages cited.

7. For periodical entries include author (if given), article title in quotation marks, periodical title underscored, date, volume, and page or pages cited.

8. For newspaper entries include author or description of article (such as "editorial"), main heading of article in quotation marks, newspaper title underscored, date, page or pages cited, and columns (optional).

Here are some of the most frequently used footnote forms.

Book, One Author

[1]Richard Bolles, *What Color Is Your Parachute?* (Berkeley, CA: Ten Speed Press, 1982), p. 18.

Book, Many Authors

[2]J. A. Mayleas, Thomas Jackson, and Margaret Palmer, *The Hidden Job Market for the Nineties* (New York: Times Books, 1990), pp. 138–145.

Magazine Article

[3]Hilary Ann Irish, "Sweaty Palms: The Neglected Art of Being Interviewed," *U.S. News & World Report*, 30 July 1989, Vol. 14, No. 7, pp. 48–51.

Newspaper Article

[4]Jay Singleton, "Job-Hunting Success for the New Professional," *Los Angeles Times*, 15 January 1991, Sec. V, p. 1, cols. 3–5.

Government Publication

[5]*Occupational Outlook Handbook*, U.S. Department of Labor (Washington, D.C.: U.S. Government Printing Office, 1989), p. 203.

Encyclopedia Article Without Author

[6]"Escrow," *Encyclopedia Brittanica*, Vol. V, 1988, p. 694.

Interview

[7]Personal interview with Kimberly Lopez, supervisor, Information Services Division, Rocketwell, Inc., 4 October 1991.

In referring to a previously mentioned footnote, cite the page number along with the author's last name or a shortened form of the title if no author is given (see Footnote 3 in Figure A3.1). The Latin forms *ibid., op. cit., loc. cit.,* and *et al.* are rarely seen in business reports today.

~~~~

FIGURE A3.1   Portion of Report Page Showing Footnoting

.
.
.

Despite accusations, no link "between radiation emissions from VDTs and reported spontaneous abortions, birth defects, cataracts, and other injuries" was reported by an American Medical Association panel that conducted a comprehensive review of research evidence.[1]

To reduce real and perceived negative effects of VDTs, companies should design and set up ergonomically sound workstations. Observe the following guidelines:

> Make sure tables provide adequate leg room and are adjustable. Select VDT systems with detachable keyboard, rotatable/tiltable monitor, and contrast and brightness controls. Consider the noise factor when selecting a VDT system. For instance, laser and electronic printers are quieter than daisy wheel printers.[2]

Numerous cases have been cited to indicate that glare is a major irritation in operating VDTs. It causes eye fatigue and discomfort. Indirect lighting is recommended to prevent glare, along with antiglare hoods.[3]

---

[1]Jeffrey L. Bowers, "Effects of Video Display Terminals," Journal of American Medical Association, 20 March 1990, p. 1151.

[2]Sylvia W. Snyder, Michael McDonald, and Jennifer Lee-Sims, Ergonomics for Today's Offices (Boston: PWS-KENT Publishing Company, 1989), pp. 256–261.

[3]Snyder and others, p. 289.

≈

Endnote Method

A second method for documenting reports is the endnote method. Like the footnote method, superscript numerals within the text identify data to be cited. However, instead of appearing at the bottom of each page, source notes are located at the end of the report on a separate page. The title starts on line 13. Figure A3.2 illustrates endnotes. Notice that no superscripts are used.

The endnote method is easier for the author than the footnote method because notes do not have to be placed on the same page where they are cited. Word processing further simplifies the task. As the author keys each reference, the computer software automatically numbers references and renumbers if changes are made. When the text is completed, the system prints a numbered list of all references.

≈

Parenthetic, or MLA, Method

The third method of documentation, recommended by the Modern Language Association, uses parenthetical data to identify references. Within the text a

≈

FIGURE A3.2   Portion of Report Page Showing Endnotes

NOTES

1. Jeffrey L. Bowers, "Effects of Video Display Terminals," Journal of American Medical Association, 20 March 1990, p. 1151–1167.

2. Sylvia W. Snyder, Michael McDonald, and Jennifer Lee-Sims, Ergonomics for Today's Offices (Boston: PWS-KENT Publishing Company, 1989), pp. 256–261.

3. Snyder and others, p. 289.

4. Personal interview with Dr. Meredith Wagner, director, Department of Occupational Research, Carnegie Institute, 24 November 1990.

5. Bowers, p. 1154.

6. Theodore A. Chester, "An Ounce of Prevention," Infosystems, June 1987, p. 54.

.
.
.

brief reference to identify a source is inserted. This parenthetical comment usually consists of the author's last name and the page on which the reference is found. If no author is available, an abbreviated title is used to identify the reference. The following excerpt illustrates the parenthetic documentation method.

> Several private studies on the subject of occupational health are now
>
> being conducted (Peters 127). In addition, the U.S. Office of
>
> Management and Budget plans to develop its own study at a cost of
>
> $500,000 ("Uneasy Silence" 54).

When the author is mentioned in the textual material, it is unnecessary to include the name again in the parenthetical reference. Just insert the page reference, as shown here.

> Peters also notes that stress could be a contributing factor in the
>
> health problems reported thus far (135).

At the end of the report, all references are included on a page entitled "Works Cited," as illustrated in Figure A3.3.

≋

FIGURE A3.3   Works Cited, MLA Method

WORKS CITED

Barton, Bertram, "Use of Ergonomics No Guarantee That Workers Will Benefit," Occupational Safety Health Reporter June 1988: 125–130.

"Computing." Encyclopedia Americana. 1985 ed.

Gomez, Carlos. "Link Between Computer VDTs and Birth Defects Suspected," Cleveland Plain Dealer 20 May 1986: 3.

Peters, Winifred Ellen. Health and Employment. Garden City, NY: Anchor Books, 1989.

Shicoff, Evita. Personal interview. 12 February 1991.

"An Uneasy Silence." Editorial. Infosystems. March 1988: 54.

~~

The Bibliography

A bibliography is an alphabetic list of materials on a topic. If used, it appears after appendix items. Although it looks similar to footnotes or endnotes, the bibliography is different in these ways:

1. The bibliography is optional. It is often included in a long report as an added resource to the reader. It may be omitted if the total number of footnotes is fewer than ten.

2. Its entries are arranged alphabetically by author for easy reference.

3. It may include all the works consulted as well as those actually cited.

4. For readability, entries are displayed in hanging indented form—that is, the second and succeeding lines are indented five spaces from the left margin.

5. The arrangement and punctuation of each entry is somewhat different from footnote form.

Study the following entries to note their differences from footnote form. See page 297 for an example of a complete bibliography as part of a long report.

Book, One Author

Bolles, Richard. *What Color is Your Parachute?* Berkeley, CA: Ten Speed Press, 1982.

Book, Same Author

————. *Go Hire Yourself an Employer.* Berkeley, CA: Ten Speed Press, 1990.

Book, Many Authors

Mayleas, J. A., Thomas Jackson, and Margaret Palmer. *The Hidden Job Market for the Nineties.* New York: Times Books, 1990.

Magazine Article

Irish, Hilary Ann. "Sweaty Palms: The Neglected Art of Being Interviewed," *U.S. News & World Report,* 30 July 1989, 48–51.

Newspaper Article

Singleton, Jay. "Job-Hunting Success for the New Professional," *Los Angeles Times,* 15 January 1991, Sec. V, p. 1, Cols. 3–5.

Government Publication

Occupational Outlook Handbook. U.S. Department of Labor. Washington, D.C.: U.S. Government Printing Office, 1989.

Encyclopedia Article Without Author

"Escrow." *Encyclopedia Brittanica.* Vol. V. 1988. 694.

Interview

Kimberly Lopez. Personal interview. 4 October 1990.

Grammar/Mechanics Handbook

The Grammar/Mechanics Handbook consists of

1. Grammar/Mechanics Diagnostic Test
   - To assess students' strengths and weaknesses in eight areas of grammar and mechanics.
2. Grammar/Mechanics Profile
   - To pinpoint specific areas in which students need remedial instruction or review.
3. Grammar Review with Review Exercises
   - To review basic principles of grammar, punctuation, capitalization, and number style.
   - To provide reinforcement exercises allowing students to interact with the principles of grammar and test their comprehension.
   - To serve as a systematic reference to grammar and mechanics throughout the writing course.
   - To be used for classroom-centered instruction or self-guided learning.

Grammar/Mechanics Diagnostic Test

Name _____

This diagnostic test is intended to reveal your strengths and weaknesses in using the following:

plural nouns	prepositions
possessive nouns	conjunctions
pronouns	punctuation
verbs	capitalization style
adjectives	number style
adverbs	

The test is organized into sections corresponding to these categories. In sections A through H, each sentence is either correct or has one error related to the category under which it is listed. If a sentence is correct, write *C*. If it has an error, underline the error and write the correct form in the space provided. Use ink to record your answers. When you finish, check your answers with your instructor and fill out the Grammar/Mechanics Profile on page 384.

A. Plural Nouns

branches

Example: The newspaper named editors in chief for both <u>branchs</u>.

C

1. Three of the <u>attornies</u> representing the defendants were from cities in other states.

freshmen

2. Four <u>freshmans</u> discussed the pros and cons of attending colleges or universities.

companies

3. Since the 1970s, most <u>companys</u> have begun to send bills of lading with shipments.

Morises

4. Neither the Johnsons nor the Morris's knew about the changes in beneficiaries.

Saturdays

5. The manager asked all secretaries to work on the next four <u>Saturday's</u>.

B. Possessive Nouns

jury's'

6. We sincerely hope that the <u>jurys</u> judgment reflects the stories of all the witnesses.

C

7. In a little over two months' time, the secretaries had finished three reports for the president.

FRANKLIN'S

8. Mr. <u>Franklins</u> staff is responsible for all accounts receivable contracted by customers purchasing electronics parts.

STOCKHOLDERS'

9. At the next <u>stockholders</u> meeting, we will discuss benefits for employees and dividends for shareholders.

Smith's

10. Three months ago several employees in the sales department complained of Mrs. <u>Smiths</u> smoking.

C. Pronouns

me

Example: Whom did you ask to replace Tom and <u>I</u>?

I

11. My manager and <u>myself</u> were willing to send the copies to whoever needed them.

MR. Benson *me*

12. Some of the work for Mr. Benson and I had to be reassigned to Mark and <u>him</u>.

myself *its*

13. Although it's motor was damaged, the car started for the mechanic and <u>me</u>.

C

14. Just between you and me, only you and I know that she will be transferred.

15. My friend and I applied for employment at Reynolds, Inc., because of their excellent employee benefits. *C its*

D. Verb Agreement

Example: The list of arrangements <u>have</u> to be approved by Tim and her. *has*

16. The keyboard, printer, and monitor <u>costs</u> less than I expected. *cost*
17. A description of the property, together with several other legal documents, <u>were</u> submitted by my attorney. *C was*
18. There <u>was</u> only two enclosures and the letter in the envelope. *were*
19. Neither the manager nor the employees in the office think the solution is fair. *C*
20. Because of the holiday, our committee <u>prefer</u> to delay its action. *prefers*

E. Verb Mood, Voice, and Tense

21. If I was able to fill your order immediately, I certainly would. *C were*
22. To operate the machine, first open the disk drive door and then <u>you</u> insert the diskette. *delete "you"*
23. If I could chose any city, I would select Honolulu. *C choose*
24. Those papers have <u>laid</u> on his desk for more than two weeks. *lain*
25. The auditors have <u>went</u> over these accounts carefully, and they have found no discrepancies. *gone*

F. Adjectives and Adverbs

26. Until we have a more clearer picture of the entire episode, we <u>shall</u> proceed cautiously. *clear, will / more*
27. For about a week their newly repaired copier worked just <u>beautiful</u>. *beautifully*
28. The recently elected official benefited from his coast-to-coast campaign.
29. Mr. Snyder <u>only has</u> two days before he must complete the end-of-the-year report. *has only*
30. The architects submitted <u>there</u> drawings in a last-minute attempt to beat the deadline. *C their*

G. Prepositions and Conjunctions

31. Can you tell me where the meeting is scheduled <u>at</u>? *delete*
32. It seems <u>like</u> we have been taking this test forever. *that or if*
33. Our investigation shows that the distribution department is more efficient <u>then</u> the sales department. *C than*
34. My courses this semester are totally different <u>than</u> last semester's. *C from*
35. Both of the managers were aware of and<u> </u>interested in the proposal. *were out of the*

were

H. Commas

For each of the following sentences, insert any necessary commas. Count the number of commas that you added. Write that number in the space provided. All punctuation must be correct to receive credit for the sentence. If a sentence requires no punctuation, write *0*.

2

Example: However, because of developments in theory and computer applications, management is becoming more of a science.

2 3   36. For example, management determines how orders, assignments and responsibilities are delegated to employees.

3 4   37. Your order, Mrs. Swift, will be sent from Memphis, Tennessee, on July 1.

1 2   38. When you need service on any of your pieces of equipment we will be happy to help you, Mr. Lopez.

2 2   39. Keven Long, who is the project manager at Techdata, suggested that I call you.

0 1   40. You have purchased from us often and your payments in the past have always been prompt.

I. Commas and Semicolons

Add commas and semicolons to the following sentences. In the space provided, write the number of punctuation marks that you added.

2   41. The salesperson turned in his report; however, he did not indicate what time period it covered.

1   42. Interest payments on bonds are tax deductible, dividend payments are not.

0   43. We are opening a branch office in Kettering and hope to be able to serve all your needs from that office by the middle of January.

1 2   44. As suggested by the committee, we must first secure adequate funding then we may consider expansion.

1 3   45. When you begin to conduct research for a report consider the many library sources available; namely books, periodicals, government publications, and newspapers.

J. Commas and Semicolons

2   46. After our office manager had the printer repaired it jammed again within the first week, although we treated it carefully.

1   47. Our experienced, courteous staff has been trained to anticipate your every need.

48. In view of the new law that went into effect April 1 our current liability insurance must be increased; however, we cannot immediately afford it. — 2 3

49. As stipulated in our contract your agency will supervise our graphic arts and purchase our media time. — 0 1

50. As you know, Mrs. Simpson, we aim for long-term business relationships; not quick profits. — 3 3

K. Other Punctuation

Each of the following sentences may require dashes, colons, question marks, quotation marks, periods, and underscores, as well as commas and semicolons. Add the appropriate punctuation to each sentence. Then, in the space provided, write the total number of marks that you added.

Example: Price, service, and reliability—these are our prime considerations. — 3

51. The following members of the department volunteered to help on Saturday: Kim, Carlos, Dan, and Sylvia. — 1

52. Mr. Danner, Miss Reed, and Mrs. Garcia usually arrived at the office by 8:30 a m. — 3 4

53. Three of our top managers; Tim, Marcy, and Thomas received cash bonuses. — 1 2

54. Did the vice president really say "All employees may take Friday off"? — 2

55. We are trying to locate an edition of Newsweek that carried an article entitled "Microcomputers Beat the Office Crunch". — 3

L. Capitalization

For each of the following sentences, circle any letter that should be capitalized. In the space provided, write the number of circles that you marked.

Example: Vice president Daniels devised a procedure for expediting purchase orders from area 4 warehouses. — 4

56. although english was his native language, he also spoke spanish and could read french. — 4

57. on a trip to the east coast, uncle henry visited the empire state building. —

58. karen enrolled in classes in history, german, and sociology. — 1 2

59. the business manager and the vice president each received a new apple computer. — 2

60. james lee, the president of kendrick, inc., will speak to our conference in the spring. — 4

M. Number Style

Decide whether the numbers in the following sentences should be written as words or as figures. Each sentence either is correct or has one error. If it is correct, write *C*. If it has an error, underline it and write the correct form in the space provided.

five _____   **Example:**   The bank had <u>5</u> branches in three suburbs.

C _____   61. More than <u>2,000,000</u> people have visited the White House in the past five years.

THIRTY-FIVE _____   62. Of the <u>35</u> letters sent out, only three were returned.

_____   63. We set aside forty dollars for petty cash, but by December 1 our fund was depleted.

THREE _____   64. The meeting is scheduled for <u>May 5th</u> at <u>3</u> p.m.

_____   65. In the past <u>20</u> years, nearly 15 percent of the population changed residences at least once.

≈

Grammar/Mechanics Profile

In the spaces at the right, place a check mark to indicate the number of correct answers you had in each category of the Grammar/Mechanics Diagnostic Test.

		Number Correct*				
		5	4	3	2	1
1–5	Plural Nouns	_____	_____	_____	_____	_____
6–10	Possessive Nouns	_____	_____	_____	_____	_____
11–15	Pronouns	_____	_____	_____	_____	_____
16–20	Verb Agreement	_____	_____	_____	_____	_____
21–25	Verb Mood, Voice, and Tense	_____	_____	_____	_____	_____
26–30	Adjectives and Adverbs	_____	_____	_____	_____	_____
31–35	Prepositions and Conjunctions	_____	_____	_____	_____	_____
36–40	Commas	_____	_____	_____	_____	_____
41–45	Commas and Semicolons	_____	_____	_____	_____	_____
46–50	Commas and Semicolons	_____	_____	_____	_____	_____
51–55	Other Punctuation	_____	_____	_____	_____	_____
56–60	Capitalization	_____	_____	_____	_____	_____
61–65	Number Style	_____	_____	_____	_____	_____

*Note: 5 = have excellent skills; 4 = need light review; 3 = need careful review; 2 = need to study rules; 1 = need serious study and follow-up reinforcement.

~~

Grammar Review

Parts of Speech (1.01)

1.01 Functions. English has eight parts of speech. Knowing the functions of the parts of speech helps writers better understand how words are used and how sentences are formed.

a. **Nouns** name persons, places, things, qualities, concepts, and activities (for example, *Kevin, Phoenix, computer, joy, work, banking*).

b. **Pronouns** substitute for nouns (for example, *he, she, it, they*).

c. **Verbs** show the action of a subject or join to the subject words that describe it (for example, *walk, heard, is, was jumping*).

d. **Adjectives** describe or limit nouns and pronouns and often answer the questions *what kind? how many?* and *which one?* (for example, *fast* sale, *ten* items, *good* manager).

e. **Adverbs** describe or limit verbs, adjectives, or other adverbs and frequently answer the questions *when? how? where?* or *to what extent?* (for example, *tomorrow, rapidly, here, very*).

f. **Prepositions** join nouns or pronouns to other words in sentences (for example, desk *in* the office, ticket *for* me, letter *to* you).

g. **Conjunctions** connect words or groups of words (for example, you *and* I, Mark *or* Jill).

h. **Interjections** express strong feelings (for example, *Wow!, Oh!*).

Nouns (1.02–1.06)

Nouns name persons, places, things, qualities, concepts, and activities. Nouns may be classified into a number of categories.

1.02 Concrete and Abstract. Concrete nouns name specific objects that can be seen, heard, felt, tasted, or smelled. Examples of concrete nouns are *telephone, dollar, IBM, apple*. Abstract nouns name generalized ideas such as qualities or concepts that are not easily pictured. *Emotion, power,* and *tension* are typical examples of abstract nouns.

Business writing is most effective when concrete words predominate. It's clearer to write "We need 16-pound bond paper" than to write "We need office supplies." Chapter 4 provides practice in developing skill in the use of concrete words.

1.03 Proper and Common. Proper nouns name specific persons, places, or things and are always capitalized (*General Electric, Baltimore, Jennifer*). All other nouns are common nouns and begin with lowercase letters (*company, city, student*). Rules for capitalization are presented in Section 3.01 through Section 3.16.

1.04 Singular and Plural. Singular nouns name one item; plural nouns name more than one. From a practical view, writers seldom have difficulty with singular nouns. They may need help, however, with the formation and spelling of plural nouns.

1.05 Guidelines for Forming Noun Plurals

a. Add *s* to most nouns (*chair, chairs*; *mortgage, mortgages*; *Monday, Mondays*).

b. Add *es* to nouns ending in *s, x, z, ch,* or *sh* (*bench, benches*; *boss, bosses*; *box, boxes*; *Lopez, Lopezes*).

c. Change the spelling in irregular noun plurals (*man, men*; *foot, feet*; *mouse, mice*; *child, children*).

d. Add *s* to nouns that end in *y* when *y* is preceded by a vowel (*attorney, attorneys*; *valley, valleys*; *journey, journeys*).

e. Drop the *y* and add *ies* to nouns ending in *y* when *y* is preceded by a consonant (*company, companies*; *city, cities*; *secretary, secretaries*).

f. Add *s* to the principal word in most compound expressions (*editors in chief, fathers-in-law, bills of lading, runners-up*).

g. Add *s* to most numerals, letters of the alphabet, words referred to as words, degrees, and abbreviations (*5s, 1990s, Bs, ands, CPAs, qts.*).

h. Add *'s* only to clarify letters of the alphabet that might be misread, both uppercase (*A's, I's, M's, U's*) and lowercase (*i's, p's,* and *q's*). An expression like *c.o.d.s* requires no apostrophe because it would not easily be misread.

1.06 Collective Nouns. Nouns such as *staff, faculty, committee, group,* and *herd* refer to a collection of people, animals, or objects. Collective nouns may be considered singular or plural depending upon their action. See Section 1.10i for a discussion of collective nouns and their agreement with verbs.

Review Exercise A—Nouns

In the space provided for each item, write *a* or *b* to complete the following statements accurately. When you finish, compare your responses with those shown below. For each item on which you need review, consult the numbered principle shown in parentheses.

_____ (1.05f)
1. Nearly all (a) *editor in chiefs,* (b) *editors in chief* demand observance of standard punctuation.

_____ (1.05d)
2. Several (a) *attorneys,* (b) *attornies* worked on the case together.

_____ (1.05b)
3. Please write to the (a) *Davis's,* (b) *Davises* about the missing contract.

_____ (1.05e)
4. The industrial complex has space for nine additional (a) *companys,* (b) *companies.*

_____ (1.05e)
5. That accounting firm employs two (a) *secretaries,* (b) *secretarys* for five CPAs.

_____ (1.05b)
6. Four of the wooden (a) *benches,* (b) *benchs* must be repaired.

_____ (1.05d)
7. The home was constructed with numerous (a) *chimneys,* (b) *chimnies.*

8. Tours of the production facility are made only on (a) *Tuesdays*, (b) *Tuesday's*. _____ (1.05a)

9. We asked the (a) *Lopez's*, (b) *Lopezes* to contribute to the fund-raising drive. _____ (1.05b)

10. Both my (a) *sister-in-laws*, (b) *sisters-in-law* agreed to the settlement. _____ (1.05f)

11. The stock market is experiencing abnormal (a) *ups and downs*, (b) *up's and down's*. _____ (1.05g)

12. Is it possible that the two (a) *foremans*, (b) *foremen* both misunderstood the time of the meeting? _____ (1.05c)

13. This office is unusually quiet on (a) *Sundays*, (b) *Sunday's*. _____ (1.05a)

14. Several news (a) *dispatchs*, (b) *dispatches* were released during the strike. _____ (1.05b)

15. Two major (a) *countries*, (b) *countrys* will participate in arms negotiations. _____ (1.05e)

16. Some young children have difficulty writing their (a) *bs and ds*, (b) *b's and d's*. _____ (1.05h)

17. The (a) *board of directors*, (b) *boards of directors* of all the major companies participated in the survey. _____ (1.05f)

18. In their letter the (a) *Metzes*, (b) *Metzs* said they intended to purchase the property. _____ (1.05b)

19. In shipping we are careful to include all (a) *bill of sales*, (b) *bills of sale*. _____ (1.05f)

20. Over the holidays many (a) *turkies*, (b) *turkeys* were consumed. _____ (1.05d)

---

1. b, 3. b, 5. a, 7. a, 9. b, 11. a, 13. a, 15. a, 17. b, 19. b

Pronouns (1.07–1.09)

Pronouns substitute for nouns. They are classified by case.

1.07 Case. Pronouns function in three cases, as shown in the following chart.

Nominative Case (Used for subjects of verbs and subject complements)	Objective Case (Used for objects of prepositions and objects of verbs)	Possessive Case (Used to show possession)
I	me	my, mine
we	us	our, ours
you	you	your, yours
he	him	his
she	her	her, hers
it	it	its
they	them	their, theirs
who, whoever	whom, whomever	whose

1.08 Guidelines for Selecting Pronoun Case

a. Pronouns that serve as subjects of verbs must be in the nominative case.

   He and *I* (not *Him* and *me*) decided to apply for the jobs.

b. Pronouns that follow linking verbs (such as *am, is, are, was, were, be, being, been*) and rename the words to which they refer must be in the nominative case.

   It must have been *she* (not *her*) who placed the order. (The nominative-case pronoun *she* follows the linking verb *been* and renames *It*.)

   If it was *he* (not *him*) who called, I have his number. (The nominative-case pronoun *he* follows the linking verb *was* and renames *It*.)

c. Pronouns that serve as objects of verbs or objects of prepositions must be in the objective case.

   Mr. Andrews asked *them* to complete the proposal. (The pronoun *them* is the object of the verb *asked*.)

   All computer printouts are sent to *him*. (The pronoun *him* is the object of the preposition *to*.)

   Just between you and *me*, profits are falling. (The pronoun *me* is one of the objects of the preposition *between*.)

d. Pronouns that show ownership must be in the possessive case. Possessive pronouns (such as *hers, yours, ours, theirs,* and *its*) require no apostrophes.

   We found my diskette, but *yours* (not *your's*) may be lost.

   All parts of the machine, including *its* (not *it's*) motor, were examined.

   The house and *its* (not *it's*) contents will be auctioned.

   Don't confuse possessive pronouns and contractions. Contractions are shortened forms of subject-verb phrases (such as *it's* for *it is*, *there's* for *there is*, and *they're* for *they are*).

e. When a pronoun appears in combination with a noun or another pronoun, ignore the extra noun or pronoun and its conjunction. In this way, pronoun case becomes more obvious.

   The manager promoted Jeff and *me* (not *I*). (Ignore *Jeff and*.)

f. In statements of comparison, mentally finish the comparative by adding the implied missing words.

   Next year I hope to earn as much as *she*. (The verb *earns* is implied here: *. . . as much as she earns*.)

g. Pronouns must be in the same case as the words they replace or rename. When pronouns are used with appositives, ignore the appositive.

A new contract was signed by *us* (not *we*) employees. (Temporarily ignore the appositive *employees* in selecting the pronoun.)

We (not *us*) citizens have formed our own organization. (Temporarily ignore the appositive *citizens* in selecting the pronoun.)

h. Pronouns ending in *self* should be used only when they refer to previously mentioned nouns or pronouns.

Robert and *I* (not *myself*) are in charge of the campaign.

i. Use objective-case pronouns as objects of the prepositions *between, but, like,* and *except*.

Everyone but John and *him* (not *he*) qualified for the bonus.

Employees like Miss Gillis and *her* (not *she*) are hard to replace.

j. Use *who* or *whoever* for nominative-case constructions and *whom* or *whomever* for objective-case constructions. In making the correct choice, it's sometimes helpful to substitute *he* for *who* or *whoever* and *him* for *whom* or *whomever*.

For *whom* was this book ordered? (*This book was ordered for him/whom?*)

Who did you say would drop by? (*Who/he . . . would drop by?*)

Deliver the package to *whoever* opens the door. (In this sentence the clause *whoever opens the door* functions as the object of the preposition *to*. Within the clause itself *whoever* is the subject of the verb *opens*. Again, substitution of *he* might be helpful: *He/Whoever opens the door.*)

1.09 Guidelines for Making Pronouns Agree with Their Antecedents. Pronouns must agree with the words to which they refer (their antecedents) in gender and in number.

a. Use masculine pronouns to refer to masculine antecedents, feminine pronouns to refer to feminine antecedents, and neuter pronouns to refer to antecedents without gender.

The man opened *his* office door. (Masculine gender applies.)

A woman sat at *her* desk. (Feminine gender applies.)

This computer and *its* programs fit our needs. (Neuter gender applies.)

b. Use singular pronouns to refer to singular antecedents.

Any customer who writes us should have *his* (not *their*) letter answered promptly. (The singular pronoun *his* refers to the singular subject *customer*.)

Common-gender (masculine) pronouns traditionally have been used when the gender of the antecedent is unknown. Sensitive writers today, however, prefer to recast such constructions to avoid the need for common-gender pronouns. Study these examples for alternatives to the use of common-gender pronouns.[1]

Customers' letters should be answered promptly.

Customers who write us should have their letters answered promptly.

Any customer who writes us should have *his or her* letter answered promptly. (This alternative is the least acceptable since it is wordy and calls attention to itself.)

c. Use singular pronouns to refer to singular indefinite subjects and plural pronouns for plural indefinite subjects. Words such as *anyone, something,* and *anybody* are considered indefinite because they refer to no specific person or object. Some indefinite pronouns are always singular; others are always plural.

Always Singular		Always Plural
anybody	everything	both
anyone	neither	few
anything	nobody	many
each	no one	several
either	somebody	
everyone	someone	

"any single Body"

Somebody in the group of touring women left *her* (not *their*) purse in the museum.

Either of the companies has the right to exercise *its* (not *their*) option to sell stock.

d. Use singular pronouns to refer to collective nouns and organization names.

The engineering staff is moving *its* (not *their*) facilities on Friday. (The singular pronoun *its* agrees with the collective noun *staff* because the members of *staff* function as a single unit.)

Jones, Cohen, & James, Inc., has (not *have*) cancelled *its* (not *their*) contract with us. (The singular pronoun *its* agrees with *Jones, Cohen, & James, Inc.* because the members of the organization are operating as a single unit.)

e. Use a plural pronoun to refer to two antecedents joined by *and*, whether the antecedents are singular or plural.

Our company president and our vice president will be submitting *their* expenses shortly.

[1]Note: See Chapter 3, p. 47 for additional discussion of common-gender pronouns.

f. Ignore intervening phrases—introduced by expressions like *together with, as well as*, and *in addition to*—that separate a pronoun from its antecedent.

One of our managers, along with several salespeople, is planning *his* retirement. (If you wish to emphasize both subjects equally, join them with *and*: "One of our managers *and* several salespeople are planning *their* retirements.")

g. When antecedents are joined by *or* or *nor*, make the pronoun agree with the antecedent closest to it.

Neither Jackie nor Kim wanted *her* (not *their*) desk moved.

Review Exercise B—Pronouns

In the space provided for each item, write *a, b,* or *c* to complete the statement accurately. When you finish, compare your responses with those shown below. For each item on which you need review, consult the numbered principle shown in parentheses.

1. Mr. Behrens and (a) *I,* (b) *myself* will be visiting sales personnel in the Wilmington district next week. _____ (1.08h)

2. James promised that he would call; was it (a) *him,* (b) *he* who left the message? _____ (1.08b)

3. Much preparation for the seminar was made by Mrs. Washington and (a) *I,* (b) *me* before the brochures were sent out. _____ (1.08c)

4. The Employee Benefits Committee can be justly proud of (a) *its,* (b) *their* achievements. _____ (1.09d)

5. A number of inquiries were addressed to Jeff and (a) *I,* (b) *me,* (c) *myself.* _____ (1.08c, 1.08e)

6. (a) *Who,* (b) *Whom* did you say the letter was addressed to? _____ (1.08j) *He, Him* *who   whom* *(objective) (subjective)*

7. When you visit Sears Savings Bank, inquire about (a) *its,* (b) *their* certificates. _____ (1.09d)

8. Copies of all reports are to be reviewed by Mr. Sanders and (a) *I,* (b) *me,* (c) *myself.*   *(b) = object of the preposition* _____ (1.08c, 1.08e)

9. Apparently one of the female applicants forgot to sign (a) *her,* (b) *their* application. _____ (1.09b)

10. Both the diskette and (a) *it's,* (b) *its* cover are missing.   *usually* _____ (1.08d)

11. I've never known any man who could work as fast as (a) *him,* (b) *he.* _____ (1.08f)

12. Just between you and (a) *I,* (b) *me,* the stock price will fall by afternoon.   *w/ preposition use objective* _____ (1.08c, 1.08i)

13. Give the supplies to (a) *whoever,* (b) *whomever* ordered them. _____ (1.08j)

14. (a) *Us,* (b) *We* employees have been given an unusual voice in choosing benefits. _____ (1.08g)

15. On her return from Mexico, Mrs. Sanchez, along with many other passengers, had to open (a) *her,* (b) *their* luggage for inspection. _____ (1.09f)

(1.09g)

(1.09b)

(1.08d)

(1.08i)

(1.08f)

16. Either James or Robert will have (a) *his*, (b) *their* work reviewed next week.

17. Any woman who becomes a charter member of this organization will be able to have (a) *her*, (b) *their* name inscribed on a commemorative plaque.

18. We are certain that (a) *our's*, (b) *ours* is the smallest wristwatch available.

19. Everyone has completed the reports except Debbie and (a) *he*, (b) *him*.

20. Lack of work disturbs Mr. Thomas as much as (a) *I*, (b) *me*.

object of prep.

1. a,   3. b,   5. b,   7. a,   9. a,   11. b,   13. a,   15. a,   17. a,   19. b

Verbs (1.10–1.15)

Verbs show the action of a subject or join to the subject words that describe it.

1.10 Guidelines for Agreement With Subjects.   One of the most troublesome areas in English is subject-verb agreement. Consider the following guidelines for making verbs agree with subjects.

a. A singular subject requires a singular verb.

   The stock market *opens* at 10 a.m. (The singular verb *opens* agrees with the singular subject *market*.)

   He *doesn't* (not *don't*) work on Saturday.

b. A plural subject requires a plural verb.

   On the packing slip several items *seem* (not *seems*) to be missing.

c. A verb agrees with its subject regardless of prepositional phrases that may intervene.

   This list of management objectives *is* extensive. (The singular verb *is* agrees with the singular subject *list*.)

   Every one of the letters *shows* (not *show*) proper form.

d. A verb agrees with its subject regardless of intervening phrases introduced by *as well as, in addition to, such as, including, together with,* and similar expressions.

   An important memo, together with several letters, *was* misplaced. (The singular verb *was* agrees with the singular subject *memo*.)

   The president as well as several other top-level executives *approves* of our proposal. (The singular verb *approves* agrees with the subject *president*.)

e. A verb agrees with its subject regardless of the location of the subject.

   Here *is* one of the letters about which you asked. (The verb *is* agrees with its subject *one*, even though it precedes *one*. The adverb *here* cannot function as a subject.)

There *are* many problems yet to be resolved. (The verb *are* agrees with the subject *problems*. The adverb *there* cannot function as a subject.)

In the next office *are* several word processing machines. (In this inverted sentence, the verb *are* must agree with the subject *machines*.)

f. Subjects joined by *and* require a plural verb.

Analyzing the reader and organizing a strategy *are* the first steps in letter writing. (The plural verb *are* agrees with the two subjects, *analyzing* and *organizing*.)

The tone and the wording of the letter *were* persuasive. (The plural verb *were* agrees with the two subjects, *tone* and *wording*.)

g. Subjects joined by *or* or *nor* may require singular or plural verbs. Make the verb agree with the closer subject.

Neither the memo nor the report *is* ready. (The singular verb *is* agrees with *report*, the closer of the two subjects.)

h. The following indefinite pronouns are singular and require singular verbs: *anyone, anybody, anything, each, either, every, everyone, everybody, everything, many a, neither, nobody, nothing, someone, somebody,* and *something*.

Either of the alternatives that you present *is* acceptable. (The verb *is* agrees with the singular subject *either*.)

i. Collective nouns may take singular or plural verbs, depending on whether the members of the group are operating as a unit or individually.

Our management team *is* united in its goal.

The faculty *are* sharply *divided* on the tuition issue. (Although acceptable, this sentence sounds better recast: The faculty *members* are sharply divided on the tuition issue.)

j. Organization names and titles of publications, although they may appear to be plural, are singular and require singular verbs.

Clark, Anderson, and Horne, Inc., *has* (not *have*) hired an automation consultant.

Thousands of Investment Tips is (not *are*) again on the best-seller list.

1.11 Voice. Voice is that property of verbs that shows whether the subject of the verb acts or is acted upon. Active-voice verbs direct action from the subject toward the object of the verb. Passive-voice verbs direct action toward the subject.

Active voice: Our employees *write* excellent letters.

Passive voice: Excellent letters *are written* by our employees.

Business writing that emphasizes active-voice verbs is generally preferred because it is specific and forceful. However, passive-voice constructions can help a writer be tactful. Strategies for effective use of active- and passive-voice verbs are presented in Chapter 4.

1.12 Mood.   Three verb moods express the attitude or thought of the speaker or writer toward a subject: (1) the indicative mood expresses a fact; (2) the imperative mood expresses a command; and (3) the subjunctive mood expresses a doubt, a conjecture, or a suggestion.

Indicative:	I *am looking* for a job.
Imperative:	*Begin* your job search with the want ads.
Subjunctive:	I wish I *were* working.

Only the subjunctive mood creates problems for most speakers and writers. The most common use of subjunctive mood occurs in clauses including *if* or *wish*. In such clauses, substitute the subjunctive verb *were* for the indicative verb *was*.

> If he *were* (not *was*) in my position, he would understand.
>
> Mr. Simon acts as if he *were* (not *was*) the boss.
>
> I wish I *were* (not *was*) able to ship your order.

The subjunctive mood may be used to maintain goodwill while conveying negative information. The sentence "I wish I *were* able to ship your order" sounds more pleasing to a customer than "I cannot ship your order," although, for all practical purposes, both sentences convey the same negative message.

1.13 Tense.   Verbs show the time of an action by their tense. Speakers and writers can use six tenses to show the time of sentence action; for example:

Present tense:	I *work*; he *works*.
Past tense:	I *worked*; she *worked*.
Future tense:	I *will work*; he *will work*.
Present perfect tense:	I *have worked*; he *has worked*.
Past perfect tense:	I *had worked*; she *had worked*.
Future perfect tense:	I *will have worked*; he *will have worked*.

1.14 Guidelines for Verb Tense

a. Use present tense for statements that, although they may be introduced by past-tense verbs, continue to be true.

> What did you say his name *is*? (Use the present tense *is* if his name has not changed.)

b. Avoid unnecessary shifts in verb tenses.

> The manager *saw* (not *sees*) a great deal of work yet to be completed and *remained* to do it herself.

Although unnecessary shifts in verb tense are to be avoided, not all the verbs within one sentence have to be in the same tense; for example:

> She *said* (past tense) that she *likes* (present tense) to work late.

1.15 Irregular Verbs. Irregular verbs cause difficulty for some writers and speakers. Unlike regular verbs, irregular verbs do not form the past tense and past participle by adding *-ed* to the present form. Here is a partial list of selected troublesome irregular verbs. Consult a dictionary if you are in doubt about a verb form.

Troublesome Irregular Verbs

Present	Past	Past Participle (Always use helping verbs.)
begin	began	begun
break	broke	broken
choose	chose	chosen
come	came	come
drink	drank	drunk
go	went	gone
lay (to place)	laid	laid
lie (to rest)	lay	lain
ring	rang	rung
see	saw	seen
write	wrote	written

a. Use only past-tense verbs to express past tense. Notice that no helping verbs are used to indicate simple past tense.

The auditors *went* (not *have went*) over our books carefully.

He *came* (not *come*) to see us yesterday.

b. Use past participle forms for actions completed before the present time. Notice that past participle forms require helping verbs.

Steve had *gone* (not *went*) before we called. (The past participle *gone* is used with the helping verb *had*.)

c. Avoid inconsistent shifts in subject, voice, and mood. Pay particular attention to this problem area, for undesirable shifts are often characteristic of student writing.

Inconsistent: When Mrs. Taswell read the report, the error was found. (The first clause is in the active voice; the second, passive.)

Improved: When Mrs. Taswell read the report, she found the error. (Both clauses are in the active voice.)

Inconsistent: The clerk should first conduct an inventory. Then supplies should be requisitioned. (The first sentence is in the active voice; the second, passive.)

Improved:	The clerk should first conduct an inventory. Then he or she should requisition supplies. (Both sentences are in the active voice.)
Inconsistent:	All workers must wear security badges, and you must also sign a daily time card. (This sentence contains an inconsistent shift in subject from *all workers* in first clause to *you* in second clause.)
Improved:	All workers must wear security badges, and they must also sign a daily time card.
Inconsistent:	Begin the transaction by opening an account; then you enter the customer's name. (This sentence contains an inconsistent shift from the imperative mood in first clause to the indicative mood in second clause.)
Improved:	Begin the transaction by opening an account; then enter the customer's name. (Both clauses are now in the indicative mood.)

Review Exercise C—Verbs

In the space provided for each item, write *a* or *b* to complete the statement accurately. When you finish, compare your responses with those shown below. For each item on which you need review, consult the numbered principle shown in parentheses.

(1.10c)

1. A list of payroll deductions for our employees (a) *was*, (b) *were* sent to the personnel manager.

(1.10e, 1.10f)

2. There (a) *is*, (b) *are* a customer service engineer and two salespeople waiting to see you.

(1.10f)

3. Increased computer use and more complex automated systems (a) *is*, (b) *are* found in business today.

(1.10j)

4. Crews, Meliotes, and Bove, Inc., (a) *has*, (b) *have* opened an office in Boston.

(1.15a)

5. Yesterday Mrs. Phillips (a) *choose*, (b) *chose* a new office on the second floor.

(1.14a)

6. The man who called said that his name (a) *is*, (b) *was* Johnson.

(1.10j)

7. *Modern Office Procedures* (a) *is*, (b) *are* beginning a campaign to increase readership.

(1.10h)

8. Either of the flight times (a) *appears*, (b) *appear* to fit my proposed itinerary.

(1.15b)

9. If you had (a) *saw*, (b) *seen* the rough draft, you would better appreciate the final copy.

(1.10e, 1.10f)

10. Across from our office (a) *is*, (b) *are* the parking structure and the information office.

(1.15b)

11. Although we have (a) *began*, (b) *begun* to replace outmoded equipment, the pace is slow.

(1.10d)

12. Specific training as well as ample experience (a) *is*, (b) *are* important for that position.

(1.10f)

13. Inflation and increased job opportunities (a) *is*, (b) *are* resulting in increased numbers of working women.

14. Neither the organizing nor the staffing of the program (a) *has been*,   _____ (1.10g)
    (b) *have been* completed.

15. If I (a) *was*, (b) *were* you, I would ask for a raise.   _____ (1.12)

16. If you had (a) *wrote*, (b) *written* last week, we could have sent a brochure.   _____ (1.15b)

17. The hydraulic equipment that you ordered (a) *is*, (b) *are* packed and will   _____ (1.10a)
    be shipped Friday.

18. One of the reasons that sales have declined in recent years (a) *is*, (b) *are*   _____ (1.10c)
    lack of effective advertising.

19. Either of the proposed laws (a) *is*, (b) *are* going to affect our business   _____ (1.10h)
    negatively.
                                    plural subject = plural verb
20. Merger statutes (a) *requires*, (b) *require* that a failing company accept bids   _____ (1.10b)
    from several companies before merging with one.

---

1. a,   3. b,   5. b,   7. a,   9. b,   11. b,   13. b,   15. b,   17. a,   19. a

Review Exercise D—Verbs

In the following sentence pairs, choose the one that illustrates consistency in use
of subject, voice, and mood. Write *a* or *b* in the spaces provided. When you finish, compare your responses with those shown below. For each item on which
you need review, consult the numbered principle shown in parentheses.

1. (a) You need more than a knowledge of equipment; one also must be able to   _____ (1.15c)
       interact well with people.
   (b) You need more than a knowledge of equipment; you also must be able to
       interact well with people.

2. (a) Tim and Jon were eager to continue, but Bob *wanted* to quit.   _____ (1.14b)
   (b) Tim and Jon were eager to continue, but Bob *wants* to quit.

3. (a) The salesperson should consult the price list; then you can give an accu-   _____ (1.15c)
       rate quote to a customer.
   (b) The salesperson should consult the price list; then he or she can give an
       accurate quote to a customer.

4. (a) Read all the instructions first; then you install the printer program. ?   _____ (1.15c)
   (b) Read all the instructions first, and then install the printer program.

5. (a) She was an enthusiastic manager who always had a smile for everyone.   _____ (1.14b)
   (b) She was an enthusiastic manager who always has a smile for everyone.

---

1. b,   3. b,   5. a

Adjectives and Adverbs (1.16–1.17)

Adjectives describe or limit nouns and pronouns. They often answer the questions *what kind? how many?* or *which one?* Adverbs describe or limit verbs, adjectives, or other adverbs. They often answer the questions *when? how? where?* or *to
what extent?*

1.16 Forms. Most adjectives and adverbs have three forms, or degrees: positive, comparative, and superlative.

	Positive	Comparative	Superlative
Adjective:	clear	clearer	clearest
Adverb:	clearly	more clearly	most clearly

Some adjectives and adverbs have irregular forms.

	Positive	Comparative	Superlative
Adjective:	good	better	best
	bad	worse	worst
Adverb:	well	better	best

Adjectives and adverbs composed of two or more syllables are usually compared by the use of *more* and *most*; for example:

The Payroll Department is *more efficient* than the Shipping Department.

Payroll is the *most efficient* department in our organization.

1.17 Guidelines for Use

a. Use the comparative degree of the adjective or adverb to compare two persons or things; use the superlative degree to compare three or more.

Of the two letters, which is *better* (not *best*)?

Of all the plans, we like this one *best* (not *better*).

b. Do not create a double comparative or superlative by using *-er* with *more* or *-est* with *most*.

His explanation couldn't have been *clearer* (not *more clearer*).

c. A linking verb (*is, are, look, seem, feel, sound, appear,* and so forth) may introduce a word that describes the verb's subject. In this case, be certain to use an adjective, not an adverb. [predicate adjective]

The characters on the monitor look *bright* (not *brightly*). (Use the adjective *bright* because it follows the linking verb *look* and modifies the noun *characters*. It answers the question *What kind of characters?*)

The company's letter made the customer feel *bad* (not *badly*). (The adjective *bad* follows the linking verb *feel* and describes the noun *customer*.)

d. Use adverbs, not adjectives, to describe or limit the action of verbs.

The business is running *smoothly* (not *smooth*). (Use the adverb *smoothly* to describe the action of the verb *is running*. *Smoothly* tells how the business is running.)

Don't take his remark *personally* (not *personal*). (The adverb *personally* describes the action of the verb *take*.)

e. Two or more adjectives that are joined to create a compound modifier before a noun should be hyphenated.

> The *four-year-old* child was tired.

> Our agency is planning a *coast-to-coast* campaign.

✳ Hyphenate a compound modifier following a noun only if your dictionary shows the hyphen(s).

> Our speaker is very *well-known*. (Include the hyphen because most dictionaries do.)

> The tired child was four years old. (Omit the hyphens because the expression follows the word it describes, *child*, and because dictionaries do not indicate hyphens.)

f. Keep adjectives and adverbs close to the words that they modify.

> She asked for a cup of *hot* coffee (not *a hot cup of coffee*).

> Patty had *only* two days of vacation left (not *Patty only had two days*).

> Students may sit in the *first* five rows (not *in the five first rows*).

> He has saved *almost* enough money for the trip (not *He has almost saved*).

g. Don't confuse the adverb *there* with the possessive pronoun *their* or the contraction *they're*.

> Put the documents *there*. (The adverb *there* means "at that place or at that point.")

> *There* are two reasons for the change. (The adverb *there* is used as an expletive or filler preceding a linking verb.)

> We already have *their* specifications. (The possessive pronoun *their* shows ownership.)

> *They're* coming to inspect today. (The contraction *they're* is a shortened form of *they are*.)

Review Exercise E—Adjectives and Adverbs

In the space provided for each item, write *a* or *b* to complete the statement accurately. If two sentences are shown, select *a* or *b* to indicate the one expressed more effectively. When you finish, compare your responses with those shown below. For each item on which you need review, consult the numbered principle shown in parentheses.

1. After the interview, Tim looked (a) *calm*, (b) *calmly*.   _____ (1.17c)

2. If you had been more (a) *careful*, (b) *carefuler*, the box might not have broken.   _____ (1.17b)

3. Because a new manager was appointed, the advertising campaign is running very (a) *smooth*, (b) *smoothly*.   _____ (1.17d)

4. To avoid a (a) *face to face*, (b) *face-to-face* confrontation, she wrote a letter.   _____ (1.17e)

(1.17d)

5. Darren completed the employment test (a) *satisfactorily*, (b) *satisfactory*.

(1.17c)

predicate adverb

6. I felt (a) *bad*, (b) *badly* that he was not promoted.

(1.17a)

7. Which is the (a) *more*, (b) *most* dependable of the two models?

(1.17g)

8. Can you determine exactly what (a) *there*, (b) *their*, (c) *they're* company wants us to do?

(1.17a)

9. Of all the copiers we tested, this one is the (a) *easier*, (b) *easiest* to operate.

(1.17f)

10. (a) Mr. Aldron almost was ready to accept the offer.
    (b) Mr. Aldron was almost ready to accept the offer.

(1.17f)

11. (a) We only thought that it would take two hours for the test.
    (b) We thought that it would take only two hours for the test.

(1.17f)

12. (a) Please bring me a glass of cold water.
    (b) Please bring me a cold glass of water.

(1.17f)

13. (a) The committee decided to retain the last ten tickets.
    (b) The committee decided to retain the ten last tickets.

(1.17e)

Because comes before word modifies = hyphen

14. New owners will receive a (a) *60-day*, (b) *60 day* trial period.

(1.17d)

15. The time passed (a) *quicker*, (b) *more quickly* than we expected.

(1.17e)

16. We offer a (a) *money back*, (b) *money-back* guarantee.

(1.17a)

17. Today the financial news is (a) *worse*, (b) *worst* than yesterday.

(1.17d)

adjective   adverb

18. Please don't take his comments (a) *personal*, (b) *personally*.

(1.17e)

19. You must check the document (a) *page by page*, (b) *page-by-page*.

(1.17f)

20. (a) We try to file only necessary paperwork.
    (b) We only try to file necessary paperwork.

---

1. a,   3. b,   5. a,   7. a,   9. b,   11. b,   13. a,   15. b,   17. a,   19. a

Prepositions

Prepositions are connecting words that join nouns or pronouns to other words in a sentence. The words *about, at, from, in,* and *to* are examples of prepositions.

1.18 Guidelines for Use

a. Include necessary prepositions.

What type *of* software do you need (not *what type software*)?

I graduated *from* high school two years ago (not *I graduated high school*).

b. Omit unnecessary prepositions.

Where is the meeting? (Not *Where is the meeting at?*)

Both printers work well. (Not *Both of the printers.*)

Where are you going? (Not *Where are you going to?*)

c. Avoid the overuse of prepositional phrases.

Weak: Your application for credit at our branch in the Fresno area is before me.

Improved: Your Fresno credit application is before me.

d. Repeat the preposition before the second of two related elements.

Applicants use the résumé effectively *by* summarizing their most important experiences and *by* relating their education to the jobs sought.

e. Include the second preposition when two prepositions modify a single object.

George's appreciation *of* and aptitude *for* computers led to a promising career.

(The use of prepositions in idiomatic expressions is discussed in Chapter 2, p. 32.)

Conjunctions

Conjunctions connect words, phrases, and clauses. They act as signals, indicating when a thought is being added, contrasted, or altered. Coordinate conjunctions (such as *and, or, but*) and other words that act as connectors (such as *however, therefore, when, as*) tell the reader or listener in what direction a thought is heading. They're like road signs signaling what's ahead.

1.19 Guidelines for Use

a. Use coordinating conjunctions to connect only sentence elements that are parallel or balanced.

Weak: His report was correct and written in a concise manner.

Improved: His report was correct and concise.

Weak: Management has the capacity to increase fraud, or reduction can be achieved through the policies it adopts.

Improved: Management has the capacity to increase fraud or to reduce it through the policies it adopts.

b. Do not use the word *like* as a conjunction.

It seems *as if* (not *like*) this day will never end.

c. Avoid using *when* or *where* inappropriately. A common writing fault occurs in sentences with clauses introduced by *is when* and *is where*. Written English ordinarily requires a noun (or a group of words functioning as a noun) following the linking verb *is*. Instead of acting as conjunctions in these constructions, the words *where* and *when* function as adverbs, creating faulty grammatical equations (adverbs cannot complete equations set up by linking verbs). To avoid the problem, revise the sentence, eliminating *is when* or *is where*.

Weak: A bullish market is when prices are rising in the stock market.

Improved: A bullish market is created when prices are rising in the stock market.

Weak:	A flowchart is when you make a diagram showing the step-by-step progression of a procedure.
Improved:	A flowchart is a diagram showing the step-by-step progression of a procedure.
Weak:	Word processing is where you use a computer and software to write.
Improved:	Word processing involves the use of a computer and software to write.

A similar faulty construction occurs in the expression *I hate when*. English requires nouns, noun clauses, or pronouns to act as objects of verbs, not adverbs.

Weak:	I hate when we're asked to work overtime.
Improved:	I hate it when we're asked to work overtime. OR
Improved:	I hate being asked to work overtime.

d. Don't confuse the adverb *then* with the conjunction *than*. *Then* means "at that time"; *than* indicates the second element in a comparison.

We would rather remodel *than* (not *then*) move.

First, the equipment is turned on; *then* (not *than*) the program is loaded.

Review Exercise F—Prepositions and Conjunctions

In the space provided for each item, write *a* or *b* to indicate the sentence that is expressed more effectively. When you finish, compare your responses with those shown below. For each item on which you need review, consult the numbered principle shown in parentheses.

(1.18b)   1. (a) Do you know where this shipment is being sent?
        (b) Do you know where this shipment is being sent to?

(1.18e)   2. (a) She was not aware of nor interested in the company insurance plan.
        (b) She was not aware nor interested in the company insurance plan.

(1.18a)   3. (a) Mr. Samuels graduated college last June.
        (b) Mr. Samuels graduated from college last June.

(1.19c)   4. (a) "Flextime" is when employees arrive and depart at varying times.
        (b) "Flextime" is a method of scheduling worktime in which employees arrive and depart at varying times. *grammatical rule caused more wordiness here*

(1.18b)   5. (a) Both employees enjoyed setting their own hours.
        (b) Both of the employees enjoyed setting their own hours.

(1.19c)   6. (a) I hate when the tape sticks in my VCR.
        (b) I hate it when the tape sticks in my VCR.

(1.18a)   7. (a) What style of typeface should we use?
        (b) What style typeface should we use?

(1.19a)   8. (a) Business letters should be concise, correct, and written clearly.
        (b) Business letters should be concise, correct, and clear.

parallelism

9. (a) Mediation in a labor dispute occurs when a neutral person helps union and management reach an agreement.
   (b) Mediation in a labor dispute is where a neutral person helps union and management reach an agreement.   (1.19c)

10. (a) It looks as if the plant will open in early January.
    (b) It looks like the plant will open in early January.   (1.19b)

11. (a) We expect to finish up the work soon.
    (b) We expect to finish the work soon.   (1.18b)

12. (a) At the beginning of the program in the fall of the year at the central office, we experienced staffing difficulties.
    (b) When the program began last fall, the central office experienced staffing difficulties.   (1.18c)

13. (a) Your client may respond by letter or a telephone call may be made.
    (b) Your client may respond by letter or by telephone.   (1.19a)

14. (a) A résumé is when you make a written presentation of your education and experience for a prospective employer.
    (b) A résumé is a written presentation of your education and experience for a prospective employer.   (1.19c)

15. (a) Stacy exhibited both an awareness of and talent for developing innovations.
    (b) Stacy exhibited both an awareness and talent for developing innovations.   (1.18e)

16. (a) This course is harder then I expected.
    (b) This course is harder than I expected.   (1.19d)

17. (a) An ombudsman is an individual hired by management to investigate and resolve employee complaints.
    (b) An ombudsman is when management hires an individual to investigate and resolve employee complaints.   (1.19c)

18. (a) I'm not certain where to take this document to.
    (b) I'm not certain where to take this document.   (1.18b)

19. (a) By including accurate data and by writing clearly, you will produce effective memos.
    (b) By including accurate data and writing clearly, you will produce effective memos.   (1.18d)

20. (a) We need computer operators who can load software, monitor networks, and files must be duplicated.
    (b) We need computer operators who can load software, monitor networks, and duplicate files.   (1.19a)

---

1. a,   3. b,   5. a,   7. a,   9. a,   11. b,   13. b,   15. a,   17. a,   19. a

Punctuation Review

Comma (Part I) (2.01–2.04)

2.01 Series. Commas are used to separate three or more equal elements (words, phrases, or short clauses) in a series. To ensure separation of the last two elements, careful writers always use a comma before the conjunction in a series.

> Business letters usually contain a dateline, address, salutation, body, and closing. (This series contains words.)

> The job of an ombudsman is to examine employee complaints, resolve disagreements between management and employees, and ensure fair treatment. (This series contains phrases.)

> Trainees complete basic keyboarding tasks, technicians revise complex documents, and editors proofread completed projects. (This series contains short clauses.)

2.02 Direct Address. Commas are used to set off the names of individuals being addressed.

> Your inquiry, *Mrs. Johnson,* has been referred to me.

> We genuinely hope that we may serve you, *Mr. Lee.*

2.03 Parenthetical Expressions. Skilled writers use parenthetical words, phrases, and clauses to guide the reader from one thought to the next. When these expressions interrupt the flow of a sentence and are unnecessary for its grammatical completeness, they should be set off with commas. Examples of commonly used parenthetical expressions follow:

all things considered	however	needless to say
as a matter of fact	in addition	nevertheless
as a result	incidentally	no doubt
as a rule	in fact	of course
at the same time	in my opinion	on the contrary
consequently	in the first place	on the other hand
for example	in the meantime	therefore
furthermore	moreover	under the circumstances

> *As a matter of fact,* I wrote to you just yesterday. (Phrase used at the beginning of a sentence.)

> We will, *in the meantime,* send you a replacement order. (Phrase used in the middle of a sentence.)

> Your satisfaction is our first concern, *needless to say.* (Phrase used at the end of a sentence.)

Do not use commas if the expression is necessary for the completeness of the sentence.

> Kimberly had *no doubt* that she would finish the report. (Omit commas because the expression is necessary for the completeness of the sentence.)

2.04 Dates, Addresses, and Geographical items. When dates, addresses, and geographical items contain more than one element, the second and succeeding elements are normally set off by commas.

a. Dates

> The conference was held February 2 at our home office. (No comma is needed for one element.)

> The conference was held February 2, 1986, at our home office. (Two commas set off the second element.)

> The conference was held Tuesday, February 2, 1986, at our home office. (Commas set off the second and third elements.)

> In February 1986 the conference was held. (This alternate style omitting commas is acceptable if the month and year only are written.)

b. Addresses

> The letter addressed to Mr. Jim W. Ekman, 600 Via Novella, Agoura, CA 91306, should be sent today. (Commas are used between all elements except the state and zip code, which in this special instance are considered a single unit.)

c. Geographical items

> She moved from Toledo, Ohio, to Champaign, Illinois. (Commas set off the state unless it appears at the end of the sentence, in which case only one comma is used.)

In separating cities from states and days from years, many writers remember the initial comma but forget the final one, as in the examples that follow:

> The package from Austin, Texas {,} was lost.

> "We opened June 1, 1985 {,} and have grown steadily since."

Review Exercise G—Comma (Part I)

Insert necessary commas in the following sentences. In the space provided write the number of commas that you add. Write *C* if no commas are needed. When you finish, compare your responses with those shown below. For each item on which you need review, consult the numbered principle shown in parentheses.

1. As a rule we do not provide complimentary tickets. _____ (2.03)

2. You may be certain, Mr. Martinez, that your policy will be issued immediately. _____ (2.02)

_____ (2.03)

3. I have no doubt that your calculations are correct.

_2_____ (2.03)

4. The safety hazard, on the contrary, can be greatly reduced if workers wear rubber gloves. *At the beginning or end = emphasis*

_____ (2.01)

5. Every accredited TV newscaster radio broadcaster and newspaper reporter had access to the media room.

_3_____ (2.04c)

6. Deltech's main offices are located in Boulder, Colorado, and Seattle, Washington.

_____ (2.01)

7. The employees who are eligible for promotions are Terry Evelyn Vicki Rosanna and Steve.

_2_____ (2.03)

8. During the warranty period, of course, you are protected from any parts or service charges.

_____ (2.01)

9. Many of our customers include architects engineers attorneys and others who are interested in data-base management programs.

_2_____ (2.02)

10. I wonder, Mrs. Stevens, if you would send my letter of recommendation as soon as possible.

_____ (2.01)

11. The new book explains how to choose appropriate legal protection for ideas trade secrets copyrights patents and restrictive covenants.

_3_____ (2.04b)

12. The factory is scheduled to be moved to 2250 North Main Street, Ann Arbor, Michigan 48107, within two years.

_____ (2.03)

13. You may however prefer to correspond directly with the manufacturer in Hong Kong.

_C_____ (2.03)

14. Are there any alternatives in addition to those that we have already considered?

_____ (2.04a)

15. The rally has been scheduled for Monday January 12 in the football stadium.

_1_____ (2.02)

16. A check for the full amount will be sent directly to your home, Mr. Jefferson.

_____ (2.03)

17. Goodstone Tire & Rubber for example recalled 400,000 steelbelted radial tires because some tires failed their rigid tests.

_2_____ (2.01)

18. Kevin agreed to unlock the office, open the mail, and check all the equipment in my absence.

_____ (2.03)

19. In the meantime thank you for whatever assistance you are able to furnish.

_____ (2.04c)

20. Research facilities were moved from Austin, Texas to Santa Cruz, California.

---

1. rule,   3. C   5. newscaster, radio broadcaster,   7. Terry, Evelyn, Vicki, Rosanna,   9. architects, engineers, attorneys,   11. ideas, trade secrets, copyrights, patents,   13. may, however,   15. Monday, January 12,   17. Rubber, for example,   19. meantime,

Comma (Part 2) (2.05–2.09)

2.05 Independent Clauses. An independent clause is a group of words that has a subject and a verb and that could stand as a complete sentence. When two such clauses are joined by *and, or, nor,* or *but,* use a comma before the conjunction.

> We can ship your merchandise July 12, *but* we must have your payment first.

> Net income before taxes is calculated, *and* this total is then combined with income from operations.

Notice that each independent clause in the preceding two examples could stand alone as a complete sentence. Do not use a comma unless each group of words is a complete thought (*i.e.,* has its own subject and verb).

> Net income before taxes is calculated *and* is then combined with income from operations. (No comma is needed because no subject follows *and.*)

2.06 Dependent Clauses. Dependent clauses do not make sense by themselves; for their meaning they depend upon independent clauses.

a. **Introductory Clauses.** When a dependent clause precedes an independent clause, it is followed by a comma. Such clauses are often introduced by *when, if,* and *as.*

> *When your request came,* we immediately responded.

> *As I mentioned earlier,* Mrs. James is the manager.

b. **Terminal Clauses.** If a dependent clause falls at the end of a sentence, use a comma only if the dependent clause is an afterthought.

> The meeting has been rescheduled for October 23, *if this date meets with your approval.* (Comma used because dependent clause is an afterthought.)

> We responded immediately *when we received your request.* (No comma is needed.)

c. **Essential and Nonessential.** If a dependent clause provides information that is unneeded for the grammatical completeness of a sentence, use commas to set it off. In determining whether such a clause is essential or nonessential, ask yourself whether the reader needs the information contained in the clause to identify the word it explains.

> Our district sales manager, *who just returned from a trip to the Southwest District,* prepared this report. (This construction assumes that there is only one district sales manager. Since the sales manager is clearly identified, the dependent clause is not essential and requires commas.)

> The salesperson *who just returned from a trip to the Southwest District* prepared this report. (The dependent clause in this sentence is necessary to identify *which* salesperson prepared the report. Therefore, use no commas.)

The position of assistant sales manager, *which we discussed with you last week*, is still open. (Careful writers use *which* to introduce nonessential clauses. Commas are also necessary.)

The position *that we discussed with you last week* is still open. (Careful writers use *that* to introduce essential clauses. No commas are used.)

2.07 Phrases.   A phrase is a group of related words that lacks both a subject and a verb. A phrase that precedes a main clause is followed by a comma only if the phrase contains a verb form or has five or more words.

> *Beginning November 1*, Worldwide Savings will offer two new combination checking/savings plans. (A comma follows this introductory phrase because the phrase contains the verb form *beginning*.)

> *To promote their plan*, we will conduct an extensive direct-mail advertising campaign. (A comma follows this introductory phrase because the phrase contains the verb form *to promote*.)

> *In a period of only one year*, we were able to improve our market share by 30 percent. (A comma follows the introductory phrase—actually two prepositional phrases—because its total length exceeds five words.)

> *In 1985* our organization installed a multiuser system that could transfer programs easily. (No comma needed after the short introductory phrase.)

2.08 Two or More Adjectives.   Use a comma to separate two or more adjectives that equally describe a noun. A good way to test the need for a comma is this: Mentally insert the word *and* between the adjectives. If the resulting phrase sounds natural, a comma is used to show the omission of *and*.

> We're looking for a versatile, programmable calculator. (Use a comma to separate *versatile* and *programmable* because they independently describe *calculator*. *And* has been omitted.)

> Our *experienced, courteous* staff is ready to serve you. (Use a comma to separate *experienced* and *courteous* because they independently describe *staff*. *And* has been omitted.)

> It was difficult to refuse the *sincere young* telephone caller. (No commas are needed between *sincere* and *young* because *and* has not been omitted.)

2.09 Appositives.   Words that rename or explain preceding nouns or pronouns are called *appositives*. An appositive that provides information not essential to the identification of the word it describes should be set off by commas.

> James Wilson, *the project director for Sperling's*, worked with our architect. (The appositive, *the project director for Sperling's*, adds nonessential information. Commas set it off.)

Review Exercise H—Comma (Part 2)

Insert only necessary commas in the following sentences. In the space provided, indicate the number of commas that you add for each sentence. If a sentence requires no commas, write *C*. When you finish, compare your responses with those shown below. For each item on which you need review, consult the numbered principle shown in parentheses.

1. A corporation must be registered in the state in which it does business and it must operate within the laws of that state. *sub./verb* _____ (2.05)

2. The manager made a point-by-point explanation of the distribution dilemma and then presented his plan to solve the problem. _____ (2.05)

3. If you will study the cost analysis you will see that our company offers the best system at the lowest price. _____ (2.06a)

4. Molly Epperson, who amassed the greatest number of sales points, was awarded the bonus trip to Hawaii. *dep clause* 2 _____ (2.06c)

5. The salesperson who amasses the greatest number of sales points will be awarded the bonus trip to Hawaii. _____ (2.06c)

6. To promote goodwill, and to generate international trade, we are opening offices in the Far East and in Europe. _____ (2.07)

7. On the basis of these findings I recommend that we retain Jane Rada as our counsel. _____ (2.07)

8. Mary Bantle is a dedicated, hard-working employee for our company. _____ (2.08)

9. The bright young student who worked for us last summer will be able to return this summer. _____ (2.08)

10. When you return the completed form, we will be able to process your application. *INTRODuctory adv clause* _____ (2.06a)

11. We will be able to process your application when you return the completed form. _____ (2.06b)

12. The employees who have been with us over ten years automatically receive additional insurance benefits. *Restrictive clause (no commas)* _____ (2.06c)

13. Knowing that you wanted this merchandise immediately I took the liberty of sending it by Express Parcel Services. _____ (2.07)

14. The central processing unit requires no scheduled maintenance and has a self-test function for reliable performance. _____ (2.05)

15. Foreign competition nearly ruined the American shoe industry but the textile industry remains strong. _____ (2.05)

16. Stacy Wilson, our newly promoted office manager, has made a number of worthwhile suggestions. *modifier* _____ (2.09)

17. For the benefit of employees recently hired we are offering a two-hour seminar regarding employee benefit programs. _____ (2.07)

18. Please bring your suggestions and those of Mr. Mason when you attend our meeting next month. _____ (2.06b)

19. The meeting has been rescheduled for September 30 if this date meets with your approval. _____ (2.06b)

20. Some of the problems that you outline in your recent memo could be rectified through more stringent purchasing procedures. _____ (2.06c)

---

1. business,   3. analysis,   5. C   7. findings,   9. C   11. C   13. immediately,   15. industry,
17. hired,   19. September 30,

Comma (Part 3) (2.10–2.15)

2.10 Degrees and Abbreviations.   Degrees following individuals' names are set off by commas. Abbreviations such as *Jr.* and *Sr.* are also set off by commas unless the individual referred to prefers to omit the commas.

> Anne G. Turner, *M.B.A.*, joined the firm.
>
> Michael Migliano, *Jr.*, and Michael Migliano, *Sr.*, work as a team.
>
> Anthony A. Gensler *Jr.* wrote the report. (The individual referred to prefers to omit commas.)

The abbreviations *Inc.* and *Ltd.* are set off by commas only if a company's legal name has a comma just before this kind of abbreviation. To determine a company's practice, consult its stationery or a directory listing.

> Firestone and Blythe, *Inc.*, is based in Canada. (Notice that two commas are used.)
>
> Computers *Inc.* is extending its franchise system. (The company's legal name does not include a comma just before *Inc.*)

2.11 Omitted Words.   A comma is used to show the omission of words that are understood.

> On Monday we received 15 applications; on Friday, only 3. (Comma shows the omission of *we received*.)

2.12 Contrasting Statements.   Commas are used to set off contrasting or opposing expressions. These expressions are often introduced by such words as *not*, *never*, *but*, and *yet*.

> The consultant recommended hard-disk storage, *not* floppy-disk storage, for our operations.
>
> Our budget for the year is reduced, *yet* adequate.
>
> The greater the effort, the greater the reward.

If increased emphasis is desired, use dashes instead of commas, as in "Only the sum of $100—not $1,000—was paid on this account."

2.13 Clarity.   Commas are used to separate words repeated for emphasis. Commas are also used to separate words that may be misread if not separated.

> The building is a long, long way from completion.
>
> Whatever is, is right.
>
> No matter what, you know we support you.

2.14 Quotations and Appended Questions

a. A comma is used to separate a short quotation from the rest of a sentence. If the quotation is divided into two parts, two commas are used.

The manager asked, "Shouldn't the managers control the specialists?"

"Not if the specialists," replied Tim, "have unique information."

b. A comma is used to separate a question appended (added) to a statement.

You will confirm the shipment, won't you?

2.15 Comma Overuse.   Do not use commas needlessly. For example, commas should not be inserted merely because you might drop your voice if you were speaking the sentence.

One of the reasons for expanding our West Coast operations is {,} that we anticipate increased sales in that area. (Do not insert a needless comma before a clause.)

I am looking for an article entitled {,} "State-of-the-Art Communications." (Do not insert a needless comma after the word *entitled*.)

A number of food and nonfood items are carried in convenience stores such as {,} 7-Eleven and Stop-N-Go. (Do not insert a needless comma after *such as*.)

We have {,} at this time {,} an adequate supply of parts. (Do not insert needless commas around prepositional phrases.)

Review Exercise 1—Comma (Part 3)

Insert only necessary commas in the following sentences. Remove unnecessary commas with the delete sign (⌀). In the space provided, indicate the number of commas inserted or deleted in each sentence. If a sentence requires no changes, write *C*. When you finish, compare your responses with those shown below. For each item on which you need review, consult the numbered principle shown in parentheses.

1. We expected Charles Bedford not Tiffany Richardson to conduct the audit.   _____ (2.12)

2. Brian said, "We simply must have a bigger budget to start this project."   _____ (2.14a)

3. "We simply must have " said Brian, "a bigger budget to start this project."   _____ (2.14a)

4. In August, customers opened at least 50 new accounts; in September, only about 20.   _____ (2.11)

5. You returned the merchandise last month didn't you?   _____ (2.14b)

6. In short, employees will now be expected to contribute more to their own retirement funds.   _____ (2.13)

7. The better our advertising and recruiting the stronger our personnel pool will be.   _____ (2.12)

8. Mrs. Delgado investigated selling her stocks, not her real estate, to raise the necessary cash.   _____ (2.12)

_____ (2.14a)   9. "On the contrary " said Mrs. Mercer "we will continue our present marketing strategies."

_____ (2.15)   10. Our company will expand into surprising new areas such as, women's apparel and fast foods.

_____ (2.12)   11. What we need is more not fewer suggestions for improvement.

_____ (2.10)   12. Randall Clark , Esq., and Jonathon Georges, M.B.A, joined the firm.

_____ (2.14a)   13. "America is now entering " said President Saunders "the Age of Information."

_____ (2.15)   14. One of the reasons that we are inquiring about the publisher of the software is, that we are concerned about whether that publisher will be in the market five years from now.

_____ (2.10)   15. The talk by D. A. Spindler Ph.D. was particularly difficult to follow because of his technical and abstract vocabulary.

_____ (2.13)   16. The month before, a similar disruption occurred in distribution.

_____ (2.15)   17. We are very fortunate to have, at our disposal, the services of excellent professionals.

_____ (2.13)   18. No matter what, you can count on us for support.

_____ (2.11)   19. Mrs. Sandoval was named legislative counsel; Mr. Freeman executive advisor.

_____ (2.15)   20. The data you are seeking can be found in an article entitled, "The Fastest Growing Game in Computers."

---

1. Bedford, Richardson,   3. have," said Brian,   5. month,   7. recruiting,   9. contrary," Mercer,
11. more, not fewer,   13. entering," Saunders,   15. Spindler, Ph.D.,   17. have at our disposal
19. Freeman,

Semicolon (2.16)

2.16 Independent Clauses, Series, Introductory Expressions

a. **Independent Clauses With Conjunctive Adverbs.** Use a semicolon before a conjunctive adverb that separates two independent clauses. Some of the most common conjunctive adverbs are *therefore, consequently, however,* and *moreover.*

Business letters should sound conversational; *therefore,* familiar words and contractions are often used.

The bank closes its doors at 3 p.m.; *however,* the walk-up window is open until 6 p.m.

Notice that the word following a semicolon is *not* capitalized (unless, of course, that word is a proper noun).

[handwritten notes:]
Bill bought a car last week; (He) wrecked it last week.

S-V ; S-V
SEPARATED, but closely related
(linking, but separating

b. **Independent Clauses Without Conjunctive Adverbs.** Use a semicolon to separate closely related independent clauses when no conjunctive adverb is used.

> Bond interest payments are tax deductible; dividend payments are not.

> Ambient lighting fills the room; task lighting illuminates each workstation.

Use a semicolon in *compound* sentences, not in *complex* sentences.

> After one week the paper feeder jammed; we tried different kinds of paper. (Use a semicolon in a compound sentence.)

> After one week the paper feeder jammed, although we tried different kinds of paper. (Use a comma in a complex sentence. Do not use a semicolon after *jammed*.)

The semicolon is very effective for joining two closely related thoughts. Don't use it, however, unless the ideas are truly related.

c. **Independent Clauses With Other Commas.** Normally, a comma precedes *and*, *or*, and *but* when those conjunctions join independent clauses. However, if either clause contains commas, change the comma preceding the conjunction to a semicolon to ensure correct reading.

> If you arrive in time, you may be able to purchase a ticket; but ticket sales close promptly at 8 p.m.

> Our primary concern is financing; and we have discovered, as you warned us, that money sources are quite scarce.

d. **Series With Internal Commas.** Use semicolons to separate items in a series when one or more of the items contain internal commas.

> Delegates from Miami, Florida; Freeport, Mississippi; and Chatsworth, California, attended the conference.

> The speakers were Kevin Lang, manager, Riko Enterprises; Henry Holtz, vice president, Trendex, Inc.; and Margaret Slater, personnel director, West Coast Productions.

e. **Introductory Expressions.** Use a semicolon when an introductory expression such as *namely*, *for instance*, *that is*, or *for example* introduces a list following an independent clause.

> Switching to computerized billing are several local companies; namely, Ryson Electronics, Miller Vending Services, and Black Advertising.

> The author of a report should consider many sources; for example, books, periodicals, government publications, and newspapers.

Colon (2.17–2.19)

2.17 Listed Items

a. **With Colon.** Use a colon after a complete thought that introduces a formal list of items. A formal list is often preceded by such words and phrases as *these, thus, the following,* and *as follows.* A colon is also used when words and phrases like these are implied but not stated.

> Additional costs in selling a house involve *the following*: title examination fee, title insurance costs, and closing fee. (Use a colon when a complete thought introduces formal list.)

> Collective bargaining focuses on several key issues: cost-of-living adjustments, fringe benefits, job security, and hours of work. (The introduction of the list is implied in the preceding clause.)

b. **Without Colons.** Do not use a colon when the list immediately follows a *to be* verb or a preposition.

> The employees who should receive the preliminary plan are James Sears, Monica Spears, and Rose Lopez. (No colon is used after the verb *are*.)

> We expect to consider equipment *from* IBM, Wang, Exxon, and Lanier. (No colon is used after the preposition *from*.)

2.18 Quotations.   Use a colon to introduce long one-sentence quotations and quotations of two or more sentences.

> Our consultant said: "This system can support up to 32 users. It can be used for decision support, computer-aided design, and software development operations at the same time."

2.19 Salutations.   Use a colon after the salutation of a business letter.

> Gentlemen: Dear Mrs. Seaman: Dear Jamie:

Review Exercise J—Semicolons, Colons

In the following sentences, add semicolons, colons, and necessary commas. For each sentence indicate the number of punctuation marks that you add. If a sentence requires no punctuation, write *C*. When you finish, compare your responses with those shown below. For each item on which you need review, consult the numbered principle shown in parentheses.

_____ (2.16a)

1. A strike in Canada has delayed shipments of parts consequently our production has fallen behind schedule.

_____ (2.16b)

2. Our branch in Sherman Oaks; specializes in industrial real estate our branch in Canoga Park concentrates on residential real estate.

_____ (2.01, 2.17a)

3. The sedan version of the automobile is available in these colors Olympic red metallic silver and Aztec gold.

4. If I can assist the new manager, please call me; however, I will be gone from June 10 through June 15.

_(2.06a, 2.16a)_

5. The individuals who should receive copies of this announcement are Henry Doogan Alicia Green and Kim Wong.

_(2.01, 2.17b)_

6. We would hope, of course, to send personal letters to all prospective buyers; but we have not yet decided just how to do this.

_(2.03, 2.16c)_

7. Many of our potential customers are in Southern California therefore our promotional effort will be strongest in that area.

_(2.16a)_

8. Since the first of the year, we have received inquiries from one attorney, two accountants and one information systems analyst.

_(2.01, 2.07, 2.17b)_

9. Three dates have been reserved for initial interviews January 15 February 1 and February 12.

_(2.01, 2.17a)_

10. Several staff members are near the top of their salary ranges, and we must reclassify their jobs.

_(2.05)_

11. Several staff members are near the top of their salary ranges; we must reclassify their jobs.

_(2.16b)_

12. Several staff members are near the top of their salary ranges therefore we must reclassify their jobs.

_(2.16a)_

13. If you open an account within two weeks you will receive a free cookbook moreover your first 500 checks will be imprinted at no cost to you.

_(2.16a)_

14. Monthly reports from the following departments are missing Legal Department Personnel Department and Engineering Department.

_(2.01, 2.17a)_

15. Monthly reports are missing from the Legal Department Personnel Department and Engineering Department.

_(2.01, 2.17b)_

16. Since you became director of that division, sales have tripled; therefore, I am recommending you for a bonus.

_(2.06a, 2.16a)_

17. The convention committee is considering Portland Oregon New Orleans Louisiana and Phoenix Arizona.

_(2.16d)_

18. Several large companies allow employees access to their personnel files; namely, General Electric, Eastman Kodak and Infodata.

_(2.01, 2.16e)_

19. Sherry first asked about salary; next she inquired about benefits.

_(2.16b)_

20. Sherry first asked about the salary, and she next inquired about benefits.

_(2.05)_

---

1. parts; consequently, 3. colors: Olympic red, metallic silver, 5. Doogan, Alicia Green,
7. California; therefore, 9. interviews: January 15, February 1, 11. ranges; 13. weeks, cookbook;
moreover, 15. Department, Personnel Department, 17. Portland, Oregon; New Orleans, Louisiana;
Phoenix, 19. salary;

Apostrophe (2.20–2.29)

2.20 Basic Rule. The apostrophe is used to show ownership, origin, authorship, or measurement.

Ownership:	We are looking for *Brian's* keys.
Origin:	At the *president's* suggestion, we doubled the order.
Authorship:	The accountant's annual report was questioned.
Measurement:	In two years' time we expect to reach our goal.

a. **Ownership Word Does Not End in *s*.** To place the apostrophe correctly, you must first determine whether the ownership word ends in an *s* sound. If it does not, add an apostrophe and an *s* to the ownership word. The following examples show ownership words that do not end in an *s* sound:

the employee's file	(the file of a single employee)
a member's address	(the address of a single member)
a year's time	(the time of a single year)
a month's notice	(notice of a single month)
the company's building	(the building of a single company)

b. **Ownership Word Ends in *s*.** If the ownership word does end in an *s* sound, usually add only an apostrophe.

several employees' files	(files of several employees)
ten members' addresses	(addresses of ten members)
five years' time	(time of five years)
several months' notice	(notice of several months)
many companies' buildings	(buildings of many companies)

A few singular nouns that end in *s* are pronounced with an extra syllable when they become possessive. To these words, add *'s*.

my boss's desk
the waitress's table
the actress's costume

Use no apostrophe if a noun is merely plural, not possessive.

All the sales representatives, as well as the secretaries and managers, had their names and telephone numbers listed in the directory.

2.21 Names. The writer may choose either traditional or popular style in making singular names that end in an *s* sound possessive. The traditional style uses the apostrophe plus an *s*, while the popular style uses just the apostrophe. Note that only with singular names ending in an *s* sound does this option exist.

Traditional Style	Popular Style
Russ's computer	Russ' computer
Mr. Jones's car	Mr. Jones' car
Mrs. Morris's desk	Mrs. Morris' desk
Ms. Horowitz's job	Ms. Horowitz' job

The possessive form of plural names is consistent: the Joneses' car, the Horowitzes' home, the Lopezes' daughter.

2.22 Gerunds. Use *'s* to make a noun possessive when it precedes a gerund, a verb form used as a noun.

> Mr. Smith's smoking prompted a new office policy. (*Mr. Smith* is possessive because it modifies the gerund *smoking*.)

> It was Betsy's careful proofreading that revealed the discrepancy.

Review Exercise K—Apostrophes

Insert necessary apostrophes in the following sentences. In the space provided for each sentence, indicate the number of apostrophes that you added. If none were added, write *C*. When you finish, compare your responses with those shown below. For each item on which you need review, consult the numbered principle shown in parentheses.

1. Your account should have been credited with six months interest. _____ (2.20b)

2. If you go to the third floor, you will find Mr. Londons office. _____ (2.21)

3. All the employees personnel folders must be updated. _____ (2.20b)

4. In a little over a years time, that firm was able to double its sales. _____ (2.20a)

5. The Harrises daughter lived in Florida for two years. _____ (2.21)

6. An inventors patent protects his or her patent for seventeen years. _____ (2.20a)

7. Both companies headquarters will be moved within the next six months. _____ (2.20b)

8. That position requires at least two years experience. _____ (2.20b)

9. Some of their assets could be liquidated; therefore, a few of the creditors were satisfied. _____ (2.20b)

10. All secretaries workstations were equipped with terminals. _____ (2.20b)

11. The package of electronics parts arrived safely despite two weeks delay. _____ (2.20b)

12. Many nurses believe that nurses notes are not admissable evidence. _____ (2.20b)

13. According to Mr. Cortez [or Cortezs] latest proposal, all employees would receive an additional holiday. _____ (2.21)

14. Many of our members names and addresses must be checked. _____ (2.20b)

_____ (2.21)   15. His supervisor frequently had to correct Jacks financial reports.

_____ (2.20a)   16. We believe that this firms service is much better than that firms.

_____ (2.20a)   17. Mr. Jackson estimated that he spent a years profits in reorganizing his staff.

_____ (2.20b)   18. After paying six months rent, we were given a receipt.

_____ (2.21)   19. The contract is not valid without Mrs. Harris [or Harriss] signature.

_____ (2.22)   20. It was Mr. Smiths signing of the contract that made us happy.

---

1. months'   3. employees'   5. Harrises'   7. companies'   9. C   11. weeks'
13. Cortez' or Cortez's   15. Jack's   17. year's   19. Harris' or Harris's

Other Punctuation (2.23–2.29)

2.23 Period

a. **Ends of Sentences.** Use a period at the end of a statement, command, indirect question, or polite request. Although a polite request may have the same structure as a question, it ends with a period.

> Corporate legal departments demand precise skills from their work force. (End a statement with a period.)

> Get the latest data by reading current periodicals. (End a command with a period.)

> Mr. Rand wondered if we had sent any follow-up literature. (End an indirect question with a period.)

> Would you please reexamine my account and determine the current balance. (A polite request suggests an action rather than a verbal response.)

b. **Abbreviations and Initials.** Use periods after initials and after many abbreviations.

R. M. Johnson	c.o.d.	Ms.
M.D.	a.m.	Mr.
Inc.	i.e.	Mrs.

Use just one period when an abbreviation falls at the end of a sentence.

> Guests began arriving at 5:30 p.m.

2.24 Question Mark.   Direct questions are followed by question marks.

> Did you send your proposal to Datatronix, Inc.?

> Statements with questions added are punctuated with question marks.

> We have completed the proposal, haven't we?

2.25 Exclamation Point. Use an exclamation point after a word, phrase, or clause expressing strong emotion. In business writing, however, exclamation points should be used sparingly.

> Incredible! Every terminal is down.

2.26 Dash. The dash (constructed at a keyboard by striking the hyphen key twice in succession) is a legitimate and effective mark of punctuation when used according to accepted conventions. As an emphatic punctuation mark, however, the dash loses effectiveness when overused.

a. **Parenthetical Elements.** Within a sentence a parenthetical element is usually set off by commas. If, however, the parenthetical element itself contains internal commas, use dashes (or parentheses) to set it off.

> Three top salespeople—Tom Judkins, Tim Templeton, and Mary Yashimoto—received bonuses.

b. **Sentence Interruption.** Use a dash to show an interruption or abrupt change of thought.

> News of the dramatic merger—no one believed it at first—shook the financial world.

> Ship the materials Monday—no, we must have them sooner.

Sentences with abrupt changes of thought or with appended afterthoughts can usually be improved through rewriting.

c. **Summarizing Statement.** Use a dash (not a colon) to separate an introductory list from a summarizing statement.

> Sorting, merging, and computing—these are tasks that our data processing programs must perform.

2.27 Parentheses. One means of setting off nonessential sentence elements involves the use of parentheses. Nonessential sentence elements may be punctuated in one of three ways: (1) with commas, to make the lightest possible break in the normal flow of a sentence; (2) with dashes, to emphasize the enclosed material; and (3) with parentheses, to deemphasize the enclosed material. Parentheses are frequently used to punctuate sentences with interpolated directions, explanations, questions, and references.

> The cost analysis (which appears on page 8 of the report) indicates that the copy machine should be leased.

> Units are lightweight (approximately 13 oz.) and come with a leather case and operating instructions.

> The IBM laser printer (have you heard about it?) will be demonstrated for us next week.

A parenthetical sentence that is not imbedded within another sentence should be capitalized and punctuated with end punctuation.

> The Model 20 has stronger construction. (You may order a Model 20 brochure by circling 304 on the reader service card.)

2.28 Quotation Marks

a. **Direct Quotations.** Use double quotation marks to enclose the exact words of a speaker or writer.

> "Keep in mind," Mrs. Frank said, "that you'll have to justify the cost of automating our office."

> The boss said that automation was inevitable. (No quotation marks are needed because the exact words are not quoted.)

b. **Quotations Within Quotations.** Use single quotation marks (apostrophes on the typewriter) to enclose quoted passages within quoted passages.

> In her speech Mrs. Deckman remarked, "I believe it was the poet Robert Frost who said, 'All the fun's in how you say a thing.'"

c. **Short expressions.** Slang, words used in a special sense, and words following *stamped* or *marked* are often enclosed within quotation marks.

> Jeffrey described the damaged shipment as "gross." (Use quotation marks for slang words.)

> Students often have trouble spelling the word "separate." (Quote words used in a special sense.)

> Jobs were divided into two categories: most stressful and least stressful. The jobs in the "most stressful" list involved high risk or responsibility. (Quote words used in a special sense.)

> The envelope marked "Confidential" was put aside. (Words following *marked* are often enclosed in quotation marks.)

In the four preceding sentences, the words enclosed within quotation marks can be set in italics, if italics are available.

d. **Definitions.** Double quotation marks are used to enclose definitions. The word or expression being defined should be underscored or set in italics.

> The term *penetration pricing* is defined as "the practice of introducing a product to the market at a low price."

e. **Titles.** Use double quotation marks to enclose titles of literary and artistic works, such as magazine and newspaper articles, chapters of books, movies, television shows, poems, lectures, and songs. Names of major publications—such as books, magazines, pamphlets, and newspapers—are set in italics (underscored) or typed in capital letters.

> Particularly helpful was the chapter in Smith's EFFECTIVE WRITING TECHNIQUES entitled "Right Brain, Write On!"

In the <u>Los Angeles Times</u> appeared John's article, "Corporate Raiders"; however, we could not locate it in a local library.

f. **Additional Considerations.** Periods and commas are always placed inside closing quotation marks. Semicolons and colons, on the other hand, are always placed outside quotation marks.

Mrs. James said, "I could not find the article entitled 'Technology Update.'"

The president asked for "absolute security": all written messages were to be destroyed.

Question marks and exclamation points may go inside or outside closing quotation marks, as determined by the form of the quotation.

Sales Manager Martin said, "Who placed the order?" (The quotation is a question.)

When did the sales manager say, "Who placed the order?" (Both the incorporating sentence and the quotation are questions.)

Did the sales manager say, "Ryan placed the order"? (The incorporating sentence asks question; the quotation does not.)

"In the future," shouted Bob, "ask me first!" (The quotation is an exclamation.)

2.29 Brackets. Within quotations, brackets are used by the quoting writer to enclose his or her own inserted remarks. Such remarks may be corrective, illustrative, or explanatory.

Mrs. Cardillo said, "OSHA [Occupational Safety and Health Administration] has been one of the most widely criticized agencies of the federal government."

Review Exercise L—Other Punctuation

Insert necessary punctuation in the following sentences. In the space provided for each item, indicate the number of punctuation marks that you added. Count sets of parentheses and dashes as two marks. Emphasis or deemphasis will be indicated for some parenthetical elements. When you finish, compare your responses with those shown below. For each item on which you need review, consult the numbered principle shown in parentheses.

1. Will you please stop payment on my Check No. 233   (2.23a)

2. (Emphasize.) Your order of October 16 will be on its way — you have my word—by October 20.   (2.26b)

3. Mr Sirakides, Mrs Sylvester, and Miss Sanchez have not yet responded   (2.23a, 2.23b)

4. Mrs Franklin asked if the order had been sent c o d   (2.23b)

5. Interviews have been scheduled for 3:15 p m , 4 p m , and 4:45 p m   (2.23b)

_____ (2.27)

6. (Deemphasize.) Three knowledgeable individuals the plant manager, the construction engineer, and the construction supervisor all expressed concern about soil settlement.

_____ (2.25)

7. Fantastic The value of our stock just rose 10 points on the stock market exchange

_____ (2.28d)

8. The word de facto means exercising power as if legally constituted.

_____ (2.27)

9. (Deemphasize.) Although the appliance now comes in limited colors brown, beige, and ivory , we expect to see new colors available in the next production run.

_____ (2.28f)

10. Was it the manager who said, "What can't be altered must be endured "?

_____ (2.28c)

11. The stock market went bonkers over the news of the takeover.

_____ (2.28c)

12. Because the envelope was marked "Personal," we did not open it.

_____ (2.26c)

13. Price, service, and reliability these are our prime considerations in equipment selection.

_____ (2.28b, 2.28f)

14. The lettercarrier said, "Would you believe that this package was marked 'Fragile' ?"

_____ (2.26a)

15. (Emphasize.) Three branch managers Carmen Lopez, Stan Meyers, and Ivan Sergo will be promoted.

_____ (2.27)

16. (Deemphasize.) The difference between portable and transportable computers see Figure 4 for weight comparisons may be considerable.

_____ (2.28c)

17. All the folders marked Current Files should be sent to the Personnel Division.

_____ (2.28e)

18. I am trying to find the edition of Newsweek that carried an article entitled "The Future Without Shock."

_____ (2.23b)

19. Martin Simon M D and Gail Nemire R N were hired by Healthnet, Inc

_____ (2.28a)

20. The computer salesperson said, "This innovative, state-of-the-art computer sells for a fraction of the big-name computers.

---

1. 233.   3. Mr.   Mrs.   responded.   5. p.m.   p.m.   p.m.   7. Fantastic!   exchange!
9. (brown   ivory),   11. "bonkers"   13. reliability—   15. managers—   Sergo—
17. "Current Files"   19. Simon, M.D.,   Nemire, R.N.,   Inc.

Style and Usage

Capitalization (3.01–3.16)

Capitalization is used to distinguish important words. However, writers are not free to capitalize all words they consider important. Rules or guidelines governing capitalization style have been established through custom and use. Mastering these guidelines will make your writing more readable and more comprehensible.

3.01 Proper Nouns. Capitalize proper nouns, including the *specific* names of persons, places, schools, streets, parks, buildings, religions, holidays, months, agreements, programs, services, and so forth. Do *not* capitalize common nouns that make only *general* references.

Proper Nouns	Common Nouns
Michael DeNiro	a salesman in electronics
West Germany, Japan	two countries that trade with the United States
El Camino College	a community college
Sam Houston Park	a park in the city
Phoenix Room, Statler Inn	a meeting room in the hotel
Catholic, Presbyterian	two religions
Memorial Day, New Year's Day	two holidays in the year
Express Mail	a special package delivery service
George Washington Bridge	a bridge
Consumer Product Safety Act	a law to protect consumers

When a common-noun element is used in combination with two or more proper nouns, do not capitalize the common noun. For example, "Our markets include countries across both the Pacific and the Atlantic *oceans*."

3.02 Proper Adjectives. Capitalize most adjectives that are derived from proper nouns.

Greek symbol	British thermal unit
Roman numeral	Norwegian ship
Xerox copy	Hispanic markets

Do not capitalize the few adjectives that, although originally derived from proper nouns, have become common adjectives through usage. Consult your dictionary when in doubt.

manila folder	mimeograph copies
india ink	china dishes

3.03 Geographic Locations. Capitalize the names of *specific* places such as cities, states, mountains, valleys, lakes, rivers, oceans, and geographic regions.

New York City	Great Salt Lake
Allegheny Mountains	Pacific Ocean
San Fernando Valley	Delaware Bay
the East Coast	the Pacific Northwest

3.04 Organization Names.   Capitalize the principal words in the names of all business, civic, educational, governmental, labor, military, philanthropic, political, professional, religious, and social organizations.

Inland Steel Company

The Wall Street Journal*

New York Stock Exchange

United Way

Commission to Restore the Statue of Liberty

Board of Directors, Midwest Savings and Loan Association

Securities and Exchange Commission

National Association of Letter Carriers

Association of Information Systems Professionals

3.05 Academic Courses and Degrees.   Capitalize particular academic degrees and course titles. Do not capitalize references to general academic degrees and subject areas.

Professor Bernadette Ordian, Ph.D., will teach *Accounting* 221 next fall.

Mrs. Snyder, who holds *bachelor's* and *master's* degrees, teaches *marketing* classes.

Jim enrolled in classes in *history, English,* and *management.*

3.06 Personal and Business Titles

a. Capitalize personal and business titles when they precede names.

Vice President Ames

Board Chairman Frazier

Governor G. W. Thurmond

Professor McLean

Uncle Edward

Councilman Herbert

Sales Manager Klein

Dr. Samuel Washington

b. Capitalize titles in addresses, salutations, and closing lines.

Mr. Juan deSanto
Director of Purchasing
Space Systems, Inc.
Boxborough, MA 01719

Very truly yours,

Clara J. Smith
Supervisor, Marketing

c. Capitalize titles of high governmental rank or religious office, whether they precede a name, follow a name, or replace a name.

The President of the United States

the Premier's palace

the Governor of Ohio

J. W. Ross, Attorney General

James Lee, Senator

the Secretary of State

an audience with the Pope

the Chief Justice

*Note: Capitalize *the* only when it is part of the official name of an organization, as printed on the organization's stationery.

d. Do not capitalize more common titles following names.

The speech was delivered by Wayne Barcomb, *president*, PWS-KENT Publishing Company.

Lois Herndon, *chief executive officer*, signed the order.

e. Do not capitalize more common titles appearing alone.

Please speak to the *supervisor* or the *office manager*.

Neither the *president* nor the *vice president* was asked.

However, when the title of an official appears in that organization's minutes, bylaws, or other official document, it may be capitalized.

f. Do not capitalize titles when they are followed by appositives naming specific individuals.

We must consult our *director of research*, Ronald E. West, before responding.

g. Do not capitalize family titles used with possessive pronouns.

my mother	our aunt
your father	his cousin

h. Capitalize titles of close relatives used without pronouns.

Both *Mother* and *Father* must sign the contract.

3.07 Numbered and Lettered Items. Capitalize nouns followed by numbers or letters (except in page, paragraph, line, and verse references).

Flight 34, Gate 12	Plan No. 2
Volume I, Part 3	Warehouse 33–A
Invoice No. 55489	Figure 8.3
Model A5673	Serial No. C22865404–2
State Highway 10	page 6, line 5

3.08 Points of the Compass. Capitalize *north*, *south*, *east*, *west*, and their derivatives when they represent *specific* geographical regions. Do not capitalize the points of the compass when they are used in directions or in general references.

Specific Regions	General References
from the South	heading north on the highway
living in the Midwest	west of the city
Easterners, Southerners	western Nevada, southern Indiana
going to the Middle East	the northern part of the United States
from the East Coast	the east side of the street

3.09 Departments, Divisions, and Committees. Capitalize the names of departments, divisions, or committees within your own organization. Outside your organization capitalize only *specific* department, division, or committee names.

> The inquiry was addressed to the *Legal Department* in our *Consumer Products Division*.
>
> John was appointed to the *Employee Benefits Committee*.
>
> Send your résumé to their *personnel division*.
>
> A *planning committee* will be named shortly.

3.10 Governmental Terms. Do not capitalize the words *federal*, *government*, *nation*, or *state* unless they are part of a specific title.

> Unless *federal* support can be secured, the *state* project will be abandoned.
>
> The *Federal* Deposit Insurance Corporation protects depositors from bank failure.

3.11 Product Names. Capitalize product names only when they refer to trademarked items. Except in advertising, common names following manufacturers' names are not capitalized.

Trademarked Names	Common Names
IBM Selectric	Apple computer
Ford Thunderbird	Swingline stapler
BASF FlexyDisk	3M diskettes
Dictaphone Thought Tank	Sony dictation machine
DuPont Teflon	Canon camera

3.12 Literary Titles. Capitalize the principal words in the titles of books, magazines, newspapers, articles, movies, plays, songs, poems, and reports. Do *not* capitalize articles (*a*, *an*, *the*), short conjunctions (*and*, *but*, *or*, *nor*), and prepositions of fewer than four letters (*in*, *to*, *by*, *for*, etc.) unless they begin or end the title.

> Jackson's *What Job Is for You?* (Capitalize book titles.)
>
> Gant's "Software for the Executive Suite" (Capitalize principal words in article titles.)
>
> "Performance Standards to Go By" (Capitalize article titles.)
>
> "The Improvement of Fuel Economy With Alternative Motors" (Capitalize report titles.)

3.13 Beginning Words. In addition to capitalizing the first word of a complete sentence, capitalize the first word in a quoted sentence, independent phrase, item in an enumerated list, and formal rule or principle following a colon.

> The business manager said, "*All* purchases must have requisitions." (Capitalize first word in a quoted sentence.)

Yes, if you agree. (Capitalize an independent phrase.)

Some of the duties of the position are as follows:

1. *Transcribing* dictation from recording equipment

2. *Receiving* and routing telephone calls

3. *Verifying* records, reports, and applications (Capitalize items in an enumerated list.)

One rule has been established through the company: *No* smoking is allowed in open offices. (Capitalize a rule following a colon.)

3.14 Celestial Bodies. Capitalize the names of celestial bodies such as *Mars*, *Saturn*, and *Neptune*. Do not capitalize the terms *earth*, *sun*, or *moon* unless they appear in a context with other celestial bodies.

Where on *earth* did you find that manual typewriter?

Venus and *Mars* are the closest planets to *Earth*.

3.15 Ethnic References. Capitalize terms that refer to a particular culture, language, or race.

Oriental	Hebrew
Caucasian	Indian
Latino	Judeo-Christian
Persian	Negro

3.16 Seasons. Do not capitalize seasons.

In the *fall* it appeared that *winter* and *spring* sales would increase.

Review Exercise M—Capitalization

In the following sentences correct any errors that you find in capitalization. Circle any lowercase letter that should be changed to a capital letter. Draw a slash (/) through a capital letter that you wish to change to a lowercase letter. In the space provided, indicate the total number of changes you have made in each sentence. If you make no changes, write *0*. When you finish, compare your responses with those shown below. For each item on which you need review, consult the numbered principle shown in parentheses.

Example: Bill McAdams, currently Assistant Manager in our Personnel department, will be promoted to Manager of the Employee Services division.   5

1. The social security act, passed in 1935, established the present system of social security.   (3.01)

2. Our company will soon be moving its operations to the west coast.   (3.03)

3. Marilyn Hunter, m.b.a., received her bachelor's degree from Ohio university in athens.   (3.01, 3.05)

_____ (3.06e, 3.12)   4. The President of Datatronics, Inc., delivered a speech entitled "Taking Off Into the Future."

_____ (3.06e, 3.06g)   5. Please ask your Aunt and your Uncle if they will come to the Attorney's office at 5 p.m.

_____ (3.01, 3.07)   6. Your reservations are for Flight 32 on American Airlines leaving from Gate 14 at 2:35 p.m.

_____ (3.01)   7. Once we establish an organizing committee, arrangements can be made to rent holmby hall.

_____ (3.05)   8. Bob was enrolled in history, Spanish, Business communications, and physical education courses.

_____ (3.06e, 3.11)   9. Either the President or the Vice President of the company will make the decision about purchasing xerox copiers.

_____ (3.01, 3.07)   10. Rules for hiring and firing Employees are given on page 7, line 24, of the Contract.

_____ (3.02)   11. Some individuals feel that american management does not have the sense of loyalty to its employees that japanese management has.

_____ (3.01, 3.14)   12. Where on Earth can we find better workers than Robots?

_____ (3.06c, 3.10, 3.13) 13. The secretary of state said, "we must protect our domestic economy from Foreign competition."

_____ (3.01, 3.08)   14. After crossing the Sunshine Skyway Bridge, we drove to Southern Florida for our vacation.

_____ (3.01)   15. All marketing representatives of our company will meet in the empire room of the red lion motor inn.

_____ (3.01, 3.05, 3.06e) 16. Floyd Elkins, Ph.D., has been named director of research for Spaceage Strategies, Inc.

_____ (3.01, 3.02, 3.11) 17. The special keyboard for the IBM Computer must contain greek symbols for Engineering equations.

_____ (3.05, 3.09)   18. After she received a master's degree in electrical engineering, Joanne Dudley was hired to work in our product development department.

_____ (3.01, 3.03, 3.16) 19. In the Fall our organization will move its corporate headquarters to the franklin building in downtown los angeles.

_____ (3.13)   20. Dean Amador has one cardinal rule: Always be punctual.

---

1. Social Security Act   3. M.B.A.   University   Athens   5. aunt   uncle   attorney's
7. Holmby Hall   9. president   vice president   Xerox   11. American   Japanese
13. Secretary   State   We   foreign   15. Empire Room   Red Lion Motor Inn
17. computer   Greek   engineering   19. fall   Franklin Building   Los Angeles

Number Style (4.01–4.13)

Usage and custom determine whether numbers are expressed in the form of figures (for example, *5, 9*) or in the form of words (for example, *five, nine*). Numbers expressed as figures are shorter and more easily understood, yet numbers expressed as words are necessary in certain instances. The following guidelines are observed in expressing numbers in written *sentences*. Numbers that appear on business forms—such as invoices, monthly statements, purchase orders—are always expressed as figures.

4.01 General Rules

a. The numbers *one* through *ten* are generally written as words. Numbers above *ten* are written as figures.

   The bank had a total of *nine* branch offices in *three* suburbs.

   All *58* employees received benefits in the *three* categories shown.

   A shipment of *45,000* light bulbs was sent from *two* warehouses.

b. Numbers that begin sentences are written as words. If that number involves more than two words, however, the sentence should be written so that the number does not fall at the beginning.

   Fifteen different options were available in the annuity programs.

   A total of *156* companies participated in the promotion (not *One hundred fifty-six companies participated in the promotion*).

4.02 Money.   Sums of money $1 or greater are expressed as figures. If a sum is a whole dollar amount, omit the decimal and zeros (whether or not the amount appears in a sentence with additional fractional dollar amounts).

   We budgeted *$30* for diskettes, but the actual cost was *$37.96*.

   On the invoice were items for *$6.10, $8, $33.95,* and *$75*.

Sums less than $1 are written as figures that are followed by the word *cents*.

   By shopping carefully, we can save *45 cents* per diskette.

4.03 Dates.   In dates, numbers that appear after the name of the month are written as cardinal figures (*1, 2, 3,* etc.). Those that stand alone or appear before the name of a month are written as ordinal figures (*1st, 2d, 3d,** etc.).

   The Personnel Practices Committee will meet *May 7*.

   On the *5th* day of February and again on the *25th*, we placed orders.

   In domestic business documents, dates generally take the following form: *January 4, 1991*. An alternative form, used primarily in military and foreign correspondence, begins with the day of the month and omits the comma: *4 January 1991*.

---

*Many writers today are using the more efficient *2d* and *3d* instead of *2nd* and *3rd*.

4.04 Clock Time.   Figures are used when clock time is expressed with *a.m.* or *p.m.* Omit the colon and zeros in referring to whole hours. When exact clock time is expressed with the contraction *o'clock*, either figures or words may be used.

Mail deliveries are made at *11 a.m.* and *3:30 p.m.*

At *four* (or *4*) *o'clock* employees begin to leave.

4.05 Addresses and Telephone Numbers

a. Except for the number *one*, house numbers are expressed as figures.

540 Elm Street	17802 Washington Avenue
One Colorado Boulevard	2 Highland Street

b. Street names containing numbers *ten* or lower are written entirely as words. For street names involving numbers greater than *ten*, figures are used.

330 Third Street	3440 Seventh Avenue
6945 East 32 Avenue	4903 West 103 Street

If no compass direction (*North, South, East, West*) separates a house number from a street number, the street number is expressed in ordinal form (*-st, -d, -th*).

256 42d Street	1390 11th Avenue

c. Telephone numbers are expressed with figures. When used, the area code is placed in parentheses preceding the telephone number.

Please call us at *(818) 347–0551* to place an order.

Mr. Sims asked you to call *(619) 554–8923, Ext. 245*, after 10 a.m.

4.06 Related Numbers.   Numbers are related when they refer to similar items in a category within the same reference. All related numbers should be expressed as the largest number is expressed. Thus if the largest number is greater than *ten*, all the numbers should be expressed as figures.

Only *5* of the original *25* applicants completed the processing. (Related numbers require figures.)

The *two* plans affected *34* employees working in *three* sites. (Unrelated numbers use figures and words.)

Getty Oil operated *86* rigs, of which *6* were rented. (Related numbers require figures.)

The company hired *three* accountants, *one* customer service representative, and *nine* sales representatives. (Related numbers under *ten* use words.)

4.07 Consecutive Numbers. When two numbers appear consecutively and both modify the same following noun, words are used to express the smaller or less complex number.

> We need *250 five-page* colored inserts (not *two hundred fifty 5-page* inserts).

> The magazine was devoted to *two 25-page* articles (not *2 twenty-five-page* articles).

4.08 Periods of Time. Periods of time are generally expressed in word form. However, figures may be used to emphasize business concepts such as discount rates, interest rates, warranty periods, credit terms, loan or contract periods, and payment terms.

> This business was incorporated over *fifty* years ago.

> Any purchaser may cancel a contract within *72* hours. (Use figures to explain a business concept.)

> The warranty period is *5* years. (Use figures for a business concept.)

> Cash discounts are given for payment within *30* days. (Use figures for a business concept.)

4.09 Ages. Ages are generally expressed in word form unless the age appears immediately after a name or is expressed in exact years and months.

> At the age of *twenty-one*, Elizabeth inherited the business.

> Wanda Tharp, 37, was named acting president.

> At the age of 4 years and 7 months, the child was adopted.

4.10 Round Numbers. Round numbers are approximations. They may be expressed in word or figure form, although figure form is shorter and easier to comprehend.

> About *600* (or *six hundred*) stock options were sold.

> It is estimated that *1,000* (or *one thousand*) people will attend.

For ease of reading, round numbers in the millions or billions should be expressed with a combination of figures and words.

> At least *1.5 million* readers subscribe to the ten top magazines.

> Deposits in money market accounts totaled more than *$115 billion*.

4.11 Weights and Measurements. Weights and measurements are expressed with figures.

> The new deposit slip measures *2* by *6* inches.

> Casio desktop calculators weigh only *2* pounds *4* ounces.

> Toledo is *60* miles from Detroit.

4.12 Fractions. Simple fractions are expressed as words. Complex fractions may be written either as figures or as a combination of figures and words.

Over *two thirds* of the stockholders voted.

This microcomputer will execute the command in *1 millionth* of a second. (Combination of words and numbers is easier to comprehend.)

She purchased a *one-fifth* share in the business.*

4.13 Percentages and Decimals. Percentages are expressed with figures that are followed by the word *percent*. The percent sign (%) is used only on business forms or in statistical presentations.

We had hoped for a *10 percent* interest rate, but we received a loan at *12 percent*.

Over *50 percent* of the residents supported the plan.

Decimals are expressed with figures. If a decimal expression does not contain a whole number (an integer) and does not begin with a zero, a zero should be placed before the decimal point.

The actuarial charts show that *1.74* out of 1,000 people will die in any given year.

Inspector Norris found the setting to be *.005* inch off. (Decimal begins with a zero and does not require a zero before the decimal point.)

Considerable savings will accrue if the unit production cost is reduced *0.1 percent*. (A zero is placed before a decimal that neither contains a whole number nor begins with a zero.)

Quick Chart—Expression of Numbers

Use Words	Use Figures
Numbers *ten* and under	Numbers *11* and over
Numbers at beginning of sentence	Money
Periods of time	Dates
Ages	Addresses and telephone numbers
Fractions	Weights and measurements
	Percentages and decimals

Review Exercise N—Number Style

Circle *a* or *b* to indicate the preferred number style. Assume that these numbers appear in business correspondence. When you finish, compare your responses

---

*Note: Fractions used as adjectives require hyphens.

with those shown below. For each item on which you need review, consult the numbered principle shown in parentheses.

1. (a) 2 alternatives	(b) two alternatives	(4.01a)
2. (a) Seventh Avenue	(b) 7th Avenue	(4.05b)
3. (a) sixty sales reps	(b) 60 sales reps	(4.01a)
4. (a) November ninth	(b) November 9	(4.03)
5. (a) forty dollars	(b) $40	(4.02)
6. (a) on the 23d of May	(b) on the twenty-third of May	(4.03)
7. (a) at 2:00 p.m.	(b) at 2 p.m.	(4.04)
8. (a) 4 two-hundred page books	(b) four 200-page books	(4.07)
9. (a) at least 15 years ago	(b) at least fifteen years ago	(4.08)
10. (a) 1,000,000 viewers	(b) 1 million viewers	(4.10)
11. (a) twelve cents	(b) 12 cents	(4.02)
12. (a) a sixty-day warranty	(b) a 60-day warranty	(4.08)
13. (a) ten percent interest rate	(b) 10 percent interest rate	(4.13)
14. (a) 4/5 of the voters	(b) four fifths of the voters	(4.12)
15. (a) the rug measures four by six feet	(b) the rug measures 4 by 6 feet	(4.11)
16. (a) about five hundred people attended	(b) about 500 people attended	(4.10)
17. (a) at eight o'clock	(b) at 8 o'clock	(4.04)
18. (a) located at 1 Wilshire Boulevard	(b) located at One Wilshire Boulevard	(4.05a)
19. (a) three computers for twelve people	(b) three computers for 12 people	(4.06)
20. (a) 4 out of every 100 licenses	(b) four out of every 100 licenses	(4.06)

---

1. b,   3. b,   5. b,   7. b,   9. b,   11. b,   13. b,   15. b,   17. a or b,   19. b

INDEX